THE ORIGINS OF YOU

THE ORIGINS OF YOU

How Childhood Shapes Later Life

Jay Belsky • Avshalom Caspi • Terrie E. Moffitt • Richie Poulton

Harvard University Press

Cambridge, Massachusetts & London, England

First Harvard University Press paperback edition, 2023
First printing

Library of Congress Cataloging-in-Publication Data
Names: Belsky, Jay, 1952– author. | Caspi, Avshalom, author. |
Moffitt, Terrie E., author. | Poulton, Richie, 1962– author.
Title: The origins of you : how childhood shapes later life / Jay Belsky,
Avshalom Caspi, Terrie E. Moffitt, Richie Poulton.
Description: Cambridge, Massachusetts : Harvard University Press, 2020. |
Includes bibliographical references and index.
Identifiers: LCCN 2019050707 | ISBN 9780674983458 (hardcover) |
ISBN 9780674293854 (pbk.)
Subjects: LCSH: Developmental psychology. | Developmental biology. |
Nature and nurture. | Child development.
Classification: LCC BF713 .B445 2020 | DDC 155—dc23
LC record available at https://lccn.loc.gov/2019050707

CONTENTS

V. GENETICS

VI. AGING IN MIDLIFE

VII. CONCLUSION

PREFACE

The first time I met Terrie Moffitt was in the late 1980s, during a visit to a city in northern Finland where both of us were attending an international conference on human development. Temi, as she likes to be called, was sitting at the hotel bar, talking to Avshalom Caspi, whom I knew—but more as a younger colleague than a close friend, as he and Temi would become. As I approached Avshalom, who was deep in conversation with Temi, I overheard them discussing pubertal development. In my impulsive New York manner, I butted in and said, "Hi, Avshalom, I've got a hypothesis about puberty for you."

I had recently become enamored with evolutionary biology's argument that the *purpose* of life is to pass on genes to the next generation and future descendants (grandchildren, great-grandchildren, and so on). Although this idea is central to the thinking of virtually all biological scientists studying nonhuman life, it remains foreign to most students of human development, especially those investigating whether and how experiences in the family affect the developing child. Their more traditional frame of reference emphasizes health, happiness, and well-being, leading most developmental scholars to view life in terms of healthy versus unhealthy or "optimal" versus compromised development rather than in terms of reproductive success.

Although I was intrigued by evolutionary thinking, I struggled to come up with a hypothesis that, if confirmed, would convince me—and, I hoped, others—that an evolutionary perspective had much to offer students of human development. This led eventually to the hypothesis that I shared with Temi and Avshalom, which no traditional development perspective had ever stimulated or could account for if true: *Because growing up under adverse conditions increases the risk of dying or having one's development compromised before reproducing, adverse childhood experience should accelerate pubertal development and thereby sexual maturation and fertility.* In other words, family economic and social conditions should regulate physical development—by influencing the timing of puberty—not just, as has long been appreciated by traditional developmental reasoning, psychological and behavioral development.

I knew immediately after sharing my hypothesis with Avshalom and Temi that I would become fast friends with both of them, though perhaps Temi in particular. Why? Because of how the person who turned out to be Avshalom's fiancée responded to my potentially outrageous proposition that family processes would influence pubertal development. Temi didn't make a face that said "who is this impolite guy interrupting our conversation?"—a response that my New York style had provoked before. Nor did she, as so many others had, dismiss the idea out of hand because it challenged sacred theoretical cows about who was healthy, what was optimal development, and thus the fundamental nature of human development. (Sadly, academia is far less open-minded than many presume.) Rather, Temi responded enthusiastically and open-mindedly by immediately saying, "We can test that!" And so we did, as detailed in Chapter 7, using data from the Dunedin Multidisciplinary Health and Development Study, the focus of most of this book.

It is critical to appreciate that neither Temi nor Avshalom was embracing my evolutionary perspective or the puberty hypothesis it yielded. Instead, they evinced a scientific mind-set, agreeing that "it's a potentially interesting, certainly provocative idea, and one that can be subject to empirical evaluation." I was, of course, both eager to see the hypothesis tested and anxious that I could be proven wrong. But, like my newfound friends, I live in a scientific world—the empirical chips would fall wherever they might and that would be that. After all, what was the worst that could happen? I could be wrong!

Anyway, this was the beginning of a long-lasting and lovely friendship. As I came to follow my friends' and colleagues' work, I kept feeling that however much (deserved) attention it received in the most prestigious scholarly journals and however many journalists wrote about it in newspapers, magazines, and social media posts, too few people understood and appreciated the scope of their many contributions to our understanding of how we develop. I kept hoping that a Pulitzer Prize–winning science writer would come along and write a popular book about their research. I had no doubt that such a book could prove to be a great seller, but as the years went by and no such professional writer materialized to harvest the fruits of Avshalom and Temi's (and their collaborators') labors, I decided that I would try my hand at it. I appreciated that I was not the writer I was hoping for, so I proposed to my friends that I would write what I hoped would be an engaging book summarizing for a lay audience many—but by no means all—of their contributions. I wanted to share the insight, even excitement, that comes from investigating how humans develop, while also informing readers how such work is done. That is why I initially thought we would use as the title for the book *Adventures in Human Development: How We Become Who We Are.* I decided that a book that didn't require the reader to read the chapters in order might be the best way to realize these goals. Not only would it be doable for the writer, but more importantly it could prove attractive to today's readers, whose attention spans seem to be growing shorter and whose interests are not the same.

My original intent was to be the "voice" of Moffitt, Caspi, and their friend and collaborator Richie Poulton, now my friend, too, but as the proposal for the volume developed, it seemed reasonable to make two slight modifications to the original plan. First, in addition to sharing work on the Dunedin Multidisciplinary Health and Development Study, based in New Zealand, which I was involved in to a very limited extent (covered in Chapters 5 and 7), it seemed appropriate to include some of Moffitt and Caspi's other groundbreaking research by drawing on their UK-based Environmental-Risk Study (see Chapters 9, 10, and 17). Second, it dawned on me that a project that I worked on with many others over the course of almost twenty years might be worth covering, too. That is why Chapter 8 addresses the effects of day care on child and adolescent development, a topic not investigated by my coauthors, and why Chapter 7, focused on family influences on female pubertal development, also includes evidence from this third research project.

Given that I was the principal writer of this volume—but writing about work carried out almost entirely by others—we all agreed that writing in the first person plural made the most sense. All of us contributed to the birth of the research ideas in this book, in many late-night sessions of idea bouncing, and, of the hundreds of research reports on numerous topics related to human development emanating from the Dunedin and Environmental-Risk studies, I decided which to cover.

In view of all this, my wife asked me one day why I was taking the time to write a book about the work of others, good friends though they are. My best answer was that this effort was—and remains—a "labor of love." I wanted to convey my fondness for my colleagues, my admiration of their dedication to their science, the insight that their research has generated about how humans develop, and my strong feeling that others should come to know and thereby appreciate their many outstanding accomplishments. I certainly hope this volume serves the latter purpose; it has already served the former ones.

Jay Belsky
December, 2019

THE ORIGINS OF YOU

PART I

INTRODUCTION

1

Lives through Time

Does a child's temperament at age three forecast that child's personality in young adulthood? How important is self-control early in life for success in later life? Is attention-deficit/hyperactivity disorder (ADHD) just for kids? Do adolescent delinquents grow out of their antisocial behavior? Why do parents parent the way they do? Does family conflict promote female sexual activity by accelerating sexual maturation? Does regular marijuana use affect physical and mental health decades later? Is cigarette smoking or even success in life written in our genes? Does genetic makeup determine who proves resilient in the face of stress and who succumbs to childhood adversity? Why do some individuals at midlife look, feel, and act much older than they are, whereas others look, feel, and act noticeably younger? How does stress in childhood and adolescence become biologically embedded so that it undermines health in midlife?

These are some of the questions that will be asked and answered in this book. In fact, our aspiration in writing it was to take the reader on the same journeys that we have been on for decades. Guiding our intellectual travels is the central question we have long wondered about regarding human development: "why are we the way we are and different from others?" Curiosity about this issue has led us to follow the lives of more than four thousand individuals for many years, beginning in infancy or early childhood, through adolescence, and in some cases well into adulthood. As far as supplies are concerned, the journey requires us to gather at many points in childhood, adolescence, and adulthood information that we can use to ask and answer questions like those in the preceding paragraph, but it further requires us not just to interrogate the information gathered, often at great expense, time, and effort, but also to question the answers that we secure. By doing so, we can increase our confidence that what we are discovering about "why we are the way we are" is on target, being more likely true and trustworthy. Ultimately, we hope to show that much of what we discover both challenges and confirms widespread ideas about the nature of human development and thus how we become who we end up being.

Many nonfiction books about psychology, behavior, and health focus on a single topic, addressing it in-depth. Think about books focused on bullying, sexual behavior, or marital relations. That will not be the way with this book. Because it is based on our research following individuals across many years, we focus on a variety of topics that have fascinated us rather than just one or two. What is of central importance at one point in developmental time, say early childhood, often differs greatly from what is important at a later time, say middle childhood or adolescence. Indeed, this is why we address topics such as temperament and day care in early childhood, bullying and ADHD in middle childhood, marijuana use and tobacco smoking in adolescence, and health in middle age. It might be helpful to think of this book more in terms of Jules Verne's classic novel *Journey to the Center of the Earth* rather than Ernest Hemingway's *The Old Man and the Sea*. Whereas the former is about a series of challenging—and varied—experiences of explorers after entering a volcano and following its lava tubes to the center of the earth, the latter is about a poor fisherman's experience during a single day in which he caught and tried to bring home one very large fish.

Because we focus on many topics, we should make clear that you need not progress through the book in the sequence in which it is organized. Think of it as a smorgasbord that allows you to choose to eat what you want to eat when you want to eat it rather than a more traditional restaurant dinner that progresses from appetizer to dessert. The topics covered early in the book are not only about childhood, nor are those covered later only about adulthood. Likewise, the book is not ordered in terms of when the research discussed was carried out over the many decades covered. Thus, some of the early chapters address topics we studied quite some time ago, whereas others were investigated much more recently. The same holds for the later chapters. We purposefully constructed this book appreciating that some topics will prove more interesting to some readers than to others. So, while reading the chapters in sequence is most certainly fine, there should be little intellectual cost to jumping around from chapter to chapter. Indeed, because this book is all about individual differences in development—how people are different and what makes them so—there is no reason why this orientation should not be brought to bear on how this book is read. Read it your way! In fact, because of this flexible approach to reading it, a particular chapter will often refer to prior or subsequent chapters so that interested readers can follow a lead that captures their attention in other parts of the book.

In addition to sharing our excitement about—and adventures studying—human development, a second goal of this book is to challenge the way many think about development. Despite frequent stories in the press and on social media, popular understanding of how humans develop from birth through adulthood remains mired in platitudes, often embraced simply because they confirm what some of us want to believe. These include claims that "it is all in our genes"; that "family experiences in childhood make us who we are"; "that day care is bad (or good) for children"; and that "adolescent trouble-making is just a passing phase." This book seeks to disabuse readers of these simplicities in the course of detailing hard-won insights about some fundamental themes of this book. These are addressed in Parts II through VI of the book:

- Whether and how children think, feel, and behave in their first five, ten, and fifteen years of life forecasts who they become later in life.
- Whether and how experience in the family while growing up shapes—or fails to shape—who they become later in life.
- Whether and how experience beyond the family while growing up shapes—or fails to shape—who they become later in life.
- Whether and how genetics influences human development.
- Whether and how adult health is rooted in childhood.

Even though none of the work we present directly involves intervention or clinical or community-service delivery, virtually all chapters make clear how insights achieved in addressing the issues just highlighted can inform such efforts. In fact, throughout the book, we strive to show that the basic science of human development generates knowledge that can and does inform efforts to promote physical and mental health, prevent problems from developing, and treat problems that have already emerged. As such, the science of human development is based on the same logic that underlies many other scientific disciplines: if you know how something works, then you are in a much better position to maintain it in good working order and address any problems that might arise.

WHAT IS HUMAN DEVELOPMENT?

By this point, the reader might be wondering what human development actually is. Well, to begin with, it's a field of study that addresses questions as diverse as those posed in the opening paragraph of this chapter. That makes it a multidisciplinary science. It is a psychological science, given its interest in emotion, cognition, and behavior. It is a neuroscience, given its focus on the mind and brain. It is a sociological science, given its attention to the family, neighborhood, employment, and crime. Finally, it is a biological and public-health science, given its focus on genetics, physiology, health, and even the role that evolution still plays in how we grow and change.

The discipline of human development is perhaps most like meteorology, the study of weather and climate, in that there are many factors and forces to consider that interact in complex ways over time and space. Humans have their hurricanes and rainy days, and bright, sunshiny ones, all of which developmental science seeks to illuminate, especially in terms of what causes them and what their effects are. That is why we focus on cognitive, social, emotional, behavioral, biological, and physical development, including health, from birth to midlife, while considering the influence of nature and nurture. Despite the fact that our capacity to predict how children will look and behave decades from now is not yet on a par with meteorologists' ability to forecast the weather, it is indisputable that scientists and scholars studying human development are making progress, as we hope to show.

Meteorology makes a good point of comparison also because, like human development, it is a *probabilistic,* not *deterministic,* science. Excluding quantum mechanics, which deals with phenomena at the subatomic level, physics is the prototypical deterministic science. It has rigorous laws—

including precise formulas—to explain, for example, how temperature affects the state of H_2O (ice, liquid, or gas); how the size of a container affects gas pressure (Boyle's law); or how gravity affects the acceleration of a falling object (thanks to Isaac Newton). It is rarely the case, however, that research in human development yields such real-world certainty. In fact, that is why we have confidence that engineers can design and build bridges that we are willing to cross and high-rise buildings that we are prepared to live in, but we cannot be sure that a specific approach to child-rearing, educational instruction, or clinical treatment will exert the same developmental effects on every child who experiences it.

Thus, even though being subjected to harsh physical punishment can and often does foster aggression in the child, whether it does so for a particular child may depend on other factors. These might include, for example, whether the child has a very sensitive nervous system or has another parent whose love and affection can compensate for the harsh treatment to which the child is exposed. Of course, weather works in the same probabilistic manner. Whether a storm will turn into a hurricane may depend not only on its characteristics but also on whether air pressure in another locale will increase the time that the hurricane spends out at sea, picking up moisture, before making landfall. In other words, in the case of a probabilistic science like human development, we should not expect the kind of one-to-one correspondence between would-be cause (for example, hostile parenting) and would-be consequence (for example, child aggression) that we can expect with the effect of temperature on the state of H_2O or of container volume on gas pressure.

Ultimately, there are just too many moving parts when it comes to the life sciences—and we regard human development as a life science, not "merely" a social science—because the effect of most sources of influence depends on others, whether acknowledged and measured or not. Although this can be very frustrating to those who seek certainty, it can be a rather hopeful fact, as we hope we make clear throughout the book. Indeed, it is central to one of the book's themes that we will return to repeatedly—resilience. Even if, say, bullying fosters obesity (Chapter 10), child maltreatment promotes male violence (Chapter 14), or multiple life stressors contribute to depression (Chapter 15), this does not mean that such effects are inevitable. The probability that such adverse outcomes will occur increases in the face of these conditions, so risk is certainly heightened under certain conditions. But it is also often possible to identify countervailing forces that reduce their probability, sometimes eliminating it entirely. And these may open up avenues for intervention to reduce the likelihood that this risk will be realized. The research we share herein is ideally suited to uncovering these countervailing forces. Insights such as these will make clear that human development is both a basic and an applied science. It should be regarded as the former because it addresses our curiosity about why we are the way we are and the latter by yielding insights we can use to prevent problems from developing, treat those that have developed, and promote well-being more generally.

THREE RESEARCH PROJECTS FOLLOWING
YOUNG LIVES THROUGH TIME

Throughout this book, we share probabilistic insights we gleaned by studying more than four thousand individuals over several decades as part of three different research projects carried out on three different continents.

The Dunedin Multidisciplinary Health and Development Study follows virtually all one thousand or so New Zealanders born in the town of Dunedin in a twelve-month period in the early 1970s, with assessments of children and their developmental experiences made at birth and when children, adolescents, and eventually adults were three, five, seven, nine, eleven, thirteen, fifteen, eighteen, twenty-one, twenty-six, thirty-two, and thirty-eight years of age. At the last assessment wave, 95 percent of those study members still living took part. As we write, we just concluded the latest phase of this effort, studying Dunedin Study members once again, this time at age forty-five. This effort is so recent that we do not yet have findings to share in this volume.

Over the years, Dunedin study data has been gathered in a variety of ways, centered on study members' visits to the research project's offices at the University of Otago in Dunedin, with the exception of work reported in Chapter 5, in which visits were made to the homes of study members who were rearing their own children. Data come from interviews with parents when study members were children, as well as with children themselves as they got older. Observations of children's behavior and formal assessments of their abilities were also undertaken, including medical exams and biological measurements. During study members' late adolescence and adulthood, people who knew them well also provided information about them. Police were helpful in sharing information on criminal behavior, and the New Zealand government has assisted with administrative data, such as electronic medical records and social welfare records. Authors Moffitt, Poulton, and Caspi direct this research, and author Belsky has had some limited involvement in the study (Chapters 5 and 7). The Dunedin Study is the principal or exclusive focus of all chapters in this book except Chapters 8, 9, 10, and 17. Not surprisingly, given its long-term scope, the study addresses all three core issues highlighted earlier that are central to this book: links between a child's functioning and later development, the effects of childhood and adolescent experiences on future development, and the influence of childhood on health in midlife.

Readers may be interested in the backstory of the Dunedin Study and how we became involved in it. It began in the 1970s as a survey of all the babies born in one year in one hospital, with the purpose of counting how many mothers and their babies had complicated births. A follow-up at age three was undertaken to check whether the babies with birth complications were meeting their developmental milestones. This effort was led by Phil Silva, who today is considered the visionary founder of the longitudinal study. From the beginning, Silva recruited investigators to the study to expand data collection to track the children on scientific topics as diverse as educational attainment, injuries, and dental, respiratory, sexual, and mental health. Data collection ran on "the smell of an oily rag," as they say Down Under, testing children in a church hall. The research team had to clear out on weekends for Sunday school.

Silva met Moffitt in the 1980s on a round-the-world tour seeking new talent for the study. He persuaded her to join the team, aiming to expand the data collection into new topics such as delinquency and drug use when study members entered adolescence. Moffitt moved to Dunedin in 1985 and developed a deep commitment to the scientific enterprise, eventually securing grants from the National Institutes of Health (NIH) in the United States that helped to secure its financial future. Needing help to interview one thousand teenagers, Moffitt recruited Richie Poulton, a young student who was attending the University of Otago in Dunedin. Avshalom Caspi's involvement developed quite differently. He watched Moffitt present Dunedin data at a conference and approached her with the worst pickup line of all time: "What a beautiful data set you have there." Moffitt brought Caspi to visit Dunedin in the 1990s, and Silva recognized an opportunity to add expertise in personality and social relationships to the study's data cupboard. Shortly thereafter, Moffitt and Caspi, by then married Dunedin study collaborators, introduced Silva to Jay Belsky. Belsky visited Dunedin in 1993 (bringing his ten-year-old son Daniel, who in his thirties would come to work on the study as a young scientist—see Chapters 12, 13, and 19). Study members were now old enough to begin having their own babies. Under Belsky's leadership, a study of Dunedin Study members' parenting of their three-year-olds was launched (see Chapter 5). At about this time, onetime student Richie Poulton completed his PhD in Australia, and Moffitt lured him home to Dunedin, where Silva welcomed the newly minted doctor and schooled him to step into the study director's role upon his own retirement. Between the four of us friends, we have by now spent almost a hundred person-years working together on the study.

The Environmental-Risk Study (E-Risk), which so far has followed more than one thousand pairs of British twins across their first two decades of life, assessed children and their experiences growing up when they were five, seven, ten, twelve, and eighteen years of age. At the last assessment wave, 93 percent of the study members still living took part. Besides its focus on twins, the E-Risk Study, as it is called, contrasts with the Dunedin Study in a number of ways. Whereas the participants in the Dunedin Study are virtually all the children born in a single twelve-month period in Dunedin and thereby representative of the population, E-Risk focused disproportionately on re-cruiting economically disadvantaged families living all over England and Wales. Another contrast is that most E-Risk data were gathered during the course of visits to the homes of the families by research workers who con-ducted (separate) interviews with mothers and each twin, administered ques-tionnaires, made observations, and carried out standardized testing. People who lived in the neighborhood were also surveyed about each twin family's local area. The E-Risk Study is the focus of Chapters 9, 10, and 17. Moffitt and Caspi founded this research in the 1990s. When it comes to the major goals of this book, the E-Risk Study enabled us to gain insight into how child-hood functioning and experiences shape (somewhat) later development.

In planning the E-Risk Study, investigators Moffitt and Caspi in essence sought to repeat the Dunedin Study but this time with twins. They built in two design features that were novel and that were aimed at giving the environment a chance to compete against genetics in the causation sweepstakes. First, Moffitt and Caspi insisted on collecting E-Risk data during visits in the twins' homes and collecting video observations and interviewer ratings of the homes and local area. Most large twin studies collected data through the mail, phone, or internet, causing them to miss important environmental measurements. Second, Moffitt and Caspi ensured that E-Risk families represented the full range of socioeconomic status, from advantaged to severely disadvantaged. They accomplished this by underrecruiting twins born to older mothers, who tend to be well-educated women who use assisted reproduction, and overrecruiting twins born naturally to teenage mothers, who tend to be poor. Many twin samples until then had been biased toward the middle class, because middle-class families are more likely to volunteer and maintain long-term study participation. The recruitment strategy resulted in a sample that today almost perfectly represents the distribution of Britain's families on its demographic Index of Multiple Deprivations.

The *NICHD Study of Early Child Care and Youth Development*, carried out in collaboration with the National Institute of Child Health and Development (NICHD), followed about one thousand three hundred children growing up in ten American locales from birth to age fifteen. Children and their families, along with children's experiences in child care and/or at school, were assessed when children were one, six, fifteen, twenty-four, thirty-six, and fifty-four months of age, as well as across the elementary school years and, for the last time, when fifteen years of age. In some respects, this project integrates the two investigatory approaches outlined in the Dunedin and E-Risk studies in that scientific procedures involved bringing children into university laboratories on a regular basis (as in the Dunedin Study) and going into their homes (as in the E-Risk Study), but supplemented such efforts with assessments of children's day-care settings and even their primary-school classrooms. At the same time, it cannot claim to be representative of any population other than those born in the local hospitals from which families were recruited. This study is the focus of Chapters 7 and 8; Belsky was involved in this research from its inception. Like the E-Risk Study, it addresses the first two goals of this book but not the third (childhood influences on midlife health).

The backstory of the NICHD Study is rather different from those of the Dunedin Study and E-Risk Study, as it was conceived to address one particular issue: the effects of day care on child development. Doing so, however, necessitated collecting many different data that, as we will see in Chapter 7, could be used for purposes far beyond that primary focus. Chapter 8 tells the backstory of this collaborative enterprise, as well as what it revealed about the effects of day care, so further details will be omitted here.

It is important to appreciate that despite the work covered in this book having been conducted in geographically diverse locales—New Zealand, the United Kingdom, and the United States—it does not address development in much of the rest of the world. Developmental science has been justifiably criticized for being almost exclusively focused on the world of children growing up in white, educated, industrialized, rich, and democratic (WEIRD) societies. As should be evident, we, too, are guilty of this investigatory sin. To us, that means two important things. First, it is not really surprising that research has been conducted principally in those places where funding for scientific investigation has been generously available. Second, it is not really a sin if work in such WEIRD places leads to research in more varied places in the world, just as it is currently doing, not only to learn new things but also to determine how much hard-won knowledge that has emerged from studying the WEIRD world can be generalized to rather different locales. What we do know, though, is that much of what we have learned by studying human development in New Zealand, Great Britain, and the United States is generally applicable to much of the WEIRD world. That discovery should not be dismissed, even if it cannot—and should not—be glibly generalized to non-WEIRD societies. Only future research can determine whether what we have been finding and share throughout this volume accurately portrays development in places like Kenya, China, or New Guinea. We suspect that in some cases it will and in other cases it won't. We trust that readers will come to appreciate this if they do not already, given how much this book will reveal about the importance of the environmental conditions in which individuals grow up when it comes to determining the kind of people they turn out to be.

THE POWER OF LONGITUDINAL RESEARCH

One might wonder why we have devoted our working lives to studying human development, following about four thousand people for years and years while needing to master diverse academic disciplines, including psychology, neuroscience, sociology, biology, and statistics. In some respects, that is an easy question to answer: each of us finds the phenomena of human development fascinating. Why are we the way we are? How did we become who we are? What roles do nature and nurture play in this process? On the other hand, the answer to the question of why we do this work is also more complicated, and here we explain what makes the research that is the focus of this book seductively powerful.

Observational versus Experimental Research

The answer to the question of why we follow lives through time has to do with two important scientific characteristics that all three research enterprises that are the focus of this book share—besides the involvement of the authors. The first is that they are nonexperimental and observational in character. By this, we mean that no effort has been made to enhance or modify child, adolescent, or adult development. Our research therefore does not involve interventions designed to modify the nature and course of human development. We are "watchers," not interveners; historians, not policymakers. Therefore, central to all three research projects are monitoring and recording—that is, observing—what goes on in study members' lives and how they develop and change over time. As one member of the Dunedin Study noted about his long-standing involvement in the research, "Being a study member in the Dunedin Study is like being in one of those nature documentaries where the lion stalks the gazelle; the scientists never try to save the gazelle or stop the lion, they just observe." However much we may like this characterization, it is not entirely accurate. If and when it becomes clear that persons being studied pose an imminent threat to themselves or someone else, we meet our legal and ethical responsibilities to secure assistance for the individual and/or family involved. Otherwise, we just sit back and watch.

In any event, our employment of an observational approach is almost entirely because most of the questions addressed in the three projects—and presented in all chapters of this book—cannot really be subject to experimental manipulation and thus investigation. Who would agree to abuse their child so we could study the effects or to have their child placed in day care of high or low quality on a random basis in order to evaluate the effects of day care on children? Who would allow their daughter to be given drugs to slow down or speed up her physical development so that the effects of early versus later sexual maturation could be investigated? And, as a final example, who would let their child be bullied, again on a random basis, just so the effects of such harsh treatment could be evaluated?

Some scientists, scholars, citizens, and policymakers are inclined to look down on observational research like our own. This is because they view experimental research, often in the form of randomized clinical trials (RCTs), as the "gold standard" of scientific inquiry. As the terminology stipulates, these involve participants in a research enterprise who are randomly assigned to one treatment condition or another and a control group who don't get the treatment, so that comparisons between them can be made. Random assignment is carried out to ensure, or at least increase the likelihood, that the groups receiving different treatments are not different to begin with. Consequently, one can draw the "strong inference" that any post-treatment differences between groups were the result of the treatment being studied. Treatments themselves might involve the administration of a drug or a placebo (for example, to reduce appetite), participation in one form of training or another (for example, to be less harsh in parenting), or exposure to a particular set of experiences (for example, a trip to a park to learn about nature). Such research designs typically afford greater confidence that causal effects are being documented than is the case in observational research, but the truth is that not everything students of human development are interested in is amenable to experimental manipulation, as noted in the preceding paragraph. This is also why meteorology, astronomy, and geology are principally observational sciences—because we can't change the weather, the planets, or the Earth to see what the consequences of doing so would be. In other words, observational science is science—and not a lesser scientific enterprise than those that rely heavily or exclusively on experimentation.

One final point we should highlight in making this claim concerns the putatively gold-standard approach that is often pitted against observational inquiry. The assignment of individuals to a presumed helpful treatment or control condition on a random basis is central to the utility of RCTs, but the rarely heralded fact about this approach to empirical inquiry is that not everyone is willing to put themselves in a position to be potentially randomly assigned to a control condition—especially if the experimental treatment is intended to be beneficial, as it almost always is. "Sure," someone might say,

"I'm happy to participate, so long as I am randomly assigned to the treatment condition rather than the control condition." Any such assertion, however, will preclude an individual from being enrolled in an RCT—because enrollees must be willing to go along with whatever condition they are assigned, experimental or control.

This means that the generalizability of findings of clinical trials is rarely as broad as often assumed—because people who are not ready to risk being randomized to the control condition rarely agree to participate in RCTs. People also drop out of RCTs at alarming rates. This of course means that just because some treatment is found to result in some outcome does not necessarily mean that it would do so if made available to a large population. After all, there will be many in the population who would not have been willing to participate in the original experimental version of the treatment. Therefore, one cannot be certain that what worked with those willing to be randomized in an experiment would also work with those who were or would have been unwilling to do so. Sometimes such a generalization would not be a problem, but at other times it surely could be. From this perspective, "gold" would seem a mistaken way to characterize experimental work; "silver" might be more accurate. But our purpose here is not to throw the RCT baby out with the experimental bathwater, only to make clear that those who might be inclined to pooh-pooh observational science give the issue some more thought.

Of course, observational scientists have to be keenly aware of the limits of their investigatory strategy when it comes to drawing conclusions based on their empirical findings. In the case of human development researchers like us, this means being cautious about inferring causality when documenting statistical associations linking developmental experiences and environmental exposures, as well as functioning early in life, with later development. Everyone should know that correlation—a statistical association—does not necessarily document a causal effect of one thing on another, say marijuana use in adolescence and cognitive functioning later in adulthood. Even though we appreciate that strong causal inferences are virtually impossible to draw on the basis of observational research like that which is the focus of this book, we believe, as we hope to show throughout the book, that efforts can be made to reduce the likelihood that inferences drawn about causal effects with respect to human development will be misguided. Indeed, readers will discover that we repeatedly challenge our initial findings and the conclusions to which they lead by considering and empirically evaluating alternative explanations of our results. Only when we have done so and found these latter accounts wanting can we embrace the evidence we present. In fact, one of our reasons for writing this book was to bring this point home, thereby documenting the utility of an observational science for understanding human development while showing how knowledge generated this way can be used to guide interventions and the development of services to prevent or treat developmental problems and/or foster well-being.

Prospective versus Retrospective Research

Beyond their observational character, the second common feature of the three research projects that form the basis of this book is that they all *prospectively* follow lives through time. What exactly do we mean by that? The key term is "prospective," the opposite of which is "retrospective." In retrospective research on human development, one studies the functioning of individuals at some point in time and then endeavors to link what is observed—in childhood, adolescence, or adulthood—back to earlier experiences, exposures, or ways of functioning that are recalled. Consider in this regard so much recent research on adverse childhood experiences (ACEs), such as being a victim of child abuse or the child of a drug-addicted parent. Most of this work conducted by physicians trying to understand the developmental origins of health and disease in adulthood involves querying adults about what they experienced in childhood—ten, twenty, or thirty years earlier. In such retrospective research, the potential causes of later social, emotional, and cognitive functioning, or even of physical health, are not measured when they occur; they are based on "looking-back" reports of what (supposedly) happened earlier in life. In contrast, in prospective research, which characterizes all the work presented in this book, experiences, exposures, and early-life functioning are measured when (or close to when) they actually occur and then individuals are followed forward in time as they grow and develop. This allows investigators like us to link such antecedent and potentially causal factors and processes with future "outcomes." Indeed, it is this following of study members over time that makes the research longitudinal.

One might reasonably wonder whether it actually matters whether one studies development prospectively, as we have done, or retrospectively, as many others have and still do. Let us use two examples to illustrate the functional differences between these two approaches—which are central to why we do what we do as prospective researchers. The first example is about the early-life origins of problem behavior in childhood, the kind that often leads children to fail academically and have trouble getting along with peers. Let's imagine that the hypothesis guiding some retrospective research is that children who are aggressive and uncooperative during their elementary-school years are just behaving in ways that are a continuing reflection of how they functioned much earlier in life. In other words, when a child has an early difficult temperament characterized by much crying and problems sleeping, eating, and adjusting to new situations as an infant, he or she grows up to behave in elementary school in the problematic fashion that we have described. By the way, this relation between functioning early and later in life is the focus of Part II of the book, which addresses the first of our core goals and themes, determining whether how children think, feel, and behave in their first five, ten, or fifteen years of life forecasts who they become later in life and, if so, how.

If we set out to evaluate the hypothesis under consideration by using a retrospective approach, we might collaborate with service providers working at a clinic treating aggressive, uncooperative, and antisocial children. Given our hypothesis about early temperament, a fundamental question we would surely ask parents of children in the clinic would be, "When did your child start behaving in such a problematic manner?" Evidence indicates that many parents would answer something like, "Oh, he has always been this way, a handful of trouble from the moment he was born, crying, struggling, just being difficult, sometimes impossible." If enough parents recollected such early onset of their child's problematic behavior, we might conclude that the evidence supported our hypothesis that problems in childhood have their origins in temperamental difficulty in infancy.

Before we confidently embrace this conclusion based on the collection of retrospective information on how the child who is now behaving problematically behaved as a baby, let's take a moment to consider who is not studied in the kind of investigation we just described: children who as babies had temperaments that were just as difficult and challenging as those of the ones who ended up in the psychological clinic needing treatment *but who never developed problems requiring treatment!* Had such children been included, the strength of any detected link between difficult and challenging infant behavior and later problems in childhood would no doubt be much weaker than a retrospective approach might indicate. Only by implementing a prospective study in which temperament is measured early in life and children are followed forward in time—prospectively—could we have confidence that we didn't fail to consider difficult infants who became well-adjusted school pupils. Consequently, any discerned association between early difficult temperament and later behavior problems in a prospective study would be much more likely to be accurate and meaningful rather than an artifact of looking at development through a rear-view mirror.

This is not just a theoretical, academic, or ivory tower problem. As already noted, the last several years have witnessed an outpouring of research—and discovery—concerning ACEs. This is our second example exploring the potential limits of retrospective studies and the scientific advantages of prospective ones. Much exciting research has been reported by physicians who have found that patients who have certain illnesses, more illnesses, or particular health conditions that cause illness recall, more than other individuals, having been abused, badly treated, and/or exposed to dangerous environments, including domestic violence, while growing up. Indeed, this work has been embraced to such an extent that many doctors today routinely require adult patients to share not just their medical histories but also their experiences while growing up, giving them a short questionnaire listing adversities to which they might have been exposed. This is presumed to afford the physician better understanding of their patient, perhaps even providing insight into the early-life determinants of the patient's poor health.

Because psychologists have wondered (and worried) for decades about the accuracy of adults' recollections of childhood—which too many believe they can report with great accuracy—psychological scientists have carried out research on this subject. Intriguingly, it shows that our memories of what we experienced while growing up, perhaps especially how our parents treated us, can be biased by our moods and mental health when reporting on our childhoods. Thus, people who are depressed tend to report worse childhood experiences than those who are not depressed. But couldn't this be because those who are depressed actually had worse childhoods? Sure it could be, but retrospective investigations are poorly positioned to illuminate this issue because of the risk of emotional bias.

In the Dunedin Multidisciplinary Health and Development Study, we were thus led to evaluate (a) the similarity of measurements of children's experiences obtained *during their childhoods* and reported by study members *decades later;* and (b) how each portrayal of childhood related to objective measures of physical health (such as blood pressure) and subjective appraisals of health (for example, "Overall, how would you rate your health today—excellent, good, fair, poor, or terrible?"). Is there much agreement between such assessments? Are they telling the same story? Are retrospective reports as good as prospective measurements of childhood experience when it comes to predicting health in adulthood? To find out the answers to the questions just raised, you'll have to read Chapter 16! Given this preliminary enticement, let us turn to what we cover herein.

OVERVIEW

This book is organized into five major parts (Parts II–V), all of which follow this introductory one and precede the final one, in which we draw some conclusions based on the work covered in these substantive parts. Before outlining the topics that will be covered, we need to make crystal clear that all the work described and discussed in this book was carried out by the authors, always in collaboration with many colleagues, so this book is not a review, survey, or summary of the state of knowledge in the field of human development today. As we trust our opening comments on this point have made clear, this volume is about the scientific adventures we have had in studying human development. Having said that, readers should be aware that our work, like that of all other scholars, builds on the insights and understandings achieved by those who preceded us. The specific research on which each chapter is based can be found, with full scholarly citations, in the bibliography at the end of the book.

A related point concerns a critical early decision made when conceptualizing this book: do we review and refer to the work of many other investigators, including many colleagues and even friends, who have toiled in the same investigatory vineyards that we have and whose work has influenced our own thinking and investigatory approach, or do we focus principally on our own work? From a scientific perspective, the question is, "How much review of the preexisting scholarly literature do we consider before presenting our own research?" Like so much in the sciences, as in life, open-minded thinkers—and book writers—can have honest differences of opinion on this matter. We decided early on not to spend time and space presenting a scholarly "literature review" of the numerous topics we address in this book but rather make clear what conceptual issues and scientific questions guided our work (and that of others), presenting details only of our work.

This should not be read to mean that the research that preceded our own is not important. Except in very rare instances—think of Einstein's theory of relativity—virtually all scientists "stand on the shoulders" of those who preceded them, hoping to see further than would otherwise be the case. We are no different (we are not Einsteins). All the work we share in this book builds on and we hope extends that of others, while providing similar grist for future investigatory efforts. This will become clear to anyone who consults our scholarly publications listed in the bibliography, as every one lays out the scholarly foundations on which each of our distinct investigations was based. Seventeenth-century English poet John Donne famously wrote, "No man is an island, entirely to itself; every man is a piece of the continent, a part of the main" (Meditation XVII in *Devotions Upon Emergent Occasions,* 1624). This certainly applies to modern science, and we remain honored to be part of the main.

As we hope to show, carrying out longitudinal, observational research is sometimes like being a pomologist, the person who runs an orchard; sometimes like being a chef preparing a meal; sometimes like a detective trying to solve a mystery; and, of course, sometimes like an explorer going places where few or no others have gone or even a treasure hunter, who expects to find something but cannot be certain this will happen. Like the pomologist, those of us who begin to study human development very early in life sometimes have to wait years for the "tree" to grow so that its "fruit" can be harvested. Before we can ask, much less answer, many developmental questions—such as whether people change or stay the same from childhood to later in life or whether supportive or adverse experiences early in life affect who we become—we need to wait for young children to become adolescents and adults. Like chefs, we longitudinal researchers collect much information that we keep in a data archive—think of a food pantry—and when we want to investigate, for example, an issue concerning development, we go to that pantry to select the necessary "ingredients" (read measured variables) so we can prepare a "meal" that is, carry out the necessary data analyses to empirically illuminate the issue under consideration.

As we plan our work, we often function like detectives or treasure hunters, but sometimes just as explorers. Typically, we draw on prior work that provides clues as to where to look and what to expect. In science, this is called the "premise" behind a piece of research. Of course, the clues are rarely so straightforward that we can be certain we will find what we are looking for. So, in these cases, we put on our detective or treasure-hunter hats, "read the tea leaves" provided by others, and make educated guesses. These are our predictions as to what we expect to find. But sometimes the clues are so confusing, if even available, that we are not well positioned even to advance a hypothesis, so we end up simply asking questions, hoping to get an answer. In that sense, we are like explorers delving into the unknown.

Today, when there is much skepticism about science, some of it certainly reasonable (dealing with the replicability of findings), this has become an important issue. Many, sadly, believe that scientists only find what they want to find, so ideology and advocacy contaminate scientific inquiry. While this is certainly true to some extent, when applied to the world of science more generally it represents a serious mistake in understanding. As we make clear repeatedly in this book, good science involves the dispassionate pursuit of objective knowledge. Even though no scientist can be 100 percent certain that unconscious biases are not undermining such objectivity, perhaps especially in the case of topics like those covered herein, careful scientists work hard to ensure that this is not the case.

Part II of the book addresses a claim that we have already touched on to some extent—that "the child is the father of the man." This old adage (coined by Romantic poet William Wordsworth in his 1802 poem "My Heart Leaps Up") refers, of course, to the claim that children's psychological and behavioral dispositions provide insight into who they will become as they get older, including as adults. It succinctly advances a long-standing hypothesis that how children think, feel, and behave forecasts who they become later in life. Thus, in the first chapter of this part, Chapter 2, we focus on temperament at age three as the predictor of development in young adulthood, discovering that some children we studied seem to "move against the world" early and later in life, whereas some others seem to "move away from the world" and still others are much more likely to engage the world in a confident, friendly, and open manner. In Chapter 3, we look further along the life span to middle age, asking about the long-term influence of self-control manifested—or not—in the first decade of life. We title this chapter "To Be Or Not To Be Self-Controlled." Chapter 4, the final chapter in Part II, addresses links or connections between being diagnosed with ADHD in childhood and the same disturbance in midlife. Here the developmental question concerns whether ADHD in adulthood represents the continuation of ADHD earlier in life.

In providing support for the adage that "the child is the father of the man," Part II of the book sets the stage for the next four parts, all of which address the question of why children and adolescents develop the way they do. In so doing, they build on Part I, addressing the second major theme and goal of this book: determining whether and how experience in the family shapes—or fails to shape—children's and adolescents' future development. Given the widespread view that parenting exerts a considerable impact on child and adolescent development, we begin Part III, on family influences, by asking, in Chapter 5, why parents treat their children the way they do. Building on extensive work showing that abusive and neglectful parenting is often even if not always passed down from one generation to the next, we evaluate in the Dunedin Study whether the same is true of warm, stimulating, supportive mothering and fathering, the kind of parenting that much research shows fosters child and adolescent well-being, broadly conceived. In Chapter 6, we investigate the family conditions that promoted delinquency among boys growing up in Dunedin, distinguishing between those who begin breaking rules on a regular basis in childhood and those whose rule-breaking careers begin in adolescence—because even if both groups behave rather similarly as teenagers, their experiences in their families while growing up turn out to be rather different, influencing their future development. The third family-related chapter, Chapter 7, turns attention to girls, examining the causes and consequences of early pubertal development. Results emanating from both the Dunedin Study and the NICHD Study of Early Child Care and Youth Development are considered. They indicate, perhaps surprisingly, that problematic family dynamics appear to accelerate female pubertal development and thereby adolescent sexual behavior. Like several subsequent chapters, Chapter 7 illuminates factors and forces that promote resilience—the capacity to experience adversity without succumbing to its negative effects. By considering resilience, we offer insight into conditions that might prevent problems from developing when children grow up under conditions of adversity. This is yet another theme or goal of this book—to illuminate when otherwise detected environmental effects (for example, early-life adversity leading to early onset of sexual behavior) do not materialize, and the implications of such insights for intervention and service delivery.

Part IV of the book takes the reader beyond the family to further address the third theme and goal of our book—determining whether and how developmental experiences and exposures beyond the family shape future functioning. We address the effects of day care (Chapter 8) and neighborhoods (Chapter 9) on child and adolescent development, as well as two topics pertaining to the influence of peers: bullying in childhood (Chapter 10) and cannabis smoking initiated in adolescence (Chapter 11). Chapter 10 is based on the NICHD Study, providing both good and bad news about the influence of day care on child and adolescent development. Our chapter on bullying, based on our study of children from the United Kingdom through their teenage years as part of the E-Risk Study, highlights its shorter- and longer-term effects on mental and physical health, while Chapter 11, also based on this UK study, focuses on how growing up in economically disadvantaged communities affects children's development. Intriguingly, we discover that the physical proximity of more affluent families turns out to matter. Does closer proximity benefit the child growing up in a disadvantaged household in England, as many policymakers and social activists have presumed, or does the experience of relative deprivation undermine well-being? The final chapter in this part, Chapter 11, shows that cannabis smoking, which typically emerges under the influence of peers in adolescence, can undermine cognitive functioning as well as mental health, especially when cannabis use persists into the fourth decade of life. Notably, all these chapters underscore the probabilistic nature of development—yet another theme of this book—in that not all children succumb to the adverse effects of risky circumstances. Once again, observations about factors promoting resilience afford insight into what could be done to prevent problematic functioning in the face of problem-inducing developmental experiences and environmental exposures.

Today it is widely appreciated that genetics must be considered if we hope to understand why individuals develop in such different ways. After all, there is no nurture without nature (and vice versa). So, in the first two chapters of Part V of the book, Chapters 12 and 13, addressing our fourth theme and goal of this book—determining whether and how an individual's genetic makeup shapes development—we evaluate whether certain genes can help explain who does and who does not get addicted to nicotine once they start smoking tobacco and whether a different set of genes can be used to predict success in life (as indicated, for example, by a high-status occupation, upward social mobility, and wealth accumulation). The results will raise the specter of genetic determinism, but as we will make clear, given the probabilistic nature of development, genetic effects are not inevitable. This is not to say that they are not important. To argue otherwise would be so outdated as to be silly. In Chapters 14 and 15, which also deal with genetics, we move beyond direct genotype-phenotype associations, as they are called, to investigate gene-by-environment interaction. Such a focus involves consideration of how nature and nurture collectively and interactively conspire to undermine human development by promoting male violence (Chapter 14) and depression (Chapter 15). Extending the interest in resilience in the face of stress, we identify those who do and those who do not prove vulnerable to adversity because of their genetic makeup. All the genetics-related work just outlined is based on the Dunedin Study.

We turn to the Environmental-Risk Study, however, for the final chapter dealing with genetics, focused as it is on what might be called the "new genetics," epigenetics. In Chapter 16, we evaluate whether, as theory and some evidence now suggest would be the case, the experience of being victimized in adolescence actually "turns off" the influence of some genes (gene expression) via a process of epigenetic methylation. If so, this would indicate that genes are not only "first causes" eventually affecting particular aspects of human functioning but also that developmental experiences and environmental exposures actually influence whether particular genes affect development. Indeed, should this be the case, we can think of genes as dependent variables, being affected by other factors.

Given the focus in the preceding chapters on diverse sources of influence shaping human development and whether "the child is the father of the man," we turn attention in Part VI, the last major part of the book, to the process of aging and, thereby, determining whether and how health in midlife is rooted in childhood. In Chapter 17, we provide evidence—from the Dunedin Study—that midlife health does have its roots in childhood and we address the issue of ACEs measured prospectively and retrospectively. In Chapter 18, which draws on the E-Risk Study, we look at how adversity "gets under the skin" and becomes "biologically embedded" by considering the immune system, stress physiology, and genetics. Finally, in Chapter 19, focused on aging in midlife, we examine variation in biological aging and report on how and why individuals in the Dunedin Study who are chronologically the same age nevertheless age biologically at different rates.

In the book's concluding chapter, Chapter 20, which comprises Part VII, we take stock of all that has preceded it. Here we highlight themes that have emerged in the course of conducting the three prospective, longitudinal studies that form the basis of this book. These themes include that childhood functioning is often a reasonably good prognosticator of future development; that no single source of influence is typically deterministic—because development is shaped by multiple interacting factors and forces, including experiences within and beyond the family, as well as genetics; that some children prove more resilient to adversity than others do, for a variety of reasons (for example, supportive parenting, neighborhood collective efficacy, and individual genetic makeup); and that all these conclusions provide reasons for hope that problems can be prevented or even remediated and that well-being, broadly conceived, can be promoted. Nevertheless, we make clear that we have "miles to go before we sleep" in that human development is a discipline still in its infancy—or at least its early childhood. There is much still to learn, so what we share in this volume can be regarded as a progress report. We trust that the reader will appreciate that progress in understanding human development is being made, especially via large, informative, prospective studies like our own that follow lives through time, beginning at or near birth.

PART II

THE CHILD AS THE FATHER OF THE MAN

2

Moving Against the World, Moving Away from the World

My heart leaps up when I behold
A rainbow in the sky;
So was it when my life began;
So is it now I am a man;
So be it when I shall grow old,
Or let me die!
The Child is father of the Man;
And I could wish my days to be
Bound each to each by natural piety.

—William Wordsworth, "My Heart
Leaps Up When I Behold"

The poet's assertion that "the child is the father of the man" implies that who we are as adults reflects, more or less, who we were as children. From this perspective, the child's behavior and functioning foreshadows—and forecasts—that of the adult. In some real sense, this is a nondevelopmental view of human development; after all, it suggests that we do not change very much but remain pretty much the same over time, and just becoming bigger and more complex versions of our younger selves. It is a view held, for example, by the forty-fifth president of the United States, Donald Trump. While running for the presidency in 2016, he claimed that he was the same person at seventy that he was as a preschooler. Given his emotionally reactive and impulsive behavior during the electoral campaign and even as holder of the most powerful position in the world, this doesn't seem hard to believe. But what about the rest of us? To what extent does how we behave and function as adults reflect who we are as children? And, reciprocally, does who we are as children forecast who we will be as adults?

This issue of continuity versus discontinuity—that is, sameness versus change—in development is an old one, though not always cast in such terms. More than fifty years ago, two New York child psychiatrists, Stella Chess and Alexander Thomas, helped launch the study of early temperament in an effort to address this issue. They championed the view of continuity, which was also picked up and further developed over many years by Harvard University developmental psychologist Jerome Kagan, now retired but still writing scholarly articles in his eighties, including on the subject of temperament. Whereas developmental scholars like Kagan underscore the striking continuities in development, the ways in which children remain who they are long into adolescence and even adulthood, others zero in on the remarkable ways in which people change—the surprising leaps, twists, and turns that often occur during a person's opening decades of life.

One thing almost everyone agrees on is that from very early ages children differ remarkably from one another in their psychological and behavioral dispositions—that is, their temperaments. While some infants are stoic in the face of adversity, seeming unperturbed by what can cause distress in others their age, others are vulnerable and easily upset. Whereas some toddlers are curious and readily approach novel and unfamiliar people, places, and things in a bold manner, others hold back, watching and waiting before doing so. And whereas some are ready to smile and laugh, others are hard pressed to express, at least overtly, such positive emotions. Dispositional differences such as these can be observed at very early ages, including the first year of life. Thomas and Chess distinguished three types of temperaments in early childhood: easy, difficult, and slow to warm up. The differences in the behavior of children with varying temperaments will become apparent as we proceed through this chapter.

For many students of child development today, inborn or early temperamental characteristics serve as the first hints of developmental phenomena that we can observe later in life—such as aggression or anxiety. But it often takes a second child to make many parents believers in temperament, especially when they have an "easy" rather than a "difficult" baby to care for the first time around. This is because with their "easy" child first-time parents often attribute their child's easygoing style to their own skills in child-rearing. Indeed, it is not unusual for these parents to presume that there is some problem with other people's parenting when they witness their compatriots struggling with babies who are challenging to put to sleep and have trouble adjusting to new situations. They often think, "If we had that child, she wouldn't be so difficult; the problem is with the parenting, not the child." But when a second child comes along who is dramatically different temperamentally from their first, easy-to-manage one, all of a sudden the idea of inborn, temperamental differences is appreciated. In such cases, parents often switch theories, from nurture, emphasizing the influence of parenting, to nature, emphasizing inborn temperament. A more nuanced view emerges: "It's not, or at least not entirely, how the child is cared for that matters but rather what the child brings into the world."

This observation struck one of this book's authors quite powerfully when raising two sons, except that rather than the first child being easy to care for and the second quite difficult, it was the other way around. In fact, the first child proved to be so demanding behaviorally, so difficult to soothe, so challenging to put to sleep, that his parents could not help but wonder: "Why isn't there more child abuse in the world?" That's how frustrating caring for this child could be. At the same time, they appreciated that it was a good thing that they were the ones who got to raise this patience-depleting individual, as some other parents with fewer psychological, economic, and educational resources might easily have been provoked into behaving in harsh and insensitive ways, perhaps even to the point of abuse. That certainly has been known to happen.

When this author's second child proved to be so much easier than the first, the child's parents now wondered: What kind of shock do parents go through when they first experience an incredibly easy child that leaves them feeling efficacious—that they have this parenting thing under control—only to be confronted the second time around with an incredibly challenging, willful child? If you could pick, would you choose to have the easy child first and the difficult child second, or vice versa? Obviously, there is no correct answer.

Students of child development regard the question of whether the child is the father of the man, and thus whether temperament early in life forecasts developmental functioning later in life, as an empirical issue, not a philosophical one. Do temperament-like behavioral characteristics that children manifest at an early age forecast—that is, statistically predict—how they will behave later in life? Or, cast somewhat differently, does adult personality have its developmental roots in temperament early in life? Given the Dunedin Multidisciplinary Health and Development Study's long-term and intensive character, it was perfectly positioned to address this question. In this chapter, we start by considering whether and how temperament measured at age three relates to personality measured a decade and a half later, at age eighteen. We then examine whether and how such early temperament forecasts real-life interpersonal relationships—with friends, family, and partners—when the study members were twenty-one years of age. Eventually, we even consider whether temperament at age three is related to having problems with gambling three decades later, at age thirty-two.

EARLY TEMPERAMENT AND YOUNG-ADULT PERSONALITY

When it comes to thinking about early temperament, there are at least two ways a developmental scholar can proceed. These can be understood—and distinguished—by contrasting the two observations "some people are more active than others" and "some people are active and some are sedentary." Note how the first observation treats activeness as a *dimension* that ranges from high to low, whereas the second highlights *types* of people, placing them into distinct categories—like Chess and Thomas's easy, difficult, and hard-to-warm-up children. Neither way of thinking about how people differ from one another is inherently better than the other. Each can be useful. For example, if I am going to take a bath, I treat the temperature of the water dimensionally, asking myself: "Is it warm enough yet to get in or do I need to add more hot water?" But if I want to cook some pasta, then the question is not whether the water is too warm or too cold but rather whether it is boiling. Both dimensions and categories can be used productively to study childhood temperament.

As we planned our adventure of examining the legacy of early temperament as it related to later functioning, we applied the typological approach, following the lead of Chess and Thomas and classifying children at age three as having one type of temperament or another, as will be explained shortly. We decided to proceed in this manner because we wanted to consider multiple aspects of temperament simultaneously rather than focus on one at a time. We would be asking questions like: "Does a child who is shy, active, *and* difficult to comfort when distressed develop differently than a child who is active, highly sociable, *and* easy to comfort?" Rather than investigating separately the legacy of shyness, activity level, or soothability, we considered a package or mosaic of multiple traits so that the whole person could be characterized, not just component parts or traits.

Just to be clear, we do not contend that our approach, which is referred to as a "person-centered" one, is better than what is referred to as a "variable-centered approach," which focuses on one dimension at a time, such as shyness or activity level. One may be more appropriate than the other, depending on the developmental outcome being predicted. If one wanted to predict athletic ability, for example, it might make very good sense to focus on the individual dimension of activity level to test the proposition that children who are more active than others early in life are more likely than others to become athletes later in life. But if one wanted to predict the quality of a person's romantic partner or spouse, for example, then focusing simultaneously on physical appearance, intellectual ability, and friendliness might be a more promising way to proceed. Studying temperament can be like what physicists have learned when studying the nature of light: sometimes treating light as a wave is the way to go, but at other times treating it as a particle (that is, a photon) makes more sense.

One of the interesting questions raised by the multifaceted, person-centered approach to temperament concerns how multiple distinctive traits might go together. Imagine that we have three different temperamental traits—call them A, B, and C—and that a child could score either high or low on each of them. This means, at least theoretically, that there could be eight different types of children, because when two possible versions of trait A (that is, high scorers, low scorers) are crossed with two possible versions of trait B and the resulting four possibilities are crossed with two possible versions of trait C, the result is a total of eight possible combinations of traits and thus types of individuals. If we scored children as high, medium, and low on each trait, then twenty-seven different types of temperaments could theoretically emerge (that is, $3 \times 3 \times 3 = 27$). And if there were five aspects of temperament, measured as high or low, there could be thirty-two different temperamental types (that is, $2 \times 2 \times 2 \times 2 \times 2 = 32$)!

But would this many distinct types really emerge? It is critical to appreciate that just because there could *theoretically* be eight, twenty-seven, or thirty-two possible temperament types does not necessarily mean that all would emerge in the Dunedin Study or any other investigation. The theoretical "design space" of temperament would not necessarily be completely "filled," such that each of possible types of children was represented. In other words, it wouldn't necessarily "map onto" the actual arrangement of multiple individual traits. This is just like the evolution of animals and their traits. Whereas some combinations of traits often go together in diverse animals, being large and aggressive, for example, or small and fast (to escape larger, more aggressive predators), some combinations (of many more than just two traits) are simply not found in nature. For example, we have no aggressive birds that are as large as an elephant (for obvious reasons). So the first challenge we faced related to the developmental legacy of early temperament was to identify, using information collected at age three, different types of children, based on temperament-related information.

TEMPERAMENTAL TYPES

As with most adventures, preparations were called for before we could begin. Several preliminary steps had to be taken before launching the first stage of our mission, identifying types of children at age three, so that we could, in the second stage, determine whether and how their personalities differed fifteen years later. First, we took advantage of twenty-two different ratings of child behavior made by an examiner who worked with each child for ninety minutes upon the child's arrival at the University of Otago lab at age three. These evaluations were based on how the child behaved across multiple situations designed to assess cognitive, language, and motor abilities. In these assessments, children were instructed to perform certain actions, such as standing on one leg, or to solve certain problems, such as putting an object in its correct place on a shape board (for example, the square object goes in the square space and the triangular object goes in the triangular space). Examiner ratings captured multiple aspects of children's psychological and behavioral functioning, including how much the child expressed different emotions and how restless, impulsive, and willful the child was. How much the child actively engaged in or withdrew from the tasks presented during testing and displayed persistent or fleeting attention were also rated, as was how negative, self-critical, cautious, friendly, self-confident, self-reliant, shy, verbally communicative, and fearful the child was.

The examiner, who was with the child through all phases of testing and observation, waited until the end of the ninety-minute period before making any ratings. Each trait was rated dimensionally, with each child receiving a score for each trait. For example, a child who was very impulsive but not very fearful would get a high score for impulsiveness but a low score for fearfulness. Another child might get rated high on both of these traits, another child low on both, and still another child the reverse of the first, low on impulsiveness and high on fearfulness. Given the longitudinal nature of the Dunedin Study, it is important to appreciate that these ratings were made in 1975—so we would not use them to predict adult functioning until a decade and a half later. This kind of prospective work, following individuals as they develop, obviously takes time. Recall the analogy used in Chapter 1, highlighting how studying development is like planting fruit trees: the pomologist has to wait before harvesting the fruit.

Therefore, when, well after 1975, we decided to examine the developmental legacy of temperament in early childhood, we took the twenty-two ratings made of each child from our data archive to determine whether we could identify different types of children and relied on a sophisticated multivariate statistical technique. In this case, *multivariate* refers to the twenty-two individual ratings made of each child—that is, these multiple variables, or distinct measurements. Essentially, the statistical method groups together children whose scores *across multiple traits* are similar to one another and different from those of other children. This procedure enabled us to identify five types of children in a person-centered way.

Undercontrolled children, who comprised 10 percent of the Dunedin sample, were irritable and distractible, and appeared not to enjoy their experiences at the university lab at age three. They had a difficult time focusing on the tasks they were asked to complete, including sitting still. They also behaved impulsively rather than taking their time to reflect on what was being asked of them. These children therefore proved quite similar to Chess and Thomas's "difficult" child.

Inhibited children, who made up 8 percent of the sample, were shy, fearful, barely communicative, at least verbally, and became upset when dealing with the unfamiliar examiner. Like their undercontrolled counterparts, they were also very distractible, having difficulty sustaining attention, but they were not impulsive. These children therefore proved quite similar to Chess and Thomas's "slow-to-warm-up" child.

Confident children, who comprised 27 percent of the sample, were especially willing and eager to tackle and explore the activities that they were asked to engage in. They displayed little or no concern about separating from their parents, which was required for some of the testing. Interpersonally, they were very responsive to the examiner. In other words, they seemed to adjust very quickly to the laboratory context and the demands made on them. These children therefore proved quite similar to Chess and Thomas's "easy" child.

Reserved children, who made up 15 percent of the sample, were uncomfortable with the testing situation, being shy, fearful, and self-critical. Unlike inhibited children, however, they were reasonably responsive when dealing with the examiner, and their discomfort did not interfere with their doing what was asked of them. So, despite being somewhat timid, they were able to orient toward and focus on the tasks they confronted.

Finally, *well-adjusted* children, who comprised 40 percent of the sample, were capable of being reserved and in control when it was required of them. They were reasonably self-confident and attempted to cope with difficult tasks, but they did not become unduly upset when a task (such as completing a puzzle) proved too difficult for them. They did display some initial hesitancy during testing, however, but warmed up and became friendly after a while.

Some might reasonably ask whether these types of children that we identified would also be found if research like our own was carried out someplace other than Dunedin, New Zealand. This is actually a more general issue that is routinely raised about our work in what many might regard as a faraway and thus strange and unusual place, but the truth is that New Zealand is very much like many other modern, industrialized Western nations, and certainly English-speaking ones such as the United States. Therefore, we are not surprised that findings like those reported in this chapter and throughout the book prove remarkably similar to those detected by scholars studying child, adolescent, and adult development in many other places around the WEIRD world. In fact, returning to the issue of types of temperaments, it seems noteworthy that when we studied in other work a sample of poor African American children growing up in a major northeastern American city, we obtained the same temperament groups as in Dunedin. Researchers elsewhere have also reported results similar to ours.

PERSONALITY IN YOUNG ADULTHOOD

Fifteen years after the children came to the laboratory as three-year-olds, we measured the personalities of most of them, using a standard questionnaire that study members completed as a means of describing themselves. This second stage of our adventure yielded ten dimensions of personality at the variable level, on which we compared the five groups of children. Only some of the ten traits distinguished one group of children from another, now as eighteen-year-olds. Those are the only ones we consider as we describe what we found regarding whether the child is the father of the man—that is, whether early temperament predicts later personality.

Overall, at age eighteen, the five groups of children differed on half the individually measured personality dimensions, but it was young adults who had been categorized as either undercontrolled or inhibited as toddlers who proved most similar to themselves fifteen years earlier by the time they finished or should have been finishing high school. Let's consider the continuity in development we observed in the undercontrolled children before proceeding to address the developmental legacy of early inhibited temperament.

Continuity in Undercontrolled Children

As young adults, the formerly undercontrolled toddlers showed limited behavioral restraint or control. At age eighteen, they described themselves as danger seeking and impulsive and were the least likely of all young adults to avoid harmful, exciting, and dangerous situations or to behave in reflective, cautious, careful, or planful ways—thinking and reflecting before doing. They also experienced and expressed a great deal of negative emotion in that they were prone to respond negatively—and strongly—to many everyday events. Thus, if they lost a game or if a friend proved unhelpful when assistance was sought, these youths were very likely to get upset and even lose their tempers. Additionally, they characterized themselves as mistreated and victimized, likely to be betrayed by others, and to be the targets of false rumors.

Could this paranoia have been why these formerly undercontrolled toddlers were also the most aggressive young adults? After all, the now eighteen-year-olds freely acknowledged that they were willing to hurt other people for their own advantage and would frighten and cause discomfort in others as a result. Or could it have been the other way around, with their aggressive inclinations provoking mistreatment from others? In all likelihood, the interpersonal door swung both ways, with the aggressiveness of formerly undercontrolled young children contributing and being a response to problems they had with others in young adulthood and earlier in life. Given these observations and reflections, we characterized these study members, both as toddlers and as young adults, as *"moving against the world."*

Continuity in Inhibited Children

Development looked decidedly different in the case of the formerly inhibited children, even if continuity also characterized the relationship between their functioning in toddlerhood and at age eighteen. Recall that as three-year-olds these study members were shy and fearful and had difficulty concentrating on tasks during their visit to the university laboratory. In adulthood, they proved to be overcontrolled, restrained behaviorally, and manifesting a nonassertive interpersonal orientation. As young adults, they preferred safe activities to dangerous ones more than all other eighteen-year-olds did. They also were the most cautious, most careful, and least impulsive. For example, when asked if they would take a risk if friends challenged them to do something scary—such as jump off a big boulder into a lake—they indicated that even the disrespect of their peers would not be sufficiently motivating to make them engage in such an activity. On what could be regarded as a more positive note, these formerly inhibited toddlers were the most likely of all young adults to refrain from taking advantage of others and were least likely to be aggressive toward others. Notably, though, they lacked social potency in that they were the least forceful and decisive of all eighteen-year-olds; they were not interested in influencing others or assuming leadership roles—in the classroom, on a team, or even when out with friends. As in the case of young adults who were undercontrolled as three-year-olds, these formerly inhibited children provided support for the claim "show me the child and I'll show you the man." Indeed, we came to view them as *"moving away from the world"* in both early childhood and young adulthood.

Continuity in Other Children

Young adults who fell into one of the three other, less extreme temperament groups as three-year-olds did not display adult personalities that were as strikingly consistent with their earlier selves as those who moved against or away from the world. Nonetheless, our efforts to view them as eighteen-year-olds through the lens of their functioning in early childhood provided some evidence of continuity from early temperament to later personality. Recall that confident young children evinced an enthusiastic approach to the novel testing session at the university laboratory. As adults, they turned out to be more impulsive than every other temperament group except those who had been undercontrolled in early childhood and were judged as moving against the world later in life. The reserved young children who were apprehensive in the same novel testing situations at age three were, as adults, significantly less forceful and decisive than all other children, with the exception of those who had been inhibited in early childhood and were judged as moving away from the world later in life. Finally, the eighteen-year-olds whose emotions and behavior had been characterized as appropriate to their age and situation at age three and were thus considered well adjusted developed into what could only be described as normal, healthy young adults. They proved to be neither extremely planful nor timid, aggressive, or impulsive.

HOW EARLY TEMPERAMENT COMES TO BE RELATED TO LATER PERSONALITY

Given the continuity that we discerned linking three-year-old temperament with eighteen-year-old personality, one is forced to wonder what accounts for it. How does early inhibition or lack of control early in life end up predicting—and contributing to—personality fifteen years later? One possibility is that we are dealing with temperament and personality styles that are genetically heritable, with the same genes that contribute to early temperament also influencing later personality. This could explain why child temperament and adult personality are related. There is certainly evidence from other research that is consistent with this claim. In Chapters 12 and 13 we directly address the effects of genetic makeup on functioning in adolescence and adulthood, if only to make clear that nature, not just nurture, plays an important role in influencing how we become who we are.

Even after granting a considerable role to genetics, it cannot answer the question of *how* the differences we observed in early temperament are preserved and flower into the personality traits we measured a decade and a half later. Here we are dealing with the issue of developmental processes responsible for continuity. To illuminate this issue, it is useful to think about "development in context"—and thus the interaction of growing children and their environment, especially those around them. We are developmental scholars, so it is no surprise that "development in context" has been a central organizing principle of our work. Two of the authors, Belsky and Caspi, cut their developmental teeth in graduate school at Cornell University, almost ten years apart, and both were influenced by the thinking and writings of Urie Bronfenbrenner, the developmental scholar at Cornell famous for his contextual model of the "ecology of human development." Like others before him, Bronfenbrenner believed that you could no more take a child or adult out of context if you want to understand its development than you can take a fish out of water if you want to understand it. Perhaps what Bronfenbrenner added to this understanding when it came to the importance of person-environment interaction in the process of development was his articulation of the multiple ecological layers in which humans are embedded. These range from the immediate environment that the child directly experiences (for example, family, day care, school) to the broader societal and historical context (for example, democratic versus totalitarian or the history of slavery) in which these more immediate contexts are embedded, like those Russian nested dolls that fit one inside the other.

Three Person-Environment Developmental Processes

For the Dunedin Study, it proved helpful to distinguish three distinct developmental processes capable of fostering continuity in personality. We suspected that all were operative in the case of undercontrolled and inhibited children, which accounts for the striking continuity so evident in their development.

The first process involves the child's temperament *evoking* responses from others that contribute to *maintaining and even amplifying* the child's early disposition. Consider, for example, how an undercontrolled child might challenge parents, teachers, and peers so much that they react with hostility toward the offender, thereby promoting future aggressiveness. Here we see the first mechanism by which the child can be said to be a "producer of his own development" even when others are contributing to the developmental process.

With respect to the second developmental process to be considered, we need to think in terms of a *reactive* person-environment process. Such a perspective calls attention to the possibility—no doubt probability—that individuals with different psychological and behavioral inclinations experience, interpret, and react to the same situation differently—just as the Dunedin Study members did to being tested at the university at age three. So imagine a teacher asking a question in class and the confident child raising her hand, while the reserved child—who also knows the answer—hangs back. To the extent that such a process is repeated in different contexts with different people, is it any wonder that formerly confident and formerly reserved children continue to look so different as young adults—and so much like themselves so many years earlier? Here again, we see the child engineering his or her own development, even if not knowingly.

Finally, consider the third temperament-to-personality process, a *proactive* person-environment process that involves individuals selecting or creating their own experiences and thereby maintaining, perhaps even amplifying, their early dispositions. In such "niche picking," a well-adjusted child might look forward to the transition to middle school. Knowing that she will make new friends, which she does, her sense that she can control the world only increases. In contrast, the inhibited child is made anxious by the same transition. As a result, he withdraws from opportunities to meet and befriend new people and ends up lacking the ability to influence others or assume leadership roles. So niche picking becomes a third process by which early temperament develops into adult personality and the child becomes the father of the man.

This interpretive analysis is very important because it challenges notions of children as wet clay, shaped exclusively by experiences that others generate. Whether we are talking about evocative, reactive, or proactive developmental processes, the child can no longer be conceived of as a passive agent that others mold to their needs and ideals. To mix metaphors, or at least switch from one involving wet clay to one involving a chalkboard, the child is not simply a blank slate that others write on. Rather, at least to some extent, the child plays the roles of the slate being written on, the chalk doing the writing, and the person holding the chalk.

Notably, it is not just environmentally minded developmentalists who emphasize this role of the child in shaping his or her own world, which can subsequently influence the child's growth and development. Although genetics will not be discussed until Chapters 12–16, we would be remiss if we failed to highlight what goes by the term *gene-environment correlation* in the study of human development. This phenomenon poses challenges to research, including some of our own, which does not always take into consideration genetic differences between individuals (sometimes because the work was undertaken before it was possible to measure genes). Gene-environment correlation refers to the fact that genetic differences between individuals can result in the different individuals experiencing different environments while growing up. Thus, the child genetically disposed to being highly active will be more likely than others to enjoy phys-ed class and to seek out sports activities, whereas the child predisposed in the opposite direction for genetic reasons could be less likely to engage in sports and more likely to play computer games. If this is the case, then it becomes possible that detected statistical links between particular environments and ways of developing that suggest effects of nurture may have as much to do with genetic differences between children, reflecting effects of nature.

EARLY TEMPERAMENT AND INTERPERSONAL RELATIONSHIPS

Further consideration of the three person-environment processes just highlighted that contribute to continuity in development, along with the notion of the child as an active agent producing his or her own development, motivated us to take a second look at the legacy of early temperament when we next saw study members, at age twenty-one. In the second stage of our adventure investigating the developmental legacy of early temperament, our focus was on relationships with other people rather than on individual personality traits. We focused on this aspect of development because whether and how we get along with others is central to the environments in which we find ourselves, some that we no doubt help create and others that continue to shape who we are and become. If temperament early in life is related to relationship functioning later in life, this would imply that early temperament can be an important life force shaping other important life forces. One then might think of early temperament in metaphorical terms: as a machine that designs another machine, which goes on to influence development.

To investigate whether the developmental legacy of early temperament extends to the quality of relationships we have with others in young adulthood, we returned to the Dunedin "data pantry" (that is, archive) to gather and analyze information about interpersonal relations. Metaphorically, then, it was time to bake another cake. In doing so, it was important to us to move beyond self-reports of study members themselves, obtained through questionnaires and face-to-face interviews. We thus supplemented these approaches to measurement with reports from friends, relatives, and partners whom the study member indicated knew them well, so-called informants. Obtaining such "ingredients" for our metaphorical cake was a very expensive and time-consuming process that was rarely implemented in other long-term studies. Upon making contact with such significant others in the lives of study members, we used mailed questionnaires to query them about their relationships with the study member and their impressions of the study member's typical behavior. This dual approach involving reports both from study members and from people who knew them well provided us with both "insider" and "outsider" views of the interpersonal world of the study member.

When we examined links between early temperament and many aspects of study members' interpersonal worlds at the start of their third decade of life, distinctive patterns of functioning emerged. These links between early and later life proved most striking in the case of individuals we already described as moving against or away from the world. Indeed, few differences could be detected in the social worlds of those who as toddlers had been categorized as well adjusted, reserved, and average. These three groups of individuals were more similar than different, just as they had been at younger ages.

It would be a mistake to leave the impression that twenty-one-year-olds who had been undercontrolled or inhibited as 3-year-olds functioned entirely the same way when it came to the young-adult interpersonal world. We say this because these two groups of children proved more different from each other than either did from the three other temperament groups. In general, the formerly inhibited children experienced less social support as young adults than others did, perhaps because they had smaller social networks—that is, fewer friends and acquaintances whom they spent time with and enjoyed the company of. Reputationally, according to those who knew them well, these study members appeared as less sociable than others, limited in their social agency or power to make things happen, and lacking lively interest and engagement in their worlds. Again, they appeared to be moving away from the world. Notably, though, these same individuals experienced reasonably well-functioning romantic relationships, reported minimal antisocial behavior, and had pretty good social experiences at work. Obviously, being inhibited in early childhood did not seem to undermine all relationships and relationship experiences.

Things could not have been more different for the twenty-one-year-old study members characterized as undercontrolled eighteen years earlier. Indeed, they showed even more evidence of moving against the world. Most notably, perhaps, they had highly conflicted relationships across four different social contexts that we studied: their social network of friends and acquaintances, their families, their romantic relationships, and their workplaces. As just one example, they were more likely than all other study members were to get fired from a job—even by the young age of twenty-one! No doubt, this had something to do with their engaging in the most antisocial behavior directed toward others. They were also the most likely to be victimized by others and to be considered highly unreliable by people who knew them well.

In sum, and no doubt because of the developmental processes previously reviewed dealing with evocative, reactive, and niche-picking effects, we found that early temperament was related not only to aspects of personality measured at age eighteen but also to interpersonal relations at age twenty-one, especially in the case of those study members categorized as undercontrolled or inhibited almost two decades earlier. This led us to wonder about the early temperamental origins of one particular form of problematic functioning.

EARLY TEMPERAMENT AND GAMBLING

Having discovered that at least some of the adults we encountered at ages eighteen and twenty-one behaved in ways very consistent with what we saw when they were three, we decided to reinvestigate the issue of continuity in development when study members were a decade older. This was the fourth and final stage of our adventure investigating the developmental legacy of early temperament. Because we desired to study a way of behaving that could prove very problematic not just to the study member but also to his or her family, we chose gambling behavior as our target of inquiry. We measured it when we restudied the Dunedin cohort at age thirty-two, when they were approaching middle age.

Historians have observed that gambling in some form has been nearly ubiquitous around the world and throughout history. But though gambling is a long-standing and common practice, only a small fraction of people who gamble end up losing control over their betting behavior to the point of developing a gambling disorder. Given that many engage in gambling in one form or another—whether it's weekly poker games, sports betting, or trips to Las Vegas—and that only a small segment of those who partake in it develop a disorder, there is reason to suspect that there are important differences between those who gamble to excess and those who don't. Because others have linked problems with gambling to personality characteristics like those we studied at age eighteen, it seemed reasonable that we might be able to predict problematic gambling at age thirty-two from our temperament assessment at age three. Indeed, we predicted specifically that the adults who at age three had undercontrolled temperaments and were inclined to move against the world would be most at risk three decades later.

As we made clear in Chapter 1, the Dunedin Study positioned us to advance understanding of the determinants of problematic gambling because our study is not retrospective. Thus, instead of being designed to look backward into the recalled lives and developmental histories of adults with a serious gambling problem, we could follow children forward in time to see who ended up suffering from a gambling disorder. The great benefit of this approach, which allows us to investigate potential determinants of gambling before any problem with gambling emerges, is revealed by considering the fundamental problem inherent in the retrospective method that we highlighted in Chapter 1: that it is poorly positioned to consider adults whose earlier lives, including their ways of behaving, were very much like those of people who became problem gamblers, yet they did not turn out to be problem gamblers. Therefore, the consequence of this backward-looking approach is that it might indicate that those who are problem gamblers are more likely to have been, for example, school dropouts when, looking forward, being a school dropout simply does not predict who will develop a gambling problem—because most dropouts never develop a gambling problem.

In addition to using the temperament measurements already considered in this final stage of our first adventure, we drew on what we learned from interviews with study members about their gambling behavior when we saw them at age thirty-two. We characterized study members as having a gambling disorder based on their responses to two measures of gambling behavior. These tapped impaired control or the inability to stop gambling; severity of harm, such as being in serious debt because of gambling; and recognized need for treatment. Almost 80 percent of study members at age thirty-two reported gambling in the past year, but only a little more than 4 percent met the criteria for a diagnosis of a serious gambling problem.

Because we wanted to be cautious and conservative in illuminating links between temperament at age three and gambling at age thirty-two, we addressed the question of the relation between the two after taking into account the study member's IQ as a child and the social class of the family when the study member was growing up. This means that before statistically examining links between early temperament and gambling at age thirty-two, we "discounted" the effects of these other potential sources of influence. Statistically, this involves "adjusting" the gambling scores of all individuals to reflect what they would have been if all individuals had the same IQ and grew up in identical conditions, at least as indexed by socioeconomic status (SES). This allowed us to be sure that any detected relation between child and adult functioning was not caused by either of these potentially "confounding" factors. A confounding factor is scientific lingo for a pretty good alternative explanation of the outcome being investigated—in this case, disordered gambling. Scientists who conduct observational research, including us, are obligated to evaluate alternative explanations in hopes of being able to rule them out—or at least discount them—before concluding that the primary factor under investigation actually influences the outcome in question.

In the context of our gambling study, consider the possibility that children who grow up poor or are not very intelligent are attracted to gambling and that such children tend to have undercontrolled temperaments. Were this the case and we did not seek to rule out or take into account these alternative influences on gambling behavior before linking early temperament with later gambling, we would risk misattributing the cause of problematic gambling to early temperament. As will become evident throughout the book, we implement this strategy in virtually all our work in one way or another. Actually, it takes two forms. In one, which we use in many chapters, we first evaluate the primary association of interest, such as the link between early temperament and gambling, and thereafter, in a second step, determine whether it remains robust when alternative explanatory factors are taken into account (that is, statistically discounted). In the other form, implemented in the gambling study and in Chapter 3 on self-control, we integrate these two steps into a single step in which we discount alternative explanatory factors while evaluating the primary association of interest (early temperament predicting gambling).

As predicted, study members characterized as undercontrolled in their temperaments at age three were most likely to have a gambling disorder at age thirty-two (see Figure 2.1). In fact, such individuals were three times

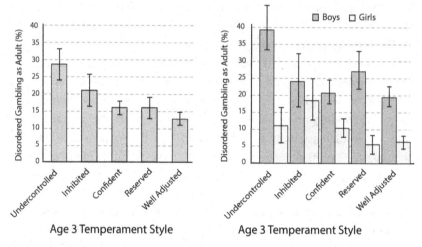

FIGURE 2.1. Percentage of adults who met the criteria for disordered gambling at age thirty-two as a function of temperament at age three for the full sample (left panel) and for boys and girls separately (right panel). Reformatted from Slutske, W.S., Moffitt, T.E., Poulton, R., & Caspi, A. (2012). Undercontrolled temperament at age 3 predicts disordered gambling at age 32. *Psychological Science 23*, 510–516, figure 1. © 2012 The Authors. Reproduced with permission from SAGE Publications, Inc.

as likely as all other study members to meet criteria for the disorder. But, as we examined the data more closely, it became apparent that this effect was principally found in boys. Girls with an undercontrolled temperament in early childhood were only one-third as likely as boys with such a childhood temperament to become problem gamblers. In some respects, that is not all that surprising, because men are more likely than women to develop gambling problems—in our study as well as in other research.

CONCLUSION

Throughout our adventure investigating the developmental legacy of early temperament and addressing the first theme and goal of our book— determining whether and how characteristics of children forecast functioning later in life—we discerned evidence of continuity in development. At least to some extent, this confirmed the claim that the child is the father of the man. Consistent with this view were the findings linking early temperament with personality traits measured at age eighteen, interpersonal relations in multiple domains of life assessed at age twenty-one, and then disordered gambling at age thirty-two. The evidence of continuity proved strongest in the case of the two groups of children with undercontrolled or inhibited temperaments as three-year-olds.

These results suggest that the continuity detected likely was fostered by the active role that the child played in his or her own development. On the one hand, it seems likely that the antisocial behavior of formerly undercontrolled children provoked negative responses from others that further undermined their capacity to get along in a highly social world. On the other hand, it seems that the limited social networks of formerly inhibited children likely derived from their own tendency to withdraw from the social world and isolate themselves. In the former example, continuity is driven by what individuals do to others, and, in the latter example, what individuals do to themselves. It is because of such evocative and nichepicking developmental processes that it seems appropriate to speak of children with undercontrolled temperaments as having spent their lives "moving against the world" and those with inhibited temperaments as "moving away from the world," just as we have done.

Developmental scholars who study lives through time, as we do, always bemoan what they did not or could not measure but wish they had. They are probably not alone. Just imagine what Darwin might have surmised had he known about genes, or what Galileo would have discovered had he possessed a more powerful telescope. After completing the work summarized in this chapter, we are left with two mysteries, one based on what we could not measure because our temperament assessments were not made for the first time until age 3 and the second based on what we found and its implications for what we did not find.

Age three is indisputably young, but it is also true that a lot goes on developmentally between birth, or even before, and the end of the third year of life. Today we know that temperament in the opening months and years of life can be measured reliably, something that was not known back in 1972, when our study members were born and the Dunedin Study was launched. So the question we are forced to grapple with, but cannot answer in the case of the Dunedin Study, is what our well-adjusted, reserved, undercontrolled, inhibited, and confident three-year-olds looked like in their first and second years of life. How did they behave? What experiences did they have? And therefore, what accounts for the behavioral styles we measured in the university laboratory when they were three? Were the temperaments we identified at this age already clearly or even somewhat evident years earlier, thus perhaps underscoring the importance of genetic influence? Or did certain very early experiences, including during fetal development, influence the temperaments we measured at age three, thereby implicating the role of nurture rather than nature? Of course, one must appreciate that these seemingly alternative possibilities are not actually mutually exclusive, an issue we return to in Chapters 14 and 15, which deal with gene-environment interaction.

Evidence gathered over the past forty years, perhaps most notably by behavioral geneticist Robert Plomin of Kings College London, a friend and colleague of ours, indicates that a child's genetic makeup plays an important role in shaping the temperaments even of infants. But we also know that genetics doesn't account for all the differences we see in infants and toddlers, so all we can do is ponder the extent to which nature, nurture, and their interplay contributed to making our three-year-olds who they were when we saw them in the lab at that young age. Presumably, it should be clear why scholars remain frustrated that we did not have good information on infant temperament in the Dunedin Study.

The second mystery we are left with has to do not with what went unmeasured but rather with what we did not find. Although we detected clear evidence of the child as the father of the man, it would be a developmental error to leave the impression that documented associations linking early-life temperament with eighteen-year-old personality and twenty-one-year-old relationship experience applied equally to all children, with the same being true of the connection linking undercontrolled temperament at age three with disordered gambling at age thirty-two. This is because we did not find anything close to perfect continuity. While we detected notable associations between early temperament and later development, these were probabilistic (see Chapter 1). Simply put, it was by no means the case that later in life every undercontrolled or inhibited toddler looked very similar to themselves earlier in life. Thank goodness! But this does not mean that what we discerned was not notable, only that change as well as continuity characterized the development of study members.

This lack of perfect prediction, or even anything close to it, is a cause for hope and optimism. After all, it would seem a very good thing that not all those children who were moving against or away from the world as three-year-olds functioned similarly decades later. Sadly, though, we remain in the dark when it comes to accounting for why *some* children who were undercontrolled or inhibited became much less so over time, or even why some of those who were reserved, confident, or well adjusted didn't turn out to be relatively average in their functioning up to eighteen years after our assessments of their early temperament.

Of course, we can speculate on what accounted for the change over time, given that early temperament was by no means a perfect predictor of later personality, relationship functioning, or problematic gambling. More importantly, we can infer some things based on work done by others that was carried out after our own. There is some indication, for example, that a supportive, intimate relationship with a partner or spouse can function as a "corrective emotional experience," attenuating the legacy of a problematic pattern of functioning earlier in life. Experiences with close friends or influential mentors might operate in a similar fashion. But it is also true that trauma, loss, disappointment, and other forms of adversity can alter the developmental trajectory of someone who was developing well so that in the future they function more problematically than would otherwise have been expected. Therefore, the moral of our adventure studying the legacy of early temperament should not be that only continuity characterizes development across the first two decades of life. While it is rather remarkable that evidence of continuity or sameness in the behavior and functioning of some individuals spans many decades, especially if a child was undercontrolled or inhibited early in life, our research also shows that such sameness over time does not apply to everyone equally.

To Be or Not to Be
Self-Controlled

et's begin by stating the obvious. Just as people vary in their height,
children, like adults, vary greatly in their self-control. Consider in this
regard some of the variation we witnessed in the course of conducting the
Dunedin Study. One child, when asked if he had ever started a fight and
tried to hurt someone as a result of some affront experienced at the hands
of another child, responded, "Only Catholics—do they count?" When another boy, thirteen years of age, was asked whether he had ever been in
trouble with the police, he replied, "Not yet ma'am, but no worries; it's
a-coming to me." And a daring girl snuck out of our research office with a
game tucked under her sweater that she stole from the examiner. But consider also the great effort and commitment another girl with severe disabilities displayed when struggling to complete a simple drawing task as part
of one of the developmental assessments administered, or the quiet boy who
recited multiplication tables for fun, obviously having spent long hours of
concentration memorizing them. Clearly, as already stipulated, children
vary immensely in their self-control—just like adults.

It is one thing to illustrate variation in self-control, as we just did, but
another to define and operationalize it so that it can be measured and
studied. In addressing these issues, we need to go beyond responses like that
of a famous Supreme Court justice who, when asked to define pornography

as part of a case involving freedom of speech, found it difficult to do but added, "I know it when I see it." Let's see if we can do better as we share our developmental adventure investigating the future consequences of childhood self-control.

Interest in self-control, it turns out, unites virtually all the social and behavioral sciences, though concepts and measurements can and do differ across disciplines. Whereas some conceptualize it in terms of impulsivity, others do so in terms of conscientiousness, self-regulation, delay of gratification, inattention-hyperactivity, executive function, and will power. Neuroscientists study self-control as an "executive function" subserved by the brain's frontal cortex and have uncovered brain structures and systems involved when research participants exert self-control. Behavioral geneticists have shown that self-control is under both genetic and environmental influences, and they have been searching for specific genes related to variation in self-control. Psychologists have described how young children develop self-control skills and, as we do herein, have investigated patterns of stability and change in self-control throughout life. Health researchers have focused on the legacy of (or lack of) self-control vis-à-vis mortality, psychiatric disorders, and unhealthy behaviors, such as overeating, smoking, unsafe sex, driving drunk, and noncompliance with medical regimens. Sociologists focus on low self-control as a determinant of unemployment and criminality.

Even though self-control is an umbrella construct that bridges concepts and measurements from different scientific disciplines, it can be usefully defined as *the ability to manage or regulate impulses and desires in a socially appropriate way rather than be managed or regulated by them*. Thus, lack of self-control can manifest itself in many ways, including elevated emotional lability, tendency to fly off the handle, low tolerance for frustration, lack of persistence, short attention span, high distractibility, frequent shifting from activity to activity, being restless, being overactive, acting before thinking, having problems waiting for something good, and having difficulty taking turns. Clearly, though, these examples do not exhaust the myriad ways in which limited self-control can be displayed.

In recent years, interest in the development of self-control and in its consequences for success later in life has arisen for a number of reasons. The capacity for self-control over our thoughts and actions is a fundamental human faculty, but the inability to make use of that capacity can be our greatest failure, especially in today's fast-paced, fast-food, social-media-obsessed world of endless possibilities, distractions, and temptations.

It is also important to appreciate that people are living longer than ever. To avoid disability, dependency on family, reliance on state benefits, and poverty, people must remain attentive to their long-term health and wealth. Managing retirement savings demands incredible foresight at the same time that one is bombarded with seductive advertising that can be a challenge to resist. Delectable, high-calorie foods are readily available on every corner, even as today's jobs leave many people exercising little besides their fingers and minds. Should it be any surprise, then, that westerners face an epidemic of obesity at least partially because of the limited self-control of many individuals?

Consider, too, the fact that as more citizens receive more years of education, intellectual achievement alone no longer wins the competition for good jobs. Employers now screen graduates for signs of conscientiousness and perseverance—or lack thereof—sometimes by monitoring their Facebook pages. Have you ever bragged, or at least shared stories with friends on social media, about drinking too much, falling behind on credit-card payments, or being late for work or in handing in a school paper? The remarkable historical shifts we are experiencing are enhancing the value of individual self-control, not only for well-being but also for survival.

Our home lives are not much different. The prevalence of two working parents or of a single parent employed outside the home requires a delicate balance of ever-shifting roles, responsibilities, and priorities. When times get tough at home, divorce is now a ready and socially acceptable option—as are a wide range of addictive substances, prescription or otherwise. Keeping a family healthy and intact requires tremendous acts of will. Skilled parents teach their children to control themselves and manage their emotions and impulses, along with teaching them their ABCs.

Besides these realities of the modern world that highlight the benefits of self-control and the costs associated with a lack of this important skill, we were drawn to study the developmental consequences of self-control after learning about the effects of the well-known Head Start program launched more than fifty years ago to enhance the development of young children growing up in economically disadvantaged circumstances. While it has long been appreciated that the program did not succeed, at least over the longer term, in increasing measured intelligence as some presumed it would and should, much research has challenged the notion that Head Start "failed." This is because some work examining developmental outcomes other than IQ that might be associated with enrollment in Head Start revealed important long-term, positive effects of this national program. In contrast to children who did not attend a Head Start program in early childhood, those who did proved less likely to become teenage parents, to drop out of school, to engage in delinquent behavior, and even in adulthood to miss days of work. Clearly, any conclusion that Head Start "failed" simply because it did not yield enduring gains in intelligence misses the mark by focusing too narrowly on only one of the potential benefits of this early-childhood experience.

The findings from the more recent and longer-term evaluations of the developmental legacy of Head Start led James Heckman, a Nobel laureate in economics from the University of Chicago, to wonder, in an important paper published in the prestigious journal *Science,* whether these findings could result from the effect of Head Start on self-control. Rather than increased intelligence being the route to a better life, Heckman surmised, Head Start's promotion of the ability to regulate impulses and be planful explained its documented longer-term benefits. Thus, when Heckman discovered that we investigators held in the Dunedin Study "data pantry" many potential measures of self-control early in life, he wondered whether these could be used to predict adult outcomes in the Dunedin Study like those found to be associated with enrollment in Head Start. From his point of view, that would be a further way of evaluating his hypothesis that it was Head Start's impact on the development of self-control, which went unmeasured in childhood in the Head Start evaluations, that benefited its recipients decades later.

To be honest, we were skeptical. To our way of thinking, the socioeconomic circumstances of a child's family and the child's intelligence rather than self-control would exert greater long-term influence on so many aspects of functioning later in life. Because we were worried that findings we might generate could embarrass such a distinguished scholar—by revealing that self-control was not the magic bullet Heckman suspected it was—we politely tried to avoid addressing the problem. He was quite persistent, however, so in the end we decided to let the empirical chips fall where they may by undertaking research to determine whether self-control in childhood would prove a powerful predictor of later development in the Dunedin

Study, just as Heckman hypothesized it would. Thus, we sought to determine whether study members who displayed higher levels of self-control across a myriad of assessments administered between ages three and eleven looked different in adulthood, at age thirty-two, from those who evinced lower levels in childhood. Given our interest in adult functioning in the real world, we focused this empirical adventure on determining whether childhood self-control predicted health, wealth, and criminal behavior. In so doing, we were clearly extending our work beyond a focus on the predictive power of temperament at age three while extending the range of adult outcomes potentially related to childhood functioning.

In carrying out this work, we appreciated, as we always did when drawing on the nonexperimental data from our longitudinal study, the need to consider alternative explanations for any findings we might generate. In testing Heckman's hypothesis, that meant being cognizant of the fact that some "third variables"—that is, alternative explanatory factors—could explain any associations over time we might detect that links self-control in the first decade of life with adult functioning in the fourth decade. These alternative explanatory factors are referred to as "third variables" because the predictor, in our case childhood self-control, is considered a "first variable" and the outcome to be predicted, say criminal behavior, is considered a "second variable." Anything that explained the association between the first (predictor) and second (outcome) variables could be a third variable. For example, when people go swimming (predictor), this predicts they will eat ice cream (outcome), so a third variable might be hot temperatures, as it could explain both predictor and outcome and thus account for any relation between them.

It didn't take much imagination to appreciate that if we found that higher levels of self-control in childhood forecast greater health and wealth in adulthood, as Heckman predicted, this association could be spurious. It could actually be a function of some other factors—in particular, as already noted, growing up in a socioeconomically advantaged home or simply being more rather than less intelligent. In the former case, we might find early self-control is associated with greater health and wealth in adulthood simply because a family's socioeconomic resources contributed to both our predictor, early self-control, and our self-control-related outcomes. If so, this could imply that any detected associations between the self-control predictor and our outcomes were simply an artifact of the influence that family socioeconomic advantage exerted on both predictor and outcome. The same thinking held for intelligence. After all, some children might have more self-control than others simply because they are more intelligent than others, and such children might prove healthier and wealthier as adults for the same reason.

Appreciation of these possibilities necessitated taking into account the potentially confounding factors of family socioeconomic status and child-hood intelligence *before* even evaluating the effects of self-control in childhood on adult development. In the findings we share, this is exactly what we did, by adopting the integrated, two-step process outlined in Chapter 2 to discount the effects of these alternative explanatory factors in step one before evaluating, in step two, predictive links between childhood self-control and adult development. Thus, the empirical question central to our self-control adventure became whether Heckman (who championed the influence of self-control) or our group (who suspected that once family social class and child intelligence were taken into account, childhood self-control would exert little, if any, predictive power) would prove more in-sightful. The developmental journey we go on in this chapter was not just a scientific adventure but also a competing-ideas horse race.

GETTING OUR DUCKS IN ORDER

Once again, it was necessary to assemble "provisions" before we could launch our adventure investigating the developmental legacy of self-control. Thus, before we could proceed to evaluate the power of childhood self-control to predict health, wealth, and criminality in adulthood after dis-counting effects of family socioeconomic status and child intelligence, we had to create measures of these constructs so that they could be subject to statistical analysis. One of the great things about the Dunedin Study is how rich in "ingredients" the data pantry is, thus enabling us to select from the cupboard robust measurements of the constructs of importance as we need them. Indeed, one of the fascinating things about a long-term study like ours is that one can use measurements to ask and answer developmental questions—that is, to go on developmental adventures—that were not even entertained when the original "shopping" was done for the "ingredients" eventually included in the "meal" to be prepared. This is perhaps a too convoluted way of saying that when some assessments of child behavior were obtained, none of us had any idea that they would be used to predict criminality decades later. (An added advantage of prospective data is that they keep researchers honest; it wasn't possible for us to collect measures in ways that would favor a pet hypothesis not crafted until decades later.) Similarly, when adult measurements of health and wealth were secured, it was not necessarily assumed by any of us that we would undertake research to determine whether these would end up being related to self-control in childhood. It was only because our well-stocked data pantry held the necessary provisions that we were positioned to launch our self-control adventure and test Heckman's thinking.

In order to create a dimensional measure of childhood self-control to use to predict functioning in adulthood, we drew on assessments obtained at a variety of ages and via a range of methods and combined them to create a composite index of self-control on which some children scored higher and others lower. Our self-control index was thus comprised of diverse measurements of children obtained across the first decade of life. These included ratings of child behavior based on observations made by research staff when children visited our offices at Otago University for testing at ages three and five years; ratings of child behavior made by parents when children were five, seven, nine, and eleven years of age; and similar behavioral evaluations provided by four schoolteachers when children were these same ages. Thus, our composite self-control score—which actually captured lack of self-control—reflected the degree to which a child displayed low frustration tolerance, lack of reserve, restlessness, impulsivity, limited attention, and lack of persistence in reaching goals when observed at ages three and five. Drawing on information obtained at older ages from parents and teachers, our composite index also captured impulsive aggression, as indexed by questions about flying off the handle and fighting with others; hyperactivity, reflecting frequent running and jumping, inability to follow a set of instructions, short attention span, being "on the go" as if "driven by a motor," and difficulty sitting still; lack of persistence, as indexed by a failure to finish tasks, being easily distracted, and having difficulty sticking to an activity; impulsivity, reflecting acting before thinking, difficulty waiting one's turn, and shifting excessively between activities. Notably, we did not rely exclusively on reports by others in creating our measure of (lack of) self-control. We also included the child's own self-evaluations at age eleven—about being fidgety and restless, being inattentive (for example, trouble sticking to a task), and behaving in impulsive ways (for example, difficulty waiting to take a turn, talking when others are still talking).

Ultimately, it was our view that by combining information obtained from observers, parents, teachers, and even the children themselves we would secure a robust measure of self-control manifested across a variety of settings, including our research offices, at the family's home, and in school. Decades ago, developmental scholars may have been inclined to consider separately the predictive power of each of the various measurements—or indicators—of self-control that we composited. Some still do. But extensive work has made it clear that because each individual measurement is typically limited in some way, combining together many that are conceptually related is often a better way to go.

The same "lumping" rather than "splitting" strategy informed how we dealt with multiple indicators of the developmental outcomes we sought to predict using childhood self-control, so when it came to physical health, we combined a series of biomarkers gathered during study member visits to our research offices at age thirty-two. These reflected cardiovascular, respiratory, dental, and sexual health, as well as inflammatory status. Measurements were based on physical examinations and laboratory tests to assess metabolic abnormalities, including being overweight, airflow limitation, periodontal disease, sexually transmitted infection, and C-reactive protein level, an index of inflammation. When these clinical measures were summed to create a measure of poor physical health, 43 percent of study members had none of the biomarkers, 37 percent had one, and 20 percent had two or more, at age thirty-two.

Because we were also interested in psychological and behavioral health, we took advantage of standardized psychiatric interviews administered at age thirty-two. These enabled us to examine the effects of childhood self-control on depression and substance dependence, including dependence on tobacco, alcohol, and cannabis, as well as other street and prescription drugs. Importantly, we also obtained from people who knew the study member well their appraisals of the study member's well-being. As we reported in Chapter 2, this enabled us to secure "inside" and "outside" perspectives on the thirty-two-year-olds we had been studying for decades.

When it came to measuring wealth at age thirty-two, we had available measures of the social class or socioeconomic status of study members as adults, based on their level of education, the status or prestige of their occupation (for example, doctor greater than teacher, secretary greater than garbageman), and their income. We had also assessed how financially planful study members were, based on whether they were savers or spenders and whether they had acquired financial building blocks for the future, including owning a home, participating in retirement plans, and having other investments. Study members were also queried as to whether they had difficulties managing money or had problems with credit and debt. Once again, these multiple measures were combined to create a single score reflecting wealth.

Let us take a moment to share a fascinating story about how we got interested in study members' credit ratings, the basis of our measurements of credit and debt. Terrie Moffitt found herself sitting next to an insurance executive on a plane one day, conversing about how companies decide whether to sell life and health insurance to someone. "People who don't take care of their money don't take care of their health," the executive asserted. This claim seemed like a hypothesis we could test. Thus, in response to this serendipitous encounter on a plane, we decided to secure credit ratings on study members, with their permission, of course, to add to our data pantry. This is what positioned us to include credit information in our composite measure of wealth at age thirty-two as we assembled provisions for our adventure evaluating the developmental legacy of childhood self-control.

Finally, when it came to criminal behavior, we secured records of every study member's court convictions in New Zealand and Australia, if they had any. This was accomplished by searching the central computer systems of the New Zealand Police. Virtually one in four study members had been convicted of a crime by age thirty-two. Although this rate may seem high, it is actually consistent with those of other developed countries.

THE LONG ARM OF CHILDHOOD SELF-CONTROL

Now that we had our provisions assembled, we were ready to launch our developmental adventure. Metaphorically, this is kind of like taking all the ingredients one has—childhood self-control, health, wealth, criminality— to make different dishes and serve up a meal, with the ultimate goal being to determine how nutritious it is or how good it tastes. As it turned out, our cooking proved delicious, at least for those who scored high on self-control as children. As we will show, Heckman ended up consuming a five-star meal, whereas we ended up eating crow! This was because our research compellingly revealed the power of childhood self-control—or lack thereof—to forecast real-world functioning decades later. When it came to health, we discovered that poorer childhood self-control predicted more health problems, as reflected in our composite biomarker index, even after discounting the effects of our third variables, childhood socioeconomic status and intelligence. Thus, adults with limited self-control in childhood grew up to have more cardiovascular, respiratory, dental, and sexual health problems, as well as more inflammation. And this was not simply because of the social and economic resources available to them as children or their measured intelligence.

When it came to mental health, variation in childhood, self-control failed to predict depression, but those study members who had less self-control as children were more likely to become dependent on substances, even after discounting the effects of our third variables. In fact, when individuals nominated by the study members as people who knew them well were asked about the substance dependence of study members, these reports by friends, partners, and relatives revealed that those individuals who scored more poorly on self-control in childhood had more problems with alcohol and drugs at age thirty-two.

Social and economic wealth accumulated by the fourth decade of life also proved to be related to childhood self-control. In fact, even with childhood social class taken into account, study members with less self-control in childhood found themselves in a lower social class in adulthood than their peers who evinced greater self-control in childhood. Given this observation, it should not be surprising that these same thirty-two-year-olds with a childhood history of limited self-control had less savings and had acquired fewer financial building blocks, such as home ownership and investments. They also were struggling more than others financially, reporting more money-management problems and more credit problems. Reports by informants about study members' economic conditions and behavior revealed much the same story. As an aside, we should also report that the insurance executive mentioned earlier knew what he was talking about. Our future work uncovered not only that a poor credit rating measured at age thirty-two was related to poor heart health at age thirty-two, but also that this connection itself was explained by limited self-control in early childhood.

The developmental legacy of childhood self-control also emerged when we studied crime. Children who had limited self-control grew up to be adults with more criminal convictions by their fourth decade of life. In fact, of the 5 percent of study members who had actually been incarcerated, more than 80 percent of these imprisoned individuals scored low in childhood self-control, falling in the bottom 40 percent of the Dunedin sample.

It is especially important to appreciate that our findings revealed a *gradient* of self-control ranging from high to low and thus provided evidence of dose-response relations (see Figure 3.1). In other words, it was not just that there were two groups of individuals with divergent developmental trajectories, one with low and one with high levels of self-control and competent functioning in adulthood. Instead, having a little more self-control resulted in slightly better outcomes, having moderately more self-control predicted moderately better outcomes, and having still more self-control forecast still better outcomes.

Despite this consistent observation, grounds for questioning the results of our research existed. First, they might have been "driven" principally by the small number of children who had been diagnosed with attention-deficit/hyperactivity disorder (ADHD, discussed in detail in Chapter 4), a psychiatric disorder of impaired impulse control. To address this concern, we deleted from our sample sixty-one study members who had been diagnosed with ADHD and we reexamined the effects of childhood self-control on health, wealth, and crime. The findings remained unchanged. Clearly, it was not the case that limited self-control forecast problems in adulthood only if children suffered from a psychiatric disorder involving limited self-control.

But is it mainly or only when childhood self-control is extremely limited that it undermines adult development? To address this most reasonable question, we analyzed our data again, this time excluding from the sample the 20 percent of study members who had the *lowest* self-control scores on our composite childhood measure. This, too, did not affect the findings. In fact, results remained the same even when we further excluded those study members who scored in the *top* 20 percent of self-control in childhood, thereby leaving only the study members who were among the 60 percent with moderate self-control scores. Clearly, the evidence linking childhood self-control with adult functioning did not simply reflect the adverse

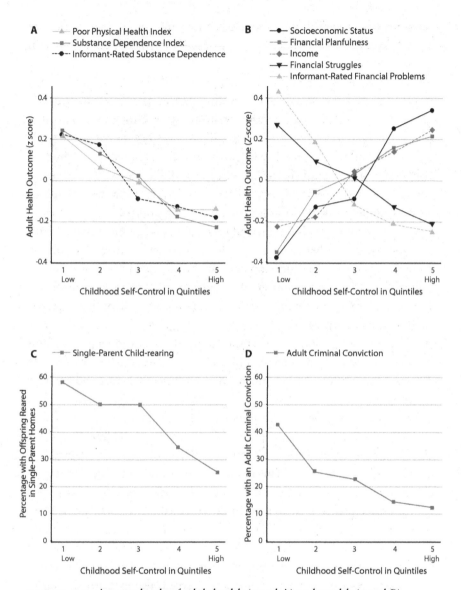

FIGURE 3.1. Average levels of adult health (panel A) and wealth (panel B) and percentage of study members with offspring reared in single-parent homes (panel C) and with adult criminal convictions (panel D) as a function of childhood self-control. Reformatted from Moffitt, T.E., Arseneault, L., Belsky, D., Dickson, N., Hancox, R.J., Harrington, H., Houts, R., Poulton, R., Roberts, B.W., Ross, S., Sears, M.R., Thomson, W.M., & Caspi, A. (2011). A gradient of childhood self-control predicts healthy, wealth and public safety. *PNAS*, *108*, 2693–2698, figure 2.

consequences of very low self-control or the substantial benefits of very high self-control. Even moderate levels of self-control had developmental consequences.

Because we also had in the data pantry an index of self-control at age twenty-six, we were positioned to address yet another interesting developmental issue, that of discontinuity in development—or the effect of changes in functioning over time. Recall that we briefly considered this topic at the end of Chapter 2, when we considered, for example, children with inhibited temperaments at age three who did not follow the developmental trajectory predicted by this behavioral style. Now we wanted to know what happened if a study member's self-control *increased* from childhood to young adulthood. Would the individual be functioning better in adulthood than others who also scored low on self-control in childhood but did not show positive development by the middle of their third decade of life? To address this question, we supplemented our measurements already described by combining two indicators of self-control that we measured at age twenty-six. One was an index tapping self-control that was part of a broader personality inventory completed by study members, and the other was a related index completed by a friend, partner, or relative about the study member. Once again, we drew on both insider and outsider perspectives.

After taking into account childhood self-control, we discovered that those study members who increased in self-control from childhood to young adulthood functioned better at age thirty-two than those who remained low in self-control to this point. This is a most important result because it documents that the child need not always be "father of the man," while underscoring the probabilistic nature of development. This latter point is reflected in the fact that poor self-control in childhood was not entirely deterministic of later functioning. This is because its developmental legacy was dependent on further developments in the future, in this case an increase in self-control over time. While we discerned clear evidence that levels of self-control across childhood predicted diverse aspects of functioning decades later, such results do not mean that poor childhood self-control leads—in an inevitable manner—to compromised development by age thirty-two. Indeed, even if this is generally true on a probabilistic basis, it is also true that childhood functioning need not be destiny. Development is a continuous process, even into the third decade of life.

HOW DOES CHILDHOOD SELF-CONTROL COME TO INFLUENCE ADULT FUNCTIONING?

It is one thing to find that self-control-related functioning in the first decade of life forecasts functioning decades later, just as James Heckman hypothesized, but another to illuminate why this is so. We addressed this issue next, extending our program of research determining whether childhood functioning forecasts functioning in adulthood. Thus, we "turned up the power of the microscope" so that we could delve into the developmental process, pathway, or mechanism by which childhood functioning came to influence functioning in adulthood. The point we make here, then, is related to the one just made: development is a dynamic, ongoing process whereby things occurring within the child and/or within the environment in which the child develops after childhood serves as a pathway that accounts for how childhood functioning comes to predict adult functioning. Developmental scholars typically conceptualize such intervening phenomena as "mediators" that link antecedents to their future consequences.

When it came to thinking about mediators, pathways, or developmental processes that may account for how childhood self-control came to influence adult development, we were intrigued by a hypothesis advanced by Terrie Moffitt that can be posed as a question: might mistakes made in adolescence, during the second decade of life, play a particularly influential role in linking poor self-control in the first decade of life with problematic functioning in the fourth decade? Because we had collected relevant information at ages thirteen, fifteen, eighteen, and twenty-one, we were positioned to discover, as we did, that study members with poor childhood self-control were more likely to make mistakes as adolescents, experiencing what Moffitt liked to refer to as "snares" that caught and trapped them in harmful lifestyles. Consider in this regard that children with low self-control were more likely than others to begin smoking by age fifteen, to leave school early without educational qualifications, and to become teenage parents because of an unplanned pregnancy. In fact, the lower an individual's childhood self-control, the more such snares they encountered as teenagers.

But it was not simply that lack of self-control early in life predicted adolescent snares. What is even more noteworthy is that these snares helped to account for why poor childhood self-control predicted poor adult development in the first place. When we statistically took into account—or discounted—the number of adolescent snares experienced, the strength of the previously discerned association linking childhood self-control and many adult outcomes was substantially reduced. In the case of childhood self-control predicting health and social class, predictive power was reduced by about one-third; when predicting substance dependence and financial planfulness, the reduction was about twice as great, hovering around two-thirds; and when predicting crime, the reduction was more than 40 percent.

To help understand our analysis and interpretation of these findings that mediate the effect of childhood self-control on later development by age thirty-two, imagine three dominos lined up in sequence, separated by only limited space. Domino 1 represents low self-control in childhood, domino 2 the number of snares encountered in adolescence, and domino 3 poor functioning in adulthood. Knocking over domino 1 knocks over domino 3 by first knocking over domino 2, but if you take domino 2 out of the sequence—as our statistical reanalysis did—the power of domino 1 to knock over domino 3 is reduced, although it could still have some effect via some other process—such as making the table vibrate. The point is that adolescent snares appear to be an important link connecting limited self-control in childhood and compromised development in adulthood. Just think what the consequences could be for adult development if there was a means of reducing the chance that adolescents with childhood histories of limited self-control will be caught in the snares of adolescence.

CONCLUSION

That we found better health and wealth and less criminal behavior was associated with greater childhood self-control even with childhood IQ and family social class taken into account means that the benefits of high levels of self-control and the costs of low levels of it cannot be attributed to these other—plausibly confounding—factors. Indeed, in our work, self-control predicted health, wealth, and criminal activity to the same extent as IQ and childhood social class did. To repeat, James Heckman was right and we were wrong. Not only was losing to a Nobel laureate not embarrassing, but it reminded us of an adage of a distinguished senior colleague, Michael Rutter: "When data conform to expectations that is boring, but when data prove you wrong, you really learn something." We suspect that Sir Michael may have been exaggerating a bit when it came to the first part of this claim; James Heckman was not bored by our findings!

The distinct influence of self-control that we chronicled should be regarded as especially important given the likelihood that it is much easier to foster self-control than it is to influence the two other "strong forces" in child development that we initially presumed would account for any effect of self-control: family social class and child IQ. Recall that in the case of IQ, that is exactly what the long-term evaluations of Head Start revealed. Even though enrollment in this early-childhood program did not result in enduring gains in measured intelligence, it did affect aspects of adult development that are dependent on self-control—in fact, the very ones that we found to be related to childhood self-control in the Dunedin Study: teenage pregnancy, school dropout, and delinquent behavior.

Because Head Start is a program for young children, even if not for infants and toddlers, it seems conceivable that it was already affecting self-control in early childhood rather than only later, during the elementary-school years. The basis of that inference comes from findings we have not yet shared: when we reran our prediction analyses including only the self-control measurements secured at ages three and five and based on only ninety minutes of observation of the child during assessments at the Dunedin research unit (see Chapter 2), these measurements very early in life forecast, *all by themselves,* adult functioning almost three decades later. Such findings do not imply, however, that intervention efforts will only be successful in promoting self-control if initiated in early childhood or even during the infant and toddler years. Even if efforts at these young ages prove to be less expensive, easier to implement, and more effective than ones provided at older ages—and this is a question of evidence, not of theory or belief—other results presented suggest that adolescence might also be a promising time to intervene.

Recall that adolescent "snares" caught more study members in the second decade of life who displayed limited self-control in the first decade of life. They were more likely than their more controlled agemates to have begun smoking by age fifteen, to have dropped out of high school before graduating, and to have become teenage parents. That these events helped explain rather substantially, though incompletely, the detected effects of lower social control on poorer health, less wealth, and more trouble with the police by age thirty-two strongly suggests that preventing teens from being snagged in these ways could largely ameliorate the otherwise anticipated adverse effects of limited self-control in childhood on adult development. Also recall our findings indicating that children with low self-control who had increased their self-control by their mid-twenties were doing better at age thirty-two than those who had not.

One of the frequent mistakes that parents, teachers, policymakers, and even developmental scholars make when thinking about interventions to promote well-being, broadly conceived, is to think in terms of and look to identify a "silver bullet" that will make all children grow up to be healthy, wealthy, and wise—or at least fulfill their potential. There are several problems with this view that need to be corrected. The first is that this view of how we develop is too deterministic. The second and related problem is that development is lifelong, not over by age three, seven, or even seventeen, which is not to say that it is as easy to intervene effectively at a later age as at an earlier one. But even if interventions prove more effective earlier in life, say at Head Start age or even earlier, than later, such as the teenage years, that does not mean that intervening at the earlier age will be sufficient to achieve beneficial effects that last a lifetime. Again, this is because of the probabilistic nature of development. Nor does it mean that intervening only at a later age will be a waste of time, money, and effort. The true moral of the development story is that because the effects of early life and most experiences growing up are not deterministic but instead are likely to exert their effects in a probabilistic manner, in part because of the role of various mediators in maintaining or deflecting established development trajectories, we should not expect a single intervention effort at any point in time to get the entire developmental job done when it comes to promoting future well-being. In other words, administering a vaccine at one time that provides protection across the life span for a particular illness is not a relevant model or metaphor when it comes to affecting many aspects of human development.

The point is that even if a child develops more self-control than would otherwise have been the case because of an intervention administered sometime during the first five years of life, that does not guarantee protection from the negative effects of adversities, including the snares of adolescence, later in life. While such an individual may be less at risk of succumbing to these future adversities—such as peer pressure to smoke, use drugs, and skip school—than an agemate who did not have the same beneficial early-intervention experience, that does not mean that later adversities could or would not undermine the development of the child with the early-intervention experience. Resilience, after all, is not all or none. By analogy, being in tolerably good physical condition because of training may enable one runner to finish a five-mile race that another runner lacking that training could not complete, but it doesn't necessarily mean that the first runner could complete a twenty-six-mile marathon. That would surely necessitate more and different training than that required for a five-mile race.

In other words, if we want to foster future success, including good health, reasonable wealth, and the absence of criminal behavior, we need to think about efforts to foster self-control across childhood and adolescence and even during adulthood. Doing so will undoubtedly prove more successful than just targeting one developmental period and using one particular intervention strategy. Some evidence for at least the first part of the preceding claim actually emerged from our study, though we haven't shared that information yet: even if self-control measured exclusively in *early childhood* did predict adult development, it did not do so as well as self-control measured across the *first decade of life*. In other words, self-control in early childhood matters, but it is not all that matters. Recall again that increases in self-control from the first to third decade of life also enhanced health, wealth, and public safety, the latter by reducing criminal behavior.

The developmental imperative that our findings and developmental perspective lead to is to endeavor to promote self-control early, often, and continuously. There is unlikely to be a "critical period" for doing so, meaning that attempts to do so at other times will not invariably fail or that only one strategy for doing so is likely to prove effective. It also is not difficult to appreciate that strategies for promoting self-control with three-year-olds are unlikely to prove effective with seven- or thirteen-year-olds. Intervention efforts must be appropriately suited to the child's age and the developmental challenges that the child faces.

Another issue that merits attention in light of our findings concerns who to target for intervention. One view might be that efforts to promote self-control should target those who most lack it. The alternative is to endeavor to treat all children. This contrast underscores a core issue in intervention and service delivery: serve everyone or target those most in need? The "serve everyone" view is based on notions of equity. Treating everyone the same is the only fair way to operate. The "targeting" view, in contrast, privileges efficacy rather than equity: serve those most likely to benefit, thereby maximizing efficiency of resources devoted to preventing problems from developing in the first place or remediating those already evident. Had we discovered that our findings were "driven" by or caused by those children with ADHD or who scored especially low in self-control as children, such evidence could have provided support for the targeted approach. But that is exactly what we did not find. Even when we eliminated these two subgroups from the sample, as well as those who manifested the most self-control in childhood, results linking childhood self-control with adult development remained largely unchanged. Thus, our findings imply that that there is room to enhance adult development even among the segment of the population whose childhood self-control skills are somewhat above average. Universal interventions designed to promote self-control could thus benefit everyone while avoiding stigmatizing certain children who are low in self-control. It is also an approach likely to attract widespread citizen support.

When it comes to how one might promote self-control, even in adulthood, let us make one more point. We do not need to think only in terms of long-lasting, complicated, and expensive interventions such as Head Start. So-called nudges could prove useful, too. These are mini-interventions that are almost effortless to go along with. Think about retirement accounts that require an employee to "opt out" rather than "opt in" to put some income earned on the job toward retirement. Whereas a person low in self-control might fail to "opt in" when given the choice—because of a desire to have some more money today rather than even more money tomorrow— that same individual might never bother to say, as required of the opt-out method, "I want my money today so I am not going to defer receipt and let it grow in a retirement account."

Now consider a kind of nudge that might work in childhood. If you want to get children to eat healthier because fast food appeals especially to those with limited self-control, put healthy foods on the most accessible shelves in stores. Many other mini-interventions like these have been proposed and are certainly worth considering, whether one is a parent or policymaker. Just google *nudges* and see what turns up.

4

ADHD in Childhood
and Adulthood

Attention-deficit/hyperactivity disorder (ADHD) is a mental disorder characterized by problems paying attention, excessive activity, or difficulty controlling behavior that is not appropriate for a person's age. Boys are far more likely than girls to be diagnosed with ADHD. This could be because the symptoms displayed by girls differ from those of boys or because cultural beliefs about behavior differ for the two sexes. Either way, virtually all experts agree that ADHD is rare in girls. It can be hard to distinguish ADHD from other disorders, and even mental health professionals sometimes have difficulty deciding whether a high level of activity or a limited attention span is within the normal range. Nevertheless, worldwide estimates of the overall prevalence of childhood ADHD hover around 5 percent of the population, depending on the criteria used in making a formal diagnosis of the disorder. According to a 2013 World Health Organization estimate, this means that ADHD affects almost forty million people around the world!

One of us, Jay Belsky, recalls encountering what certainly appeared to be an early-emerging and unambiguous case for the first time while observing a fifteen-month-old boy in his home—let's call him Sean—as part of a study of family life and early child development. The research protocol called for observing behavior for ten seconds, recording what was observed for later analysis over the ensuing five-second period, and repeating this process across a series of ten-minute epochs, each separated by five minutes of just observing, with no behavioral recording. Although this process demanded a great deal of attention from the observer, observing and recording was not typically a challenging task for a well-trained researcher—except in the case of Sean. Now, decades later, Belsky vividly recalls Sean's incessant movement, jumping on his rocking horse and rocking so fast and hard that it seemed inevitable that the horse would tip over backward. Sean would then run around, climbing on and over the couch and then the coffee table, only to race back to the rocking horse for another life-threatening ride. By the time the ninety-minute home visit and observation were over, Belsky was exhausted. He could only imagine what the parents of this child must go through; and apparently Sean didn't need much sleep.

One might think that in the many years since this doctoral-dissertation research was conducted, the causes of ADHD would have become well understood, as would its developmental course over the life span, with a clear consensus emerging regarding its treatment. Nothing could be further from the truth. Ritalin, a stimulant otherwise presumed to increase arousal and activity, has long been used to treat ADHD because of its apparent counterintuitive effects on children and adolescents with ADHD—downregulating activity while enhancing attention. Many high-school and college students never diagnosed with ADHD now take this "prescription-only" medication for its supposed benefits in enhancing concentration and thereby studying and test taking.

But the efficacy of this frequently prescribed drug has not gone unquestioned, even when prescribed for those diagnosed with ADHD. For many who are critical of the widespread practice of administering powerful psychiatric drugs to children to treat their supposed behavioral problems, the problem is less with children than with the contexts in which the modern world places them, along with the inappropriate expectations it has for them. Asking children at ever-younger ages to sit quietly for extended periods is just misguided, many critics of ADHD diagnoses and the use of Ritalin contend.

Perhaps one reason treatments are still debated, whether pharmacological, as in the case of Ritalin administration, or behavioral, using rewards to train the child to remain focused and reduce activity, is because the causes of ADHD also remain a subject of great controversy. As just noted, some believe that it is a socially constructed disorder that plagues the modern world because of unrealistic demands placed on children today, but there is also evidence from studies of twins that the disorder has a genetic component. The relevant finding here is that the probability of one twin having the disorder if the other twin has it is substantially greater in the case of identical twins, who share 100 percent of their genes, than in the case of fraternal twins, who share only 50 percent of their genes. But beyond such comparisons of twins, there also exists some evidence linking specific genes to the disorder. Many environmental factors have been implicated in the etiology of ADHD. These include exposure during pregnancy to high levels of maternal stress, exposure to toxic substances in the home, such as insecticides and artificial food dyes, and problematic parenting that takes the form of child abuse and neglect, to cite just a few.

In this chapter, we focus our developmental adventure not on the causes or treatments of ADHD but rather, as in Chapters 2 and 3, on the issue of developmental legacy. Once again, we address whether and how functioning in childhood forecasts functioning later in life. Current research indicates that ADHD is not just a disorder of childhood, as many adults now receive this psychiatric diagnosis. So a critical developmental question is whether such functioning in adulthood represents the maintenance of problematic behavior that originated in childhood or emerges in adulthood. Indeed, diagnosing ADHD in adults draws much of its legitimacy from the assumption that it is the same disorder as childhood ADHD, with the same neurodevelopmental etiology, affecting the same individuals in childhood and adulthood. The "neuro" in neurodevelopmental refers to the cardinal ADHD indicator of low test scores on cognitive functions such as learning, memory, and attention. The "developmental" in neurodevelopmental refers to the received wisdom that in order to be ADHD, the symptoms must emerge in childhood.

But the more we considered the evidence that adults with ADHD had cognitive deficits and symptoms dating from childhood, the more concerned we became with the state of knowledge purporting to support it. This was because the evidence supposedly documenting a connection between childhood and adulthood ADHD was seriously limited, relying on two research strategies, each with severe weaknesses. One approach involved following up in adulthood individuals diagnosed with ADHD in childhood, in order to determine whether they still manifest the disorder. Two problems plague this approach to investigating the developmental legacy of childhood ADHD—or any childhood condition. First, not all children who would meet the criteria for ADHD receive a diagnosis, so this first strategy, which relies exclusively on children who were diagnosed, is disadvantaged by "referral bias." Therefore, adults with ADHD who also had it in childhood but were not then diagnosed would mistakenly be judged to have it for the first time in adulthood. This would lead to the conclusion that ADHD in childhood is *less* associated with ADHD in adulthood than is actually the case. A second problem with following up only children diagnosed with ADHD in childhood is the failure to study children who did not have ADHD in childhood but developed it in adulthood. Therefore, the problem would be the reverse of the one already highlighted—a conclusion that ADHD in childhood is *more* associated with ADHD in adulthood than is actually the case.

The second approach to studying continuity in ADHD from childhood to adulthood that we regard as severely limited involves interviewing adults diagnosed with the disorder in adulthood about their recollected behavior in childhood to see whether they also had the disorder early in life. This is what is called a retrospective study, which we discussed in Chapter 1 when introducing the logic and benefits of carrying out prospective longitudinal research (research that measures individuals in childhood and then continues to study them as they age). While a strength of retrospective studies of ADHD relative to the "referral-biased" ones already considered is that they typically include a comparison group of adults who have not been diagnosed with ADHD—to see whether the two groups report different childhood experiences—their major weakness is their reliance on retrospective recall. The sad truth, as Chapter 1 made clear, is that memories are strikingly fallible, making recall problematic. If you doubt this, just consider the (many?) times you and a friend, sibling, or partner had different recollections of something that happened to both of you or that both of you witnessed.

For example, consider the situation in which two individuals had sufficient symptoms in childhood to have been diagnosed with ADHD, even if they did not actually receive a formal psychiatric diagnosis, but are diagnosed as having ADHD in adulthood. Whereas one accurately recalls his way of functioning as a child, the other does not. So, even though both experienced continuity in ADHD symptomology, the data collected only indicate this for one of these two individuals. If this problem occurred with enough frequency, investigators could conclude that there is minimal continuity in diagnosed ADHD from childhood to adulthood when there is actually much more than discerned. A not unrelated problem is that individuals without ADHD in adulthood could mistakenly recall being hyperactive and having a difficult time concentrating as a child when that was really not so—or at least not to such an extent as to result in a formal psychiatric diagnosis. Notably, the issues just raised are not merely hypothetical; the Dunedin Study presented evidence in the 1990s that false memories of ADHD can and do occur.

Given the developmental and clinical significance of investigating whether ADHD proves stable from childhood to adulthood and the inherent limits of existing research seeking to assess the connection between childhood and adulthood ADHD, the Dunedin Study was once again ideally positioned to advance understanding. An intensive population-based study like ours, with its numerous measurements made across childhood and adolescence and into adulthood, could overcome all the limits just highlighted that plague so much prior work. We could not only distinguish adults who do and do not meet criteria for the formal psychiatric disorder but could also return to the "data pantry" to see how these adults functioned as children. We could even compare such evidence with what adults recalled about their childhoods to determine whether such recollections proved accurate, which we suspected they would not. Because the Dunedin sample is of an entire birth cohort, there is no problem with "referral bias" or only select individuals being studied, as the study members are fully representative of the population from which they were drawn. They were enrolled at birth and thus before any would or even could be diagnosed with ADHD. All this enabled us to not only examine the relation between child and adult ADHD but also determine how those with these diagnoses functioned in adulthood, drawing on lots of information in our data pantry.

Whatever the scientific utility of conducting a prospective study of links between ADHD in childhood and adolescence, there was a personal experience—but not with the disorder itself—that motivated the developmental adventure that is the focus of this chapter. As many readers will know, the *Diagnostic and Statistical Manual of Mental Disorders (DSM)* has gone through a number of revisions. The latest is the fifth edition—*DSM5*. Like its predecessors, it stipulates the definitional boundaries of numerous psychiatric disorders and serves as the basis, at least in the United States, for determining whether an insurance company will cover the cost of mental health services. Like earlier versions, *DSM5* was years in the making and proved highly controversial once it was released. One of us, Terrie Moffitt, spent three years on one of the numerous subcommittees charged with reviewing and revising diagnostic criteria. After listening to endless debates by self-anointed pundits about what ADHD in adulthood was and was not, she had heard enough. This should not be a theoretical, ideological, or subjective issue but instead an empirical one, she reasoned. That led to the scientific journey we will now share, our third effort after Chapters 2 and 3 focused on age-three temperament and childhood self-control to address the issue of whether, as many believe and some of our evidence already clearly indicates, "the child is the father of the man."

GATHERING THE NECESSARY INGREDIENTS

To determine whether a formal psychiatric diagnosis of ADHD in childhood was related to such a diagnosis in adulthood, we drew on standard psychiatric interviews administered at ages eleven, thirteen, fifteen, and thirty-eight by trained interviewers lacking all other information about the study members. A standard psychiatric interview involves administering a set of standard questions (for example, Do you ever feel . . . ?), followed by standard probes in response to certain answers (for example, How long did it last? Did it interfere with your family life or work life?) All responses are then collectively judged in a standard manner in order to arrive at a formal psychiatric diagnosis. The availability of these provisions for our ADHD adventure ensured that subtle or not so subtle biases would not contaminate the psychiatric evaluation at any time. It is not hard to imagine that if the person conducting the psychiatric assessment knew other things about the study member—such as their parents being divorced or the child being required to repeat a grade—this could undermine the objectivity of the psychiatric evaluation. This risk would certainly be heightened if the interviewer was aware of the child's ADHD status, which is of course why we kept our adult interviewers "blind" to information about study members' childhoods.

To supplement what we learned from the interviews, we also had information on child behavior provided by parents and teachers who completed behavioral checklists that we used to also characterize children's behavior when they were five, seven, eleven, thirteen, and fifteen years of age. Even if a parent's previous reports might influence and bias their later ones, this was unlikely to be the case with teacher ratings, as children typically had different teachers reporting on them at different ages. Thus, whereas a parent reporting on a child at age eleven might be influenced by what they experienced and reported two years earlier, this limitation would not typically plague teacher reports. This was one reason why we focused on multiple sources of information about child hyperactivity and inattention.

Symptoms of ADHD in childhood include behavioral characterizations such as "very restless, often running about or jumping up and down, hardly ever still," "squirmy, fidgety," and "poor concentration or short attention span." Of course, each of these potential symptoms might apply to many children. To receive a formal ADHD diagnosis, however, many of these symptoms had to characterize the individual. By analogy, sneezing once or twice on a spring day is not enough to suggest a hay fever allergy, but doing so often, especially when other symptoms are evident—such as itchy or teary eyes—is another matter.

When it came to diagnosing ADHD in adulthood at age thirty-eight, pertinent symptoms included getting bored easily; not being able to concentrate; being messy and disorganized; being easily distracted; feeling fidgety, restless, or squirmy; talking too much; having difficulty waiting; and acting without thinking about future consequences. But, to be formally diagnosed with the disorder in adulthood, there also had to be evidence that the behaviors in question interfere with an individual's life, resulting in problems in the family, at work, with friends, and/or with other adults.

We also obtained information at age thirty-eight on how satisfied study members were with their lives; whether they experienced specific problems in life, such as underachieving; whether they were exhausting to be with (or "hard work," as a friend of one of the authors used to characterize such individuals); and whether they had accidents and injuries or engaged in risky driving. Careful interviewing, as well as information gathered on study members' medical histories, further enabled us to determine whether they had sought or received treatment for a mental health problem or taken any medication for specific psychological problems, such as anxiety or depression. Data that functioned as "ingredients" in the continuity-in-ADHD "meal" we were preparing also addressed the educational achievement of study members, their income, their tendency to save money rather than spend it, any troubles with debt and cash flow, their credit score, and whether they received welfare benefits in adulthood, submitted insurance claims for injuries, or had criminal convictions (based on central computer systems of the New Zealand Police). To test for the "neuro" part of the claim that adult ADHD is also a neurodevelopmental disorder, we administered an extensive battery of tests of neurocognitive function, including memory and attention. Similarly, to gain information on childhood neurocognitive functioning that might be related to ADHD in childhood or adulthood, we drew on data we archived on tested intelligence and reading achievement when children were seven, nine, and eleven years of age.

THE DEVELOPMENTAL LEGACY
OF CHILDHOOD ADHD

The first thing we learned during our ADHD adventure was that the diagnostic assessments of children and adults revealed that 6 percent of the children (by age fifteen) and 3 percent of thirty-eight-year-olds met psychiatric criteria for ADHD. Importantly, these prevalence rates are in line with those from other research conducted outside New Zealand. This again makes clear that even though our investigation was conducted in an English-speaking country far away from where most of our readers live, this does not mean it is not applicable to many other places. Childhood cases were predominantly male, as boys comprised just under 80 percent of ADHD cases. This observation is also consistent with prior work carried out in other locales. By adulthood, however, things had changed somewhat, with only 60 percent of adult cases of ADHD being male. Thus, twice as many females were diagnosed with ADHD in adulthood (40 percent of Dunedin's ADHD cases) as had been diagnosed in childhood (20 percent of ADHD cases). This was our first evidence that childhood ADHD and adult ADHD might not be as strongly linked as many psychiatrists, psychologists, and clinical researchers suspected. When it came to addressing this issue in more formal and direct ways, we adopted three approaches, each of which we now consider in turn.

Formal ADHD Diagnosis in Childhood and Adulthood

Our first formal and direct test of continuity, which sought to link formal psychiatric diagnoses of ADHD in childhood and adulthood, revealed no evidence of continuity. Thus, knowing that someone was *formally diagnosed* with ADHD in childhood proved statistically unrelated to receiving an ADHD diagnosis decades later. Of the sixty-one study members diagnosed in childhood, only three—or 5 percent—still met diagnostic criteria at age thirty-eight! And these three individuals diagnosed at both developmental periods constituted only 10 percent of the thirty-one adult ADHD cases at age thirty-eight. Indeed, nine of ten adults with ADHD had been free from it throughout their childhoods, according to their parents and teachers interviewed repeatedly *at that time.* So, clearly, *in terms of formal diagnostic criteria,* ADHD in childhood evinced very little continuity with respect to ADHD in adulthood. The evidence to this point therefore indicated that adult ADHD was not "developmental," because diagnosed individuals did not have sufficient symptoms in childhood to receive a formal diagnosis at that time.

Beyond this discovery, more insights were forthcoming from our adventure studying the developmental legacy of childhood ADHD—or lack thereof. The first was that adult ADHD did not seem to have a "neuro" basis. Even though Dunedin children with ADHD had the problematic and requisite memory and attention-deficit scores on tests administered in childhood that theory predicted they would, the Dunedin adults with ADHD did not show such deficits when they were tested at age thirty-eight. It would seem notable, especially today, when many scientists and citizens are rightfully concerned about the "crisis of (non)replication" in science—in which empirical findings prove different when other investigators address the same scientific question—that the results just summarized also emerged when we investigated the same issue in the Environmental-Risk Study being carried out in the United Kingdom (which is the focus of Chapters 9, 10, 16, and 18). In the UK case, however, we examined links between ADHD diagnosis at any time between the ages of five and twelve and later in young adulthood, at age eighteen (see Figure 4.1). Thus, even though a late-onset ADHD group could be identified both in New Zealand and in the United Kingdom, it proved to be unrelated to an ADHD diagnosis much earlier in childhood. Just as importantly, in both studies, no cognitive deficits proved evident

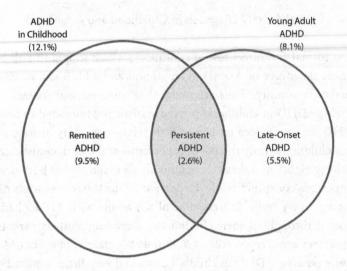

FIGURE 4.1. Proportion of study participants who met diagnostic criteria for childhood ADHD only, adult ADHD only, and both childhood and adult ADHD (shaded portion). Reformatted from Agnew-Blais, J.C., Polanczyk, G.V., Danese, A., Wertz, J., Moffitt, T.E., & Arseneault, L. (2016). Evaluation of the persistence, remission, and emergence of attention-deficit/hyperactivity disorder in young adulthood. *JAMA Psychiatry, 73*, 713–720, figure 1. Reproduced with permission from American Medical Asssociation.

among those receiving ADHD diagnoses at older ages. Such replicated findings raise the question of whether the term ADHD should even be applied to both childhood and adult disorders. Certainly, based on the findings considered to this point, it would seem that it should not. After all, the Dunedin findings revealed virtually no continuity in formal diagnoses between childhood and adulthood, as well as different results in childhood and adulthood with respect to sex differences in ADHD and neuropsychological correlates of ADHD.

Dimensional ADHD Assessment in Childhood and Formal Diagnosis in Adulthood

Despite the Dunedin findings, we recognized a need to journey further as part of our ADHD adventure before coming to any conclusions about whether the disorders in childhood and adulthood should both be called

ADHD. In fact, despite the repeatability of our findings across New Zealand and the United Kingdom, it occurred to us that perhaps the lack of consistency from childhood to adulthood in the behavior we chronicled resulted from the fact that we were linking formal, *categorical* diagnoses: ADHD versus no ADHD. What if instead of adopting such a typological approach, we implemented a dimensional one? Recall that we distinguished such alternative approaches to conceptualizing a developmental phenomenon when discussing ways to think about temperament in Chapter 2 and made clear that each can be useful. Thus, the question became, "What if we just considered the behavior ratings that parents and teachers made at ages five, seven, nine, and eleven and thus mostly before any child was formally diagnosed with ADHD at ages eleven, thirteen, and fifteen?" Would such dimensional measurements—as opposed to categorical classifications—be related to a formal (and typological) ADHD diagnosis in adulthood? Perhaps we failed to detect continuity in development because we were relying on formal and categorical psychiatric diagnoses (that is, you have it or you don't) at both times of measurement.

When we examined the issue of continuity in ADHD using dimensional measures of ADHD symptoms in childhood, we discovered that study members diagnosed with ADHD *in adulthood* did not score higher than nondiagnosed adults on dimensional parent and teacher ratings of inattention and hyperactivity in childhood. In other words, those diagnosed in adulthood did not look especially hyperactive, inattentive, or impulsive in childhood according to those who knew them well at the time. There was no strong evidence of continuity in development of "the child being the father of the man." And this was so irrespective of how we investigated the relation between childhood and adulthood ADHD. We got the same answer to the issue at hand whether we tried to link a formal diagnosis of ADHD in adulthood to a similar formal—and categorical (yes or no)—diagnosis in childhood or treated childhood ADHD symptoms dimensionally.

Upon first consideration, these results would seem to imply that childhood ADHD and ADHD in adulthood are unrelated, independent ways of functioning, so the same label probably should not be used for both of them, as this risks implying continuity from childhood to later in life. It would seem that the child is not "the father of the man" when it comes to the developmental legacy of ADHD. In some sense, this is not surprising, given all that has been said to this point in the book about the probabilistic rather than deterministic nature of development, in this case the legacy of child-hood ADHD when it comes to ADHD in adulthood. But before we could firmly embrace even this conclusion, there was at least one more possibility we needed to consider.

Formal Diagnoses in Childhood and Adulthood and Adult Behavioral Symptoms

In all the findings shared to this point, we have focused on formal psychiatric diagnoses of ADHD, whether both in childhood and adulthood, in our initial analysis, or only in adulthood, in our subsequent analysis. In the latter case, we linked the ADHD *diagnosis in adulthood* to behavioral symptoms, *measured dimensionally, only in childhood*. What if we turned things around and sought to link childhood ADHD or adult ADHD *diagnosis* with behavioral symptoms measured *dimensionally* in adulthood? Would children or adults formally diagnosed with ADHD function differently than those not diagnosed when we considered their behavior or symptoms in adulthood, all measured dimensionally (that is, from low to high)? It turned out that they did differ, resulting in a very different story of developmental continuity than reflected in our preliminary conclusions to this point.

In this regard, first consider reports about study members provided by friends or relatives who knew them well in adulthood. These revealed that study members diagnosed with ADHD in childhood were regarded in adult-hood as more inattentive and hyperactive/impulsive than study members who were not diagnosed as having ADHD in childhood. Furthermore, study members diagnosed in childhood, when compared to their peers who had not been diagnosed in childhood, proved to be less satisfied with their adult lives, perhaps because they were less likely to have completed a university degree, had significantly lower incomes, carried more debt, spent more time receiving social-welfare benefits, made more injury-related insurance claims, and were more often convicted of crimes. This means, of course, that even if children receiving a formal psychiatric diagnosis of ADHD were unlikely to be formally diagnosed with the same disorder again in adulthood, they nevertheless functioned differently—and more problematically—than their adult agemates who had not been diagnosed in childhood. Clearly, the devel-

opmental legacy of childhood ADHD looks troubling, despite a formal childhood diagnosis failing to predict the same formal diagnosis decades later.

But what about an adult diagnosis of ADHD at age thirty-eight? How
did that relate to functioning in the real world in adulthood, once more as
measured dimensionally? Here things also looked worse than for those individuals who had been diagnosed with ADHD in adulthood: Those study
members who received a psychiatric diagnosis of ADHD in adulthood were
more likely than other adult study members to have a long-term dependence
on alcohol, cannabis, or other drugs, as well as tobacco. In addition to such
apparent "self-medicating" tendencies, these adults with ADHD were also
highly likely—to the tune of 70 percent of them—to have had contact with
professionals for a mental health problem between the ages of twenty-one
and thirty-eight. And almost half had taken medication for a problem other
than ADHD, including depression, anxiety, psychological trauma, substance abuse, and eating disorders. It would seem, once again, that when it
comes to adult functioning, both childhood and adult ADHD are associated with problems and impairment in many, even if not all, areas of life.

CONCLUSION

We can imagine that the contrasting findings we have shared regarding the
developmental legacy of childhood ADHD might be confusing. Whereas,
on the one hand, a formal childhood diagnosis of ADHD did not predict a
formal adulthood diagnosis of ADHD, being diagnosed with ADHD in
childhood, on the other hand, did predict elevated levels of hyperactivity,
inattentiveness, and impulsivity, as rated by friends and family members in
adulthood. One item frequently endorsed by these informants of children
who had been diagnosed with ADHD was, "The person is exhausting to
be around." There were also some problems in life reported by the study
members themselves. There are two ways of thinking about these seemingly
inconsistent findings.

In considering the first, it might be helpful to think in terms of the following analogy. Suppose we measured obesity in childhood and wanted to
determine whether obese children grow up to be obese adults and to function more poorly than adults who were not obese in childhood. Even if we

discovered that being obese in childhood did not predict obesity in adult-hood, it could still be the case that formerly obese children still weighed more, on average, than others as adults, even if they didn't meet formal criteria for adult obesity. They could also experience less success in life than those who were not obese as children.

Once again, the point is that sometimes assessing a phenomenon in cat-egorical terms—ADHD diagnosis or not, obese or not—can be a useful way to proceed, but at other times it is not, because it masks variation across individuals as much as it illuminates it. This is why although we did not find that a childhood ADHD diagnosis predicted a formal ADHD diagnosis in adulthood, it did forecast being more hyperactive and inattentive in midlife, both of which were dimensional, not categorical, measurements. Had we not examined reports of attention and hyperactivity of study mem-bers provided by people who knew them well in adulthood and instead relied only on formal psychiatric evaluations, we would have had a very different—and misleading—story to tell. Instead of concluding that child-hood ADHD is unrelated to adult ADHD, we found that childhood ADHD was related to more inattentiveness and hyperactivity decades later and functioning more poorly in life, with this even more true for those diag-nosed with ADHD in adulthood. This observation underscores the value of our approach to measurement and assessment, moving beyond formal psychiatric assessment to consider dimensional behavioral and psycholog-ical evaluations provided by the study member's family, friends, others who knew them well, and themselves. In so doing, it also provides evidence of the scientific utility—even necessity—of challenging findings that first emerge to ensure that they reflect what is actually going on.

There is also a broader scientific moral to this story. It is increasingly appreciated in the world of psychiatry and behavioral science that few phe-nomena of interest are truly categorical—you have it or you don't—as most of the things we are interested in, whether disorders such as ADHD or competencies such as emotional intelligence, are continuous in character. Thus, it is not simply that some individuals are hyperactive and others are not or that some people are obese and others are not. Rather, it is that some are highly active or weigh a lot, others moderately so, and still others hardly at all. Whether diagnosing ADHD or obesity, we often fail to appreciate that categorical appraisals are based on some conventional cutoff points that are widely agreed on. Nevertheless, they are still fundamentally arbitrary; they do not reflect some natural category boundary. To be obese, one must have a body-mass index (BMI) greater than 30, but no thoughtful person would really expect someone with a BMI of 29 to be necessarily in better health, for example, than someone with a BMI of 31, even though the first individual is not formally obese while the second one is.

Ultimately, behavioral and psychological functioning is not like physics, in which there are truly qualitative "state changes" as continuous measurements change. Everyone knows that when water is cooled from thirty-three to thirty-one degrees Fahrenheit, thus passing the thirty-two-degree threshold for freezing, it changes qualitatively—from liquid to ice. But, to our knowledge, this kind of qualitative state change does not occur in behavioral or psychological phenomena. Thus, relying exclusively on categorical designations can mask as much as it illuminates. Our intent here is not to throw the categorical baby out with the categorical bathwater, however. We only want to point out the benefits of adopting a variety of approaches when addressing an empirical question regarding human development. After all, even though the childhood ADHD diagnosis did not predict the adult ADHD diagnosis, it did predict continuous ratings of some ADHD-like behaviors in adulthood. In consequence, it would have been inaccurate to conclude, had we only relied on our initial, categorical approach, that childhood ADHD and functioning in later life are unrelated to one another.

Our adventures in human development have repeatedly taught us that development is probabilistic, not deterministic. In many of our studies, we concluded that development was probabilistic because a particular risk factor (for example, undercontrolled temperament) or condition (for example, teenage mother) did not predict very well the expected outcome years later. For example, childhood ADHD did not predict that a person would still have ADHD decades later as an adult, but, we found the even more surprising probabilistic situation that for many participants in our longitudinal studies, diagnosable ADHD popped up in their lives seemingly out of the blue, well after they reached adulthood. These people believed they had aged safely through the childhood years, with no ADHD problems, and cognitive testing had detected no risk signals of abnormal neurodevelopment either. Nevertheless, they had belatedly become overactive, impulsive, and inattentive, to the extent that this syndrome was damaging their work and family lives. Some of these study members understandably asked, "Isn't ADHD just for kids?"

Other researchers were surprised, too. Some psychiatric pundits speculated that the adult symptoms were merely side effects of addiction, but most study members with adult-onset ADHD were not substance abusers. Other pundits speculated that adult-onset ADHD symptoms might be the earliest detectible signs of future Alzheimer's! But most study members with adult-onset ADHD are far too young for dementia. Our 2015 report of late-onset ADHD in the absence of any childhood neurodevelopmental syndrome launched a new area of inquiry. Investigators are now testing many hypotheses to uncover the cause of late-onset ADHD and the best treatment for it.

Even though, as we discovered, there was some relation between ADHD in childhood and functioning in adulthood, ADHD in adulthood was more related to adult functioning than was ADHD in childhood. The adult form of ADHD may not be neurodevelopmental, but it is clearly a serious condition, warranting treatment. The final set of findings we shared made this point most clearly. Recall that adult ADHD was found to be associated with alcohol, drug, and tobacco dependence, the need for mental health services, and the taking of medication for a variety of other psychological and behavioral problems. Given these findings, most of us, if we had a choice, would probably choose to be diagnosed with ADHD in childhood rather than in midlife.

These observations force one to wonder what promoted the development of ADHD in adulthood, as it clearly was not being so hyperactive and inattentive in childhood as to receive a formal diagnosis at that time. Moreover, individuals who had adult ADHD did not display problems with learning, memory, concentration, or attention either as children or as adults. This would seem to be yet more evidence for not giving the childhood and adult conditions the same diagnostic label. Fortunately, given the many measurements we made in childhood, we were positioned to address this issue of the developmental origins of adult ADHD. Although adults diagnosed with ADHD did not differ from those not diagnosed in terms of their cognitive ability as assessed in childhood, they did show some evidence early in life of having problems related to mental health. Study members diagnosed with ADHD in adulthood had more conduct-related difficulties in childhood than those not diagnosed as adults, including being more aggressive and disobedient than other children. Notably, we were also positioned to explore the possibility that genetics played a role in the origin of adult ADHD. This was because we had measures of specific "candidate" genes that other investigations had linked to ADHD. But, in the Dunedin Study, these failed to distinguish those with and without a formal ADHD diagnosis in adulthood. Obviously, it will take more work for the developmental origins of ADHD in adulthood to be fully identified.

The final point based on our work examining connections between ADHD in childhood and adulthood concerns the risks of drawing strong conclusions from research that is not well positioned to address this issue. In contrast to prior work based on recall of childhood ADHD, results from the Dunedin Study clearly indicate that being diagnosed with ADHD in adulthood is not simply an extension of such a diagnosis in childhood or adolescence—so it should not be characterized using the same label as in childhood. Perhaps the best evidence of the importance of conducting research as we have—by following individuals prospectively as they age rather than looking backward when they are adults, based on memory and recollection—is found in evidence we have not yet shared: Many adults diagnosed with ADHD rely on information provided by their own parents, rather than on their own memories, to inform their understanding of how they behaved decades earlier in childhood, but parents themselves are not immune to memory inaccuracies. In fact, we found that about three-quarters of the parents of study members who actually were diagnosed with ADHD in childhood did not recall—when the study members were thirty-eight years of age—their offspring being diagnosed in childhood with ADHD or even having symptoms of it! This was true despite these same parents having complained extensively about their child's ADHD behaviors when interviewed as part of the study three decades earlier! Thus, most of the documented childhood ADHD cases had been forgotten by parents two decades later. This only goes to show what anyone over forty years of age should know: memory is strikingly fallible.

PART III

THE FAMILY

5

Why Parents Parent
the Way They Do

Consideration of the roles that nature and nurture play in how humans develop has long drawn attention to parenting and its effects on children's development. Does spanking children promote aggressive behavior? Does explaining to a child why he or she is being punished enable the child to internalize parental values and thereby avoid misbehavior in the future? Does regular reading to a child foster literacy? While many of us assume that parenting matters, this view has not gone unchallenged. Many best-selling books have argued otherwise, including the late David Rowe's 1993 volume *Limits of Family Influence*, well known and widely read Harvard University psychologist Steven Pinker's 1998 book *The Blank Slate*, and the late Judith Harris's Pulitzer Prize winner *The Nurture Assumption*.

Perhaps the best evidence that how parents rear their children does actually influence child development comes from experimental intervention research. Such efforts typically involve assigning parents to an experimental or control group, with those in the experimental group being provided with guidance to enhance their parenting, something not provided to those in the control group. Such guidance can take many forms. It might involve simply providing parents with material to read to their child and instructions as to how best to do so, with eventual evaluation of the child's literacy to determine whether the intervention proved effective in enhancing child development. Or it might involve encouraging parents to be consistent when disciplining their child rather than haphazard and lackadaisical, while ensuring that discipline is not too harsh, perhaps even emphasizing time out, explanations of why the child's behavior was problematical, or providing rewards for good behavior. Some have even videotaped parents interacting with their children, offering feedback to the experimental group regarding ways to be more sensitive to the needs of the child, while viewing the video with the parent. When such efforts result, as they often have, in improved parenting and thereby child functioning, they provide compelling evidence of the causal influence of parenting.

Evidence from such work and related developmental theories raise a question that is the focus—and title—of this chapter: why do parents parent the way they do? After all, some parents are sensitive, responsive, warm, and accepting and others are not; some are hostile and rejecting, and some are neglectful and detached. There are, of course, other ways to characterize the variation in how parents treat their children, but the point is that not all people parent the same way.

An anecdote recorded in the files of study members brings this observation to life. One day, when the Dunedin Study was in its early stages and the children were five years of age, two mothers and their sons were in the project's reception area, waiting to be seen. There were toys available, as well as magazines. At first, the two boys, William and Harper (whose real names have been changed, as is true of all study members mentioned throughout this book), stayed close to their mothers, but it didn't take much time for them to engage each other. And, given that each was attracted to the same toy dump truck, it didn't take much time for Harper to yank it out of William's hands. This immediately led to a tug of war between the two, resulting in Harper shoving William to the floor while claiming the prized toy. Harper's mother looked up briefly from the magazine she was paging through and said, in a harsh tone, "give it back," but then immediately returned to the magazine that had captured her attention—despite the fact that her son paid her no mind, retaining possession of the truck.

William's mother, in contrast, entered the fray seeking a way to resolve the conflict. "How do you feel about what he did to you, William?," she asked her son, to which he responded, "I want the truck; I had it first." This led William's mother to say to him, "Let the boy know that; use your words. But how about also suggesting to him that you take turns and he could have it after you use it for a short while." That led William to do just as his mother suggested. Perhaps surprisingly, Harper handed the truck back to William, a cooperative act that his own mother completely failed to notice. After a few minutes, William's mother said, "Do you think it's time for the other boy to have a turn?" With that, William handed it to Harper, who responded with a big smile. An observation like this leads one to ask why these two mothers responded so differently to the conflict they witnessed between their two sons. Our next developmental adventure addresses this issue of why parents parent the way they do. In considering this issue, we begin to address the second goal and theme of this book, illuminating whether and how children's experience in the family shapes, or fails to shape, their future development, in this case their parenting.

LESSONS FROM CHILD ABUSE?

Perhaps the most traditional way of thinking about this issue of the determinants of parenting has been to consider the parenting that parents themselves experienced during their own childhoods. The potential influence of one's childhood experience being parented on how one parents their own child is referred to as "the intergenerational transmission of parenting." Did Harper's mother's general disregard for her son's misbehavior and her own failure to follow through on her directive to him to "give it back" reflect how she was raised? Were her own parents detached, neglectful, and inconsistent in their parenting, failing to follow through on directives to her when she was a child? And was the skilled parenting of William's mother the result, at least in part, of the sensitive, responsive, and supportive care that she might have received as a child?

Diverse theories of human development provide grounds for expecting that parents will care for their children in ways that are similar to the rearing they experienced themselves while growing up. Some theories, such as attachment theory, developed by British psychiatrist John Bowlby and American developmental psychologists Mary Ainsworth and L. Alan Sroufe, emphasize emotional development, how parenting influences it, and how it then influences future parenting. Other theories, such as social learning theory, which guided the parenting research and intervention efforts of Jerry Patterson of the Oregon Social Learning Institute, emphasize behavioral development, with children repeating the kinds of behavior that were rewarded and avoiding those that had been punished. Of course, these perspectives are not mutually exclusive.

Some of the most consistent evidence seeming to document the intergenerational transmission of parenting comes from research on the causes of child abuse and neglect, with this perspective first emerging in efforts to understand the etiology of child maltreatment. Clinicians and scholars repeatedly observed that those parents who mistreated their children were disproportionately likely to have been mistreated themselves while growing up, with this mistreatment affecting their emotional development (for example, lack of empathy) and behavioral development (for example, aggression).

But the research seeming to support this intergenerational-transmission view is often limited in a number of ways, some of which we already discussed when we considered the developmental legacy of temperament at age three (in Chapter 2) and childhood ADHD (in Chapter 4). Most importantly, consider that much of this work has been retrospective in design, based on the recollections of abusing parents about how they were treated as children. It is not uncommon for such studies to find that abusive parents treat their children in a manner similar to how they report having been treated as children. In fact, it is not unusual for abusive parents to defend their approach to child-rearing by asserting, "This is how I was treated and I turned out alright!"

But the approach of asking adults who abuse their own children to recollect how they were cared for as children often has a fundamental flaw that we highlighted earlier: it doesn't include the parents who were also abused as children but did not grow up to mistreat their children—that is, individuals who have been able to "break the (intergenerational) cycle" of child abuse and neglect. If such individuals were included, the evidence might well reveal that child maltreatment is not as reliably passed down from one generation to the next as many assume, which is not to say that there is no intergenerational transmission of ordinary parenting styles within normal limits.

Even when parents who do not mistreat their children are included in retrospective studies that require them to report their own childhood experiences, additional problems arise. This is because memory is fallible, especially memory about emotionally traumatic experiences. So it is always possible, in fact probable, that at least some adults who were seriously mistreated by their own parents in childhood fail to recall such rearing experiences and thus prove unable to report accurately how they were raised, hard as that may be for some of us to imagine. In fact, some adults mistreated in childhood even "idealize" their parents, claiming, sadly and incorrectly, that they were cared for in an entirely loving way. Often, however, when such individuals are asked to provide some details to substantiate their claims—for example, "tell me about a time when you needed help and your mother was there for you"—they simply cannot come up with an actual example.

Another problem with drawing on retrospective accounts of childhood experiences when assessing parenting experienced while growing up is that some adults who recall being treated poorly by their parents were not. We know this from research that queries adults about their childhood experiences when grown up (that is, prospectively) and compares such retrospective reports to what actually happened, based on records kept during childhood. We carried out some of this research as part of the Dunedin Study. As we and others have found, collecting prospective data on parenting as children are being parented and then asking the children about their child-rearing history when they are adults often reveals a striking disconnect. This is an issue we will return to in more detail in Chapter 16. For now, it needs to be appreciated that there are serious problems with relying on memory to capture parenting that adults experienced in childhood so that the intergenerational transmission of parenting can be investigated.

BEYOND RETROSPECTIVE REPORTING

As a result of the concerns just raised about research on the causes of child abuse and neglect, most developmental scholars give much more credence to prospective evidence that links actual assessments of parenting experienced in childhood with the parenting that the child, now grown up, provides their own offspring. This approach enables one to evaluate with much greater confidence whether children who are and are not mistreated in their families of origin end up parenting in ways similar to or different from their own rearing experiences. Of course, such work takes a long time—because one must wait for children to grow up and become parents, and the latter occurs on a schedule over which the researcher has no control. Recall our comparison of longitudinal researchers like ourselves and the pomologists mentioned in Chapter 1, who must wait years before they can harvest the fruit of the trees they plant.

One way to shorten the wait before investigating the intergenerational transmission of parenting is initially to study the parenting that adolescents—rather than young children—receive and then see how that maps onto the parenting these adolescents provide to their own young children when they are adults. In some cases, there is not that long a time between these two points, as when an adolescent studied at age fifteen goes on to become a parent at age eighteen or twenty.

Even such prospective work that begins in adolescence is often limited in what it can reveal about the intergenerational transmission of parenting. This is because many studies seeking to illuminate the intergenerational transmission of parenting that begin in adolescence are not cohort studies like the Dunedin Study—which follow virtually all children in a community from birth. Instead, they often begin as investigations of "high-risk" adolescents who are growing up under dangerous and/or disadvantaged circumstances (for example, abusive parents or a violent neighborhood) or who are already showing developmental problems with aggression, delinquency, or substance abuse. All this means that what we learn about the developmental origins of how these particular adolescents parent once they have young children of their own—which they often do well before others their same age—will not necessarily generalize to and thus illuminate why most other people parent the way they do. It cannot be assumed that insight gleaned from studying the intergenerational transmission of parenting when one starts with at-risk adolescents applies to the much more numerous parents who during their teenage years did not grow up under conditions of adversity or did not have serious psychological or behavioral problems.

BEYOND PROBLEMATIC PARENTING

By appreciating this state of affairs, we realized that the Dunedin Study was well positioned to take us on another adventure, this time regarding whether and how childhood experiences in the family forecast adult functioning, in this case parenting. To begin with, we did not have to start with adolescents, because we had been studying study members and their experiences in their families since early childhood. Thus, we had measurements in our data pantry of parenting, parent-child relations, family emotional climate, and related assessments that had been prospectively collected when study members were three, five, seven, nine, eleven, thirteen, and fifteen years of age. This enabled us to do something no other study had ever been positioned to do—create measures of rearing experience specific to three distinct developmental periods: the preschool years (ages three and five), middle childhood (ages seven, nine, and eleven), and adolescence (ages thirteen and fifteen). As a result, we were uniquely positioned to determine whether rearing experience in the family during certain developmental periods proved more important in predicting future parenting than at other times. Consider that many believe it is what happens earlier rather than later in childhood that shapes who we become, including as parents.

Just as important from our perspective was the opportunity to move beyond the investigation of the intergenerational transmission of child maltreatment. Rather than focusing on dysfunctional or problematic parenting, the Dunedin Study positioned us to examine the developmental roots of competent parenting. To do this, we focused on the extent to which study members as parents of three-year-olds provided parenting that was sensitive, responsive, supportive, and cognitively stimulating rather than neglectful and detached or intrusive and overcontrolling. With such a focus, we could illuminate why parents parent the way they do in a manner that should be applicable to many more families than just those at risk for child abuse and neglect. When Jay Belsky joined the Dunedin Study, bringing his expertise on parenting, we realized there was no time to waste. Some teen study members were already having babies.

HOW TO STUDY PARENTING

When it comes to studying and measuring how people parent, many approaches can be used. These include interviewing parents about how they parent, asking them to complete questionnaires about their parenting practices, and observing them as they interact with their children. All these approaches were used in the Dunedin Study while study members were

growing up, and all have strengths and weaknesses. Although we used several of them when study members were parents themselves, we privileged
observations of parents. Ultimately, we had more confidence in parenting
behavior that we observed than in reports provided by parents themselves.

Even if observations do not suffer from rater bias—as when parents mischaracterize their parenting to make themselves look like they think we
investigators want them to—they are not foolproof. When we talk to students and others about going into homes to observe parenting or about
bringing parents into a university laboratory to be observed, many find it
difficult to believe that what we see accurately reflects what goes on day in
and day out in a child's life—and that is certainly what we are most interested in capturing. This concern is reasonable, but the truth is that informative behavioral data can still be gathered if collected in a skilled manner.
The best way to do this is to avoid saying, "Hey, we want to see what kind
of parent you are, so we are going to observe you interacting with your
child." Instead, it is useful to emphasize the child, saying something like,
"We are interested in how your child behaves and the experiences she or
he has, so we thought it would be a good idea to observe him or her while
spending time with you. Could you just go about your everyday activities
while we observe his or her life?" This is one "unstructured" way of proceeding, especially when observing the parent and child in their own home.
Another strategy, which can be implemented both at home and at a university laboratory, is to provide parent-child dyads with a standard set of
materials, as we did when we visited study members in their homes, and
ask the parent to spend time interacting with the child and using them.

One of the interesting things that can happen in situations like those just
described is, as already implied, that a parent infers you are observing their
parenting—because we certainly never say that this is not what we are doing.
So the parent puts on a show, trying to be a "good" parent. But the truth is
that putting on such a "good" show is hard; it's kind of like acting—most
people cannot do it well, which can be very revealing. In one case, we had a
parent who was so busy showing off how cognitively stimulating she was
that as she emptied out the toy chest while we watched, showing her child
every toy, it became strikingly apparent that she was not attending to the
child much at all, so intent was she in presenting herself in a particular way.

It is also the case that many, even most, parents just go about their everyday way of behaving. One of us can recall a father who came running

into the house, glanced at us doing the observation, and proceeded to say to his wife, "I've got something to tell you, but you have to swear never to tell anyone else!" The observer, Jay Belsky, couldn't help feeling like one of those eunuchs who guarded an emperor's concubines. In other cases, parents seem not to give a second thought to speaking harshly to, being impatient with, or just ignoring their child. In other words, while observing parents parent is not foolproof, it is a surprisingly good way to gain insight into the child's world.

Therefore, when it came to observing how study members behaved as parents, we made the following decisions. First, we decided to wait until their first child was three years of age. Age three was judged to be a potentially revealing time in a child's life because of rapidly developing language skills and social competencies that, individually and together, enable children to increasingly assert their desires—which can pose real challenges for parents. It was also significant that at age three was the first time study members themselves had been observed as children way back in the 1970s. The parenting study members themselves experienced while growing up had been measured repeatedly in the 1970s and 1980s, decades before they began to have their own children.

Because we appreciated that parents can behave differently in different situations and contexts, be it during dinnertime, in the supermarket, or at the playground, we created three semistructured situations and videotaped the parent and child interacting in each situation. We began first with five minutes of "free play." In this arrangement, several attractive toys are provided to the parent and child and they are instructed simply to enjoy themselves while sitting on the floor playing with them. In the second five-minute period, we sought to create a more challenging situation that mirrored one that parents often find themselves in—busy with a nonchild activity but needing to monitor the child. Thus, we took away all the nice toys from the previous play period, leaving them in a see-through bag placed near the parent, who was instructed to sit in a chair and work on what was a sham questionnaire—one provided just to keep the parent busy. At the same time, we provided the child with only a single, boring toy, a small blue elephant with no moving parts, and instructed the mother to complete the questionnaire and not allow the child to get into the bag with the much more attractive—and enticing—toys that was nearby. That wasn't very nice of us, was it?

Having thus challenged the parent-child dyad, we proceeded to a third five-minute "teaching task." Here we gave parents a series of colored blocks that had been glued together in ever more complex arrangements, along with identical blocks that had not been glued together. Parents were instructed to enable their child to use the latter blocks to make a "building" identical to the glued-together model and to move from one set of such models to the next upon completing each set. The glued-together models went from easy to difficult. Thus, the first model was of a simple inverted T made with two blocks, a red one placed horizontally on the floor and a blue one perched vertically in the middle of it. The next model included three blocks, the one after that four, and so on. Needless to say, as more blocks were added, the task of replicating the model became increasingly difficult. We presumed that this would create increasing levels of stress on the parent and child, building on that experienced in the preceding five-minute situation.

The entire fifteen-minute sequence was videotaped so we could study the parents and children and rate their behavior, using dimensional scales, at a later time. When it came to the parents, we rated separately how negative and positive they were in their emotions, whether expressed verbally or nonverbally. We also rated the extent to which their behavior was cognitively stimulating. Parents who scored high on this aspect of parenting explained things to their children in ways that were easily understandable, or they posed questions that made their children think about what they were doing in helpful ways (for example, "Where does the blue block go? Look at this building."). Beyond emotions and stimulation, we also measured the style of parenting. Thus, we evaluated whether parental involvement was sensitive, intrusive, or detached. A sensitive parent might hold the blocks steady so that the child could correctly place the next one without knocking the building down, or help the child figure out what to do next if the child seemed uncertain as to how to proceed—for example, by asking "What color is the block on top?" or "Do you see another block of the same color?" In the boring-toy situation, the sensitive parent might suggest to the child that she play a game, pretending to have the elephant eat some make-believe food, or briefly commiserate with the child, acknowledging that it was difficult to have the parent busy with the paperwork and only a single toy to play with. An intrusive parent, in contrast, might grab a toy from the child during free play to demonstrate how something, such as pouring tea from a toy teapot into a miniature cup, *should* be done rather than let the child use the teapot in whatever manner she or he desired. Another example of intrusiveness might involve holding a child's arm and moving it to where it needed to go—in a way that undermined the child's chance of succeeding on her own. Finally, detached parenting could involve failing to provide assistance when it was called for, as when a child looked at the parent for help and the parent failed to respond, or when the child seemed not to know what to do or was making a mistake yet was provided with no direction or feedback whatsoever. Think about Harper's mom, described at the beginning of this chapter.

Two considerations also led us to measure children's behavior in the three parent-child interaction episodes we orchestrated. The first was appreciation that even if parenting is shaped by how parents were reared themselves while growing up, it also is influenced by how children behave. Decades ago, this view was central to Michael Lewis's 1974 edited volume *The Effect of the Infant on its Caregivers* and Richard Q. Bell and Lawrence V. Harper's 1977 book *The Effect of the Child on the Adult*. This idea is also related to that raised in Chapter 2 when we discussed *evocative* effects that children have on those around them, resulting in parents, teachers, or peers behaving in certain ways in response to the child's behavior. Indeed, it formed the basis for our claim that the child can be the producer of his own development. Thus, if we wanted to evaluate how experiences growing up in the family affected how study members behaved as parents, it would be good to adjust for or discount the potential influence of child behavior on parent behavior in the immediate observational situation before evaluating effects of study members' own child-rearing histories on their observed parenting. We did not want one parent to appear more sensitive just because the child was very cooperative and another parent to behave intrusively just because the child was very active and distracted. By measuring child behavior and using statistics to account for differences in how children behaved, we sought to secure a "purer" measure of parenting, one unaffected by child behavior in the situations we created. Thus, we measured how positively and negatively emotional children were and how active and attentive they were. Needless to say, children differed to a great extent in this regard.

Let us say a little more about our approach to assessing parenting, as it is easy to imagine readers saying something like, "Wait a minute; how can you capture important aspects of parenting in just three five-minute sessions that are videotaped?" In the hope of persuading you that this approach, while no doubt imperfect, has merit—especially given our inability to place cameras in the home to capture parenting while parents are unaware this is going on—consider the following analogy. When a cardiologist wants to gain insight into the condition of a patient's heart, one tried and true method of doing so is the cardiovascular stress test. This involves putting the patient on a treadmill while requiring him or her to walk ever faster, with a breathing tube stuck in their mouth, until they are too out of breath to walk any farther. Clearly, this procedure is artificial, quite unlike what people experience day in and day out, but such "ecological invalidity" doesn't matter. What matters is whether the insights gleaned about the cardiovascular system from this strange procedure are informative about the condition of the patient's heart. If they are, it matters not a bit that the procedure is nothing like real life.

The same goes for our approach to measuring parenting. Ask not whether it is like everyday life but rather whether it can be used to gain insight into everyday parenting. An abundance of evidence across many studies clearly indicates that it can. For example, the approach we used has been shown to distinguish the parenting behavior of parents who are and who are not depressed, who are in more happy or more conflicted marriages, and those whose children do and do not do well in school or with their peers. Thus, even if our approach "looks" artificial and thus seems inadequate, that does not mean it would not be useful and effective for our purposes—to determine if study members' experiences with their parents growing up forecast many years later how they would parent their own three-year-old children.

PREDICTING PARENTING

The first thing we did to evaluate whether parenting was intergenerationally transmitted—that is, whether we could predict the parenting behavior we videotaped using measurements obtained while the study member was growing up—was to determine whether our many different ratings of parenting could be combined on statistical grounds to create a more robust composite measure. Note that our strategy here is just like the one we described in Chapter 4 when we discussed combining multiple indicators of ADHD-like behavior. Recall that we pointed out that compositing different measurements—being "lumpers"—can create more robust, reliable, and valid measurements than treating each one separately, as "splitters" do. To be clear, though, this strategy of combining multiple indicators, in this case of quality of parenting, is often as much a matter of taste and preference of the investigator as anything else.

Our plan to combine our multiple ratings turned out to be efficient and sensible. This was because parents—both men and women—who were more cognitively stimulating in their parenting also tended to be more sensitive and positive and less intrusive, detached, and negative when interacting with their children, so we could create a solid measure of warm, sensitive, stimulating parenting that ranged from very low to very high. Parents who scored low on our index tended to be highly intrusive, detached, and/or negatively emotional in their parenting behavior, whereas those who scored high tended to be sensitive, positive, and stimulating. If nothing else, what this preliminary step made clear was that even though our parents knew they were being videotaped, not all of them did, or could, act in a way that put them in an impressive light.

When it came to answering our core question about the intergenerational transmission of supportive—not abusive—parenting, the results were clear, consistent, and as we anticipated, but only up to a point. Put simply, how mothers in our study who had three-year-olds behaved toward their children was systematically related to their experiences as children in their families while growing up, but in the case of study members who were fathers, there was, somewhat surprisingly, no such evidence of intergenerational transmission. Exactly why that was the case was not clear, but as we will see, we made efforts to try to understand this unexpected finding.

Before saying anything more about these findings, we must acknowledge that the work that is the focus of this chapter was not "genetically informed." We had no measurement of genes, nor were we positioned to compare similarities and differences in the parenting of identical and fraternal twins or of biological and adoptive parents. As a result, there was no way to determine with certainty whether any links between how one was reared in their family of origin and how one parented one's own child resulted from the former causally influencing the latter. An alternative possibility was that such associations could be caused by the parents of study members and the study members themselves sharing genes—a "third variable"—that shaped the parenting of each generation. While this is certainly a limit of our work, we do not regard it as a fatal flaw. Laying the foundation for the study of the intergenerational transmission of warm, sensitive, stimulating parenting, as we did, provides a basis for future genetically informed work to build on.

Just before this book went to press, it became possible for us to use measures of actual DNA, as discussed in Part V of the book, devoted to genetics (Chapters 12–15), collected well after we had conducted the work reported in this chapter, to study the genetics of parenting and thereby the effects of parenting. We discovered that even after we discounted how a select set of study members' genes affected how their parents treated them (that is, an effect of the child on the parent), there remained an effect of parenting on children's development. This means that detected effects of parenting experienced on children's development are not solely an artifact of genes shared by parents and children, so there is every reason to believe that findings pertaining to the intergenerational transmission of parenting in this chapter likely reflect actual effects of experience in childhood on functioning in adulthood.

One more point may be worth making. To our—potentially misguided—way of thinking, there seems to be little reason to presume that if shared genes were driving our findings, they would only prove operative in the case of female and not male study members. Although there is certainly evidence indicating that parenting behavior is somewhat heritable, we know of no such work indicating that this is true of how females parent but not how males parent. Needless to say, we appreciate that this is by no means a foolproof defense of our inclination to interpret our results in terms of experiences growing up affecting, later in life, one's parenting. Therefore, our goal here is to alert readers to our interpretive biases rather than claim to indisputably document the intergenerational transmission of parenting through nongenetic means. Having made our perspective clear, let us share in greater detail what we discovered during our adventure investigating the intergenerational transmission of parenting.

Are Child-rearing Experiences in Some Developmental Periods More Predictive Than in Others?

In addressing the question of why parents parent the way they do, recall that we assessed effects of experiences while growing up during three separate developmental epochs: early childhood, based on measurements made when study members were three and five years of age; middle childhood, based on measurements made when children were seven and nine years of age; and adolescence, based on measurements made when children were thirteen and fifteen years of age. The parenting of female study members was more sensitive, supportive, and positive and less negative, intrusive, and/or detached when during their own early-childhood years their mothers did not overemphasize obedience, did not value strict discipline, and did not think it wise to issue unyielding edicts as to how a young child should behave. In other words, these sensitive, supportive and stimulating mothers of three-year olds had parents who were open to their young children's needs and desires, proving flexible and understanding when dealing with their children, more or less refusing to embrace the then not-uncommon view that the developing child is someone to be seen, not heard, and to whose job it is to obey.

When we considered why parents parent the way they do from the perspective of study members' experiences in their families of origin during their middle-childhood and adolescent years, further evidence of the intergenerational transmission of parenting emerged. When, during the elementary-school years, the emotional climate of the family was marked by cohesion, positive emotional expressiveness, and low levels of conflict, girls grew up to become warm, sensitive, and stimulating parents of their own young children rather than showing intrusive, negative, and overcontrolling patterns of behavior. The same was true when, during the adolescent years, daughters reported a trusting, openly communicative, and non-alienated relationship with—that is, positive attachment to—their parents.

In fact, the more the developmental experiences described characterized mothers' own lives when they were preschoolers, elementary-school children, *and* adolescents, the more likely they were to be sensitive, responsive, and stimulating when interacting with their own young children. In other words, knowing about the developmental experiences of children in their family of origin across early childhood, middle childhood, and adolescence provided more insight into how they would parent than did knowing about their experiences while growing up during any single developmental period. Importantly, then, there did not seem to be a "sensitive period" when experiences growing up proved to be all important to one's future as a parent; experiences across the first fifteen years of life appeared to matter.

The reader would do well to recall that more or less the same conclusion emerged when we studied childhood self-control and its developmental legacy, as reported in Chapter 4. Recall that while self-control during the preschool years predicted later adult development all by itself, the predictive power was substantially greater when self-control across the preschool *and* middle-childhood years was considered. This observation once again underscores the previously highlighted theme that development is a dynamic, ongoing process. It is not over at the end of the first, fifth, or tenth year of life. Even if what occurs earlier in life matters when it comes to shaping development, this does not mean that what happens later lacks subsequent influence.

SEEKING TO UNDERSTAND FATHERING

Although the findings with regard to fathers—or really the nonfindings— were surprising, two ideas led us to further examine the data we had collected. One reason for doing so was the pithy scientific rule that "the absence of evidence is not evidence of absence." In other words, just because we did not find something, in this case evidence of the intergenerational transmission of men's parenting, does not mean that boys are not affected by how they were reared when it came to parenting their own children. It simply means that we did not find evidence to this effect.

So, the first thing we did in further studying the origins of men's fathering behavior was to see whether the quality of romantic relationships (that is, study members' marriages or partnerships) played a role in the intergenerational transmission of parenting. We addressed this issue because some work on the origins of harsh parenting and even child abuse suggested that a well-functioning and supportive close relationship could serve as a "corrective emotional experience," helping to break the cycle of mistreatment in childhood leading to mistreatment of children in adulthood. Some other work had revealed that one thing that appears to keep maltreated children from mistreating their own children is being in a well-functioning intimate relationship.

Consequently, we sought to evaluate whether, in the Dunedin Study, the quality of study members' romantic relationships might illuminate the intergenerational transmission of parenting, especially in the case of men. Even though we were primarily motivated to test this this possibility because of our inability to predict men's fathering, it made sense to consider the same issue with respect to mothers, so we did. Ultimately, we wanted to know whether insight from the study of child maltreatment generalized to supportive parenting. The answer turned out to be no, at least not in the Dunedin Study. We detected no evidence that the quality of romantic relations played any role in the intergenerational transmission process. Most notably, it was not the case, as we had hypothesized, that when a study member's experiences growing up were problematic, a good partner relationship would prevent or protect that child-rearing experience from being transmitted to the next generation. This proved to be so for both male and female study members.

Because we were attracted to the idea we set out to evaluate, these results were disappointing, but once again all we can conclude is that we did not detect what we went looking for. Our null results do not lead to the conclusion that the phenomenon we were seeking to substantiate is not operative, only that we did not find evidence consistent with this line of thinking. At the same time, we were not inclined to spend time trying to explain away our null findings. As developmental scholars, we strongly believed that we needed to let the empirical chips fall where they may. Just because we did not like the answer we got was not a reason to make believe we did not get it.

This did not stop us, however, from looking elsewhere in the hope of illuminating why fathers parented the way they did. We also wondered whether our findings—and lack thereof—might have been influenced by the fact that, initially, we could only observe the parenting of study members who became parents rather early in their young-adult lives. We say this because we had no control over when study members became parents, so we just had to wait for them to do so before visiting them in their homes. And, of course, some became parents before others did. For some, parenthood just happens; for others, who often become parents at a later age, it is a planned event. Such parents-to-be wait not only until they find the right partner but perhaps also until they have finished their education and have become established occupationally. The first parents we studied to address the issue of intergenerational transmission of parenting in the Dunedin Study were those study members who first became parents at younger rather than older ages.

Could it be the case, then, that when men in particular became parents at an older age, the legacy of their own rearing histories would emerge and that our failure to detect evidence of intergenerational transmission in the initial work was because we were studying younger rather than older first-time fathers? Another possibility arose in our minds as well, probably more pertinent to mothers than to fathers, given what we had already found. Might it be the case that study members who became parents for the first time at older ages—and thus had more "distance" between their childhood experiences and their parenting—would be less affected by how they were raised while growing up when it came to how they parented? To address these possibilities, we continued to collect data on study members as they became parents for the first time at older ages. This enabled us to conduct a second study to determine whether the age at which parents became parents and thus were observed at home with their three-year-olds played some role in the intergenerational transmission of parenting, but once again this was not the case. Study members who became parents in their twenties and those who became parents in their thirties were equally affected, in the case of mothers, and unaffected, in the case of fathers, by how they were reared when it came to predicting how they would parent their own three-year-olds.

CONCLUSION

One thing that should be clear from our research on why parents parent the way they do is that one does not always find what one expects or hopes to find. That is what happens when one commits, as we have, to living in an empirical world—and trusting the data rather than our own intuitions, beliefs, and theories. But, having said that, we cannot lose sight of the problem of "embracing the null," as scientists refer to breathing meaning into nonfindings. This is because there are always many reasons for failing to detect what one goes looking for. Consider the following possibilities that could explain our nonfindings regarding fathers. Think of them as an adventurer might when it turns out she has gone down the wrong path while seeking some valuable but hidden object.

Perhaps we did not detect evidence of the intergenerational transmission of parenting in the case of fathers because it was men's own mothers and not their own fathers who provided most of the information we had on hand about what they experienced in their families while growing up. Might we have been more successful had the path we chose been based on collecting fathers' reports of how they parented their child during the study member's childhood? Another possibility is that the procedures we used to study parenting were more suited for revealing differences in mothering behavior than fathering behavior. Might we have gained more insight into men's parenting—and discerned evidence of the intergenerational transmission of their parenting—had we had parents play a competitive game with their children rather than the challenging tasks that we used? It is certainly possible. Again, this is why "the absence of evidence is not evidence of absence."

Perhaps we also failed to find evidence for the role of romantic relationships because we were focused on positive and supportive parenting more than harsh, even abusive, parenting. Conceivably, too, parental age may have turned out not to matter because we were still not positioned to study those parents who delayed becoming parents until their forties and beyond. Then, of course, there is the possibility that our failures to detect evidence of intergenerational transmission in the case of fathers, of the role of romantic relationships, or of parental age were because we were studying how parents parented three-year-olds. Perhaps we adventurers were simply in the wrong "place" metaphorically speaking at the wrong time (or is it the right place at the wrong time?). Would or could results have been different had our focus been on the parenting of eight-year-olds or adolescents? Even today, it is still the case that many fathers leave care of their young children to mothers but become more involved in their children's lives as the children grow older.

What these observations imply is that our research on the intergenerational transmission of sensitive, supportive, stimulating parenting was and is not the last word on the subject. Scientific knowledge builds over time through the accumulation of evidence. We have contributed to that fundamental scientific process in a number of ways—by prospectively, rather than retro-spectively, studying the intergenerational transmission of parenting; by focusing on an entire community of children and from an early age, not just those at risk or who are already adolescents; by investigating effects of family experiences in three different developmental epochs; and by focusing on the kind of parenting known to foster developmental well-being, not that known to undermine it.

In so doing, our long-term study, or perhaps we should say adventure pursuing the determinants of parenting, indicated that the experiences girls had growing up—in early childhood, in middle childhood, and in adolescence—appeared to affect how they parented their own three-year-old children. It also indicated that the more developmentally supportive girls' rearing environments proved to be across all three developmental epochs, the more likely they were to interact with their child in sensitive, stimu-lating, and responsive ways—those that other evidence indicates fosters the developmental well-being of offspring.

But whatever our results or those of others on the subject of the inter-generational transmission of parenting, we need to appreciate that parenting is multiply determined. In addition to a parent's own child-rearing history, parents' health and well-being, their occupational experience, the quality of their intimate relationship, and the social support they secure from friends, neighbors, relatives, and co-workers may all influence how parents parent. Recall, too, that how children themselves behave matters when ac-counting for why parents parent the way they do. Thus, even given all the hard work that went into our efforts to illuminate the intergenerational transmission of parenting, we still need to remain cognizant that we were only investigating one aspect of the dynamic process that shapes the par-enting that children experience.

6

Troubled Families and Bad Boys

Many readers of this volume, especially those who are male, will be able to recall doing something in adolescence that they would not necessarily recommend to others and would certainly not wish their children to repeat. We are referring here to things such as shoplifting or getting into a car with a drunk-driving friend while also intoxicated or engaging in unprotected sex with someone one has only recently met.

What is especially interesting about such problematic behavior in adolescence is how common it is, particularly among males. Indeed, we can recall a friend who was so intent on attending the United States Military Academy at West Point that he spent his adolescence working hard academically and athletically while becoming a leader in student government, hoping to check all the boxes needed to secure the required nomination from their congressional representative and gain admission to this elite institution. Despite this strong motivation, this "good boy" was not able to resist engaging in some petty theft and getting drunk with friends who were not so ambitious.

A second interesting feature of the developmental phenomenon considered in this chapter—delinquent behavior in adolescence—is that for some it seems to be a passing phase of rule breaking coupled with a desire to do things that are allowed of adults but not of kids, but for others it is anything but. In this regard, we can also recall a friend whose older brother hung out with the "bad kids" in high school, those who smoked cigarettes, cut classes, and got into fights with kids from neighboring communities. One day, this older brother, then 15 years old, was spotted driving his parents' car around town. Another time, while drunk with his friends, he took out the family's small boat and ended up crashing it into the dock. It was not as if this error in judgment caused him to rethink his wayward ways, though. He went on to be expelled from a small college after shooting up a dormitory—in order to maintain his "rep," he acknowledged years later.

But here is the interesting thing. Some of the very friends who joined this older brother on his teenage "pranks" never got into trouble again after leaving high school. In fact, one went on to become a high-school principal charged, of course, with maintaining the very rules he was so intent on breaking in his youth. So, for developmental scholars like us, the question becomes why some teenage boys who engage in delinquent acts "grow up," whereas others do not. When one of the authors, Terrie Moffitt, began to think about this question, she found herself developing a theory of two distinct types of delinquent teens. In this chapter, we will consider Moffitt's theory of distinct developmental trajectories of adolescent rule breaking and evidence pertaining to them. We will also integrate the first theme of this book, how functioning in childhood forecasts development later in life (Chapters 1–3), with the second theme, how experiences in and outside the family influence development (Chapter 5).

TWO TYPES OF ADOLESCENT DELINQUENTS: THE THEORY

When it came to characterizing two different types of individuals who engaged in high levels of delinquent behavior, Moffitt used labels that drew attention to when their problematic behavior began and when it tended to end. Thus, one type was referred to as "childhood-onset or life-course persistent" (LCP) and the other was called "adolescent-onset or adolescent-limited" (AL). Moffitt theorized that LCP teenagers launch their antisocial careers early in childhood as a result of subtle neuropsychological problems that disrupt the normal development of language, memory, and self-control (discussed in detail in Chapter 3). This results in toddlers whose cognitive development is delayed and who have difficult, undercontrolled temperaments (discussed in detail in Chapter 2). Moffitt further theorized that such liabilities are especially likely to emerge when children grow up in economically disadvantaged or dysfunctional families, both of which further promote the development of antisocial behavior—very early in life—that then becomes more or less self-sustaining. In this regard, recall the discussion of ineffective parenting styles in Chapter 5 and the discussion of developmental processes in Chapter 2 pertaining to how individuals "produce their own development." By putting themselves in problematic situations, such as taking something from a peer or responding to ambiguous situations in an antisocial manner, such as hitting a child who accidentally bumps you in the lunch line, early problem behavior continues to grow and develop as a result of the child's own actions.

Just as important to the LCP developmental trajectory of antisocial behavior are the "snares" of adolescence, also discussed in Chapter 3. Moffitt suspected that as a result of growing up in a high-risk family while experiencing cognitive and behavioral difficulties, early starters increase the chances of being snagged by the "snares" of adolescence, which, when encountered, further reduce the chances that teenagers will enter young adulthood in good condition. Recall that "snares" refer to things such as drinking, driving, and illegal substance use but also being alienated and disconnected from family, leaving school without qualifications, or becoming a teenage parent. Thus, as the LCP child interacts with his social environment, his antisocial style accumulates complicating features, such as hanging out with like-minded boys, being socially rejected by many other children, and failing in school. Eventually, an antisocial personality emerges that endures across time and place. Moffitt expected only a minority of children to follow this developmental trajectory or path, and when we tested these ideas central to her theory in the Dunedin Study, we discovered, perhaps not surprisingly, that boys were ten times as likely as girls to follow the LCP path. That is why our focus in this chapter is almost exclusively on boys.

Moffitt theorized that adolescent-onset or adolescent-limited (AL) delinquent behavior rather than LCP behavior characterizes the vast majority of juvenile offenders whose antisocial behavior is primarily limited to the teen years. It emerges for the first time around the age of puberty but terminates—resulting in desistance from antisocial behavior—during young adulthood, or so she theorized. Rather than arising from the combination of psychological deficiencies in early childhood and problematic family life, the delinquent behavior of AL children originates in the adolescent world of peers. According to Moffitt, normally developing children become motivated as teenagers to engage in problematic conduct when they enter adolescence because they are more or less roleless, stuck in a developmental no-man's-land between childhood and adulthood. This leads them to resent that the privileges of adulthood—such as being able to smoke, drink, drive, and have sex—are generally forbidden to them by law, family, or social convention. But upon observing LCP antisocial peers ignoring such entreaties to avoid the "forbidden fruits" of maturity, AL youths come to assert their autonomy by mimicking the delinquency of their LCP agemates. Eventually, however, when maturity brings access to adult privileges, AL youths readily desist from lawbreaking, substituting the positive skills mastered before they entered adolescence, such as self-control and persistence. Indeed, because of AL youths' healthy personality and cognitive development in childhood, they are more able than their LCP counterparts to recover from their misguided adolescent ways. Their greater attachment to family and friends is also influential in this regard.

What is especially important to appreciate about Moffitt's typological theory of adolescent delinquency is not only that it underscores the importance of both childhood psychological and behavioral functioning and experiences in and outside the family, but that when formulated originally it was just a theory. It emerged from Moffitt's piecing together of different findings from different studies while seeking to make "order out of empirical chaos," just as a detective might when faced with diverse clues to a crime and wondering how they fit together. In other words, much that we have just described about the two types of adolescent rule breakers had not been formally conceptualized and thus empirically evaluated before we set out to do just that using Dunedin study data.

That Moffitt's thinking reflected an untested theory led us to undertake two distinct studies as part of our empirical adventure investigating diverse developmental trajectories associated with adolescent delinquency. The first focused principally on the issues of developmental origins and behavioral characteristics of the two types of youths before and during adolescence, while the second, which will be considered only after the first, examined the psychological and behavioral functioning of these youths after leaving school. While we only needed to wait until study members were eighteen years of age to carry out the first piece of work, the second could not be undertaken until years later. This was because it was focused on how the two groups of youths functioned in adulthood. Because development takes time, adventurers like us have to be patient.

Before proceeding to describe what we did and what we found when adventuring in the world of adolescent delinquency, we should make clear that we regarded our efforts to evaluate Moffitt's theorizing as more than just a basic science exercise that could further understanding of human development. Indeed, from an applied science perspective, we appreciated that if Moffitt's hypotheses received empirical support, our findings would have implications for efforts to prevent and treat antisocial behavior. Not only would it be important to initiate the process of identifying and treating children at especially high risk of embarking on the LCP path well before adolescence—because of their psychological and behavioral liabilities early in life—but it would be just as important not to regard all antisocial behavior in adolescence in the same way. In fact, from the perspective of Moffitt's theory, such behavior by most adolescents should be regarded as more or less normative and thus expected rather than a reflection of some enduring developmental dysfunction. In other cases, however, given particular childhood histories, it would need to be seen in a different light.

IDENTIFYING TWO TYPES OF DELINQUENT YOUTHS AND THEIR DEVELOPMENTAL ORIGINS

In the first study testing Moffitt's ideas, we directed attention to three fundamental issues, one having to do with the behavior and attitudes of the two groups of adolescent rule breakers, another focusing on their involvement with snares that could undermine long-term healthy development, and a third dealing with the childhoods of the two different groups of adolescent boys. Turning to the first issue, we expected that the two groups of adolescents would not differ in most aspects of antisocial behavior but that LCP boys would engage in more violence than AL ones, making them more serious offenders. We further expected that LCP boys' personalities would show evidence of psychopathic traits, including a limited ability to form lasting bonds with friends or family, coupled with a tendency to be hostile and mistrustful of others while seeking to aggressively dominate them. With regard to snares, we predicted that boys on the AL path would show more developmental potential than boys on the LCP path because they would be less likely to be snared by the developmental risks associated with such experiences.

The final set of predictions concerned the childhoods of LCP and AL boys. Given the importance that Moffitt accorded neuropsychological deficits early in life (the child as the father of the man), we hypothesized that LCP boys would be more likely than AL ones to be cognitively limited in childhood and have a difficult temperament when this was first measured at age three years (as described in Chapter 2). But because Moffitt's theory also stipulated that it was growing up in troubled families that turned these childhood liabilities into more serious adolescent ones (the developmental influence of childhood experiences), we further predicted that LCP boys' childhoods would be characterized by less supportive parenting than AL boys', and that LCP parents would be more likely to suffer from mental health problems and be more likely to be raising their sons as single parents.

Once again, we had to assemble provisions for our adventure investigating adolescent delinquency before we could test the hypotheses just outlined. The first step in doing so involved gathering from our data pantry diverse information obtained every two years from ages three to fifteen and then again at age eighteen, so that we could characterize trajectories of antisocial behavior over this twelve-year stretch of time. In what follows, we only describe measurements taken from the pantry in general terms, providing more details when we share our findings related to the hypotheses already outlined.

The basic research procedures were tailored somewhat at each age, but in general they involved bringing each study member into the research unit within sixty days of his birthday for up to six hours of data collection, covering a number of topics. Importantly, each research "module"—including the mental health interview, delinquency interview, sexual behavior assessment, personality appraisal, standardized intelligence testing, and other cognitive assessments (for example, memory)—was administered by a different trained examiner to ensure that knowledge about one aspect of development did not contaminate or bias the collection of information on another one. By proceeding in this manner, we guaranteed that children did not develop a reputation within the research project that would undermine the objective assessment of their functioning.

As noted in prior chapters, parents and teachers were mailed a packet of questionnaires at each of eight assessment phases between ages five and eighteen to complement the data gathered directly from study members. These assessments provided by "outsiders" afforded additional insight into study members' personalities, attitudes, and behavior from adults who knew them well. Notably, we also had information from examiners who rated child behavior at ages three and five, with those from the earliest phase being used to generate measures of difficult temperament (see Chapter 2). Contacts were also made with police departments and the courts to gather information on criminal activity of study members.

In addition to collecting information on the cognitive, social, and behavioral development of study members when they were children and adolescents, we also gathered data on the family environment. More specifically, parents provided information on their socioeconomic circumstances, their mental health, and their parenting attitudes, values, and behavior (some of which was discussed in Chapter 5).

With all these measurement "ingredients" in hand, we set out to "cook" three different "dishes," one for each of the three general issues raised earlier about the nature and development of the two groups of delinquent boys. Thus, the first represents our efforts to identify LCP and AL groups based on their problem behavior from ages three to eighteen. The second sought to illuminate how the boys behaved as adolescents. Finally, we considered whether and how the two groups differed in childhood, in an effort to identify antecedent factors contributing to their differential developmental trajectories.

Identifying LCP and AL Boys

In order to distinguish study members who met criteria for inclusion in LCP or AL groups, we drew on data collected between ages five and eighteen years. As the first step, we distinguished boys who did and did not have histories of antisocial behavior in childhood, drawing on parent and teacher reports to identify children who were antisocial *across time*—at ages five, seven, nine, and eleven years—and *across situations,* at home and in school. Children who were antisocial in childhood frequently engaged in fighting, bullying other children, lying, disobeying adults, stealing, destroying property, and/or being irritable. In the second step, we distinguished *teenagers* who did and did not participate in many antisocial acts, based on their own reports of such behavior during confidential interviews administered when they were fifteen and eighteen years old. Teens were classified as antisocial if they engaged in nine or more distinct antisocial acts at age fifteen and/or twelve or more such acts at age eighteen. Antisocial acts included vandalism, shoplifting, buying or selling stolen goods, using or selling marijuana, driving drunk, and beating up a family member or some other person. We would be remiss if we did not note that we had great confidence in study members' answers to our questions about problematic behavior because of our history studying them. By the time they were adolescents, they knew that what they told us would not be shared with parents, school officials, or other authorities.

By putting together the information on antisocial behavior in childhood and adolescence, we discovered that 7 percent of the male study members met criteria for LCP and 23.6 percent for AL. We focus on these two groups of boys almost exclusively in this chapter. We should point out, nevertheless, that just under 6 percent of study members qualified as "recoverers," having been antisocial in childhood but not in adolescence. Another 5.5 percent qualified as abstainers, having engaged in no more than a single antisocial behavior at ages five, seven, nine, and eleven years, according to mother and teacher reports, *and* no more than a single such act according to their own self-reports at ages fifteen and eighteen years. The remainder of the study members, approximately 58 percent, did not meet criteria for membership in any of these four groups, engaging in more or less average or normative levels of antisocial behavior. Figure 6.1 displays the antisocial-behavior scores, standardized within age, for each of the groups of male study members from ages five to eighteen, including a small group of unclassified boys.

LCP and AL Groups in Adolescence

Given how we defined the two groups, it is not surprising that boys in the LCP group exhibited extreme antisocial behavior continuously from age three to age eighteen, with their lifelong antisocial behavior evident in reports by parents, teachers, and the boys themselves. Figure 6.2 makes clear that while LCP and AL boys reported essentially the same number of delinquent acts by age fifteen, numbers much higher than for other groups of

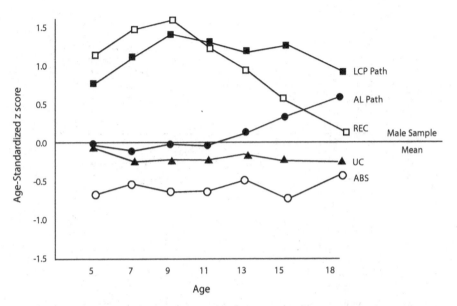

FIGURE 6.1. Males' average antisocial behavior according to reports by mother, taken at seven successive ages, as a function of diagnostic group membership. LCP path: life-course-persistent antisocial path; AL path: adolescence-limited antisocial path; REC: recoveries from childhood antisocial behavior; ABS: abstainers from antisocial behavior; UC: unclassified boys not falling into any of the other subgroups. Reformatted from Moffitt, T.E., Caspi, A., Dickson, N., Silva, P., & Stanton, W. (1996). Childhood-onset versus adolescent-onset antisocial conduct problems in males: Natural history from ages 3–18. *Development and Psychopathology, 8,* 399–424, figure 1. Reproduced with permission.

boys, it took longer for AL boys to "catch up" with their LCP counterparts. This was not the only difference between these two groups of delinquent boys. While the two groups did not differ from each other on many aspects of antisocial behavior, such as vandalism, shoplifting, and drug use, LCP boys were more violent, as Moffitt theorized would be the case. The best evidence of this was that LCP boys were convicted of a violent crime by age eighteen more often than other boys. Indeed, this was true of almost 25 percent of them.

Such behavior proved consistent with the LCP boys' own descriptions of their personalities. Based on responses to a series of questions, they characterized themselves, more often than other boys, as preferring an impulsive,

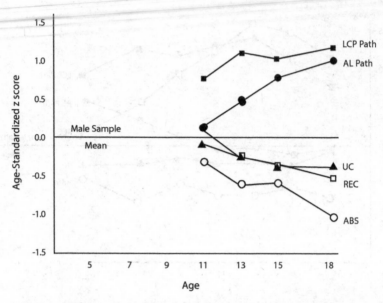

FIGURE 6.2. Males' average delinquent behavior according to self-reports taken at seven successive ages as a function of diagnostic group membership. LCP path: life-course-persistent antisocial path; AL path: adolescence-limited antisocial path; REC: recoveries from childhood antisocial behavior; ABS: abstainers from antisocial behavior; UC: unclassified boys not falling into any of the other subgroups. Reformatted from Moffitt, T.E., Caspi, A., Dickson, N., Silva, P., & Stanton, W. (1996). Childhood-onset versus adolescent-onset antisocial conduct problems in males: Natural history from ages 3–18. *Development and Psychopathology, 8,* 399–424 figure 3. Reproduced with permission.

impetuous life rather than a reflective, planful one, and as having an aggressive, hostile, alienated, suspicious, and cynical orientation toward others, while feeling distinctively callous and cold toward people. This worldview and psychological stance no doubt contributed to their getting caught up in one particular adolescent snare—restricted involvement with their family and thus weak emotional bonds.

Turning to AL boys, these study members were relative latecomers to antisocial behavior. Although some AL boys had shown some temporary or situational problems as children, none manifested a stable or pervasive pattern of childhood conduct problems. Yet their self-reports, their parents' reports, and even official records all confirmed that as a group they reached overall levels of antisocial behavior by midadolescence that rendered them indistinguishable from their LCP counterparts—except for the greater violence of the LCP boys. Nevertheless, 8 percent of AL boys had been convicted of a violent crime by age eighteen (compared to 25 percent of LCP males).

Personality characteristics and involvement in snares also distinguished AL boys from LCP ones. Although AL boys espoused aggressive attitudes, these were not as extreme as those of their LCP counterparts; rather, they described themselves as willing to dominate and intimidate others if necessary to get ahead. Consistent with this proclivity, they showed some leadership qualities that may have worked in tandem with their higher levels of completed education, resulting in AL boys' optimism about future employment prospects. But AL boys differed from LCP ones in another important—and social—way. Perhaps because they felt more closely attached to their families at age eighteen—thereby avoiding at least one important snare—they desired close relationships with intimates more than LCP boys did. Nevertheless, they showed evidence of rebelliousness. First, they had unconventional values—endorsing permissive child-rearing, eschewing traditional status hierarchies, and having little use for strict religious rules. Second, they engaged in extensive experimentation with drugs, tobacco, and alcohol, as well as unsafe sex and dangerous driving. Although they avoided more snares than LCP boys did, they were not entirely immune to them.

Childhood Origins

Having characterized similarities and differences between the two groups of antisocial teenage boys, the third phase of our adventure investigating troubled boys tested Moffitt's ideas about why the two groups of boys developed and functioned differently. Recall that in addition to proposing that LCP boys would be more antisocial as children than AL boys would be, a prediction already confirmed, Moffitt's theory also stipulated that the family environments of LCP boys would be more problematic and that these children would also show deficits in their psychological and behavioral functioning at an early age. Findings generally confirmed these expectations. Let's first consider family conditions.

Compared to AL boys, LCP boys had mothers who were younger when bearing their first child, spent more time as a single parent across the child's first eleven years of life, and were more economically and socially disadvantaged, as indicated by their lower social-class standing. Mothers of LCP boys also had more mental health problems when these were evaluated when study members were seven, nine, and eleven years of age. Perhaps because of these maternal and family conditions, mothers of LCP boys were less nurturing in their parenting than mothers of AL boys were. Indeed, when children were three years of age and mothers were observed interacting with their sons, mothers of LCP boys proved to be less supportive and caring in their parenting than mothers of AL boys; they also reported treating their sons more harshly, while the discipline they provided when the children were seven and nine years of age was less consistent. Finally, the families of LCP boys experienced more household conflict at these same ages than did families of AL boys.

While social and economic circumstances may have played a role in why LCP boys developed differently than AL boys, recall that Moffitt's theory also implicated developmental deficits in the case of LCP boys, beginning at an early age. In line with this hypothesis, we observed temperamental, cognitive, and behavioral differences between the two groups of boys as early as age two. At this young age, mothers of LCP boys described their children as more difficult; by age three we observed that they were more undercontrolled in their behavior (see Chapter 2); and from ages five through eleven, parent and teacher reports of child behavior revealed that LCP boys were more hyperactive than AL boys were (see Chapter 4).

Cognitive deficits were also evident in the case of LCP boys, again at a young age. They scored lower than AL boys did on standardized and age-appropriate tests of intelligence at age five, a difference that grew larger when intelligence tests were readministered at ages seven, nine, and eleven. Given these findings, it was no surprise that from ages seven to eleven LCP boys also had reading skills that were more limited than those of AL boys and that by age thirteen they scored lower on a test of memory.

Collectively, these psychological deficits, along with problematic family conditions, contributed to the behavioral differences between the two groups of boys that emerged from ages five through eleven. Across this period of middle childhood, which precedes adolescence, reports by parents and teachers indicated that LCP boys engaged in more fighting and, perhaps as a consequence, experienced more rejection by peers than AL boys did.

Preliminary Conclusion

In the main, Moffitt's theory of distinct developmental pathways to antisocial behavior in adolescence received substantial empirical support. First, it was clear that the two groups of children could be distinguished—those whose problem behavior was first manifested in childhood and maintained in adolescence and those whose serious problem behavior emerged for the first time in adolescence. Despite these contrasting trajectories of antisocial behavior, the two groups of boys proved to be more similar than different in adolescence. Both experienced snares, such as drug use and vandalism, and could not be distinguished on most types of antisocial behavior. Recall, however, that not only did boys whose antisocial behavior began in childhood prove more violent as adolescents than boys whose antisocial behavior was initiated in adolescence, but the LCP boys also had a hostile, alienated, suspicious, and cynical orientation toward others, whereas AL boys did not. So, even though these two groups of delinquent boys were similar in many respects, they were also different from each other in noteworthy ways. Recall that in the second part of our adventure studying troubled boys, we seek to determine whether and how these similarities or differences will play out in adulthood.

When it came to the origins of the distinctive developmental trajectories of antisocial behavior under consideration, Moffitt theorized that there would be evidence of greater problems in the families of the LCP boys, as well as in the boys' early development. This is exactly what we found. LCP boys fared poorly on background risk factors, including lower social class, greater family conflict, poor parenting, cognitive limitations, difficult temperament, and hyperactivity, beginning in early childhood and continuing through middle childhood. In fact, as the two groups of boys aged from three to eleven years, the differences in their functioning grew larger. Thus, whereas the difference between LCP and AL boys was modest at age two in terms of their being difficult to manage, it was larger at age three in terms of their being undercontrolled, and still larger at ages five to eleven in terms of their hyperactivity. Such developmental patterns are in line with Moffitt's theory, as it presumed that there would be ongoing development of the LCP boys' antisocial personality over time. Once again, it is worth thinking in terms of children's own behavior and reactions to that others serving to "produce their own development."

One final observation should be made before turning attention to the future development of LCP and AL men, and it concerns the girls we have not focused on. We chose to restrict consideration in this chapter to boys basically because they were so much more likely to develop along the LCP path—ten times as likely as girls. But despite this great difference in absolute risk or rate of becoming an LCP child, we discovered that almost all the LCP-AL differences we observed for boys held for AL and LCP girls as well. Therefore, it would seem that Moffitt's theory of LCP and AL offending is not just a theory that applies to one sex. Thus, LCP antisocial behavior—in both boys and girls—emerges when inherited or acquired developmental vulnerabilities, including cognitive limitations and difficult temperament, are present early in childhood and become exacerbated by growing up in a high-risk environment characterized by factors such as inadequate parenting, disrupted family bonds, and poverty, eventually resulting in poor relations with others outside the family, most notably peers and teachers. The relative rarity of LCP females likely results from their being less likely than males to have cognitive deficits, undercontrolled temperaments, and hyperactivity in early childhood. In both males and females, however, we see the importance for later development of both the psychological and behavioral characteristics of children and the family contexts in which they develop.

LCP AND AL MEN IN ADULTHOOD

As we make clear throughout this book, perhaps the greatest opportunity afforded by the Dunedin Study is its ability to illuminate how lives develop over time and thus when continuity and discontinuity characterize the process of human development. Thus, once we discovered what we did about LCP and AL boys through age eighteen, we could not help but wonder about how they would develop once they experienced the transition to adulthood after leaving school. Would it prove to be the case that "the teenager is the father of the man"? This question led us to the next phase of our adventure focused on troubled boys, reinvestigating the development of LCP and AL boys at ages twenty-six and thirty-two by considering a wide array of developmental attributes in order to see how they were doing. Recall that one of the core premises of Moffitt's original theory was that the AL group would prove able to desist from the antisocial behavior they engaged in for the first time in adolescence, whereas LCP boys would continue down the troublesome track they had been on since early childhood. As it turned out, the latter expectation was confirmed but the former was not entirely. Whereas the LCP boys as men functioned most poorly, the legacy of AL boys' adolescent behavior also showed some evidence of continuity in development. Let's consider first what we found at age twenty-six before turning attention to the results at age thirty-two.

LCP and AL Men at 26

About eight years after the end of high school, LCP men were significantly more involved in serious criminal offending according to their own reports than AL men were. They were two to three times more likely than AL men to have been convicted of an adult crime. And whereas AL men specialized in nonserious offenses—such as theft of less than $5, public drunkenness, and pirating computer software—LCP men tended to specialize in serious offenses, including carrying a hidden weapon, assault, robbery, and violating court orders. Such behavior was in line with how friend and family informants described LCP men and what formal psychiatric evaluations also revealed. LCP men were characterized as having significantly more symptoms of antisocial personality disorder than AL men had, according to people who knew them well, and formal psychiatric evaluations revealed they had a psychopathic personality profile (which was also evident at age eighteen). It was especially notable that LCP men continued to be violent, something that they acknowledged and that was corroborated by reports of informants, as well as by police and court records. Especially disturbing to discover was that violence was now directed at children and partners. This was despite the fact that LCP men were unlikely to stick around to help rear the large number of children they fathered. Perhaps that was not such a bad thing.

It was not just in the family and with respect to the law that LCP men were failing. By age twenty-six, they had poor work histories in low-status, unskilled jobs, lacked the minimum educational qualifications needed to get a good job, made a poor impression in an interview-type situation that we administered, and, as we have seen, had criminal records that would deter employers from hiring them. LCP men's high rate of substance-dependence problems and tendency to get into conflicts at work no doubt also undermined their chances of advancement in the low-skilled jobs they were able to secure.

While AL men were functioning better than LCP ones, there was clear evidence that they had not entirely abandoned their antisocial ways, as Moffitt's theory presumed would be the case, by taking advantage of their childhood capabilities. Let's consider the good news first: AL men had better work histories and higher-skilled jobs than LCP men did, with 80 percent having graduated from high school. They made a reasonable if not out-standing impression in an interview-type situation, and fewer of them had criminal convictions than their LCP counterparts did. No doubt, their greater success stemmed from the fact that they had agreeable personali-ties, not callous ones like their LCP counterparts, were reasonably extro-verted, retained close attachments to their parents, and had not been re-jected by peers as teenagers.

Despite these strengths, AL men fared more poorly than the Dunedin Study members who had not been classified as AL or LCP. AL men ac-counted for twice as many property and drug convictions between the ages of eighteen and twenty-six as would have been expected based on how many of them were in the total sample. And when interviewed at age twenty-six, they reported an impressive number of property and drug-related of-fenses in the past year. Such behavior was likely because of AL men's impul-sivity. Perhaps it would just take more time for AL men to mature out of their bad habits. This possibility was one big reason we reexamined the de-velopment of antisocial adolescents six years later as part of our adventure studying the nature, origins, and consequences of adolescent delinquency.

LCP and AL Men at 32

The first thing to be said about LCP men by the fourth decade of life is that there were no signs of desistance from crime. Just under one-third of these men were convicted of a violent crime between ages twenty-six and thirty-two. In fact, almost one in five had spent time in prison during these years, compared to only one in twenty AL men. Family violence also remained a part of LCP men's behavioral repertoire, but, notably, AL men were as likely as LCP ones to hit a child or direct controlling abuse toward a partner.

Mental health evaluations further revealed serious problems with LCP men. They experienced more problems with anxiety, greater incidence of major depression, and proved to be more cannabis dependent as well as more dependent on other illicit drugs than AL men were. LCP men also had attempted suicide more often. The two groups of adolescent offenders were, however, equally likely to be alcohol dependent at age thirty-two.

But it was not just in behavior and mental health that LCP men were still doing badly. They were also in poor physical health. They had the highest risk of cardiovascular disease, while showing the most evidence of inflammation. They also were the most likely to have the Type 2 herpes sexually transmitted disease and be nicotine dependent. No doubt, this latter condition played a role in their high level of chronic bronchitis symptoms, gum disease, and untreated tooth decay.

Economically, they were still doing poorly. The occupations of LCP men placed them in the lowest social class of all study members—if and when they were employed, and of all male study members they had the most months unemployed over the preceding six years. Family and friend informants rated them as having the most financial problems, such as not having enough money to pay their bills and being indebted. Perhaps as a consequence, they were the most likely to find themselves without money for food or necessities and even to be homeless.

When we turn to considering AL men, we find that they were still experiencing problems, again contrary to Moffitt's original theorizing. Indeed, even by age thirty-two, these males engaged in antisocial behavior, but, as anticipated, they were making a more successful transition to adulthood than their LCP counterparts were. Nevertheless, many were still abusing illicit substances, having economic problems, and in poor health.

Before concluding this summary of findings pertaining to the legacy of adolescent antisocial behavior in adulthood, we should again make some brief comments about LCP and AL females even though they are not the primary focus of this chapter. Those LCP women whose problems began in childhood continued to do poorly in multiple aspects of development by age thirty-two. They continued to engage in antisocial behavior, suffered from significant mental health problems, and were in poor physical health, while also experiencing substantial economic difficulties. Needless to say, this summary reads all too much like what we found for LCP men, once again suggesting that Moffitt's theory also applies to women, even if they are much less likely to find themselves on the LCP path.

Fortunately, things looked better for AL females than for AL males. These female AL study members would seem to fit Moffitt's theory even better than AL males did, as AL females demonstrated very little continuity in their antisocial behavior into adulthood. Although a small percentage of AL women became ensnared by drug use (other than marijuana), they were no more likely to meet diagnostic criteria for other psychiatric disorders than other study members were. In fact, economic status was the only domain where AL women demonstrated significant deficits in their early thirties, not differing from LCP women. In summary, the overall prognosis for LCP women at age thirty-two was poor, with the same being true of AL women because of their economic conditions but to a much lesser extent than for LCP women.

This adventure continues. A search of Dunedin Study members' police records revealed that the members of the LCP group were still being convicted of crimes. During their thirties, they were convicted five times on average, which includes two convictions for violent crimes. The AL group members were convicted only once during their thirties, on average, and not for violent crimes.

IMPLICATIONS

Two of the authors had a professor in graduate school, Urie Bronfenbrenner (mentioned in Chapter 5), who liked to quote a famous, long deceased social scientist, Kurt Lewin, who stated: "There is nothing so practical as a good theory." What exactly did Lewin mean by that? As we hope we made clear, Moffitt's theory provided us with a *road map* to follow on our developmental adventure. It first led us to seek to identify distinctive developmental trajectories of antisocial behavior, particularly two specific ones that she hypothesized would exist, LCP and AL. It also alerted us to the role that childhood cognitive and temperamental vulnerabilities, family economic disadvantage and dysfunction, and adolescent snares would play in undermining development, including distinguishing the LCP adolescents from the AL ones. Finally, it directed us to examine the adult consequences of the developmental trajectories guiding our work. As a result, our empirical tests of the theory mostly supported it. As we have noted, this was especially the case with LCP boys and girls and somewhat the case with AL males and, perhaps more so, females.

Many people find it difficult to acknowledge that their ideas are not entirely on target. Few people enjoy being wrong or misguided. And we humans are known to suffer from what social psychologists call "confirmation bias"—the tendency to filter information in ways that confirm what we already think or believe. So we often attend to and better remember observations and evidence consistent with our expectations than those that are inconsistent with them.

To our way of thinking, what distinguishes a scientist from an ideologue is the effort, indeed commitment, to recognize such human cognitive failings and endeavor to overcome them. This is why data matter, pure and simple. An open-minded investigator needs to let the empirical chips fall where they may, hoping that sometimes they will prove consistent with her thinking but understanding that sometimes they will not. There is no crime in being somewhat—or even entirely—misguided in the world of science. The only crime is sticking to a view despite contrary evidence, especially if that evidence derives from well-designed research. No one should forget that even Einstein did not get everything right! So the fact that Moffitt's theory took some hits when it came to the adult development of AL males is by no means anything to be ashamed of or embarrassed by. After all, what's wrong with being in the same league as Einstein?

Now that we have highlighted the implications of our findings for science, let's consider their implications for service and treatment. These prove to be relatively straightforward and also speak to the practical utility of a good theory. Different strategies are probably required when it comes to addressing childhood-onset and adolescence-onset delinquency, and this is so with respect to both preventing the development of problem behavior in the first place and treating it once it has emerged. With regard to prevention of the LCP path, it should be clear that such efforts must begin very early in life. After all, the LCP boys were different from AL and thus all other boys as early as two years of age and, quite conceivably, even earlier, though we were not positioned to detect such differences. It would clearly seem to be mistaken, then, to presume that "boys will be boys" or that "he will grow out of it" when early evidence of chronic antisocial behavior confronts us.

Prevention should be multifaceted, targeting not just different aspects of child development (for example, cognition and temperament) but different contexts as well, including family, day care, and school. The fact that at least some of the children who evinced high levels of problem behavior in childhood desisted by adolescence—our "recoverers"—makes clear that starting on the LCP path does not inevitably lead to continuing on it. Once again, we see that the influence of early-life functioning on adolescent delinquency is probabilistic, not deterministic. Clearly, there are grounds for hope.

Having said that, we need to be clear that when it comes to efforts to remediate antisocial behavior that begins early in childhood, this will not be easy, especially as children develop. Practitioners must be prepared to wage a vigorous extended battle against a formidable adversary. That foe is many years of accumulated problematic development, resulting in an antisocial personality structure. One of the great challenges in this regard will simply be keeping troubled teenagers in treatment, as there is extensive evidence that this is rather difficult to do.

AL boys will no doubt be more promising candidates for intervention. They lack the cumulative life history of problematic development that limits change in their LCP counterparts. Indeed, the AL boys' personality profiles included adaptive attributes such as a strong sense of agency or social potency and a preference for interpersonal closeness. That is why it is critically important for parents, physicians, schools, police, and the courts to pay serious attention to the developmental histories of adolescents who offend, in addition to what their offenses are. Treating those whose problem behavior began in adolescence in the same way as those whose behavioral problems extended back to their early childhoods—even if they have committed the same offense—would be unwise and unfair from a developmental perspective. This is why the long-term study of development, like that undertaken in the Dunedin Study, is so important. We suspect that the likely consequence of convicting and imprisoning an AL offender would be to make things worse, not better, and this itself would be a crime if these particular adolescents would be, as we further suspect, responsive to efforts to correct their behavior. Efforts should be undertaken, especially with those on the AL path, to prevent alcohol use from becoming alcohol dependence; to prevent sexual experimentation from becoming unplanned parenthood; to prevent fun in an automobile from becoming disabling injury; and to prevent truancy from becoming school dropout and unemployment.

7

Early-Maturing Girls, Troubled Families, and Bad Boys

According to file records, when Stephanie was observed at age eleven, she was different from the open and friendly, freckle-faced, curly-red-haired girl that she had been when she visited the Dunedin Study's research unit two years earlier. Now there seemed to be a premature worldliness about her. When research staff interviewed Stephanie about her relationships with peers, she no longer spoke of the board games she once enjoyed playing but rather of conflicts she was having with one-time friends; she complained that they were no longer interested in spending time with her. At the same time, she criticized them for being such "little girls," "so busy doing homework." Records also revealed that Stephanie was spending lots of time with boys, including quite a number who were older than she was. Stephanie also indicated that she had gotten drunk a few times and even tried marijuana. Staff suspected she was about to become sexually active or already had. Not only was she more physically developed than almost all the other eleven-year-olds interviewed as part of the Dunedin Study, but she asked one of the interviewers about birth control. Staff could not inquire about sexual behavior because New Zealand law prevented them from doing so.

Records further revealed that Stephanie's father had more or less abandoned the family very early in her life and that her mother had been involved with a number of men since then. Her mother was a harsh but inconsistent disciplinarian, sometimes punishing Stephanie for breaking rules and at other times seeming not to notice. Connecting these developmental dots in a cause-and-effect manner led some to conclude that Stephanie's family experiences influenced her relationships with peers, but others in our group questioned this interpretation as we reviewed the records. They suspected that genes shared by the parent and child were the cause of the harsh, inconsistent, and neglectful parenting of Stephanie's mother, as well as Stephanie's own misbehavior. Unfortunately, because the Dunedin Study did not at that time include any measurements of actual genes, we could not evaluate these alternative, nature-versus-nurture explanations when we carried out the work presented in this chapter.

Despite this limitation, we found ourselves in a position to go on another developmental adventure, once again investigating a new theoretical idea, referred to in the preface, that had intrigued Jay Belsky. We were especially interested that this new idea represented a radical alternative to prevailing social science and mental health notions about how childhood adversity affects human development. This is because it was based on the core premise of evolutionary biology, a field of inquiry central to all life sciences, that the *purpose* of life is to pass on genes to the next generation and beyond. This view of life is directly related to the illumination of effects of childhood experiences on later development. Evolutionary biology's privileging of "reproductive success" or "reproductive fitness" over all other goals of life, such as health, wealth, and happiness, to say nothing of "meaning," stimulated the novel theoretical proposition that Belsky advanced and that is the focus of this chapter—that growing up in a father-absent family or one in which conflict is frequent or parenting is harsh will accelerate girls' sexual maturation, leading them to physically mature earlier than would otherwise be the case and thereby affect their adolescent risk-taking behavior.

THE DEVELOPMENT OF FAST AND SLOW REPRODUCTIVE STRATEGIES

Although the notion of reproductive success is central to the thinking of virtually all biological scientists studying nonhuman life, it is more or less foreign to most students of human development. This is especially true, perhaps, of those interested in how experiences in the family affect the developing child. Indeed, for most psychologists, sociologists, economists, educators, policymakers, and parents, life is about health, wealth, and happiness. This leads many to conceptualize development as healthy versus unhealthy or "optimal" versus "compromised." Thus, a child who experiences nurturing care is expected to be secure, curious, friendly, and striving to achieve, eventually developing into a productive adult who, in Freud's terms, can "love and work." This represents the process and products of healthy development. In contrast, the child who is insecure, incurious, and has difficulty managing emotions and behavior because of unsupportive care represents a form of compromised development. Such an individual will not only experience limited academic and occupational success but will also be unable to establish and maintain close relationships. Central to this standard social science view of life is the presumption that the first way of developing is "natural," the way it is supposed to be, and the second represents a disturbance in development, evidence of dysfunction or even disorder, not the way it is supposed to be.

This traditional perspective on how nurture shapes development contrasts markedly with evolutionary-biological view that there is no "optimal" or best development. What succeeds in passing on genes to the next generation is best, and, critically, that depends on the context or circumstances in which a living organism exists, including those in which it develops. For example, when a member of a particular species of snail senses, while still in its larval stage, that there are predators in the water, it develops a much thicker, stronger shell than when predators are not detected. This obviously makes sense: it is "bio-logical," just as not devoting resources to building a stronger shell when no apparent need for it exists would be. Both "strategies" are optimal, each fitting the organism to its anticipated environment in a way that should facilitate its eventual reproductive success, passing on its genes to the next generation.

Therefore, from an evolutionary perspective, the best way for a child, an adolescent, or even an adult to develop is not necessarily the one valued by mental health professionals, teachers, and even policymakers. This is because what will prove most successful in passing on genes to descendants when growing up under one set of conditions, such as in a well-functioning, harmonious family, should not be presumed to do so under different conditions, such as when there is much family conflict and limited attention paid to children. This evolutionary-biological view of life implies that the forces of Darwinian natural selection have adapted our species to respond to its experiences growing up in a manner that would increase the chances of the developing child surviving, maturing, and reproducing—just as it has for the snails already mentioned.

From this perspective, what has long been regarded as evidence of "compromised" development may actually be anything but. Indeed, many of the documented consequences of growing up under conditions of adversity may also be "bio-logical": they increased our ancestors' success in passing on genes to the next generation. As a result, what many today regard as compromised, troubled, or problematic development may well have evolved as a strategic response to adversity. It is not difficult to imagine, for example, that in a world lacking safety and security, it would have been reproductively advantageous to be aggressive and take advantage of others, perhaps hitting first and asking questions only afterward.

The argument being advanced here is that during the course of human ancestral history, our species, like many others, evolved the capacity to vary its development depending on early-life experiences and exposures. Critically, such distinctive developmental responses to different contextual conditions early in life became part of the human psychobiological makeup because they fostered reproductive success, the ultimate goal of all living things. This implies that we still retain this developmental plasticity or responsiveness that emerged so long ago. But this analysis does not necessarily imply that our evolved way of responding to different developmental conditions still yields the reproductive payoffs it once did. Because the modern world is so different from our ancestral one (for example, we have birth control, abortion, and welfare benefits), and because evolution typically takes a great deal of time, we retain the responsiveness built into our species over the eons even though it is no longer as reproductively beneficial as it once was.

Evolutionary biologists speak of distinctive "reproductive strategies" or ways of developing from birth through adulthood that evolved to fit the individual to the environment it would likely inhabit as it matured. Most notably, they distinguish "fast" and "slow" strategies. When life is good—meaning the developing child experiences safety and security—there should be no rush to develop. The biologically strategic response is to grow slowly and take in all the resources that are available, including nutritional, psychological, and economic ones. Doing so will make for a more robust individual, capable of dealing with challenges, attracting a good mate, and devoting energy and effort to raising healthy children who will also have good life prospects and prove reproductively successful, passing on their own, their parents', and their ancestors' genes.

In contrast, when childhood experience teaches that others cannot be trusted, that the world is threatening, and that the chances of living a long, healthy life are limited, a reproductive strategy should involve a rush to mature—to be able to reproduce before threats put an end to life or severely compromise it. While modern, middle-class society may not embrace this latter strategy—seeing it not as an evolved developmental strategy but as an unnatural dysfunction—this does not mean it didn't pay reproductive dividends over the eons and therefore wasn't the better way to develop under the particular conditions described. Indeed, theoretically, such a seemingly "problematic" way of developing would not even have had to be extremely successful in passing on genes to have evolved as a strategic response to adversity; it only had to prove more successful in achieving this end relative to other, less problematic ways of developing. Think of it this way: imagine the problematic way of developing succeeded only 30 percent of the time when it came to passing on genes, but that this was greater, given the context of development, than the 22 percent success rate of alternative ways of developing.

It is not difficult to imagine that the fast developmental strategy would carry some costs in terms of more limited growth, potentially compromised health, and reduced ability to attract a good mate. But, according to evolutionary theorizing, such costs should be compensated for by the increased chance of maturing and reproducing before poor health or even death undermines reproductive success. Because such fast developers are presumed to be less able or less inclined to care for children well or to maintain close intimate relationships, the fast developer should also produce more children, even while "investing" less in them in terms of energy, time, and economic resources. Unlike the slow developer, who is better positioned to care for and protect progeny, the fast developer may need to produce more children in order to generate the same number of grandchildren as the slow developer. This may be especially true if the fast developer is not well positioned—for economic, physical, or social reasons—to protect and preserve their offspring's safety and security. But again we need to appreciate that bearing many children but not caring for them well may no longer yield the reproductive "payoffs" they once did. After all, culture can change much faster than evolved developmental biology.

Importantly, we should not assume that nature left it to each of us to figure all this out and consciously pursue one way of developing rather than another. Consider how when we move from a dark room into the bright light of midday our eye knows exactly what to do—narrow our pupil—and does not depend on us to consciously give it directions. Why, then, would nature leave it to the developing child to figure out which developmental "trajectory" is the correct one to follow?

A JUST-SO STORY?

However intriguing or even persuasive this reproductive-strategy view of development may sound, traditional social scientists and developmental scientists have strong grounds for questioning it. After all, extensive sociological, psychological, and even economic research has long revealed that childhood adversity—being poor, growing up in a single-parent home, being harshly treated, or even abused—often leads to problematic development. This includes aggressive behavior, poor health, limited mating prospects, sexual risk taking, unstable male-female relationships, and bearing many children who are poorly cared for from an early age. Why, then, embrace a seemingly far-fetched evolutionary story concerning our hunter-gatherer ancestors to account for why growing up under conditions of adversity should lead to particular life outcomes?

The law of parsimony, also known as Occam's razor, in the philosophy of science stipulates that when there are less and more complex explanations of a phenomenon—in this case having to do with effects of early-life adversity on development—the simpler one should be preferred. So why even consider the evolutionary history of our species when a simple learning explanation would seem to do the trick? Just consider the specific case of father absence. Girls growing up in such homes are at increased risk of becoming sexually active before other girls, even promiscuous, not because of anything having to do with our hunter-gatherer ancestors. This way of behaving simply reflects what living with their mothers has taught them: men come and go and can't be trusted but are more inclined to stick around if and when sex is available to them.

However persuasive the argument of parsimony might be, there are philosophy-of-science conditions that, if met, should lead to the acceptance of a more complex explanation—in this case having to do with evolution and reproductive strategy—over a less complex one. For a new theory or explanation to prevail over a more established one, the new perspective needs to do three things. First, it has to be able to explain what we already know, in this case that childhood adversity leads to "compromised" development. The reproductive-strategy perspective accomplishes this. Second, the new theoretical framework must generate an original hypothesis—that is, a prediction—that can be tested but that has never been proposed or evaluated by those embracing the traditional view. Finally, empirical evaluation of the new hypothesis must lead to a discovery that the traditional perspective is ill equipped to explain—and would never have anticipated. Only when all three conditions are met should a new, seemingly less parsimonious perspective trump a simpler one.

AN UNCANNY PREDICTION

Jay Belsky realized that there was at least one developmental "outcome" that could be related to childhood adversity according to the evolutionary, reproductive-strategy view of life that the social science and mental health views had never considered—the timing of puberty. He reasoned that girls who were rushing to maturity—for reproductive reasons—in response to adversity should physically mature sooner than girls growing up under more benign or benevolent conditions. This was because early pubertal development would make girls fertile sooner than would be the case for other girls. Implicit in this argument, of course, was the view that adversity-induced early puberty would promote the sexual activity needed for reproduction. Even though we were uncertain about how such puberty- and sex-accelerating effects of early-life adversity would be physiologically instantiated, we knew that if we found support for this "puberty hypothesis," it would be a result that standard social science and human-development thinking could not account for. That is why Belsky regarded it as an "uncanny" prediction, one that became the focus of another developmental adventure that is the subject of this chapter. This chapter addresses the influence of childhood experience in the family on later development by considering

how the quality of family life and parenting influences pubertal development. It also addresses the influence of early development on later development, by considering whether early- and later-developing girls differ in
the timing of their sexual debut and sexual behavior.

The Dunedin Study was well positioned to evaluate whether adverse
childhood conditions predicted accelerated pubertal development, as Belsky
theorized. We were excited to embark on this adventure because there was
no evidence about the topic when Belsky advanced his prediction and we
began our work. Information about household composition had been routinely collected, so it could be taken from the data pantry to enable us to
determine whether and how often fathers were absent from the home across
the child's first seven years of life and thus whether father absence predicted
pubertal timing. Based on reports by mothers, we also knew how much
family conflict occurred in the household, so this information could be used
for the same purpose. Finally, because we had gathered data on when girls
had their first period (menarche), we were well positioned to test the hypothesis that father absence and greater family conflict would accelerate
female pubertal development, as indicated by earlier age of menarche. This
situation reveals again one of the great strengths of research projects that
follow lives through time, such as those on which this book is based: they
are a gift that keeps giving. In other words, they afford the opportunity to
test new ideas, even ones never envisioned when the data used to evaluate
them were originally collected, such as the puberty hypothesis. It's kind of
like having in your pantry everything you need to make a new recipe even
though you never made any purchases at the grocery store with it in mind.

As it turned out, our efforts to evaluate the puberty hypothesis by linking
experiences in the family at age seven with the timing of menarche proved
consistent with predictions based on reproductive-strategy thinking in two
respects. First, girls growing up without fathers sexually matured earlier
than girls growing up in intact, two-parent families. Second, girls growing
up in high-conflict families matured earlier than their counterparts exposed
to minimal family conflict. These were empirical discoveries that had never
before been documented, no doubt because traditional thinking never raised
the possibility that early-life adversity would accelerate sexual maturation.
Just as important from the perspective of the philosophy of science, our
results were also not explicable from the standpoint of traditional theories
of family effects on human development.

As we have seen, even when findings prove to be in line with expectations, there is a need to consider alternative explanations. In the case of female pubertal development, one such alternative explanation highlights the importance of body fat. Girls must have a certain amount of body fat before they mature sexually. In fact, the "critical-fat" hypothesis explains why ballerinas and female gymnasts are typically delayed in their sexual maturation; their arduous exercise regimes eliminate virtually all the fat from their bodies. These observations raised the possibility that it was not the particular forms of adversity that we had focused on, father absence and family conflict, that influenced age of menarche but instead body fat. Fortuitously, the Dunedin Study also included measurements of physical development that we could extract from our data pantry to test this alternative explanation. This allowed us to discover that even after taking into account girls' weight, father absence and greater family conflict still predicted an earlier age of menarche, but this doesn't mean that body fat doesn't matter. It simply means that the family factors under consideration predicted age of menarche beyond weight differences between girls. With most aspects of development, it is almost always important to appreciate that they are influenced by many factors, not just one. So a hypothesis that highlights one, in this case early-life adversity, should virtually never be read as implying that there would not be others, too.

Body fat was not the only alternative explanation that we had to consider. The other, which has been raised in previous chapters, was genetic inheritance. Because it was well established that age of menarche is heritable, such that mothers who mature early are likely to have daughters who mature early, the possibility existed that the links between early-life adversity and early puberty could be a function of genes shared by parents and children. Consider that mothers of study members who themselves matured early might have been drawn into pair bonding and childbearing at too young an age, which in turn led to relationship conflict and dissolution and thus father absence for their daughters, whose early maturation might have happened for genetic reasons. Conceivably, the same genes that influence parent behavior and thus father absence or family conflict could be passed on to daughters and contribute to their early sexual maturation. Fortunately, we were able to at least partially address this concern in our next effort to evaluate and extend our uncanny puberty prediction.

BEYOND PUBERTY

The notion that psychological and behavioral development as well as physical development evolved to be responsive to rearing experiences, all in the service of passing on genes to the next generation, is central to the reproductive-strategy view of human development. In fact, Jay Belsky's evolutionary thinking that guided our work stipulated that early maturation was a step along the developmental pathway to early and even promiscuous sexual behavior. Recall that the biological reason for accelerating pubertal development is to increase the chances of sexual reproduction before becoming compromised or even dying. Thus, in an effort to extend our research on the reproductive strategies of girls growing up in troubled families, we sought to determine whether adverse rearing experiences not only accelerated pubertal development but, in so doing, influenced sexual activity as well.

With these aims in mind, we turned to the Study of Early Child Care and Youth Development highlighted in Chapter 1 and considered in greater detail in Chapter 8—for two reasons. First, it enabled us to evaluate whether we could, for a second time, document the apparent accelerating effect of early adversity on girls' pubertal development. Just as important, however, was that it afforded us the opportunity to determine whether early puberty itself was associated with sexual risk taking in adolescence. It should be appreciated that when this collaborative project involving ten research teams was launched, there was no plan to assess pubertal development or evaluate evolutionary ideas. But given the apparent promise of reproductive-strategy thinking, we decided to gather the necessary information about pubertal development in order to do so.

In fact, beyond focusing on sexual behavior, we were able to advance research in an important way related to the issue of genetic inheritance. Because of concerns that effects of shared genes might have "masqueraded" as effects of adverse family experiences in the Dunedin Study, we secured information in the child care study on the mother's age of menarche. By taking the mother's age of menarche into account before evaluating links between family experience and girls' pubertal development, we could discount at least some potential genetic influence. Unfortunately, this was not possible when it came to fathers. Even though women can recollect their age of menarche with striking accuracy—even four decades later—most men simply have no clear recollection of the timing of their pubertal development. How many male readers can recall when they first sprouted pubic hair, when their voices changed, or when they first ejaculated semen?

Ultimately, we reasoned that taking into account at least some potential genetic influence—as indexed by the mother's age of menarche—was better than not taking any into account. To our surprise, at least one critic of our work felt that we risked erring on the side of caution by treating any similarity in the mother's and daughter's ages of menarche as evidence of genetic influence. After all, it could be that a mother who matured earlier than other women did so for the same reason her daughter did: she, too, could have been exposed to adversity while growing up, thereby accelerating her own pubertal development. This brings us back to the topic of intergenerational transmission of parenting, discussed in Chapter 5. While we appreciated the concern raised by our critic, we nevertheless judged it better to be conservative and presume that any relation between the mother's and daughter's ages of menarche reflected the effect of shared genes rather than similar rearing experiences. Therefore, we statistically discounted its effect.

When we evaluated family effects on girls' pubertal development in the child care study, we discovered that harsh parenting mattered when it came to the timing of their children's pubertal development. Parents who were characterized as harsh spanked their children for doing something wrong, and they expected them to obey without asking questions and to be quiet and respectful when adults were around. Harsh parents regarded respect for authority as the most important thing for the child to learn. They also believed praise spoiled the child, so they provided few hugs and kisses. Thus, what we discovered was that the more parents regarded and treated their four-and-a-half-year-old harshly, the earlier their daughters had their first period. This was the case regardless of the age at which mothers themselves had their first period. So, the first way we extended our prior reproductive-strategy research was by discounting the effects of maternal age of menarche before evaluating the effects of harshness on the daughter's pubertal development, while still documenting what appeared to be family-environment effects.

Recall that our second means of advancing our prior work was to determine whether accelerated pubertal development itself predicted sexual behavior. It did: by age fifteen, girls who matured earlier had engaged in more sexual risk taking than other girls. The early-maturing girls who experienced harsh parenting not only had their first period before other girls

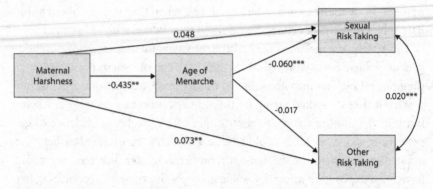

FIGURE 7.1. Statistical path model showing greater maternal harshness when the child was four and a half years old predicted earlier age of menarche (after adjusting for mother's recollected age of menarche), which itself predicted greater sexual risk taking but no other types of risk taking. Other types of risk taking were predicted directly by greater maternal harshness, though this did not directly predict sexual risk taking. Asterisks reflects statistical significance of the associations (**p,>01, ***p,>001). Reformatted from Belsky, J., Steinberg, L., Houts, R.M., Halpern-Felsher, B.L. & The NICHD Early Child Care Research Newtork (2010). The Development of Reproductive Strategy in Females: Early Maternal Harshness→Earlier Menarche→Increased Sexual Risk Taking. *Developmental Psychology*, 46, 120–128, figure 1. Reproduced with permission of American Psychological Association.

but by age fifteen were more sexually active, having engaged in more oral sex and sexual intercourse. They were not more likely, however, to engage in other risk-taking behavior, such as drinking and drug taking. Figure 7.1 graphically displays these findings.

BEYOND ADOLESCENCE

These discoveries raised a new question in our minds related to the evolutionary thinking that inspired all this work. Did the effect of girls' early maturation on their sexual behavior extend beyond midadolescence? Recall that reproductive-strategy thinking stipulates that it should. Specifically, it predicts that girls maturing earlier because of their more problematic family life would have less stable "pair bonds"—that is, close relationships with the opposite sex.

Once again, we turned to the Dunedin study to examine the longer-term sexual and relationship behavior of early-maturing girls. When study members were twenty-one, twenty-six, and thirty-two years of age, we asked questions about the number of opposite-sex partners with whom they had intercourse in the previous three years at age twenty-one, the past five years at age twenty-six, and the prior six years at age thirty-two. We did this in a way that other research indicated would promote honest reporting: we had study members answer questions on a computer rather than through a face-to-face interview, thus increasing their experience of privacy. Even if some might suspect that males in particular would exaggerate their sexual attractiveness and prowess, there was much less reason to believe that females would do the same.

When we turned our attention to the confidential information we had acquired about sexual behavior in adulthood in this next phase of our adventure investigating the development of human reproductive strategies, we discovered that early-maturing girls had more sex partners than other girls, into their thirties. The evidence further indicated that such behavior was associated with substance use. The latter observation seems quite sensible, as those who have sex often do so when they are intoxicated. Even if the finding about substance abuse was not anticipated by reproductive-strategy thinking, the association between early sexual maturity and more numerous sexual partners certainly was. Recall the earlier observation that a fast strategy was related to unstable male-female relationships. Now there was evidence, based on all the research we had conducted, that childhood adversity—indexed by father absence, family conflict, and harsh parenting—predicted accelerated pubertal development; that such early sexual maturation itself predicted more sexual risk taking in adolescence, even after taking into account a mother's age of menarche and thus some of the potential influence of genetics on girls' own somatic development; and that girls who matured earlier than others also had more sexual partners in their twenties, thirties, and forties.

RESILIENCE IN THE FACE OF RISK

Despite the results of our work, it would be an egregious error to conclude that every girl exposed to adversity or who matured early would develop in the manner just described. Here we are returning to the theme of probabilistic versus deterministic development discussed in Chapter 1. We have presented general trends, and this does not mean that they apply equally to every individual, even every early-maturing girl exposed to adversity in childhood. As an analogy, even though it is reliably hotter in New York City, on average, in July than in April, this does not mean that every day in July is always hotter than every day in April.

Throughout this book, we endeavor to make crystal clear that human development is a complex process. As previously noted, it is rare that any singular source of influence fully explains why some individuals develop one way and others develop a different way. Appreciation of this complexity led us to wonder about conditions that might prevent adverse rearing conditions and early maturity from exerting their apparent influence on how females develop. This led us to investigate factors that might attenuate or even eliminate the developmental links already documented connecting childhood adversity with girls' early sexual maturity and age of menarche with subsequent sexual activity. We addressed the first issue by returning to the NICHD Study of Child Care and Youth Development and the second by returning to the Dunedin Study. In both cases, we were pursuing the issue of resilience: what enabled girls at risk of early menarche because of problematic family backgrounds to avoid early menarche and, relatedly, what enabled girls at risk of earlier and more promiscuous sexual behavior because of their early maturity to avoid this pitfall.

Avoiding Early Maturity

Even though it was unclear exactly what physiological mechanisms might be involved in linking childhood adversity with the timing of girls' sexual maturity, we were not entirely in the dark when it came to considering what might limit the accelerating effect of family adversity on age of menarche. Some developmental scholars contend that the meaning and thus the effect of harsh parenting depends on the relationship context in which it occurs. Consider two parents from the child care study. Marilyn was inclined to be very strict with her daughter, calling on scripture to explain to us that "sparing the rod spoiled the child." That anger got the better of her sometimes when disciplining her daughter, Kathi, was especially problematic. This caused Marilyn to make disparaging comments like "you're just like your father," "you'll never amount to anything," and "I'd be surprised if anyone will ever marry you." Another parent, Sharon, who was better off economically, also shared the same biblical outlook, but she was more consistent and measured in her use of physical punishment with her daughter, Caroline, virtually never letting her anger get the better of her. Given these different experiences, might the two girls have come to view physical discipline differently? This seemed to be the case. While Kathi regarded her mother as mean and not really liking her, Caroline viewed her mother as caring and devoted.

This observation led us to wonder how girls would be affected by harsh punishment during their preschool years if they had established a secure rather than an insecure attachment to their mother in infancy. Secure children have the confidence that they are loved, a sense that provides the foundation for the view that the world is a benign if not benevolent place and that others can be trusted to be nice, kind, and caring. Theory and evidence indicate that such security is a function of the quality of care that children experience in their opening years of life. When parents are sensitive and responsive, acknowledging and accepting the feelings of their babies, while responding quickly and in a comforting manner to the fear and distress that infants often experience, infants develop a secure attachment. When parenting is less sensitive, responsive, and caring, however, insecurity becomes more likely, and with it comes a less optimistic and more distrustful outlook on life.

To the extent that this is so, we reasoned, even harsh parenting experienced in the preschool years might be less likely to accelerate girls' pubertal development if they have a history of secure attachment in infancy. In other words, a relationship history that engendered a sense of trust and security should protect a daughter from maturing early. We theorized that it would lead them to experience even harsh parenting in a more positive light than would be the case for those with insecure histories of attachment in infancy, and this is exactly what we found. The already established accelerating effect of a harsh rearing environment at age four and a half years on early pubertal development did not apply in the case of girls who were securely attached to their mothers at age 15 months; it only did so when daughters had established, as infants, insecure attachments to their mothers. These results are graphically displayed in Figure 7.2. Thus, a secure attachment operated as a resilience factor, preventing the acceleration of pubertal development when it would otherwise have been expected. This resilience-related

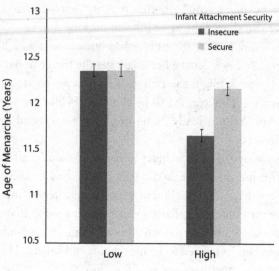

FIGURE 7.2. Average age of menarche of females who experienced low and high levels of early environmental harshness as a function of attachment security or insecurity at age fifteen months. Reformatted from Sung, S., Simpson, J.A., Griskevicius, V., Kuo, S.I., Schlomer, G.L. & Belsky, J. (2016). Secure infant-mother attachment buffers the effect of early-life stress on age of menarche. *Psychological Science, 27,* 667–674, figure 1. Reproduced with permission from SAGE Publications, Inc.

result made it clear that the accelerating effect of harsh parenting on pubertal development is not inevitable; it is probabilistic, not deterministic. Security can operate as a resilience factor. Thank goodness for the complexity of human development!

Avoiding Adolescent Problem Behavior

Having identified at least one developmental condition that protected girls exposed to harsh parenting at age four and a half years from maturing early, we wanted to know whether there were circumstances that might also prevent early-maturing girls from engaging in delinquent behavior. Recall that we could not explicitly focus on sexual behavior in the Dunedin Study because New Zealand law precluded researchers from asking teenagers about this subject back when study members were in their teens. We did not regard this as a serious limitation, however, because it was already well established—chronicled in Richard and Shirley Jessor's 1977 book *Problem Behavior and Psychosocial Development*—that teenage girls inclined to break rules by drinking, using drugs, and defying authority are the same ones likely to engage in sex at an early age.

In thinking about conditions that might prevent early-maturing girls from engaging in delinquent behavior, it didn't take a lot of insight to suspect that boys—perhaps especially older, "bad" boys—played a big role in leading early-maturing girls into temptation. Consider the sort of boy who would be attracted to an early-maturing girl, whose figure is voluptuous but who is still cognitively and emotionally a child. But how could we test this idea? We never went into the schools the girls attended or observed them in their neighborhoods in the Dunedin Study to determine who they were spending time with. And we couldn't introduce them to older boys as part of an experiment to see whether they would attract more interest than more slowly maturing agemates, even though our own experiences growing up and raising children taught us that this would be the case.

But then we realized that we really didn't need to do anything except take advantage of what might be called a "natural experiment," one that we did not design or implement but that everyday life did: some girls in the Dunedin Study attended an all-girl school, whereas others were enrolled in a coed secondary school. In New Zealand, the choice to attend a single-sex school is not a result of a family's desire that their child attend a religious or military institution; choice is primarily determined by which school the pupil can most easily walk to. If our reasoning about the role of bad boys in encouraging delinquent behavior in girls was sound, then the link between early maturity and problem behavior should prove operative in the coed school but not in the single-sex school. And that was exactly what we found.

Figure 7.3 makes clear that at age thirteen early-maturing girls in mixed-sex schools were much more likely to break rules—that is, engage in norm violations such as stealing money, going to R-rated films, and getting drunk—than those in single-sex schools, and this difference in type of school did not emerge in the case of girls who were maturing on time or later than other girls. Notably, similar results emerged when self-reported delinquency (for example, shoplifting, smoking marijuana, or using hard drugs) was measured at age fifteen. In other words, when early-maturing girls—the

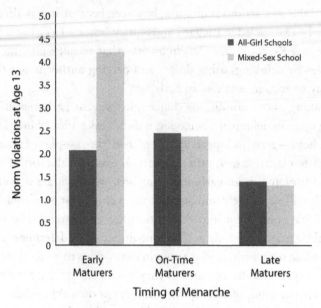

FIGURE 7.3. Norm violations in early adolescence as a function of age at menarche and school type. Reformatted from Caspi, A., Lynam, D., Moffitt, T.E., & Silva, P. (1993). Unraveling girls' delinquency: Biological dispositional, and contextual contributions to adolescent misbehavior. *Developmental Psychology, 29*, 19–30, figure 1. Reproduced with permission of American Psychological Association.

very kind we had previously found to be more likely to engage in sexual risk taking—found themselves in a boyless school environment, they were not led into temptation. This only occurred when there were boys around, including older and bad boys who would view a young teen with a developed body in a quite different light than a same-aged girl still inhabiting a child's body.

One of the things that makes these results especially important is that they reveal that it is not just maturing earlier than other girls that puts some girls at risk of delinquent behavior, including, no doubt, sexual behavior. In other words, it is not just some internal, biological process—such as surging hormones—that results in early maturity being related to problem behavior among girls. The context of development matters immensely. Put the same early-maturing girls attending a mixed-sex school into an all-girl school, and it would appear that the risks otherwise associated with early maturation would not be realized. That is, early menarche does not prove to be especially troublesome when girls do not mix with boys on an everyday basis, at least at school. Collectively, then, our findings suggest that at least two factors are necessary for the initiation and maintenance of female delinquency—puberty and boys!

CONCLUSION: WHAT IS IT ABOUT BAD BOYS?

Many a parent has experienced that helpless feeling when they discover that their daughter is involved with a boy who is likely to be going nowhere in life. Sandra was such a mother, whose daughter, Sophie, we were following in the Dunedin Study. Despite a reasonably supportive upbringing, though one fractured by a divorce, Sophie had taken up with a boy four years older. Oliver's greatest claim to fame seemed to be that he could still drive a car tolerably safely, or so he claimed, after drinking four pints of Guinness. No matter how much Sandra tried—and she tried lots of things—there seemed to be no disrupting Sophie's misguided attachment to Oliver. Even grounding her daughter didn't work. On at least one occasion, Sophie snuck out of the house, and on other occasions, with mom at work, Oliver snuck into the house. The only solace Sandra could find in this situation was the recollection that her sister had behaved in much the same way as Sophie as a teenager but nevertheless ended up finding a good man to marry.

We believe the onset of puberty operates as a "releaser" or stimulus to others in the social environment, creating a "press" among adolescent girls for new, adultlike ways of behaving. This process may result partly from the uncertain status of the adolescent in our society, which separates people as a function of their age. Recall that we discussed this issue when we considered adolescent-limited problem behavior in Chapter 6. Biological maturity used to be attained at an older age than it is now. In fact, one of the great changes that has taken place in the modern, industrialized Western world over the past two hundred years is that puberty occurs many years earlier in life than it once did. Many believe this is because improved nutrition and sanitation has led to better health.

One major consequence of this general acceleration of pubertal development is that girls and boys today end up with the bodies of adults while lacking adults' social status. In the past, adult bodies and roles went together, but in the modern world they have become decoupled. The result is a five-to-ten-year period during which adolescents are biologically mature but are (often) expected to delay assuming adult responsibilities and privileges, including driving, drinking, and having sex. The earlier onset of puberty only makes the remoteness of social maturity all the more challenging and apparent to teens. Early-maturing teenagers remain financially and socially dependent on their families and are allowed few decisions of real importance. Yet, they often have a strong desire to establish intimate bonds with the opposite sex, to make their own decisions, and to accrue their own material belongings, just as (most) adults do.

This experience of being an adult in one sense but not in another coincides with girls' entry into a secondary-school society dominated by older peers, especially boys, when attending a coed school. From the perspective of girls, older delinquents do not appear to suffer from the "maturity gap" just described. They are able to obtain possessions—such as cars, clothes, or drugs—by theft or vice that are otherwise inaccessible to teens who have no independent income. These influential delinquents, often disconnected from their families, seem to be free to go their own way. They make their own rules—to smoke, to drive, to drink and do drugs. At the same time, they appear more sexually experienced and self-confident with the opposite sex. In short, delinquency appears to offer an effective means of cutting childhood apron strings, and older delinquent boys too often prove to be ideal models for doing so, which can be especially captivating to early-maturing girls.

So, even though we have seen that adverse rearing environments can accelerate pubertal development in girls and that such physical maturity can foster early sexual behavior, delinquency, and less stable close relationships, these anticipated effects are by no means inevitable. When relationships between parents and children are built on a foundation of attachment security, the otherwise accelerating effect of harsh parenting can be buffered, resulting in resilience rather than susceptibility. And even when girls mature early, delinquency and sexual activity are not inevitable. Indeed, with regard to this latter issue, it would seem that "it takes two to tango." Maturing early is not sufficient, nor is being around boys at school day in and day out, but put the two together and bingo, the risk of trouble increases substantially.

PART IV

BEYOND THE FAMILY

8

Good News and Bad News about Day Care

In light of the fact that the study of human development touches on any number of subjects over which open-minded people—to say nothing of closed-minded ones—might disagree, it is not surprising that research on how humans develop can prove controversial. Consider some of the topics covered in this book, such as the effects of marijuana use on mental health (Chapter 11) and the influence of genetics in shaping psychological and behavioral development (Chapters 12 and 13). One of the great misunderstandings of many when it comes to such topics is the implicit if not explicit belief that reported results reflect what investigators want to find as a result of their beliefs and ideology rather than what they discover having dispassionately—and honestly—investigated the issue at hand. Thus, if findings indicate, for example, that cannabis use carries mental health risks, it is because this belief motivated the research in the first place. In other words, the research was designed and carried out to prove a point rather than to address an issue or test a hypothesis.

Experience has taught us that one way to challenge this misguided view of the scientific enterprise is by dramatizing the distinction between what emerges empirically and how one might personally want the world—and development—to operate. This can be achieved by simply entertaining the following question: "If the weatherman reports that it is going to rain tomorrow—based of course on sophisticated meteorological measurements—does this mean he is against sunshine?" The point is that students of human development do not "make the rules" about how the world works and how we develop, so their findings—and ours—should not be interpreted through a lens that presumes this is the case. Of course, what we study reflects our interests and concerns, but if we operate in good faith and carry out our work in a scientifically sound way, then the results should not be biased by how we would like development—or the world—to operate. Instead, it should simply reflect how it does. And, as honest investigators, we should always be ready to embrace findings that we might wish were otherwise.

Having said that, it is just as important to appreciate that what research reveals about how development (or the world) operates does not by any means imply that this is how it should operate. Presuming that how something is indicates how things ought to be is known in philosophy as the "naturalistic fallacy." Sadly, too many consumers of scientific information blame scholars for discovering what they do, presuming that the scientist's purpose is to affirm and encourage some way of being, behaving, or developing. Demonstrable evidence of this can be found in some reactions to early findings indicating that AIDS was rampant and being spread, at least initially, in the gay community. This led to the accusation that the scholar making this discovery was homophobic when this was by no means the case. He was just an HIV "weatherman." But one doesn't have to reach back to the early 1980s to see evidence of such misguided attributions about scientific motivation. Just consider how some today regard investigators studying—and documenting—climate change.

These comments are an important prelude to the next developmental adventure we share, investigating the effects of day care on child and adolescent development, thereby addressing the third goal and theme of this book, the effects of childhood experiences beyond the family on later development. Research in this area has been some of the most controversial in the field of human development. Many will be familiar with the seemingly never-ending "mommy wars" that pit mothers of especially young children who are employed and thus rely on others to care for their children against those who remain at home for that very purpose. For many stay-at-home mothers—and those who endorse their choice—it is often regarded as "common sense" that young children thrive best when cared for by a devoted parent, typically the mother. For others, however, it is just as commonsensical that children can thrive in the care of others, even those who are not family members, as occurs when parents place their child in a day-care center or in the care of a neighbor, often in the company of other children, an arrangement labeled "family day care." As a result of these contrasting views on what is best for mothers, families, and children, it is not uncommon for evidence seemingly consistent with one point of view to be regarded as inherently biased by those who see the world differently.

DAY CARE TODAY

What many may not fully appreciate with regard to the issue of the effects of day care is how much the rearing of children has changed in America over the past thirty to forty years. There was a time even before then when many, even most, mothers waited to return to employment following a pregnancy until their child was ready to start school, around the age of five, or go to preschool, around the age of three or four. Of course, when families were poor, mothers routinely sought employment even when their children were much younger. But over the past several decades, the experience of many more children has changed, typically because of their families' need for two incomes, or just one in the case of a single-parent household, or in response to mothers' desire to pursue careers, engage with other adults on a daily basis (rather than be isolated while home with children), or even protect themselves from the financial downside of a possible future divorce.

In fact, it is intriguing to learn that whereas the US Census Bureau once only reported rates of maternal employment for mothers of children under five years of age, over time it started to do so first for mothers with children under three, then under one, and eventually even under six months! This was in response to the dramatic change that was occurring in how American children are reared. It is now the case—because of the absence of any policy for paid parental leave at the federal level—that most mothers return to employment before their infant is six months of age and certainly before the child's first birthday. Indeed, rates of maternal employment for mothers of children under five years of age and under six months of age are virtually the same, exceeding 50 percent. Consequently, it is now the norm in the United States for children to experience some kind of "early, extensive, and continuous" child care. Here "early" refers to care initiated sometime in the first year of life, "extensive" means for twenty to thirty or more hours of care per week, and "continuous" that care lasts until the start of formal schooling. No one should infer, however, that the same care arrangements are utilized across this entire period. Indeed, multiple changes in arrangements, typically because of the changing developmental capabilities of the child or the breakdown of existing arrangements, tend to be the norm. This is true whether a child's initial care is provided by a nanny, in a family day-care home, or at a child care center.

THE DAY-CARE WARS

As the major social change—or social experiment—just described was taking place in the mid-1980s, a huge controversy broke out in the scholarly literature about the effects of day care. It spilled over into the popular press, even leading to congressional hearings—and eventually to the research described herein. The controversy arose when the mainstream—and progressive—view of university academics with expertise on the subject was challenged. The challenge involved the widely embraced claim that children could and would thrive in day care as long as it was of good quality—meaning that the care provided was attentive, responsive, affectionate, and stimulating. The age of the child when care was initiated and the number of hours the child spent in day care each week was thus deemed more or less irrelevant by most developmental scholars with expertise in early child development. It was this latter assertion that was questioned.

The counterargument, also evidence based, was that quality of care was not the only factor that mattered when it came to the effects of day care. Dosage or cumulative amount of time spent in day care across days, weeks, months, and years also mattered. And, importantly, this revisionist view was not based, as it long had been, on ideological arguments that only mothers could care for babies and young children well but rather on emerging evidence that heavy doses of day care initiated very early in life increased the risk of insecure infant-parent attachment and somewhat elevated levels of aggression and disobedience when children were three to eight years of age.

There were at least two reasons for the onset of the "day-care wars," as one observer accurately characterized the controversy. The first, already implied, was that opinions regarding effects of day care were based on ideological beliefs and desires as much as on evidence. Therefore, countering the view that only mothers could care for young children well was one that regarded such a perspective as nothing more than the long-standing—and patriarchal—effort to deny women their rights to a career while keeping them "barefoot and pregnant in the kitchen." The second contributor to the heated debate about the effects of day care was that the evidence was limited, by no means entirely conclusive, so support for alternative viewpoints could be found in the research evidence. Thus, as stipulated by the scholar who challenged the prevailing view—that as long as quality of care was good nothing else mattered—was the assertion that open-minded scholars could, would, and should view the data differently. Sadly, intellectual tolerance did not rule the day. Whereas some saw concerns about long hours spent in child care beginning in the first year of life as nothing more than misogyny masquerading as science, others regarded the obsessive concern with quality of care—and only quality of care—as little more than wish fulfillment and an expression of political correctness. The latter term, so familiar to us today, had not even been coined at the outbreak of the day-care wars.

It turned out that one of the great benefits of the scholarly controversy that broke out was that it captured the interest of the National Institute of Child Health and Human Development (NICHD), one arm of the National Institutes of Health (NIH), and led to the funding of the largest and most comprehensive study of the effects of day care ever conducted, the NICHD Study of Early Child Care and Youth Development. What that study revealed about the effects of day care is the subject of this chapter. One of the authors of this book, Jay Belsky, was not only one of the many investigators who directed this $150,000,000 project but was also the revisionist scholar who challenged prevailing dogma by contending that quantity, not just quality, of care influenced children's development, at least in the world of day care that American children experienced.

THE NICHD STUDY

To say that the NICHD Study was born in controversy and that it proceeded without any bumps and bruises would be understatements. This was because it brought together—to collaborate—developmental scholars from numerous universities who did not see eye-to-eye on what should be studied or how the research should be carried out. This was no small matter, as carrying out almost any investigation, to say nothing of one that followed more than one thousand children, growing up in ten different locales, across the first fifteen years of their lives, involves numerous decisions that open-minded investigators can think about quite differently—and have strong feelings about! As an illustration, just consider the following dilemmas: Should we study the children at six months, nine months, or twelve months of age, given that we cannot study them at every possible age? What age would be most revealing about effects of experiences outside the family on development? Should we bring them into the university laboratory, where we can exercise rigorous control over circumstances, or go to their homes to see them in their natural environment? Would the lab be too artificial or the home too "noisy" to detect what could be subtle signals of developmental effects, because of the great variation in family environments? Should we rely on parent and/or teacher reports of child behavior or actually watch and record child behavior? Whereas parents no doubt know their children better than teachers do, teachers likely have a better "point of comparison" when it comes to evaluating child behavior, given the numerous same-age children they have observed in years of teaching. Should we restrict ourselves to children in day-care centers or also include those being cared for by friends and neighbors, in what is known as family day care, or even by nannies in their own homes while their parents are employed? After all, especially at the youngest ages, day-care centers are not the norm but rather the exception regarding how infants are cared for when their parents are employed. How should we regard nonmaternal care provided by fathers or grandparents? Is this a type of day care or something else entirely? Thus, when it comes to statistically analyzing the data, should we treat such family-based, nonmaternal care in the same way as other kinds of day care, like that provided in centers? Truth be told, decision making in longitudinal, observational studies is endless, often with no truly "correct" answer. Needless to say, in a group in which individuals have strong—and often opposing—views, the possibility for conflict is virtually unlimited.

While many collaborators found the seemingly endless process of collective decision making extremely stressful, in the end it served us very well.

A truly collaborative enterprise was forged that involved research teams centered at ten universities across the country implementing exactly the same scientific protocol (that is, methods and procedures) with the particular subsample of children they were responsible for studying. At times, as we will see, this required each team to measure and investigate things it may or may not have been interested in studying and in ways that it may or may not have regarded as most appropriate. In other words, collaboration meant compromise. For most of us, this was a radically new way of working, as the traditional model was for each of us to run our own study the way we thought best rather than having to make—and go along with—group decisions. History, we believe, proved that the struggle to forge a truly collaborative investigation following some 1,364 children from birth to age fifteen was worth it, at least from a scientific perspective. As we will show, the short-term costs of conflict that collaboration engendered yielded long-term gains in terms of the scientific questions asked and answered.

Among many other things, a core goal of the NICHD Study was to evaluate the proposition that might be put rather simply and dramatically—and in a manner reminiscent of the central focus of Bill Clinton's presidential campaign in 1992. But instead of being "it's the economy, stupid," it was "it's quality, stupid." That is, the central hypothesis, at least of some investigators, was that, as already stipulated, as long as the quality of day care was high, which everyone appreciated was by no means routinely the case in the United States, children would thrive in day care and thus quantity of care—meaning age of entry and amount of hours spent in care each week—would not matter. But the alternative hypothesis, advocated by a very limited number of the more than twenty academics involved in the research, was that while quality of care mattered, it was not the only thing that mattered; quantity of care mattered, too, especially when it came to children's social and emotional development.

No matter how collaborating researchers felt about these issues, all appreciated the need to move beyond the simple thinking that had shaped so much scholarly and popular discourse on the effects of day care for decades, that day care was either good or bad for children. NICHD Study collaborators understood that the day care experience was multifaceted and needed to be studied in terms of, at the very least, both the quality and quantity of care. In the same way that nutritionists appreciate the need to distinguish the consumption of protein and carbohydrates when studying the effects of food intake on growth—rather than just how much a person eats—we developmental scientists knew that we needed to decompose the day-care experience to investigate the effects of its component parts.

Perhaps surprisingly, this had never been done before because, as the NICHD Study demonstrated, doing so was very expensive, at least if one wanted to move beyond simply asking parents to rate child care quality as good, mediocre, or poor and report on how much time the child spent in child care. In fact, what made the NICHD Study so unique—and expensive— was that it carefully measured quality of care, by sending highly trained observers into whatever nonmaternal child care arrangement a child had, if she or he had one, to observe the day-care experience of the child. Critically, these observations, lasting several hours on each of two days, focused on the extent to which a caregiver or caregivers interacted with the child in an attentive, sensitive, responsive, stimulating, and affectionate manner. This was done not at one point in a child's life but when children were six, fifteen, twenty-four, thirty-six, and fifty-four months of age. Moreover, the same approach was taken when children were in middle childhood, but now observations took place in first-, third-, and fifth-grade classrooms. This was judged necessary so that when it came to investigating the longer-term effects of day care—beyond the preschool years—we could discount detected effects of variation in schooling experiences on development. Furthermore, and again at all ages, the child's family was carefully studied, and in a myriad of ways—by having parents complete questionnaires, participate in interviews, and be videotaped interacting with their child. As with schooling, this was done, repeatedly, so that we could discount the effect of variation in family experience before evaluating day-care effects. Multiple aspects of child development—cognitive, social, emotional, and behavioral—were also measured repeatedly as children aged. This was done in order to determine whether quality and quantity differentially affected different domains of development. All this enabled the team of investigators to evaluate whether and how quality and quantity of care affected child and adolescent development, at least in the context of a nonexperimental, observational study. Obviously, this was the only way to go. After all, as noted in Chapter 1, what parents would volunteer to have their child enrolled in a neglectful child care arrangement for long hours beginning at age three months so we could investigate the anticipated deleterious effects of such care? Just as important, what investigators would participate in such unethical research?

Before sharing the major findings emanating from the scores of scholarly reports that emerged from the NICHD Study, let us point out a difference between how the study approached its empirical challenge and how the Dunedin Study and the E-Risk Study, which are the focus of all other chapters in this book, did. As previous chapters made clear and subsequent ones will as well, one way to proceed when evaluating the effects of some developmental experience or exposure—such as marijuana use or girls' early physical maturation—is in a series of steps. First determine whether the experience or exposure in question is systematically related to the outcome of interest. Then, if that is the case, see whether the association in question remains when alternative explanatory factors—such as family social class or child IQ—are taken into account, typically by statistically controlling for (that is, discounting) them.

In the NICHD Study, we did not proceed in this perfectly sound two-step manner. Instead, we began by appreciating that child care experience was not randomly assigned. Children who were cared for at home by their parents, who were in low-quality care, or who experienced moderate or high levels of care came from different families with different characteristics to begin with, including income, parent education, and quality of parenting. Thus, before we could even consider evaluating how quality or quantity of day care affected child development, we had to assess and discount the effects of many factors and forces that influenced what kind of child care, if any, the child experienced, especially those also likely to affect the child's development apart from any effects of child care. Thus, rather than proceeding in two steps, all efforts to evaluate care effects integrated such statistical controls in the same multivariate analyses that evaluated day-care effects. This resulted, more or less, in a one-step process that integrated the two-step approach already outlined.

Some of the factors and forces controlled—and thus their effects discounted before assessing effects of child care—included family income relative to the number of household members; whether the family was two parent or single parent; whether the child was white or from a minority; whether the child was a boy or a girl and had as an infant an easier or more difficult temperament; whether the mother suffered from depression to some degree; and whether the mother's own way of interacting with her child was more rather than less sensitive, responsive, and stimulating. Because these forces and factors were measured repeatedly as children aged, we discounted their potential effects both earlier and later in the child's life. Just as notable is that by the time children were in school, we also, as already indicated, controlled for what we had learned about the quality of their schooling, using classroom observations to measure both the instructional support and emotional support that children experienced in their first-, third-, and fifth-grade classrooms. To repeat, this was because we wanted to evaluate longer-term effects of child care and distinguish them from any possible effects of schooling experience, as well as of experience in the family.

Perhaps even more important to highlight is that whenever we evaluated effects of quality of care, we discounted effects of quantity, and whenever we evaluated effects of quantity of care, we discounted (that is, held constant) effects of quality—in addition to all the other factors and forces mentioned in the preceding paragraph. This ensured that any detected effect of either quality or quantity of the child care experience was not the result of the other aspect of child care. By proceeding in this manner, we could directly evaluate the claim that "it's quality stupid"—that as long as quality was good, the amount of time in care would not matter when it came to how children developed. Just as important, we could also evaluate whether spending more time in high-quality or low-quality child care environments amplified the anticipated beneficial effects of good-quality care and the anticipated deleterious effects of poor-quality child care on children's development.

THE DEVELOPING INFANT-PARENT RELATIONSHIP

A view of early child development based on attachment theory developed originally by British child psychiatrist John Bowlby had led many to presume that day care would undermine the developing child-parent relationship, perhaps especially in the earliest years of life. The thinking was that separation from the parent was inherently stressful to the child, and because being in day care involved repeated separations from parents, the child's emotional security would be undermined. Thus, the child would come to feel that he or she could not count on the parent to be there for them when needed. A not unrelated view was that lots of time away from the child would limit a parent's ability to know the child well and this, not just the experience of separation, could compromise parenting and thus the developing child-parent relationship and thereby the child's well-being.

The classic way to study the infant-parent attachment relationship is via a procedure known as the "Strange Situation," which involves bringing the parent and twelve-to-eighteen-month-old infant to an unfamiliar university laboratory, repeatedly separating the child from the parent for short periods of time (no more than three minutes), sometimes while leaving the child alone with an unfamiliar adult, and observing how the child reacts to being reunited with the parent after being (purposefully) stressed via the separation experience. On the basis of careful analysis of videotaped child behavior, especially how children react to the return of the parent following separation, attachment relationships are judged to be secure or insecure. Children who have secure relationships typically greet the returning parent from a distance in an unambiguous manner. If the child is not seriously distressed, this involves smiling, pointing, and/or vocalizing. If the child is very upset, as some are, this involves approaching the parent, seeking physical contact, and finding comfort and solace in the parent's arms, even to the point of being able to move away from the parent once soothed and return to play with toys available in the room.

Some insecure children, in contrast—the avoidant ones—tend to ignore the parent upon return or terminate a physical approach before reaching the parent. These children are typically less overtly distressed than others, which doesn't mean they are not stressed at all. A second group of insecure children, referred to as resistant, are typically very upset by the comings and goings of the mother and stranger and either cannot pull themselves together to seek comfort when the parent returns, lying on the floor and crying, or if they can mobilize an approach, push away from the parent in order to be put down after being picked up, only to insist, while still distressed, on being picked up again.

Some of the evidence central to the day-care controversy seemed to indicate that children who experienced lots of hours in day care as infants and toddlers were at increased risk of being insecure, being avoidant in their attachment relationship. But was the psychological and physical distance they maintained from their returning parent a reflection of insecurity and thus mistrust in the availability and responsiveness of the parent to meet their emotional needs, as presumed by students of attachment theory, or was it just that these infants were independent, well experienced with being apart from their parent, and thus not particularly bothered by it?

Given what has already been implied about the need for compromise among study investigators, it is perhaps not surprising that not everyone agreed on the answer to this question. Some NICHD Study collaborators who argued against using the Strange Situation to evaluate the effects of day care contended that independence was being misinterpreted as avoidance, and thus insecurity when children with lots of experience of separation from their parent as a result of going to day care did not rush to establish psychological or physical contact with their parent following separation in the Strange Situation. Other collaborators who were, we might say, attachment-theory enthusiasts insisted on it. The former group argued, more or less, that if you want to understand the infant-mother relationship, then just observe the parent and infant interacting. There is no need to stress the child, especially because the separations central to the Strange Situation would not be experienced similarly by children who had lots of experience with separation (that is, those in day care) and those who did not (that is, those cared for exclusively by mothers at home). Thus, reliance on the Strange Situation would not afford comparison of like with like. The solution to this difference of opinion turned out to be very simple: study the infant-mother relationship both ways, in the Strange Situation and just by observing the parent and infant interacting under nonstressful circumstances.

Before sharing what we discovered about the effects of day care on attachment, it is important to point out that Jay Belsky's controversial reading of the available evidence—which much mainstream thinking regarded as little more than an outdated view of child development—led him to hypothesize that lots of time in child care early in life was a "risk factor" for the development of insecure attachment. By definition, most risk factors work their (black) "magic"—in undermining development—when they co-occur with other risk factors. This is a rather familiar idea. We know, for example, that while being overweight is a risk factor for cardiovascular disease, this risk is more likely to be realized when a person also smokes, is not physically active, or comes from a family with a history of cardiovascular disease. We also saw this principle in operation in Chapter 7. Recall that it was when both risk factors of early sexual maturation and exposure to boys, especially older ones, were present that female problem behavior was most likely to characterize early-maturing girls. When applied to the study of attachment, this risk-factor view therefore implies that effects of day care may need to be considered in light of other risk factors to which the child is exposed.

Thus, when it came to the effects of day care on attachment, the results were in line with Belsky's risk-factor thinking: children who spent more time in child care (in a center, a family day-care home, or by a nanny), indeed those who averaged just ten or more hours per week across their first fifteen months of life (risk factor 1), were more likely than other children to develop an insecure attachment to their mother, as seen in the Strange Situation at fifteen months, if—and only if—they also experienced insensitive mothering (risk factor 2). Just as significant was that the same *dual-risk-factor* effect emerged in the case of quality of care: the combination of low-quality child care (alternative risk factor 1) plus insensitive mothering (risk factor 2) also increased the risk of insecure attachment. Another way of viewing the results, then, is that more time spent in child care and low-quality care each (separately) *amplified* the risk of insecurity associated with having a mother who proved to be rather insensitive in the way she interacted with the child. It is important to note that by the time the NICHD Study was launched, it had already been established that the mother's insensitivity was the best predictor of attachment insecurity in infancy.

Notably, when we reexamined the effects of day care on attachment two years later, when the children were thirty-six months of age, it was only the dual-risk combination of lots of time spent in day care (across the first thirty-six months of life) and insensitive mothering that continued to predict insecure attachment as measured using the Strange Situation. The dual risk involving low-quality care no longer seemed to influence attachment security. Not only were the findings in line with the controversial risk-factor claim central to the onset of the day-care wars, but they were inconsistent with the argument that "it's quality stupid." This was because the dual-risk effect involving lots of time in care emerged for children who experienced higher-quality as well as lower-quality care. Thus, being in even especially good-quality care did not eliminate the increased risk of insecurity associated with experiencing early and extensive care (when coupled with insensitive mothering). That is, high-quality care in this case did not promote resilience in the face of lots of time in care and insensitive mothering, as long theorized by most developmental scholars studying day care.

But remember that some, even most, NICHD Study collaborators had serious concerns about relying on the Strange Situation when it came to investigating effects of day care. Not surprisingly, then, those who argued against using this separation-based procedure to assess attachment security and thereby evaluate attachment security were not inclined to breathe too much meaning into the attachment findings just summarized. So, what emerged when we focused on videotapes of mothers interacting with their children in nonstressful situations rather than on infant attachment behavior in the Strange Situation? Even more evidence challenging the argument that "it's quality, stupid!" This was because risk factor 1—lots of time spent in child care—now predicted, all by itself, less supportive and sensitive mothering. Indeed, detailed analyses of maternal interactive behavior revealed that when infants spent more time in nonmaternal care over their first six months, their first fifteen months, their first twenty-four months, and even their first thirty-six months of life, mothers were less sensitive to their infants when observed interacting with them at six, fifteen, twenty-four, and thirty-six months of age, respectively. Conversely, less time spent in child care predicted more sensitive mothering at all these points in time, again with numerous alternative explanatory factors controlled. Such results certainly seemed consistent with the claim that extensive time away from the child might undermine the parent's capacity to know the child well and thus interact in the most development-facilitating manner. While there was some evidence, too, that exposure to low-quality care predicted less sensitive mothering, such data were less consistent and compelling than data pertaining to effects of quantity of care on maternal behavior.

In sum, no matter how we examined the developing infant-mother relationship—by using a stressful separation procedure to measure attachment security (at two different ages) or simply observing interaction under nonstressful conditions (at four different ages)—quantity of care mattered, and more so than quality of care. This proved to be the case irrespective of whether care was of good or poor quality. In other words, poor-quality care was not the reason, as mainstream thinking had long asserted, why lots of time spent in care was related to poorer-functioning infant-parent relationships.

SOCIAL, BEHAVIORAL, AND COGNITIVE DEVELOPMENT

One of the reasons for focusing on the developing parent-child relationship in the NICHD Study was not just because of ideas drawn from attachment theory. It was also a focus of inquiry because of the presumed influence of parenting and the developing parent-child relationship on child development, broadly conceived. This consideration, along with an interest in many other aspects of development, led the NICHD Study team to investigate effects of quantity and quality of day care on social, behavioral, and cognitive development. Recall in this regard that Jay Belsky's controversial risk-factor perspective calling attention to quantity of care was based on early, even though imperfect, evidence that children exposed to lots of time in child care appeared somewhat more aggressive and disobedient than other children at ages 3 to 8 years. At the same time—and before the NICHD Study was launched—evidence also called attention to developmental benefits associated with high-quality care, especially with respect to cognitive development.

Development Prior to School Entry

This scholarly background led us to ask parents and caregivers about children's social and emotional behavior at two, three, and four and a half years of age and formally assess children's intellectual development, by means of standardized developmental tests, at these same ages. Once again, the results were most interesting. Most notably, quantity and quality appeared to affect completely different aspects of development. Whether we measured intellectual functioning at age two, three, or four and a half years, higher quality of care predicted somewhat better cognitive-linguistic functioning, but quantity of care played no discernible role in influencing intellectual performance on standardized assessments at these ages of measurement. That was the "good news" about the effects of day care.

The situation was almost, though not entirely, the reverse when we examined social, emotional, and behavioral development. Although higher quality of care predicted better social functioning for some measured outcomes at some ages, the frequency of such prediction was quite limited, especially relative to the widespread effects of quality of care on cognitive functioning and the more consistent effects of quantity of care on social and behavioral functioning.

With regard to quantity effects, however, the story proved to be a bit complicated, but more consistent than inconsistent—and certainly informative. The more time children spent in day care across their first two years of life, the more aggression and disobedience they manifested at age two, according to reports by their caregivers at day care—who didn't necessarily know about their experience of child care dating back to early in their first year of life. Again, this was the case irrespective of the quality of care children experienced. But this "bad news" result failed to reemerge one year later, when children's social and behavioral functioning was reassessed at age thirty-six months. This apparent discrepancy resulted in differences of opinion among collaborating investigators, which were reflected in the discussion of these results in the scientific paper reporting these findings. We noted that although the disappearance at age three of adverse effects of lots of time in day care previously chronicled at age two would seem to indicate that there was little reason to be excessively concerned about the earlier findings, it could not yet be assumed that the effects detected at age two were, more or less, gone for good.

This situation made our next assessment of children's development—at four and a half years of age, just before the start of formal schooling—very important. Would the "bad news" effect of lots of time in day care on aggression and disobedience discerned at age two but not three reemerge? If not, that would strongly imply that the adverse effect discerned at age two was just a short-term developmental "blip" that not much meaning should be breathed into. But when we had caregivers again evaluate child behavior at age four and a half years, once again the evidence indicated that the more time spent in child care across the first four and a half years of life, the more aggressive and disobedient children proved to be. And note that these caregivers often had not been caring for children when they were two or even three years of age. Needless to say, these four-and-a-half-year findings proved controversial within the group of collaborators. As a result, efforts were made to double- and triple-check them.

Development in Kindergarten

One concern was that these latest "bad news" results might be an artifact of the caregivers' knowledge of children's day-care histories. Perhaps the children rated higher in behavior problems at preschool age received such ratings because their day-care caregivers knew that they had been in child care for a long time, beginning at a very young age, and were predisposed to regard such early, extensive, and continuous day care as bad for children—as a surprising number of them did and still do. This possibility led us to extend our investigation of children of preschool age and examine how kindergarten teachers rated the children a year later, because in virtually all cases, such teachers would only have known the children for at most one academic year when we had them complete behavioral questionnaires at the end of the school year. Thus, it would be very unlikely that they would have much if any knowledge of children's day-care experiences before starting school and dating back to their first year of life. In other words, it would be very unlikely that these teachers would be subject to day-care-related biases in evaluating children's social and emotional functioning.

When we analyzed the kindergarten data, we again detected the relation between more time in day care across the first four and a half years of life and more problems involving aggression and disobedience, so now we had evidence that more time in child care across the infancy, toddler, and preschool years predicted somewhat elevated levels of problem behavior during the first year of school as well. In fact, this adverse effect was evident whether we examined information on child behavior obtained from mothers or from kindergarten teachers. And, of course, once again, the detected quantity-of-care effect could not be attributed to exposure to low-quality child care.

Despite findings indicating that results at four and a half years of age did not appear to be an artifact of some adults knowing some children better than others or possibly having their own biases about the effects of day care, the findings were so unanticipated—and disconcerting—to some collaborating investigators that additional challenges were raised regarding the confidence that could be placed in them. So the next question became not just whether children who spent more time in day care evinced more problem behavior on average, but also whether they were more likely to score in the "at-risk" range—that is, have enough behavior problems to put them at risk of developing true psychopathology sometime in the future. Well, it turned out that they did. In fact, at both age four and a half years, prior to starting school, and at the end of the first year of schooling (kindergarten), we discerned a dose-response relation between amount of time in day care and having a behavior-problem score in the at-risk range. Figure 8.1 reveals a "stairstep" pattern, based on caregiver and kindergarten-teacher reports, indicating that as the average hours of child care per week across the first fifty-four months of life increased from zero to nine, to ten to twenty-nine, to thirty to forty-five, to more than forty-five hours per week, so did the percentage of children scoring in the at-risk range.

Despite this seemingly persuasive evidence, many collaborators still remained unconvinced that these "bad news" findings were real or kept seeking a way out of embracing results that they neither anticipated, liked, nor wanted to herald as they had excitingly heralded the good news cognitive findings. So, the next raise of the bar for the data to jump over returned us to the issue already considered when assessing attachment security. Perhaps, some argued, the children who experienced lots of day care

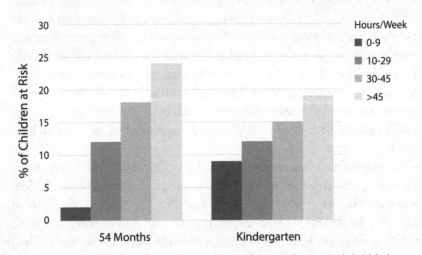

FIGURE 8.1. Proportion of children scoring in the at-risk range of child-behavior problems at age fifty-four months (left panel) and in kindergarten (right panel) as a function of quantity of child care. Data source: NICHD Early Child Care Research Network (2003). Does amount of time spent in child care predict socioemotional adjustment during the transition to kindergarten? *Child Development, 74*, 976–1005, table 8.

were not more aggressive and disobedient, as our composite, multi-item measure of different types of problem behavior indicated, but just more independent and assertive. This led us to take apart our measure, creating subsets of items reflecting indisputable aggression, noncompliance/disobedience, and assertiveness, each of which would be separately subject to analysis.

The aggression subset was comprised of behaviors such as cruelty to others, destroying one's own things, getting in many fights, threatening others, and hitting others. The noncompliance/disobedience subset was comprised of diverse behaviors, too, including being defiant, uncooperative, failing to carry out assigned tasks, throwing temper tantrums, and disrupting class discipline. Finally, the assertiveness subset included the following items, among others: brags/boasts, talks too much, demands or wants attention, and argues a lot. (One collaborator argued that this latter measure reflected "emotional neediness" rather than independent assertiveness.)

When time in child care was tested against each of these more refined outcomes, the results indicated that children who spent more time per week on average in nonmaternal care across their first four and a half years of life were not just more assertive, as some hoped would be the case, but indisputably more aggressive and disobedient as well. In other words, the evidence documenting "bad news" about the effects of day care met every empirical challenge posed by those collaborating investigators who hypothesized, repeatedly, that this would not be the case or, if so, would be a consequence of poor-quality care. Once more, the latter factor did not account for the evidence, so, once again, the conclusion had to be "it's *not* (just) quality, stupid."

FAST-FORWARD TO ADOLESCENCE

Whether considering the good news that better-quality child care promoted somewhat enhanced cognitive and language development or the bad news that lots of time in care fostered somewhat elevated levels of aggression and disobedience, it remained uncertain whether such day-care effects would endure or disappear as children got older and had many more experiences in their families, neighborhoods, and schools. This was certainly a possibility. Recall how the adverse effects of lots of time spent in day care on behavior problems at age two was no longer evident just a year later. Although we continued to evaluate day-care effects when children were in middle childhood, we are going to skip over the relevant findings, in the interest of space, to get right to the end of our evaluation. Therefore, we now turn to whether the effects of day care were evident when we saw children for the last time at fifteen years of age. To repeat something important that we said earlier, at this age we not only discounted effects of multiple aspects of children's families measured repeatedly from birth to age fifteen before evaluating the effects of day care, but did the same with measurements of children's exposure to emotionally and instructionally supportive elementary-school classrooms in the first, third, and fifth grades. This was based on our extensive in-classroom observations of study children in their schools and reflected our attempt to ensure that the effects of schooling and other factors and forces did not masquerade as effects of day care.

In most respects, the adolescent findings proved consistent with what we discerned at younger ages. Once again, better-quality child care predicted better cognitive functioning, this time measured using a standardized test tapping academic achievement. For virtually the first time since toddlerhood, there was some indication that quality of care also mattered for social functioning. Aggressive and delinquent behavior that teenagers themselves reported engaging in was more frequent among those adolescents who more than a decade earlier had been exposed to lower-quality child care.

This developmental outcome, interestingly enough, no longer was predicted, as it had been at younger ages, by quantity of care. In other words, general problem behavior, perhaps more characteristic of younger children than those at midadolescence, no longer was elevated in the case of children exposed to more time in day care across their first four and a half years of life. Instead, and perhaps in line with how behavior develops as children age, more time in care per week on average across the first four and a half years of life now predicted more teenage risk taking (e.g., sex, drugs, and rock'n'roll) and greater impulsivity, acting without thinking. So, in the end, there remained evidence of both good news and bad news when it came to the effects of day care, with most of the good news reflecting the developmental benefits of good-quality care for cognitive development and most of the bad news reflecting developmental risks to social and behavioral functioning of early, extensive, and continuous care.

A DEVELOPMENTAL MYSTERY

Recall that Jay Belsky's thinking that challenged prevailing notions about the effects of day care prior to the launch of the NICHD Study was that adverse effects of lots of time in care on the relation between infant and mother might account for why lots of time in care also was related to elevated levels of aggression and disobedience documented in some studies of older children. In other words, it was perhaps the insecurity fostered by day care or insensitive parenting resulting from so much time apart from the child that served as the developmental process by which early, extensive, and continuous care came to predict later aggression and disobedience.

Because the NICHD Study discerned evidence linking quantity of care with both insecure attachment (under dual-risk conditions) and less sensitive and stimulating parenthood (all by itself), as well as with elevated levels of aggression and disobedience in childhood and risk taking and impulsivity in adolescence, we were in an ideal position to evaluate Belsky's speculation. To our surprise, there was no evidence to support it. Even though quantity of care was related to the developing child-parent relationship and, separately, to later problematic functioning, infant-parent relations did not emerge as a pathway or mediator linking quantity of care with aggression and disobedience at ages two and four and a half years and in kindergarten, or with risk taking and impulsivity in adolescence. And, as we have repeatedly made clear, low-quality care never proved to be responsible for any of these effects of quantity of care either. So we faced a developmental mystery: why or how did lots of time in care come to affect social behavior before the transition to school, after the transition to school, and during the teenage years?

We gained some limited purchase on this conundrum when we eventually discovered that being in larger rather than smaller groups of children during the years in day care seemed to make a difference. Being in large groups of children in day-care centers or family day-care homes for long periods accounted for some of the adverse effects of quantity of care on behavioral development. What was disconcerting, though illuminating, about this finding was the discovery that most of the children who spent the most time in day care across their first four and a half years of life spent their time in large groups of children in day-care centers. This was no doubt because the earlier in life children started day care and the more hours per week they spent in day care over weeks, months, and years, the more likely the venues of care were to be day-care centers rather than other kinds of day-care arrangements (for example, a nanny or family day care). In fact, the overwhelming majority of children in day-care centers were in large groups! In other words, while a history of early, extensive, and continuous care and exposure to large groups of children did not always co-occur, these two conditions were by no means independent. They tended to come as a package.

One thing that made the large-group finding so noteworthy, though disconcerting to developmental scholars, was that it called attention to something we had perhaps not paid sufficient attention to given our obsessive—and expensive—focus on quality of care, defined in terms of how caregivers treated children: *children's experiences with other children while in day care*. Perhaps the documented developmental risks associated with lots of time in day care—including insecure attachment in infancy, aggression and disobedience in early childhood, and risk taking and impulsivity in adolescence—resulted from the influence of being with so many other children, beginning at very young ages and continuing until the start of formal schooling. After all, there was no evidence that it had anything to do with the quality of care that adults—be they mothers or paid caregivers—provided.

Having to "keep up with the Joneses"—one's peers—in large, unruly groups could have been what increased the child's risk of insecurity when reared by an insensitive mother, of being aggressive and disobedient later in childhood, and of engaging in risk taking and impulsive behavior in the middle of the second decade of life. Unfortunately, this possibility could not be investigated further because we simply did not have the detailed information about peer interactions in small and large child-care settings that might have enabled us to illuminate this issue. And this was no doubt because too many of us believed, apparently mistakenly, that it was caregiving quality that would be most influential, leaving us to apparently underestimate the importance of relations with peers at such a young age. In an earlier chapter, we called attention to the frustration that all scientists experience upon realizing that it would have been great to measure something that went unmeasured: if we only knew then what we know now!

CONCLUSION

It would appear that while the claim that "it's quality, stupid" is not entirely wrong when it comes to understanding the effects of day care, especially cognitive-linguistic development, it is not entirely correct either. Even with quality of care and many other potential child, family, and schooling influences taken into account, the developmental adventure known as the NICHD Study detected, to the surprise (and dismay) of many, that dosage of care mattered, too, even though only with respect to social and behavioral development. Thus, the good news was that better-quality care was consistently found to foster intellectual functioning, and the bad news was that early, extensive, and continuous care predicted more problem behavior at age two, as well as before and after the transition to school, and risk taking and impulsivity in adolescence. Once again, we had gained some insight into whether and how experiences in and outside the family appeared to influence children's future development.

Having emphasized what we found, it is just as important to make clear what we did not discover. Of course, we have repeatedly made clear that we failed to find any evidence, no matter how hard we looked—and we did look hard and often—that poor-quality care was responsible for the adverse effects of lots of time spent in care. Also surprising, though, was that we never found any evidence—and again we looked often—that these two fundamental dimensions of the day-care experience interacted with each other. By that, we mean we found no evidence that spending more time in high-quality care yielded greater cognitive-linguistic benefits than less time in high-quality care. By the same token, we found no evidence that spending lots of time in poor-quality care was more deleterious than limited time in poor-quality care. This was all very surprising, even counterintuitive. Why shouldn't a large dose of something apparently good— high-quality care—not yield a greater benefit than a smaller dose of such care? And why shouldn't spending lots of time in poor-quality care exert a greater adverse effect than spending limited time in such care?

But perhaps the biggest surprise was that despite long-standing claims that good-quality care benefited children, the effects of good news regarding quality of care proved to be rather modest in magnitude. The same held for the effects of bad news regarding quantity of care. Indeed, what cannot be overlooked, but has not yet been mentioned, is that the kind of family that a child grew up in proved to be much more developmentally signifi-cant than his or her day-care experience. Some of this may reflect the influ-ence of genetics, but we doubt that this fully accounts for the fact that family experience—measured by many of the variables whose effects we discounted when evaluating the effects of day care—proved more powerful in pre-dicting child and adolescent development than did all our measures of day-care experience.

One way of thinking about this matter takes the form of a thought ex-periment: if the Good Lord came to you while you were still a fetus and said you have a choice to make between growing up in a well-resourced and developmentally supportive family but spending lots of time across your first five years of life in day care that is not of particularly high quality or growing up in a poorly functioning family with limited resources but experiencing lots of high-quality day care, which should you choose from a developmental perspective? Based on the results of the NICHD Study, it would seem to be the first option. That family trumps day care is an impor-tant take-home message of the NICHD Study, one that is often lost in the debate about the effects of day care.

We do not believe, however, that this observation undermines the im-portance of our day-care findings. Please recall that early, extensive, and continuous day care is the norm in the United States today, whether that involves the use of nannies, family day-care homes, and/or day-care cen-ters. Appreciate, too, that the quality of care available to many families in the United States is by no means high and that child-care group sizes are almost always large enough to contribute to the risks associated with lots of time in care. Thus, the modesty of the effects of quality and quantity of day care detected in the NICHD Study need to be considered in light of the sizable number of children likely to be exposed to lots of time spent in day care that is of limited quality and involves large groups of children.

One might think, "What is more important, small or modest effects that affect many or larger ones that affect few?" It is therefore not just the modest effects of day care at the level of individuals that should be considered—and what the NICHD Study and most other day-care investigations focus on—but what the collective consequences might be for neighborhoods, schools, communities, and society as a whole when so many children ex-perience so much day care in a country whose policies offer so much less to families raising young children than so many other modern Western nations do. Given that the United States has neither a paid parental leave policy at the federal level nor a system of carefully regulated child care, it is difficult to argue that the United States takes good care of its most valuable national resource, its children, or the societal institution most responsible for them, the family.

It is our considered opinion that families should be offered extensive and paid parental leaves following the birth of a child. One reason for this is that survey after survey reveals that it is the preference of Americans to have their youngest children reared at home by parents rather than be coerced by economic necessity to pay others—poorly—to do that job. Likewise, there is no doubt that if infants had a say in the matter, they would tell those conducting such surveys exactly the same thing! Moreover, children should receive good-quality care not primarily because it benefits them sometime in their developmental future and thereby benefits society but because "they never asked to be here." Our youngest and most vulnerable citizens have every right to a decent quality of life, day in and day out, so we should think more in terms of the rights of children and what is moral and ethical than what the return on the investment will be of providing care of one type or another. The latter risks turning children into commodities, whereas the former reflects the inherent value of every human life.

9

What about Neighborhoods?

Up to this point, most of what we have considered when it comes to influences on child, adolescent, and eventually adult development has focused on the "near environment"—the experiences and exposures that children directly participate in, such as the family (Chapters 5 and 6) and whether a school is coed (Chapter 7). Our previously mentioned Cornell professor, Urie Bronfenbrenner, referred to this as the "microsystem" of the ecology of human development. For a long time, if developmental scholars moved beyond such contexts of development when studying factors and forces that shape our lives, they jumped—just as we regularly have—to the broad socioeconomic level of family socioeconomic status. This, of course, covers a lot of ground, capturing the education of parents, family income, and the status of parents' occupations. But, even here, to a large extent we are dealing with the near environment, as all these potential sources of influence pertain to family resources.

One of the great changes that has occurred during our careers studying human development, in large measure, even though not exclusively, because of the influence of Bronfenbrenner's nested Russian-doll model of the child's world, is ever-greater appreciation that children and families are nested in layers of context. Thus, the child is embedded in close relationships with siblings and parents; these are embedded in the family; the family is embedded in the community, which is itself embedded in the larger society; and society is embedded in a larger cultural, historical, and even evolutionary context. Thus, the forces impinging on human development extend well beyond the very near environment of family, day care, and school. Because our work is neither cross-cultural nor historical—involving comparisons of development across cultures or historical epochs—there are layers of context we have never been positioned to investigate. But we did appreciate that immediately beyond the near environment of the family was the community in which the family was embedded, and this led us on the next developmental adventure we will discuss, which deals with differences in the neighborhoods in which children grow up and how these might—or might not—influence the developing child.

Anyone who has purchased a home or even found one to rent has thought about the neighborhood. Is it safe? Are stores, especially groceries, close by? Can I get to work easily? One might even wonder why it took so long for developmentalists to focus on neighborhood given that where one lives becomes especially important when raising children—or expecting to in the not-too-distant future, particularly in the United States. Because local property taxes hugely influence school budgets, the affluence of a neighborhood affects the quality of schooling children are likely to receive—and with whom they rub shoulders when at school. But even in places like the United Kingdom, where school funding is not tied to local property taxes, neighborhood still matters when it comes to how close public transportation is, if needed, whether retail shops are within easy reach, and who children's peers are likely to be.

This latter point was brought home to us powerfully in the case of Thomas, a participant, along with his twin brother, James, in the Environmental-Risk Study, the focus of this chapter. Recall that in contrast to the Dunedin Study and the NICHD Study of Early Child Care and Youth Development, the E-Risk Study is being conducted in the United Kingdom. When we visited the twins and their mother in their home at ages five and seven, Thomas seemed to be doing just fine, but by age ten something seemed to have changed, certainly in his demeanor, apparently as a result of the family's relocation to a less attractive neighborhood following the loss of the father's job.

Now that the family lived in public housing, referred to as a "council estate" in the United Kingdom, Thomas was no longer the friendly, open, and agreeable boy we encountered in our previous visits to the family's home in what was a more affluent neighborhood. Instead, he seemed to have a chip on his shoulder, while behaving in what could only be described as a prematurely tough manner. His mother attributed Thomas's new "attitude," as she called it, to the new group of boys with whom he was hanging out. The police had even been to their home one evening to report that her son and his mates had been caught throwing stones at the still-intact windows of an abandoned building in the neighborhood. She despaired that between the fact that her husband was drinking more since losing his job and the bad influence of Thomas's newfound friends—she called them "gang members"—her son was at serious risk of turning "bad." We also wondered whether her own parenting might be contributing to the change in Thomas's behavior, as she seemed less aware than she had been at previous visits about what her son was up to.

We were not entirely surprised to hear this story, in part because we designed the E-Risk Study to afford insight into the role of neighborhood in shaping children's development, thereby enabling us to move beyond children's microenvironments. To do that, however, we appreciated the limits of our own expertise in this area and recruited collaborators to ensure that our neighborhood research would be cutting edge. In fact, this has routinely been our approach in conducting both the E-Risk Study and the Dunedin Study. We remind readers that all the work we share in this book involved very many scholars besides ourselves. This point is clearly documented in the bibliography, which lists the scholarly reports on which each chapter is based, including as coauthors of those reports our collaborators, without whom the work could not have been carried out.

In this chapter, we share the results of a developmental adventure studying not only the effects of neighborhood conditions on the development of five-to-twelve-year-old children but whether some such conditions can act as protective factors, increasing the likelihood that at least some children will prove resilient to adversity even when growing up in disadvantaged communities. In so doing, we extend our work addressing whether and how experiences beyond the family shape children's future development. Thus, along the way, we will also evaluate the role that parenting plays in potentially mediating neighborhood effects. Just as importantly, we distinguish absolute and relative disadvantage vis-à-vis one's neighbors to see which matters most when it comes to children's development. We address this latter issue by considering whether and how living alongside more affluent neighbors affects disadvantaged children.

This was especially important to us because of the prevailing assumption that mixing disadvantaged children with those growing up in more economically and educationally advantaged households was in their best developmental interest. But was that really the case? As we will see, some sociological theory actually suggests otherwise. Besides, even if mixing more and less advantaged children together is good for those growing up under more deprived conditions, shouldn't one also wonder about how such mixing affects those who happen to be more lucky in life in terms of the resources that their families afford them?

When it came to investigating these issues, we remained especially alert to two additional considerations. The first was that where families live depends to a large extent on the family itself. Thus, families with more economic and related resources typically have a greater range of alternatives to choose from. This meant, of course, that what are referred to as "selection effects" could masquerade as environmental—and, in this case, neighborhood—effects. The term *selection* in the context of this chapter means that study members' families are selectively found in particular types of neighborhoods. This is because they either choose the neighborhood, have the neighborhood forced on them, or because of limited resources end up being able to live only in certain neighborhoods. Like exposure to and experience in day care, the neighborhood one lives in is not randomly assigned. The scientific risk here is that apparent effects of neighborhood could really be a function of family resources, which strongly influence where families live, as family resources and neighborhood are typically confounded. Thus, in our work, we once again needed to disentangle actual effects of neighborhoods from the effects of families that lived in them.

We also recognized a need to move beyond some traditional strategies that others had used to measure neighborhood characteristics. In fact, we eschewed the method of asking parents of the children we studied about their neighborhoods because we were concerned that we might end up with biased views of the neighborhood. It is not hard to imagine, for example, that a depressed, anxious, or angry parent might characterize a neighborhood in more negative terms than was objectively the case. In view of this concern, we employed two less subjective methods of measurement. First, we had the good fortune to be able, by means of some sophisticated geographic-mapping software, to take advantage of socioeconomic and economic information on the areas in which E-Risk children lived that a private company had collected for marketing purposes. In addition, and at great expense and effort, we surveyed thousands of people who lived in the same neighborhoods as E-Risk Study members—but were not otherwise part of the study—to learn about quality-of-life features of these areas. As we will show, these two methods proved quite informative in answering the empirical questions central to our neighborhood adventure.

A FOCUS ON ANTISOCIAL BEHAVIOR

While it is well established that children who grow up in poor neighborhoods are less likely to graduate from high school, more likely to spend time in prison, and can expect to suffer from more health-related problems than their peers in more affluent settings, there was still much that was unknown about how neighborhoods affect children's development when we launched the E-Risk Study. Notably, most prior sociological and developmental work on the subject targeted physical health (for example, infant mortality, birth weight, and asthma) and academic achievement (for example, test scores, school readiness, and school grades) rather than social and emotional functioning. Moreover, most existing research focused on adolescents, based on the view that they are more free of parental control than younger children and thus more susceptible to neighborhood influences. This is because they can, in principle, freely roam the communities in which they live. In light of these observations, we focused our neighborhood work on the development of antisocial behavior in younger children.

For our purposes, antisocial behavior encompasses aggressive and delinquent acts that result in physical or psychological harm to others and to property. Such behavior violates the rights of others and, in some cases, violates legal codes. Thus, when E-Risk children were five, seven, ten, and twelve years of age, we had parents and teachers characterize them by completing questionnaires that tapped behaviors such as lying or cheating, swearing or bad language, stealing, truancy, having a hot temper, and physical aggression directed against others. These measurements were very much like those made at younger ages when we studied the effects of day care, as described in Chapter 8. To create a more reliable and robust index of antisocial behavior in our neighborhood work, we combined parent and teacher reports at each age of measurement. Again, the reader can see that we are more "lumpers" than "splitters" when it comes to handling many pieces of information on the same general topic.

Because the first empirical question we sought to answer concerned the economic makeup of families living in the neighborhood, one of the challenges we faced was characterizing neighborhood socioeconomic status (SES). Fortunately, a private company had solved this problem for us by creating—and sharing with us at no cost—a classification of residential neighborhoods based on over four hundred measurements obtained from the national census and from extensive consumer research databases. These measurements that are used to describe and classify areas included, for example, average educational attainment of residents, unemployment rates, percentage of single-parent households, dwelling type (for example, public versus private housing), and rate of car ownership. Five homogenous types of neighborhoods could be distinguished according to the firm from which we secured the measures, ranging from "wealthy-achiever" areas, comprised of families with high incomes, large single-family dwellings, and access to many amenities, to "hard-pressed" areas, dominated by government-subsidized housing projects, low-income families, high unemployment, and single-parent households. Roughly one-quarter of E-Risk families resided in each extreme on this neighborhood scale. For our first neighborhood study, we decided to combine some of the five types of neighborhoods by grouping together the top two, which we labeled "High SES," and the bottom two, which we labeled "Deprived," with the remaining group referred to as "Middle SES." Note how here we are adopting a combined dimensional and categorical approach in our effort to illuminate neighborhood effects on children's antisocial behavior.

Initial Findings

The first results to emerge from our neighborhood research proved consistent with our expectations—and no doubt those of many readers: a graded dose-response relationship existed between neighborhood SES and children's antisocial behavior, and this proved true at every one of the four ages at which we had measured aggressive and delinquent behavior. Thus, as neighborhood SES declined, the average level of five-, seven-, ten-, and twelve-year-olds' antisocial behavior increased (see Figure 9.1). There was also a

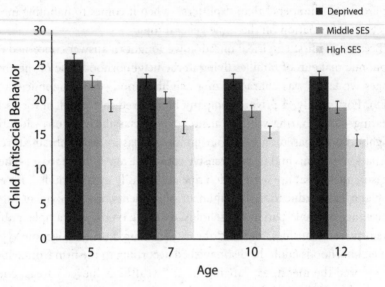

FIGURE 9.1. Average levels of antisocial behavior at ages five, seven, ten, and twelve years as a function of neighborhood socioeconomic status (SES). Odgers, C.L., Caspi, A., Russell, M.A., Sampson, R.J., Arseneault, L., & Moffitt, T. (2012). Supportive parenting mediates neighborhood socioeconomic disparities in children's antisocial behavior from ages 5 to 12. *Development and Psychopathology*, 24, 705–721, figure 2. Reproduced with permission.

noteworthy developmental trend in the data: as children got older, the behavioral gap between those living in deprived versus more affluent areas widened—by 43 percent for males and 57 percent for females, from ages five to twelve years. But this, intriguingly, was not because children living in deprived neighborhoods became more antisocial. Rather, it was because children living in high-SES and middle-SES neighborhoods experienced a normal trajectory of improvement in behavior—reductions in antisocial behavior from ages five to twelve years. Thus, in contrast to all other children, boys growing up in "deprived" neighborhoods experienced no improvement whatsoever in delinquent and aggressive behavior during this time. As twelve-year-olds, they were still behaving badly, as though they were five-year-olds. So it seems less the case that children growing up in economically disadvantaged communities become increasingly antisocial as they develop across the first decade of life and into the second than that they prove less able to inhibit their inclinations to behave in this manner—at an age when learning to inhibit is the normative developmental trend.

A Selection Effect?

Even though the evidence indicated that neighborhood contributes to antisocial behavior, there was an obvious alternative explanation to our findings—that it is not the neighborhood per se that is exerting influence but rather the children's families. In that case, we would be detecting a spurious selection effect rather than a true effect of neighborhood. To disentangle such a selection effect from a true neighborhood effect, we drew on multiple measurements in our data pantry that we now needed to statistically discount. In the case of family circumstances, these included family socioeconomic disadvantage, the father's and mother's own histories of antisocial behavior, family history of mental health problems, whether the child was physically maltreated, and the child's exposure to domestic violence. Our measurement of family SES, obtained when the child was five years old, was based on parents' years of schooling, occupational status of the head of household, household income, receipt of government benefits, residence in government-subsidized housing, and availability of a car.

At the same age-five home visit, mothers provided information, using a checklist of antisocial behaviors to report whether they or the twins' fathers had engaged in antisocial behaviors in their own lives. At the age-twelve visit, each mother was further queried as to whether she ever experienced substance-use problems, alcohol problems, depression, or psychosis, or had attempted suicide, as well as whether the close genetic relatives of the children (the twins' biological father and the mother's biological parents and siblings) had done so. A standardized clinical interview administered to the mother when children were five, seven, and ten years of age enabled us to determine whether either or both of the twins had been maltreated. Actual instances of such mistreatment that were reported to us included the following: being the victim of a legally adjudicated assault by a teenage sibling, being burned with matches, having injuries such as fractures resulting from neglectful or abusive parental care, and/or formal registration with the community child-protection team for physical abuse. It may seem that mothers would not respond forthrightly in such an interview, but by the age-twelve visit, they realized that our research team could be trusted—even though we explained, at each visit, that if we suspected any maltreatment we would, by law, have to report that to child protective services. Finally, domestic violence was evaluated by asking the mother—when the child was at ages five, seven, and ten years—whether she or her partner engaged in any of twelve physical acts of domestic violence, such as kicking the partner or threatening the partner with a knife. As should be evident, we went to great lengths to measure and consider family factors and processes that might actually account for why our neighborhood classification was related to children's antisocial behavior. We believed that simply controlling for family SES was insufficient.

So what did we find when we addressed the empirical question, "Does neighborhood deprivation predict children's antisocial behavior after all these family-selection factors and forces have been taken into account?" The answer was "yes." Even though our set of family factors collectively predicted children's antisocial behavior at age twelve, which was to be expected, neighborhood socioeconomic disadvantage also did—beyond the effect of these other predictors. In other words, children in more deprived neighborhoods were not more antisocial than those from less deprived neighborhoods just because their families were more dysfunctional. On top of this, the social and economic character of their neighborhood also mattered, such that living in more disadvantaged communities predicted children's greater engagement in more antisocial behavior. Selection effects therefore could not fully account for our initial neighborhood effects.

MECHANISM OF INFLUENCE

It is one thing to discover that neighborhood characteristics appear to influence children's development—even after taking into consideration a multitude of potentially influential family factors—but another to understand exactly why that is the case, so this issue of "how" experiences and exposures beyond the family mattered became our next focus. Specifically, we asked, "How does neighborhood deprivation come to influence children's antisocial behavior?"

Just to be clear, it would be a mistake to presume that there is a single mechanism responsible for translating neighborhood disadvantage into young people's delinquent and aggressive behavior. As we noted when discussing family effects on girls' pubertal development (Chapter 7), virtually all aspects of development are multiply determined, and a focus on one factor or source of influence should not be read to imply that there are not others. So, at the biological level, stress physiology could prove influential in linking neighborhood disadvantage with antisocial behavior. We focus on such "biological embedding" processes in Chapter 18, though not with regard to neighborhood disadvantage. It also seems likely that a "socially embedding" culprit could play a role, perhaps most notably the child's neighborhood peer group. This possibility is consistent with the view of Thomas's mother that we introduced at the beginning of this chapter. Parenting also merits consideration, and we sought to focus on that when considering mechanisms of influence by which neighborhood disadvantage influences antisocial behavior. Thus, in extending our developmental adventure investigating neighborhood effects, using E-Risk data, we tested the hypothesis that neighborhood disadvantage comes to foster antisocial behavior by first undermining supportive parenting.

To test this proposition, we measured two aspects of parenting: maternal warmth and monitoring. For the former, we relied on a procedure called the "Five Minute Speech Sample," administered to mothers during our home visits when children were ten years old. Mothers were asked to speak for five minutes about each of their twins. Recalcitrant mothers were given prompts, such as, "How do you feel when you take her out in public?" or "Is there any way you'd like him to be different?" Recordings of these parental commentaries were subsequently rated in terms of the warmth expressed by mothers toward their children. This was done, separately for each twin, by trained evaluators who knew nothing else about the families (or the other twin). The ratings of maternal warmth were based on the mother's tone of voice and the content of her comments, especially with regard to sympathy and empathy expressed toward the child. When a mother's speech showed strong evidence of enthusiasm for, interest in, and enjoyment of the child, the rating of warmth was very high. It was very low, in contrast, when there was only a slight amount of understanding, sympathy, or concern or enthusiasm about or interest in the child, or even disappointment. When a mother's speech sample fell between these extremes, so did the rating of her parental warmth.

During the same age-ten home visit, we also gathered information—again for each twin separately—on how closely the mother monitored the child's behavior when the child was away from home. Ten questions probed things such as whether the mother knows the friends the child hangs out with, knows where her child goes in his spare time, whether the child needs permission to leave home, and whether the mother knows what the child does while the child is outside the house. The more questions that mothers answered affirmatively, the higher their monitoring score.

When we looked to see whether parenting practices served as a means by which neighborhood disadvantage contributed to antisocial behavior at age twelve, we found that they did. It was because mothers in more disadvantaged neighborhoods proved less warm and supportive in their parenting and monitored their children less that their children proved to be more antisocial in their behavior. In fact, when these parenting processes were taken into account statistically (that is, controlled for), the previously detected effect of neighborhood disadvantage on children's delinquent and aggressive behavior completely disappeared! It was only because of the adverse effects of neighborhood on parenting, then, that neighborhood disadvantage predicted and presumably influenced children's antisocial behavior. By analogy, turning on the light switch on the wall results in the overhead light going on because it causes electrons to flow through a wire connecting the switch to the light, so if you discount the effect of the mediating wire—by cutting it— then turning on the switch no longer works its magic, brightening the room. In this analogy, of course, the switch represents the neighborhood, the wire parenting, and the light the child's antisocial behavior.

RELATIVE DEPRIVATION

In many places in the United States, families that are economically disadvantaged are physically segregated from those that are more affluent. As a result, the most and least affluent neighborhoods are typically not particularly close to each other. Whereas one neighborhood may be situated on one side of the tracks, the other can be situated on the other side. Of course, railroad tracks are not the only dividing lines between economically distinct residential areas.

Even though in the United States there are places where the poor and the rich live in relatively close proximity, this is much more common in the United Kingdom, especially in many cities, including its capital and largest city, London. Just days before we wrote these words, there was a terrible fire in a twenty-four-story, high-rise apartment in London. The fire swept through the building with horrific speed not long after midnight, resulting in numerous deaths and leading to a major investigation to find out exactly what happened and learn lessons to help prevent such a tragedy from happening again. In the United States, almost all news reports commented on the fact that this public-housing project—called a "council estate," as it is managed by the local council (that is, government)—was surrounded by some of the most expensive housing in the country. Rather than isolate poor citizens far away from more affluent ones, as early as the 1970s the British national government had endeavored to put richer and poorer families in close proximity, presuming that this arrangement would benefit the latter in particular.

This arrangement afforded us a great opportunity to research the effects of economically disadvantaged families living alongside rather than farther away from neighbors who were much more affluent. Two possibilities came to mind as we set out to investigate this issue. On the one hand, and consistent with expectations of the city planners, rubbing shoulders with better-off neighbors should benefit poorer families, perhaps especially their children. As they grew up, the children would be in regular contact with people who were planful, went to work every day, took care of their property, and raised cooperative children motivated to achieve academically. On the other hand, seeing more advantaged neighbors every day could prove dispiriting, even evoke anger, as it could be like having one's face rubbed in the dirt on a regular basis. Comparison of the "have nots" with the "haves" might then increase the sense—and adverse effects—of deprivation.

To evaluate these competing hypotheses—and thus the effects of "relative deprivation"—we drew on some measurements already described. We began by focusing exclusively on children who lived in those areas classified as "deprived" and whose families experienced economic hardship. The latter was indexed by things like the head of household having no educational qualifications, being employed in an unskilled job or not being employed at all, or the family living on a council estate. By using detailed geographic software to position each family's residence, it was possible to distinguish those children from deprived families living in a deprived area who lived alongside more affluent households from those who did not. This work was possible because three-quarters of E-Risk's poor children lived in neighborhoods where more than 25 percent of the neighbors were classified as well off.

Even more notably, we discovered that city planners sadly had it wrong, at least as far as antisocial behavior was concerned: low-income children surrounded by more affluent neighbors engaged—at age five—in *more* antisocial behavior, according to mother and teacher reports (combined), than their equally deprived E-Risk peers who lived embedded in concentrated disadvantage! (See Figure 9.2.) The same result emerged when antisocial behavior at ages seven, ten, and twelve was the focus of inquiry. Just as in the NICHD Study of Early Child Care and Youth Development (Chapter 8), our data pointed to the influence of the wider group of people around a child, whether in a large day-care group or a neighborhood.

But once again we needed to challenge these findings to determine whether they could be accounted for by factors other than the nearness and number of more affluent neighbors. We addressed this issue by discounting effects of a number of family and neighborhood characteristics already described, specifically family SES, the mother's and father's history of antisocial behavior, and the degree of neighborhood deprivation, as well as two additional potentially confounding factors not yet mentioned that have figured

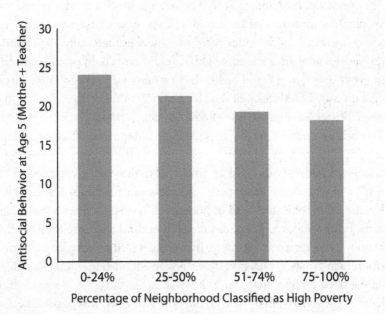

FIGURE 9.2. Average levels of antisocial behavior at age five as a function of percentage of neighborhood families living in poverty. Reformatted from Odgers, C.L., Donley, S., Caspi, A., Bates, C.J., & Moffitt, T.E. (2015). Living alongside more affluent neighbors predicts greater involvement in antisocial behavior among low income boys. *Journal of Child Psychology and Psychiatry*, 56, 1055–1064, figure 3. © 2015 Association for Child and Adolescent Mental Health.

importantly in much neighborhood-oriented sociological research: collective efficacy and neighborhood problems. These two features of a family's local area, recommended to us by sociologist Rob Sampson, a neighborhood scholar now at Harvard, were measured using surveys mailed to (cooperative) neighbors who lived on the same street or within the same apartment block as E-Risk families. The surveys captured neighborhood social cohesion and social control by including questions such as whether neighbors could be counted on to intervene in various ways if, for example, children were skipping school and hanging out on a street corner or were spray-painting graffiti on a local building. Survey respondents also evaluated whether people were willing to help their neighbors or whether they regarded their local area as close-knit.

To assess neighborhood problems, the survey included questions about whether residents regarded various types of disorder and crime in their neighborhood as a problem, including litter, broken glass, and rubbish in public places; run-down buildings, abandoned cars, and vacant shop fronts; and vandals who do things such as smashing street lamps, breaking windows, or painting graffiti on walls. Even when we discounted the effects of all these potentially confounding family and neighborhood factors, the results already reported—with one important exception—remained the same: being poor and residing in a deprived area resulted in more antisocial behavior (from ages five to twelve) *when more affluent families lived nearby* than when they did not. The exception to this finding was that with confounding factors statistically controlled, this relative-deprivation effect held only for boys, not girls.

Once we got to this point in our investigation, we could not help but wonder, "What about the children in these generally 'deprived' areas who are not from poor families? Are they also adversely affected by living in a neighborhood with less concentrated poverty and more economic mixing of households?" The answer to that question turned out to be "no." Perhaps not surprisingly, it was greater concentrations of poverty rather than greater "relative affluence" that predicted greater antisocial behavior in the case of children from more affluent families who lived in mixed areas. Once again, these results remained when the same set of neighborhood and family factors that were controlled previously had their effects statistically discounted. In other words, whereas concentrated deprivation proved unexpectedly better for poor children, particularly boys, than living near nonpoor families, the opposite was true of children from nonpoor households. Thus, whereas relative deprivation seemed to promote the antisocial behavior of boys from poor families, concentrated disadvantage rather than relative deprivation undermined the development of children if their economically advantaged family lived in a neighborhood that included many poor families. Effects of living in more versus less mixed deprived neighborhoods were different for children whose families were advantaged and disadvantaged.

Why, one might ask, does living near more rather than fewer affluent families adversely affect the development of children growing up in disadvantaged households? Decades of research on social disparities and health reveals that frequent exposure to higher-status individuals can negatively influence a lower-status person's psychological well-being and health. Indeed, such thinking as well as our own data reminded us of observations made about the experience of Russians before and after the fall of the Berlin Wall and the collapse of the Soviet Union a generation ago. For many Russian citizens, if they looked out their front door to the left and to the right before these historic changes occurred, they saw others equally disadvantaged—which made even a resource-limited life more or less tolerable. But once crony capitalism took hold, some became much more despondent because now some neighbors were far better off. This experience of relative deprivation of still-disadvantaged Russians made life feel worse— despite the fact that their own economic circumstances had not changed at all. Sometimes they even improved, just not as much as others'. In other words, those still poor felt better when everyone was disadvantaged but miserable than when some had much more than others.

When we consider antisocial behavior, long-standing theories have suggested that social comparisons of the kind just highlighted, as well as feelings of unfairness and blocked goals, may lead individuals to engage in delinquent behavior. Not only do these psychological experiences engender stress and negative emotions—such as envy and resentment—but also the "pickings" may look good nearby. Criminologists refer to this in terms of "opportunity theory": economically mixed communities may encourage youth crime by increasing the visibility and availability of high-value targets—such as more affluent neighbors. This would seem especially so if the things that other children have are highly desired by those who cannot afford them—such as expensive sneakers, called "trainers" in the United Kingdom, a laptop computer, or the latest smartphone.

Given such possibilities, one is led to ask why the relative-deprivation effect did not operate in the case of girls. One reason may be that they are less likely to be out on their own in the streets of the neighborhood because of being monitored by parents more closely than boys. Then there is the fact that, in general, boys are more likely than girls to engage in property crime, including vandalism, the destruction of property for its own sake, with nothing really to be gained—beyond an enhanced reputation in the peer group, something not to be discounted. It thus remains conceivable that relative-deprivation effects may prove more evident in the case of girls when other outcomes, such as secondary-school completion, mental health, and labor-force participation become a focus of inquiry as study members move into their young-adult years. Time will tell, but we have to wait for the E-Risk children to grow up more before we can find out. Once again, we invite the reader to recall our metaphor of the fruit farmer. Long before one can harvest the fruit that such trees can yield, one has to plant and fertilize the trees and ensure that they get sufficient water while not being damaged by insect pests.

RESILIENCE IN THE FACE OF NEIGHBORHOOD ADVERSITY

Even if growing up in more disadvantaged neighborhoods predicts more antisocial behavior, with boys being especially susceptible to the adverse effects of relative deprivation, this should not be read to imply that every child exposed to the contextual risks under consideration succumbs to them. We are again discussing probabilistic, not deterministic, effects, this time in the case of neighborhood. It is therefore critically important to illuminate factors that protect children from such adversity—circumstances that foster resilience in the face of neighborhood adversity.

When it came to addressing this issue, we drew on thinking from the emerging field of "ecometrics," which seeks to illuminate dynamic ecological factors that influence human development—beyond more static, structural features such as the concentration of economic disadvantage. Thus, ecometric considerations led us to focus on neighborhood-level social processes that might explain why some children growing up in deprived neighborhoods do better than would otherwise be expected, at least in terms of their antisocial behavior. In particular, we became intrigued by the idea that "collective efficacy," which refers to the level of social cohesion among neighbors, combined with their willingness to intervene on behalf of the common good, might promote resilience. The concept of collective efficacy emerged from research in Chicago, where some luxury high-rise apartment buildings lack it but some of the poorest African American neighborhoods have it, particularly those led by a strong church.

The level of collective efficacy within a community is not reducible to the characteristics of its individual members. Rather, collective efficacy refers to the combination of informal social control and social cohesion, and thus the willingness of community members to look out for each other and intervene when trouble arises, especially on behalf of the community's youths. This group orientation is believed to constrain deviant child and adolescent behavior and reflect a community's ability to extract resources from the larger infrastructure and mobilize social capital—that is, the skills and abilities of individuals—within a community.

Two contrasting stories shared by E-Risk home visitors nicely capture the notion of collective efficacy. Each home visitor told us about observing a similar situation upon arriving in a neighborhood to carry out a home visit. In both neighborhoods, they witnessed a group of boys perhaps ten to twelve years old giving another kid a hard time, having surrounded the victim. In one neighborhood, the few people on the same side of the street where this bullying was occurring crossed over to the other side of the street, obviously wanting no part of what was going on. Yet, in the other neighborhood, a car going down the street slowed so that the driver could call out through his window, "Leave the kid alone; I'll call the police." This resulted in the bullies breaking up, allowing the would-be victim to walk away, unimpeded by the boys who moments ago had surrounded and harassed him.

Recall that in order to characterize neighborhoods, we surveyed adults whose children were not enrolled in the E-Risk Study but who lived nearby. When each study member was eight to nine years old, we mailed questionnaires to fifteen households in the same area as each of the 1,116 E-Risk families, resulting in a total of almost seventeen thousand mailed surveys! Each of these mailed surveys included a prestamped envelope in which to return the completed survey. On average, we received three surveys for each study family. The majority of survey respondents had lived in their neighborhood for more than five years, so they knew it well.

As noted previously, collective efficacy was indexed by survey responses pertaining to social control and social cohesion. Questions about social control addressed whether neighbors could be counted on to intervene in various ways when children were misbehaving (for example, skipping school, spraying graffiti, or showing disrespect to an adult). Social cohesion and trust were indexed with questions asking whether the neighborhood was "close-knit," whether people could be trusted, and whether neighbors got along with each other and shared the same values.

To evaluate the resilience-promoting effect—or lack thereof—of collective efficacy, we first determined whether it predicted children's antisocial behavior at age five and change in such behavior over the ensuing five years. Results indicated that greater neighborhood-level collective efficacy predicted less antisocial behavior in the first year of school and, to a lesser extent, a more rapid improvement (that is, a decline) in children's antisocial behavior during schooling, from ages five to ten.

The more important and resilience-related question, however, was whether, after discounting the family and community confounding factors, the developmental benefit of collective efficacy was greater in more disadvantaged neighborhoods than in more affluent ones. This proved to be the case when predicting children's antisocial behavior at the start of school. In other words, only in "ecometric" contexts of deprivation did collective efficacy matter: If in such deprived neighborhoods collective efficacy was high, then the otherwise anticipated adverse effect of deprivation was reduced relative to when collective efficacy was low. This observation did not hold, however, in more economically advantaged communities (or with regard to change over time in antisocial behavior). In other words, only children growing up in contexts of deprivation were protected (somewhat) from its untoward effects when the community had high rather than low levels of social cohesion and social control.

This, of course, makes clear that effects of neighborhood deprivation are not the same across neighborhoods—even when they are equally deprived. At least with respect to the level of antisocial behavior that children display upon entering school, some deprived neighborhoods function in a less deprived manner than others do, as reflected in differences in collective efficacy. Consequently, so does the behavior of young children growing up in these disadvantaged neighborhoods.

When we completed the neighborhood studies whose results we have just shared, we once again found ourselves wishing we could have studied what we did not, in this case children's schooling experiences. Given that children in deprived neighborhoods with high collective efficacy proved to be less antisocial at school entry than agemates in equally deprived neighborhoods with low collective efficacies, one might imagine that the climate of the schools the two sets of children attended might also be different. Would teachers in schools serving children from deprived but high-collective-efficacy neighborhoods spend more time teaching and less time managing classroom behavior than those working in schools serving children from deprived and low-collective-efficacy neighborhoods? If so, would the effect of schooling be different across these different communities? Unfortunately, the E-Risk Study was not positioned to address this issue, which clearly merits empirical attention.

CONCLUSION

Given the important role neighborhood plays in where people, especially parents, choose to live—presuming that they have some choice—it is probably not especially surprising that we found neighborhood deprivation to be associated with children's antisocial behavior in our developmental adventure focused on the effects of the world beyond the microenvironment of the family. It seems unlikely that so many people would place so much importance on the community they reside in if it did not matter to the quality of their everyday life and to how their children develop. Recall that, despite this observation, we geared our work toward investigating whether neighborhood effects would prove evident in the preadolescent years and with respect to social-emotional development, given that most prior developmental work on neighborhood effects focused on others aspects of development during adolescence.

We think our adventure studying neighborhood as part of the E-Risk Study made several contributions to the field of "ecometrics." First, it showed that even in children as young as five years of age, neighborhood deprivation matters when it comes to understanding the determinants of children's antisocial behavior. This was true even when multiple confounding family and community factors were taken into account, implying that the effects we discerned were not simply statistical artifacts resulting from the fact that the place children live is not randomly assigned. That is, even though family factors in particular make a difference when it comes to where children grow up, the neighborhood itself—and not just a family's strengths and weaknesses—matters when it comes to how much aggression and delinquency children engage in.

Beyond this observation, three more merit review and consideration. First, family and neighborhood are not entirely independent sources of influence. We discovered in this regard that neighborhood deprivation works its developmental magic—or curse—in large measure via the parenting children received. When children live in deprived communities and also experience limited parental warmth and monitoring, they are most likely to become antisocial. This means, of course, that when parents in disadvantaged families embedded in deprived communities provide greater warmth and monitoring than would otherwise be expected given the makeup of a neighborhood, their children are less likely to become antisocial. When viewed from the perspective of resilience, then, supportive parenting functions as a protective factor that can attenuate the expected adverse effects of growing up in a disadvantaged neighborhood.

We also observed that at least in the case of boys, what may matter most is not how disadvantaged a community is but rather its relative disadvantage. Recall that disadvantaged boys were more likely to engage in delinquent and aggressive behavior—from ages five to twelve—when they lived alongside children from more affluent families. This is an observation that challenges the beliefs of many city planners. It is commonly assumed that the mixing of disadvantaged with advantaged children is in the best interests of the former. What we do not know, of course, given that the work presented in this chapter was carried out in England and Wales, is whether the same results would emerge in the United States, New Zealand, or elsewhere.

Perhaps the solution to this conundrum raised by our relative-deprivation findings—whether to develop economically mixed neighborhoods (and schools?)—is to be found in the final set of findings we shared. Not all deprived communities are the same. Their "ecometrics" differ—and matter—with some being places where community members are invested in the place they live and others less so or not at all. What our work does not illuminate, however, is what determines a neighborhood's econometrics and thus how to foster collective efficacy in communities. This, we saw, is especially important in deprived rather than more affluent neighborhoods, because it was only in the former that collective efficacy fostered resilience— leading to less antisocial behavior than would otherwise be expected. As developmental scholars studying individual differences in how and why children develop the way they do, we think this is a problem for those more knowledgeable than ourselves about community dynamics, most notably sociologists and epidemiologists. Over to such experts, then.

10

Bullying

When we visited ten-year-old Joshua and his twin brother, Jack, at their home outside Manchester, England, as part of the Environmental-Risk Study, Joshua complained repeatedly about being picked on by other boys at school. Joshua and Jack are fraternal twins, with Joshua being the (much) smaller of the two. They live with their single mother in public housing, which in the United Kingdom is rarely as dangerous as it can be in such places in the United States. Nevertheless, Joshua couldn't stop complaining about one boy after another who teased him for being such a weakling, for not being particularly bright, and for having no friends. His brother, unfortunately, wasn't much help, virtually never standing up for his co-twin, sometimes even joining in. One might imagine that if Joshua's mother had been sufficiently well off to get each of the boys a cell phone, Joshua's plight might have been even worse, with the bullying stretching into his time alone at home, where he seemed to be spending more and more time.

Bullying, sadly, is not an unusual experience for many children, either in the United Kingdom, the United States, or most other parts of the Western world. In the 2008–2009 school year, the School Crime Supplement to the National Crime Victimization Survey, administered by the National Center for Education Statistics, revealed that more than seven million twelve-to-eighteen-year-olds in the United States—some 28 percent of all students—reported that they were bullied at school. In the United Kingdom, the National Society for the Prevention of Cruelty to Children reported in 2011 that 25 percent of children claim to have been bullied. Notably, these figures are higher than an estimate of bullying worldwide, which placed the prevalence at 13 percent in 2004. The difference between these figures suggests either that bullying has increased, which certainly seems possible given the role that cyberbullying now plays in the lives of too many children and adolescents, or that bullying is much more frequent in English-speaking nations than in other parts of the world. That also seems possible.

By definition, bullying is present when children or adolescents are exposed to repeated harassment and humiliation from peers between whom there is an imbalance of power, making it difficult for victims to defend themselves. It comes in many varieties. Whereas it used to require face-to-face encounters, as when the bully knocks the victim down or makes fun of his or her appearance, all too often to the cheers of others, that is no longer the case. Cyberbullying has become a virtual epidemic, with ugly text messages sent from one or many bullies to repeatedly harass the victim. This kind of activity has even led victims to commit suicides. Many of us can surely think back to a time when we were bullied, bullied another child, or sat idly back while bullying occurred. Certainly, the latter two experiences are nothing to be proud of.

As we discussed this issue, two of us couldn't help but be reminded of our own—difficult to forget—experiences being bullied while growing up. Terrie Moffitt all too easily recalled how a boy named Topper harassed her every day after school on the long bus ride home to her family farm in North Carolina. It was his routine to shove her, knock the books out of her arms, and threaten to beat her up—as well as anyone who would sit beside her. Terrie's husband, Avshalom Caspi, also recalled being bullied as an immigrant boy in Santa Cruz, California. A guy named Jerry used to punch him in the stomach whenever he went up for a jump shot in the schoolyard basketball game. Jerry, along with a sidekick, would routinely threaten to keep doing the same after school. At irregular intervals, the two bullies would show up at one of the school entrances and either threaten to punch Avshalom or actually do so. Consequently, he spent the last period of every school day for an entire spring term trying to figure out which exit offered him the best escape route. Guess what? When we googled Jerry's name just before writing these words, we ran across his mug shot—meaning he had been arrested—from Santa Cruz. It also turned out that Temi's tormentor had an early death. These real-life outcomes are consistent with the themes of this book.

In this chapter focused on our developmental adventure studying bullying, we examine whether and how experiences growing up, in this case with peers outside the family, influence development. In particular, two distinct questions about the bullying experience are considered, drawing on data gathered as part of the E-Risk Study. The first pertained to the effects of bullying on its victims and the second to whether the adverse consequences of being bullied can be buffered or mitigated by the kind of family the bullied child grows up in. The latter issue returns us to the topic of resilience highlighted in several earlier chapters and the notion of probabilistic versus deterministic effects of developmental experiences on future functioning.

In our work on bullying victimization in primary school, we relied on interviews with mothers when children were seven and ten years of age and with children themselves when they were twelve years of age. We used these to gain insight into children's exposure to bullying. In the case of mothers, we explained that someone is bullied when another child says mean and hurtful things; makes fun of or calls a person mean and hurtful names; completely ignores or excludes someone from their group of friends or leaves them out of activities on purpose; hits, kicks, or shoves another; tells lies or spreads rumors about a person; or does other similar hurtful things. Following this description, we asked mothers whether to their knowledge either of their twin children had been treated in the ways described. During separate interviews with each twin, they indicated whether they had been bullied by another child. Whether interviews were with mothers or children, respondents were asked to describe what happened when they reported bullying. Based on such information, we learned about Joshua's bullying experience that introduced this chapter.

Before sharing what we discovered about the effects of bullying, we couldn't help but ponder a question we really hadn't thought about before: why all the attention to bullying these days? Like others, we decided to investigate its effects on children's development because it had become a "hot" topic, one that parents, teachers, policymakers and, of course, children themselves seem to be especially concerned about. But why is that? Bullying, after all, has been around for eons. Way back when, it just seemed like a regular part of childhood, in some respects a rite of passage. What, then, has made bullying such a big deal today?

We raise this issue not because we think it should not be a big issue but just because the amount of attention and concern paid to it now seems so different from what it was decades ago. One possibility is that adults in the modern era—of fewer children per family and thus fewer older siblings to come to one's defense—are simply more focused on their progeny than was the case in the past. Generations ago, children spent lots of time outside the purview of their parents, and even if they complained about being bullied, they often found parents too busy with the rest of life to spend too much time being too concerned about it. We can even recall them saying things like "you have to figure this out for yourself, just as I did."

Another possibility is that scholars, parents, and others have come to appreciate more so than in the past that when it comes to factors and forces shaping children's well-being, we have to expand our horizons beyond how parents rear their children. Experiences with peers matter, too. Not too long ago, in 1998, Judith Harris published a popular book that we mentioned in passing in Chapter 5, *The Nurture Assumption,* heralding the fact that too many of us—parents and scholars—failed to appreciate the developmental significance of experience with peers, emphasizing the role of parenting far too much while insufficiently appreciating the power and influence of friends and peers on children's development and well-being. This is one reason why in this part of the book, focused on nonfamily as well as family influences on development, we consider experiences that principally occur in the peer world: bullying in this chapter and marijuana use in Chapter 11.

But perhaps what has really moved bullying to center stage is social media. It is no longer the case that kids only get bullied face-to-face, as they did when the authors were growing up. Today, some of the worst bullying goes on via email and texting, with many kids too often joining in, perhaps even some who would never have done so before. There is also the fact that psychological pain resulting from cyberbullying can be so much more hurtful than physical pain caused by being pushed, shoved, or hit. In the final analysis, perhaps it is the confluence of these factors and forces that has brought bullying and its effects on children to the fore.

EFFECTS OF BULLYING

During the course of our research studying bullying, we carried out three separate investigations of the effects of bullying on bullied children. The first evaluated effects on children's emotional and behavior problems, the second on self-harm, and the third on being overweight. Each is discussed in turn.

Emotional and Behavior Problems

In order to evaluate effects of bullying on emotional and behavioral problems when children were ten and twelve years of age, we drew on mothers' and teachers' reports of children's behavior. The part of the behavior checklist assessing emotional problems included items such as "cries a lot," "feels too guilty," and "worries." The behavioral problems scale included items pertaining to delinquency (for example, steals) and aggression (for example, "fights a lot"). These behaviors are the same ones mentioned in Chapter 8, dealing with effects of day care, and in Chapter 9, concerned with neighborhoods, because the same measurement tool was used in both the E-Risk Study and the NICHD Study of Early Child Care and Youth Development. To enhance the reliability and thus accuracy of measurement, we once again combined the reports of parents and teachers in our bullying work, just as we had done in our neighborhood research.

As we make clear throughout this book, in nonexperimental, observational research in which children are studied over time and no efforts are made to influence their development, there is always the risk of "reverse causality." This occurs when some putative "outcome" being measured proves to be related to some suspected source of influence, but it could be because the would-be outcome actually affects the would-be causal factor. Consider the possibility that a sad, inhibited child inadvertently evokes the bullying behavior of others. In this case, the child influences the occurrence of bullying rather than just being affected by it. This is not unusual, as bullies routinely pick on the weak rather than the strong. But just to be clear and not be misunderstood, we do not mean to imply that the bullying experienced is the victim's fault.

In view of the possibility of reverse causality, we had to appreciate that even if bullying predicted children's emotional and/or behavioral problems in the future, as we hypothesized would be the case, this could be the result of earlier problem behavior evoking the bullying it would otherwise appear to cause. Therefore, we considered the level of children's problems *before* they had a chance to experience bullying in primary school. Only by doing so could we ensure that effects of child behavior eliciting bullying and continuing children's own future problematic development would not be misconstrued as effects of bullying on children's adjustment problems. Of course, it is also possible that reciprocal effects characterize the bullying process. This would entail children's emotional problems inadvertently affecting the bullying treatment they receive and, even after taking this into account, bullying further exacerbating such problems. In other words, causal influence can be bidirectional, going both from child problems to bullying and from bullying to (more) child problems.

As we have done in other chapters, to reduce the risk of inferring a bullying effect when there is only a child effect on bullying, we statistically controlled for child problems measured when we first enrolled children in the E-Risk Study at age five before evaluating effects of bullying on child problems at ages ten to twelve. Upon doing this, we found that children bullied during primary school had more emotional and more behavioral problems than children who were not bullied. In fact, given the way the analysis was carried out, the results indicated that the experience of bullying contributed to the *increase* in emotional and behavioral problems over time from age five to age twelve.

It should be appreciated that being bullied is not just painful, serving to foster emotional and behavioral problems. These very psychological and behavioral consequences of bullying have their own untoward effects on children because children showing more problems have more difficulty establishing and maintaining friendships and doing well in school. In other words, by promoting emotional and behavioral problems, bullying can be part of a downward spiral of developmental functioning, cascading to influence many aspects of development. Appreciation of this developmental reality led us to undertake the second stage of our adventure studying effects of bullying—focusing on self-harm, behavior in which children purposefully injure themselves.

Self-Harm

Earlier, we referred to the fact that bullying can be so severe and painful that it causes some children to commit suicide. Who is to blame for this heartbreaking situation? Has a crime been committed? Thinking about these matters led us to focus on self-harm. We wanted to know, consistent with anecdotal evidence that shows up in widely publicized reports in the media, whether bullying is related to children harming themselves, even if not to the point of taking their own lives. Fortunately, even in a study as large as E-Risk, with more than one thousand participating families raising twins, completed suicide is too infrequent an occurrence for us to be able to investigate it with any confidence. We did, however, include suicide attempts when assessing children's self-harm.

When it came to measuring children's self-harm, as part of the face-to-face interview we administered when children were twelve years old, we queried mothers as to whether either or both twins had ever deliberately harmed themselves or attempted suicide in the preceding six months. Ethical considerations precluded us from asking children themselves about self-harm, as we didn't want to risk planting ideas in their minds with such questioning. Examples of self-harming behavior included cutting and biting arms, pulling out clumps of hair, banging one's head against walls, and attempted suicides by strangulation (for example, hanging). Just under 3 percent of the sample qualified as self-harming, with such behavior being roughly as likely for boys as for girls.

Our first step in investigating effects of bullying on self-harm simply addressed the issue of whether frequent exposure to bullying by peers before age twelve was associated with an increased risk of self-harm at age twelve. This turned out to be the case, whether we considered the entire sample or boys and girls separately, and whether we relied on mothers' or children's reports of self-harm (see Figure 10.1).

But, as in so much of our work, we needed to go beyond just documenting an association before we could conclude that the observational evidence pointed in the direction of bullying actually causing self-harm. After all, it could be caused by something else associated with self-harm; recall that such alternative explanatory factors are referred to as "third variables." Because we appreciated that bullying and child maltreatment often co-occur and that self-harm is often associated with problematic parenting, we next evaluated whether the effect of bullying could be accounted for by children's experience of maltreatment. If so, the bullying effect we seemed to have documented would be spurious. Information on physical and sexual maltreatment by an adult was obtained during interviews conducted with mothers when children were five, seven, ten, and

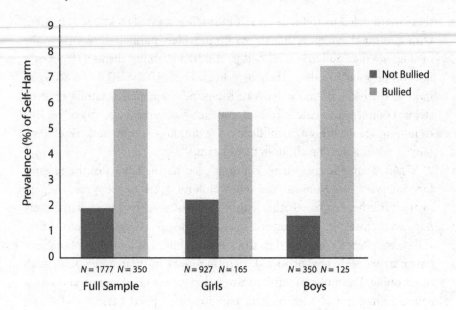

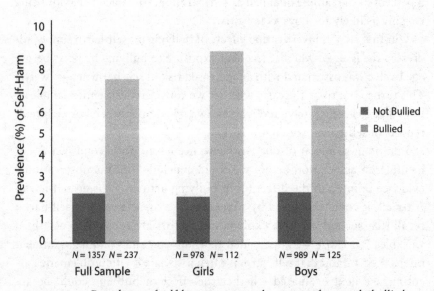

FIGURE 10.1. Prevalence of self-harm at age twelve among frequently bullied and nonbullied children, based on reports of bullying by mothers (top) and by children themselves (bottom). Reformatted from Fisher, H.L., Moffitt, T.E., Houts, R.M., Belsky, D.W., Arseneault, L., & Caspi, A. (2012). Bullying victimization and risk of self harm in early adolescence. *BMJ, 344*, e2683, Figure. CC-BY-NC.

twelve years of age. Importantly, the previously documented effects of bullying on self-harm remained even with child maltreatment taken into account. In other words, bullying contributed to self-harm beyond any effects of maltreatment.

When it came to alternative explanatory factors, we did not stop with child maltreatment. We also appreciated that children's mental health problems rather than bullying per se could contribute to self-harming behavior. We were in a position to address this second alternative explanation of the bullying effect already detected because the E-Risk data pantry included, as highlighted in the first set of bullying findings already discussed, measurements of children's emotional and behavioral problems at age five. When these were taken into account, bullying still predicted self-harm. It was not simply the case that bullying was in response to children's psychological difficulties that preceded bullying and thus that earlier problems rather than bullying influenced self-harm.

What about intelligence at age five? Could it just be that bullied children are less intelligent than others and this accounts for the bullying effect on self-harm? This third alternative explanatory factor also could not fully account for the adverse effect of bullying on self-harm.

What about the family? Maybe children harmed themselves because of problematic things other than maltreatment going on inside their homes, so attributing self-harm to bullying by peers essentially misattributed the cause to just a statistical correlate. To investigate the possibility that family factors accounted for bullying effects, we compared same-sex twins *in the same family* when one was bullied and the other was not, like the situation with Joshua and Jack discussed in the opening of this chapter. Bullying predicted self-harm even using this approach, which, by its very nature, controlled for many potential determinants of self-harm, such as household economic disadvantage, parental psychopathology, domestic violence, and having immediate and extended family members who attempted or completed suicide. This was because such potentially influential family factors would be the same for twins growing up in the same household. Thus, any differences between them related to bullying could not be because of these other experiences and exposures that twins growing up in the same family shared.

Given the findings presented to this point, one must wonder why frequent exposure to bullying by peers during childhood increases the risk of deliberate self-harm. It is known that frequent exposure to bullying is associated with high levels of distress; recall the results of our first study linking bullying to emotional problems. But why do bullied children choose to use self-harm rather than other coping strategies—such as exercise or talking—to deal with these emotions? One possibility is that twelve-year-olds lack opportunities for reducing distress that are available to adults, such as self-medication with alcohol or cigarettes, working out at the gym, or excessive food consumption. Children may use self-harm after their attempts to talk to others about their distress proved ineffective in mitigating it, so more drastic attention-seeking behavior seemed called for. That last explanation is probably more likely in abusive or neglectful family environments in which the child's voice is seldom heard, owing to their own fear of being "punished" if they spoke out or to the simple unavailability of empathic caregivers.

Overweight

The evidence considered to this point illuminates the adverse effects of bullying in childhood on children early in their second decade of life, at age twelve. Once more, we want to herald one of the great advantages of the longitudinal research that is the focus of this book—the ability to investigate whether untoward effects of adverse childhood experiences documented at one point in time prove evident later in life. In the E-Risk Study, this meant looking for such effects toward the end of the teenage years, when children were eighteen years of age, as this is as far as we have followed these children as of this writing.

In the third stage of our developmental inquiry focused on bullying, we chose to investigate adolescents' weight—specifically, whether they were overweight. More than two-thirds of American adults are currently overweight, according to standard medical definitions. A focus on being overweight with respect to the experience of bullying is important for a number of reasons. Being overweight not only increases the risk of cardiovascular disease, type 2 diabetes, and cancer but is also associated with social discrimination—in relationships, at school, and on the job. Because there is little compelling evidence that available interventions targeting the overweight, such as diet and behavioral changes, are actually effective over the longer term, it is important to identify potentially modifiable risk factors as targets for prevention. Bullying could be one of those in that it could contribute to being overweight, perhaps through self-medicating by over-eating or, at the physiological level, by slowing down metabolism. That is why we set out to evaluate bullying's effects on being overweight, even though we were not positioned to address such potential influential processes instantiating effects of bullying on weight.

Another factor motivating our focus on being overweight was evidence that early-life stress can predispose individuals toward excess body mass. Consider evidence indicating that individuals with a history of childhood maltreatment have an elevated risk of obesity in adulthood and show faster gains in body-mass index (BMI) over their lifetime relative to nonmaltreated individuals. Once again, we were cognizant of the need to rule out alternative explanations—such as being maltreated—of any detected associations linking bullying during the primary-school years with being overweight at the end of the high-school years.

In order to capture children's experience being bullied, we once again relied on the interviews with mothers when children were in primary school at ages seven and ten and with both mothers and children, separately, when children were in secondary school at age twelve. Combining information obtained from the mother and child (lumping) enabled us to distinguish three groups of children: "nonvictims," who experienced only occasional or no victimization at primary and secondary school (59 percent of study members); "transitory victims," who were frequently victimized at primary school or secondary school but not during both developmental periods (28 percent); and "chronic victims," who were frequently victimized in both primary and secondary school (13 percent). (By the way, both authors Moffitt and Caspi would qualify as transitory victims on the basis of their aforementioned childhood experiences.) When study members were seen at age eighteen, we assessed their height and weight so that we could calculate their BMI—as weight in kilograms divided by the squared value of height measured in meters (kg/m^2). *Overweight* was defined according to the US Centers for Disease Control and Prevention Criteria. Study members with a BMI in the top 15 percent of their age-sex group were classified as overweight. We also calculated their waist-hip ratio by dividing waist circumference by hip circumference. We also had available BMI measurements made when children were twelve years of age.

Once more, we began our inquiry by determining whether a simple statistical relation existed between bullying and being overweight. It did: bullied children were more likely than other children to be overweight at age eighteen, and in a dose-response manner, such that greater bullying was systematically associated with being more overweight (see Figure 10.2). Moreover, chronically bullied children had the highest BMI of all bullied children, and children categorized as transitory or chronic in their bullying exposure had greater waist-hip ratios than nonvictim comparison children did. We should note with regard to this latter finding that having a large waist circumference—the measure on which the waist-hip ratio is based—not only reflects being overweight but also denotes specific risk for metabolic problems, because visceral fat is particularly pernicious when it comes to poor health. Visceral—or "deep"—fat is stored farther underneath the skin than "subcutaneous" belly fat; it is a form of gel-like fat that's actually wrapped around major organs, including the liver, pancreas, and kidneys.

As usual, we sought to challenge our findings. We did this first by considering co-occurring maltreatment. This was important because our evidence indicated that bullied children were more likely to be maltreated than nonbullied children and that maltreatment also was related to having a larger waist-hip ratio and a greater likelihood of being overweight (for girls only). Despite these observations, being bullied remained associated with being overweight even after taking a history of maltreatment into account

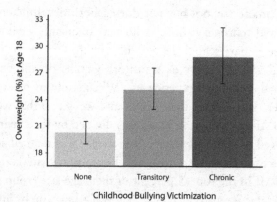

FIGURE 10.2. Percentage of children overweight at age eighteen as a function of childhood bullying victimization. Baldwin, J.R., Arseneault, L., Odgers, C., Belsky, D.W., Matthews, T., Ambler, A., Caspi, A., Moffitt, T.E., & Danese, A. (2016). Childhood bullying victimization and overweight in young adulthood: A cohort study. *Psychosomatic Medicine, 78*, 1094–1103, figure 1A.

as an alternative explanatory factor (that is, third variable). In other words, bullying predicted being overweight beyond any effects of maltreatment.

We next turned our attention to other alternative explanations of our bullying-overweight findings by taking into consideration psychosocial risks and child characteristics. This was important because being bullied also was associated with socioeconomic disadvantage and food insecurity (psychosocial risks), poor mental health (emotional and behavioral problems) and low IQ at age five, and early pubertal development. Noteworthy, too, was that each of these correlates of bullying predicted being overweight, with the exception of emotional problems. Nevertheless, when the effects of these potential confounding factors were taken into account, being bullied up to age twelve still predicted being overweight at age eighteen. As before, being bullied forecast being overweight beyond any effects of psychosocial risks and child characteristics.

But the question still arises, does bullying victimization precede being overweight—or could being overweight operate as a "selection" factor leading overweight children to be bullied? In other words, could we again be dealing with reverse causation, whereby being overweight precedes and contributes to bullying rather than the other way around—being a consequence of it? Importantly, this did not seem to be the case. Bullied children at age twelve were not more likely than other children to be overweight or to have a high BMI or high waist-hip ratio. Thus, there was little basis for believing that weight-related characteristics preceded and contributed to bullying, at least in the case of twins participating in the E-Risk Study. Just as notably, the association between childhood bullying and being overweight at age eighteen remained after accounting for childhood weight. In fact, the same was true when we discounted the effects of each child's birth weight and genetic risk for being overweight, as indexed by whether each child's co-twin was overweight.

Once again, it would appear that bullying affected children in an adverse way, this time being detectable in weight-related measurements made at age eighteen. In other words, we discovered that bullied children were at increased risk of becoming overweight. Just as important was that our findings were specific to bullying victimization by peers and were not explained by co-occurring maltreatment by adults. Recall as well that bullied children exhibited greater risk of being overweight independent of potential confounders, such as family economic disadvantage, food insecurity, child mental health, cognition, and pubertal development. Finally, the association was consistent with the hypothesized temporal priority that is critical for any causal inference, in that bullied children were not overweight at the time of victimization but became so in young adulthood independent of prior weight in childhood and preexisting genetic and fetal liability. In other words, being overweight occurred following bullying; it did not precede it.

Clearly, based on these findings, efforts should be made to support bullied children by preventing them from becoming overweight. Such efforts might focus on eating practices (for example, junk food) and activity (that is, the importance of exercise). It seems likely that, if effective, benefits could extend to children's mental health, the focus of our prior investigations of bullying's effects on emotional and behavioral problems as well as self-harm.

RESILIENCE IN THE FACE OF BULLYING

In several earlier chapters, especially Chapter 1, we highlighted the fact that, like all of biology, human development is a probabilistic, not a deterministic, science. Excluding quantum mechanics, physics is the classic deterministic science, which is why it has laws explaining how physical forces operate. These enable the confident building of bridges and high-rise buildings, to cite but two examples of the benefits of determinism. Probabilism, as explained in Chapter 1, means that causes or influences do not have inevitable effects on human development but rather ones that are more or less likely but rarely certain. Thus, they may or may not eventuate in the outcome anticipated, depending on other circumstances and factors. We all appreciate, for example, that even if smoking increases the risk of lung cancer and unprotected sex increases the risk for AIDS, not everyone who engages in these behaviors succumbs to the outcomes to which they are probabilistically related. What this means in the present context is that even if bullying increases the risk of mental health problems and self-harm in childhood and being overweight in young adulthood, it is by no means the case that every bullied child develops these liabilities. This observation calls attention to the issue of resilience in the face of adversity, raising the question of what factors or processes might protect bullied children from succumbing to the developmental risks associated with harsh treatment by peers that we have chronicled. We turned to this issue in the final stage of our research on bullying.

Our first effort to answer the question just raised involved extending our second bullying investigation, focused on self-harm, by trying to find out what differed between the bullied children who did and did not self-harm. This seemed particularly important in light of the fact that even though more than 90 percent of the bullied children did not engage in self-harm, half the children we found who self-harmed were bullied. So what distinguished the bullied self-harmers from their counterparts who were bullied but did not self-harm?

What we discovered was that bullied children who engaged in self-harming behavior were more likely than other bullied children to have in their immediate or extended family a member who had attempted or completed suicide. Self-harming bullied children were also more likely than their bullied-only counterparts to have been physically maltreated by an adult. Information on both these possibilities had been obtained during interviews with mothers. Mental health conditions of the children themselves also mattered. In fact, children who self-harmed when bullied were more likely than bullied children who did not self-harm to suffer from diagnosable conduct disorder, depression, and psychotic symptoms. Resilience in the face of bullying, it would appear, at least in the case of self-harm, was the result of being mentally healthier, coming from a family that did not have a history of suicidal behavior, and of being reared in a way that did not involve physical maltreatment.

Given these results, we decided to extend our investigation of resilience in the face of bullying by returning to our initial bullying research on the development of emotional and behavioral problems. Thus, the question became, "Why, with respect to such psychological difficulties, were some bullied children less adversely affected by it than other bullied children were?" In this second effort to illuminate resilience-related processes, we chose to focus exclusively on the family, given extensive theory and evidence that supportive family relationships can prove protective in the face of many different adversities. It also mattered to us that intervention to promote healthy family functioning could be implemented if a supportive family environment proved to protect children from the full effects of bullying, as anticipated. Indeed, we hypothesized that bullied children would be less likely to develop adjustment problems associated with bullying when the parenting they experienced was warm, when their sibling relationships were affectionate, and when the overall atmosphere of the home environment was well structured—meaning organized rather than chaotic—and emotionally supportive.

To assess maternal warmth, we relied on the Five Minute Speech Sample we introduced in Chapter 9, administered when children were five and ten years of age. Recall that in this procedure mothers are asked to speak for five minutes about each of their twins, and then recordings of their commentaries are rated, separately for each twin, in terms of the warmth expressed by mothers toward their children, based on their tone of voice and content of comments, especially with regard to sympathy and empathy expressed with respect to the child. We also relied on mothers to evaluate the warmth of their twins' sibling relationship. Thus, we asked them questions such as, "Do your twins love each other?" and "Do both your twins do nice things for each other?" Evaluation of the atmosphere of the home was based on observations made by the researchers who visited families. These focused on things such as whether the home was clean, whether children's art was displayed in the home, whether the home had a "happy feel," and whether it was chaotic or overly noisy.

With these measurements in hand, we proceeded to determine which bullied children displayed fewer emotional and behavioral problems than would have been expected given their history of being bullied. We then linked this assessment to our hypothesized family-resilience factors. We found that, as anticipated, bullied children had fewer problems than would otherwise have been expected, given the severity and chronicity of bullying they personally experienced, when mothers proved to be warm, sibling relationships were close and supportive, and the family atmosphere was positive (Figure 10.3). In fact, this evidence that such family processes could promote resilience in the face of bullying remained even when we took into account the child's IQ and adjustment problems at age five and the degree of family socioeconomic disadvantage.

Importantly, each of the three family factors we considered uniquely contributed to children's resilience in the face of adversity. This means that the more a mother was rated as warm, the more siblings were rated as caring and considerate, *and* the more positive the home environment, the fewer problems bullied children had. In sum, bullied children who had highly supportive families had fewer emotional and behavioral problems than children

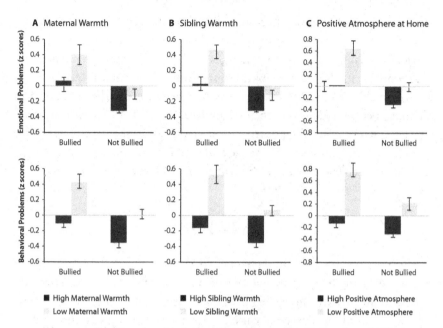

FIGURE 10.3. Emotional and behavioral problems of bullied and nonbullied children as a function of high and low maternal warmth (panel A), sibling warmth (panel B), and positive atmosphere in the home (panel C), showing that problems of bullied children were reduced when family support was high.

Reformatted from Bowes, L, Maughan, B., Caspi, A., Moffitt, T.E., & Arseneault, L. (2010). Families promote emotional and behavioural resilience to bullying: Evidence of an environmental effect. *Journal of Child Psychology and Psychiatry, 51,* 809–817, figure 1. © 2010 The Authors.

who experienced the same harsh treatment from their peers but were growing up in less supportive families.

Considered in their entirety, the results of both our efforts to better understand individual differences in self-harm and adjustment problems in the face of bullying—that is, who is more and who is less adversely affected—underscore the importance of the family. In so doing, our findings highlight the importance of including families in school-based intervention programs aimed at reducing difficulties experienced by bullied children. In addition, they call attention to targets of intervention—specifically, the organization of the home and the supportiveness of family relationships. They can even be read to suggest that if resources are limited when it comes to serving bullied children, those with supportive families should be triaged, allowing their families to provide them with the support necessary to cope with the stress of bullying. In contrast, those bullied children whose families are less supportive, have maltreated the bullied child, have histories of suicidal behavior in their family lineages, and/or are suffering from mental health problems should perhaps go to the front of the clinical-service line. It is these children who are most at risk of developing poorly—even to the extent of being dangerous to themselves. It is the families of these children, however, that will no doubt prove most challenging when it comes to effecting the kind of household change that could reduce the chances of their bullied children succumbing to bullying's probabilistic consequences.

CONCLUSION

It is imaginable that after all these pages devoted to our developmental adventure studying bullying that some might conclude that all we discovered is what is already well appreciated on the basis of common sense. To some extent, we would not disagree with this appraisal. Having said that, however, it is important to point out that common sense can be wrong. Let's consider several such possibilities.

Even though it may not be surprising that bullying is bad for children's well-being, the results of our inquiry could have been different. After all, many older adults of previous generations disparage today's worries about bullying, scoffing at the idea that it is harmful, especially in the long term, while claiming that it is a normal part of childhood. In particular, some whose common sense differs from that expressed in the previous paragraph might have contended that it is not bullying per se that is the problem but rather other factors associated with bullying. In other words, causal influence is being misattributed to bullying when it belongs elsewhere. In fact, it was because of this very real—and commonsensical—possibility that we considered multiple alternative explanations of the bullying effects we initially detected. Recall, for example, that even though being maltreated predicted bullying and problematic functioning—and thus could have been the real cause of bullied children's problems—we found this was not the case. That is, even when this most-reasonable alternative explanation of bullying effects was taken into account, bullying still predicted poor functioning—at age twelve (emotional and behavior problems, self-harm) and age eighteen (overweight).

The same applies to the effects of children's own abilities and problems that preceded the experience of primary-school bullying. Common sense might lead to the view that it is not bullying per se that contributes to children's difficulties at age twelve or being overweight at age eighteen, because problems with emotions, behavior, and weight precede bullying, contribute to bullying, and thus are actually responsible for associations detected between bullying and the negative developmental outcomes under consideration. Thus, bullying is not the cause of children's difficulties. But this, too, did not prove to be the case. The effects of bullying remained when birth weight was taken into account and when the effects of age-five IQ, psychological difficulties, and even weight were discounted. The point is that only by carefully investigating a hypothesis, which means entertaining and evaluating alternative explanations, about the effects of bullying can competing versions of common sense be evaluated.

The same, of course, goes for our research on resilience in the face of bullying. It could have been the case that children's problematic behavior at age five contributed to or evoked problematic family relationships so that once these were taken into account, supportive families would not have proven to be a source of resilience to the bullied child. But this, too, is not what we found when we turned our developmental curiosity to the subject of bullying. Having the good fortune of growing up in a caring, organized home after having the misfortune of being bullied did reduce the untoward effects of bullying, even with age-five emotional and behavioral problems taken into account. So here is another case where a commonsensical notion has been proven wrong, something that could only have been determined by undertaking the empirical investigation that we did.

Ultimately, the take-home message of our work is twofold. First, bullying has short- and longer-term adverse effects that cannot be entirely accounted for by multiple alternative—and reasonable—explanations. Second, a supportive family, in particular, functions as a protective or resilience-promoting influence in the face of bullying. Thus, even though it is better not to be bullied, if bullying does occur, it is better for it to occasion in the context of an emotionally supportive and well-functioning family. What is especially damaging is the "dual-risk" condition of being bullied by peers *and* growing up in an unsupportive family environment. These (commonsensical?) observations underscore both the importance of preventing bullying in the first place and highlighting at least some targets of intervention to reduce its untoward consequences. They also once again make clear the probabilistic nature of development. Even if bullying increases the risk of adverse developmental outcomes, this risk can be mitigated, so it is not inevitable that it will be realized. Finally, the results of our investigation of resilience underscore an important point regarding the multiple determinants of child well-being: it is a mistake to pit, as some have, the influence of the family, including parenting, against the influence of peers. Both, it turns out, matter.

11

Early and Persistent Cannabis Use

You've come a long way, baby" was the tag line to a 1970s cigarette advertising campaign specifically designed to attract modern, liberated women to the coolness of smoking a new cigarette specifically designed for them. Substituting marijuana—the most widely used illicit drug in the world—for "baby" nicely captures what we have witnessed in our own lifetimes when it comes to how cannabis is regarded. Even in the final decades of the past century, and certainly before then, pot was not just a mind-altering drug but also one that was illegal throughout the United States—and most of the rest of the world. It was also a drug whose harm was routinely heralded, perhaps nowhere more so than in the classic 1936 movie *Reefer Madness,* which claimed that smoking marijuana would make you crazy, ruin your life, and even lead to suicide. Today, however, the sale and use of marijuana is not just legal with a doctor's prescription in many states in the United States but totally legal for adults for recreational purposes in places such as Colorado, Washington, Oregon, and California, as well as Uruguay and The Netherlands. Thus, the title of this chapter could be "You've Come a Long Way, Mary Jane." ("Mary Jane," for those who do not know, was a mid- and late-twentieth-century synonym for marijuana.)

Although many have disregarded scare stories about its dangerous effects, the question does arise as to whether this mind-altering substance affects mental health and psychological functioning more generally, to say nothing of functioning in the world of employment and family life. That is certainly the case with alcohol, cocaine, and many other chemicals consumed for recreational purposes. Unfortunately, this has been a difficult issue to address, principally because the United States and other governments long restricted researchers from systematically investigating the effects of marijuana. It seemed more appropriate to claim that cannabis was bad for you than to find out whether this was the case or indeed whether it might actually have some medical benefits, which today are routinely being championed. Fortunately, this situation has recently changed in the United States, so the coming decades should see an outpouring of new research on how marijuana affects human health and development.

When we launched our developmental adventure studying effects of cannabis use as part of the Dunedin Study, there was some evidence of adverse effects on mental health. Indeed, worldwide evidence indicated that cannabis use posed a modest risk for the emergence of clinically significant mental disorders such as schizophrenia. In fact, when we initiated our research on the effects of marijuana, one large study of an entire Swedish cohort revealed that heavy cannabis use at age 18 increased the risk of schizophrenia later in life by 600 percent! Central to a diagnosis of schizophrenia are symptoms of psychosis. Psychosis occurs when thoughts and emotions are so impaired that an individual loses contact with reality. This can include delusions or seeing, hearing, and believing things that are simply not real. Hallucinations are symptoms of psychosis.

As developmental scholars, we could not help but wonder whether it mattered *when* individuals began to smoke cannabis. That was the first question we addressed in our initial research on the subject. In fact, we have situated this chapter in the part of the book dealing with family and extrafamilial influences on development because it is typically with peers in adolescence that most people try marijuana for the first time, with some smoking it thereafter on a regular basis. Data from the Dunedin Study revealed, consistent with prior work, that cannabis use in adolescence increased the likelihood of experiencing symptoms of schizophrenia in young adulthood, at age twenty-six, but our first investigation also added three new pieces of evidence relative to what was already known.

The first concerned the previously untested possibility that psychosis occurred *before* adolescents even tried marijuana for the first time. If psychotic symptoms *preceded* the onset of marijuana use, then prior research, including our own, linking marijuana use with symptoms of schizophrenia could reflect "reverse causation"—psychosis leading to cannabis use, perhaps for self-medicating purposes, rather than marijuana use leading to psychosis. Only prospective research like that undertaken in the Dunedin Study is positioned to disentangle the "temporal ordering" of factors thought to be associated with each other—that is, illuminate which came first, cannabis use or psychotic symptoms. This is because we had repeatedly administered standard psychiatric interviews to study members, so we were positioned to determine the temporal ordering of psychotic symptoms and marijuana use. Being able to show that the would-be cause, cannabis use, actually preceded the would-be consequence, psychotic symptoms, is critical when seeking to evaluate effects of any drug—or many other experiences. So, our first contribution to understanding effects of cannabis use was to discover that reverse causation did not account for links between smoking marijuana and mental health difficulties. Those study members who smoked marijuana with their peers as teenagers were *not* more likely than those who did not to have symptoms of schizophrenia *before* they began smoking marijuana.

Our second important finding was developmentally significant, as it called attention to the timing of cannabis use: smoking marijuana by age fifteen conferred a greater risk of schizophrenia-related outcomes than did onset of use after age seventeen. This result suggested to us that it may have been something about using cannabis at a time when the brain is still developing that was responsible for its problematic effects. At the time we carried out this work, neuroscience had not yet made clear what is now well appreciated: the brain, especially the prefrontal cortex, which is centrally important to planning and the regulation of impulsive behavior, continues to develop during adolescence and, in fact, into the twenties.

Our third and final discovery concerned the specificity of the cannabis-use effect with respect to mental health: young adolescents who smoked marijuana were more likely than others who did not smoke cannabis at a young age to experience psychotic symptoms—even when they were not under the influence of cannabis. They were not, however, at greater risk of becoming depressed. Again, this suggested something distinctive going on in the brain.

Before sharing more of what we discovered about the effects of cannabis—now that we have documented at least one untoward effect—we need to make something crystal clear. Our research was never designed to reveal negative effects of marijuana use or prove it was bad for health, wealth, or happiness. Nor was it designed to disprove any claims about the dangers of smoking cannabis. This is because, as with so much of our health-related work, we approached the issue of effects of cannabis as public-health-oriented developmental scientists interested in whether and how the consumption of this substance affects physical, psychological, and behavioral development. As empiricists, we always let the evidentiary chips fall where they may, reporting our findings honestly and openly, irrespective of whether our findings could or would be used by those who advocate for or against the use and legalization of cannabis. Recall what we said in Chapter 8, on day care: think of us as the weatherman stipulating what the weather forecast is based on careful analysis of relevant data. If we say it will rain, it is not because we are against sunshine; and if we say it will be sunny, it is not because we are against rain. We are simply sharing what the data indicate, pure and simple.

BEYOND MENTAL HEALTH AND ADOLESCENCE

As individuals participating in the Dunedin Study aged, we wondered whether the adverse effects of persistent cannabis use might affect development beyond adolescence and, more generally, not just in terms of their mental health. This led us to study, in subsequent stages of our developmental adventure, not just adolescent-onset cannabis use but *persistent* cannabis use in adulthood. Rather than focusing on psychosis, we turned our attention to change—or, more specifically, decline—in neuropsychological functioning from age thirteen to age thirty-eight. Neuropsychological functioning refers, among other things, to cognitive capabilities known to be associated with brain processes. So, while our measurements were not of the brain directly, as would be the case in brain imaging research (just completed in 2019—but not yet analyzed—at age forty-five in the Dunedin Study), they were of psychological capabilities that are the result of brain processes. Thus, our measures of change in neuropsychological functioning were based on age-thirteen and age-thirty-eight assessments of intelligence and memory. Additionally, we assessed visual information processing, auditory verbal learning, information-processing speed, perceptual reasoning, and verbal comprehension, all measured when study members were thirty-eight years of age.

We might point out that we had great confidence in what our neuropsychological measurements reflected so far as brain functioning goes because our resident neuropsychologist, Terrie Moffitt, had proven to be an excellent brain scientist when her aging father was showing a number of frustrating and disturbing changes in his vision, slowly going blind. Although her father's rural and aging physician concluded that there was nothing special going on, just normal aging, his daughter was not convinced. Indeed, given the collection of symptoms, she suspected that her dad had a tumor in a specific part of his brain. Sure enough, when she insisted he have his brain scanned at the Duke University Medical Center, the very tumor she hypothesized would be there was pressing against the optic nerve. After a surprisingly simple operation—going into the brain through the nasal cavity—it was gone!

Our measurement of persistent cannabis use, our predictor variable, drew on interviews conducted when study members were eighteen, twenty-one, twenty-six, thirty-two, and thirty-eight years of age. Persistent cannabis use was defined as the total number of measurement occasions—out of the five just listed—on which the individual met formal psychiatric criteria for cannabis dependence. To meet such criteria, a study member had to show a maladaptive pattern of marijuana use leading to clinically significant impairment in everyday life or distress, as manifested by multiple conditions within the same three-month period. These included things such as a need for markedly increased amounts of cannabis to achieve the desired effect (that is, tolerance for getting high); a discomforting withdrawal response when not smoking marijuana (that is, symptoms of withdrawal); unsuccessful efforts to cut down or control cannabis use; and abandonment or reduction of important social, occupational, or recreational activities because of marijuana use (for example, hanging out with nonusing friends, not going on job interviews). With criteria like these in mind, study members were scored in terms of the number of interview occasions on which they were diagnosed as cannabis dependent. This could range from zero to five.

What did we find? First, more persistent cannabis dependence was associated with a greater *decline* in IQ across the twenty-five-year study period from age thirteen to age thirty-eight. Study members who never used cannabis experienced a small increase—of just under one point, on average—in IQ over this period. But those who proved to be cannabis dependent on one, two, and three or more measurement occasions experienced IQ declines of, respectively, about one and a half points, about two and a half points, and almost six points on average. Thus, we detected a dose-response relationship, just as we reported in other chapters in this book addressing effects of other developmental experiences and environmental exposures: as the degree of exposure, in this case cannabis dependence, increased, so did the magnitude of its effect, in this case decline in IQ. While a decline of more than five points may not seem like a lot, it is not necessarily without consequence for the capabilities of the individual, perhaps especially when agemates are showing less or no decline or even a small increase. Moreover, we had asked about problems with memory and attention in a questionnaire mailed to informants who knew each study member well, and these data showed that cannabis users' cognitive problems were noticeable to other people in the users' everyday lives.

Once more, we sought to gain a deeper understanding of our initial findings by further probing the data we had collected on study members. Perhaps our result chronicling decline in intelligence was caused by the simple effect of persistent cannabis users obtaining less education, whether as a result of their marijuana smoking or for some other reason. Given this real possibility, as opposed to some more direct neurobiological effect of cannabis use on cognition, we felt compelled to check out this plausible alternative explanation of our results. As things turned out, it did not prove to be the case that the effect of persistent cannabis use on change in IQ over time resulted from persistent users having received fewer years of education. This actually surprised us, as it certainly seemed possible given the potential for cannabis to undermine achievement motivation and reduce educational ambition. Note that we are not saying here that persistent cannabis use did not affect achievement motivation or educational ambition, only that this was not the (only) reason that, or mechanism by which, cannabis use came to be associated with a decline in measured intelligence across the twenty-five-year period we were studying.

Now that we knew that persistent cannabis use did not result in declines in intelligence exclusively because persistent users had more limited educational attainment, we turned our attention to our neuropsychological assessments. We discovered, perhaps not surprisingly, that the same general dose-response pattern emerged when our targets of inquiry were specific cognitive abilities. This was so even after we took into account—that is, statistically controlled for—study members' IQ at age thirteen. This was necessary to ensure that our findings were not just an artifact of teens with lower IQs performing more poorly at age thirty-eight. With the effects of age-thirteen IQ accounted for, the evidence indicated that more persistent cannabis use undermined the ability—in midlife—to hold ideas in the mind and operate on them, known as working memory; the speed at which information is processed when solving problems; and the ability to understand spoken and written language. These, of course, are important real-life abilities that affect many aspects of daily living, whether it is talking on the phone, following a recipe, or playing a computer game.

Once more, we sought to challenge the findings to make sure that they were not a result of factors other than persistent cannabis use, those "third" or confounding variables that can always plague interpretation of the results of observational research like our own. This led us to evaluate whether the adverse effects of persistent cannabis use on neuropsychological functioning were simply a result of these persistent users getting stoned either in the twenty-four hours or in the week before we tested them when they came into the Dunedin Study project office at age thirty-eight. Thus, the question became, could our results be a simple artifact of cannabis-using study members being, more or less, "hung over"? As it turned out, getting stoned very recently did not account for our findings, thereby implying that we were detecting *enduring* effects of persistent cannabis use and not just transient or short-term effects of recent marijuana consumption. Nor was it the case that tobacco, hard-drug, or alcohol dependence or schizophrenia were responsible for the findings that emerged. When these factors were taken into account, the adverse effects of marijuana on neuropsychological functioning in midlife remained.

Given what we found in our prior studies of the effects of cannabis use—that the greatest risk of psychosis occurred when smoking marijuana occurred before age 15—we had to wonder again about the age at which study members started consuming cannabis. Did it matter whether persistent users began in adolescence or later with respect to the negative effects already highlighted? The answer to this question proved to be "yes." Results indicated that those study members who initiated cannabis use in adulthood did not suffer the effects of persistent cannabis use. In other words, the findings we have been considering regarding the neuropsychological effects of persistent cannabis use were "driven" by the subset of persistent cannabis users whose cannabis use began in adolescence. Once again, the evidence seemed to implicate a period of developmental vulnerability having something to do with the still-developing brain.

PERSISTENT CANNABIS USE AND
REAL-LIFE FUNCTIONING

It is one thing for declines in or limitations of neuropsychological functioning to show up in formal tests that psychologists administer under carefully controlled testing conditions and another to know whether effects of persistent cannabis use extend to the real world and everyday life. As we reflected on the results just summarized, it occurred to us that if persistent cannabis use contributed to poorer neurological functioning, such effects might also undermine an adult's economic and social success. This is the issue we turned to in our third study of the long-term effects of persistent marijuana use, a topic we will return to in Chapter 13, addressing the genetics of life success.

In our next marijuana-related investigation, also involving persistent cannabis use through age thirty-eight, we focused on economic and social problems evident in midlife. We first considered social mobility—by comparing the occupational status of study members at age thirty-eight with that of their parents. If parents had more prestigious occupations than the study member did—a father who is a doctor compared to a daughter who is a clerical assistant, or a mother who is an accountant compared to a son who is an auto mechanic—that would qualify as downward social mobility. The reverse would reflect upward mobility.

The next thing we examined was financial difficulties. During interviews with study members at age thirty-eight, we gathered information about their total net worth, any troubles with debt, and difficulties paying basic expenses. This information was supplemented by information on receipt of welfare benefits by searching official administrative records and on credit worthiness by searching credit ratings. Finally, to get at social functioning, we queried study members about problems in the workplace and in their intimate-partner relationships. With regard to the workplace, we gathered information on whether the study member engaged in behaviors such as lying to get a job, quitting without giving notice, having conflicts with co-workers, taking longer breaks than permitted, intentionally working more slowly than was appropriate, stealing money at work, and reporting working more days and hours than was actually the case. With regard to intimate-partner relationships, we queried study members about the general quality of their relationships—by asking them about emotional intimacy and trust, occurrence of physical abuse, and whether they or their partner engaged in controlling behavior, such as preventing the partner from working, studying, or seeing family members, as well as stalking the partner.

Given what emerged from the prior investigation of effects of persistent cannabis use on neuropsychological functioning, it seems only logical that economic and social problems would prove to be associated with this same life experience, which they did: the more persistent the study member's cannabis use across the years, the greater the likelihood that the study member experienced downward socioeconomic mobility, financial difficulties, problems in the workplace, and conflicted intimate-partner relationships at midlife. Again, the results revealed a dose-response relationship linking persistence of cannabis use with degree of problematic functioning (that is, the more use, the greater the effect).

Guess what we did next? Challenge our findings, of course! Perhaps these adverse effects of persistent cannabis use only appeared to be a result of this experience and were actually a function of other factors—such as adverse social and economic conditions in childhood, suffering from some psychopathology in childhood, being raised by a single parent, being addicted to alcohol, or, perhaps most notably, having started smoking cannabis in adolescence. Additional results revealed that none of these alternative explanatory factors could account for the results documenting yet more negative effects of persistent marijuana use from age eighteen to age thirty-eight. Perhaps most notable, even surprising, was that persistent smoking of cannabis proved to be related to poor economic and social functioning in midlife even when it began not in adolescence but later in development. These results about real-world functioning, then, differed somewhat from those we discerned when measuring neuropsychological functioning using psychometric tests administered at our research office. Recall that with regard to that set of developmental outcomes, smoking cannabis in adolescence increased the risk of poor functioning.

What might be even more surprising was that persistent cannabis use turned out to be as strongly associated with economic and social problems as alcohol dependence was, sometimes even more so. While marijuana dependence proved to be a better predictor of financial difficulties than dependency on alcohol was, the two types of dependence were associated to the same degree with downward social mobility, antisocial behavior in the workplace, and relationship conflict. In considering these findings, it is important to appreciate that many more individuals in the Dunedin Study—and around the world—suffer from alcohol dependence than from cannabis dependence. This means that the population burden posed by alcohol dependence is in all likelihood greater for the society than that posed by cannabis dependence. It does not seem strange to ask, as a result, why there have been so many more restrictions on marijuana use than on alcohol consumption.

WHAT ABOUT PHYSICAL HEALTH?

Having discovered adverse effects of early and persistent cannabis use on multiple aspects of psychological and behavioral functioning, for the final stage of our adventure studying cannabis, we turned attention toward physical health. In fact, we sought to contrast in this work the effects of smoking cannabis and those of smoking tobacco. Once again, we relied on our measurements of frequency of cannabis use and marijuana dependence at ages eighteen, twenty-one, twenty-six, thirty-two, and thirty-eight, with tobacco use assessed at these same ages. With regard to physical health, we relied on laboratory evaluations of periodontal health, lung function, system inflammation, and metabolic health, as well as self-reported physical health at ages twenty-six and thirty-eight years.

Before sharing these young-adult-to-midlife findings, we should highlight several previous health-related findings from earlier work. First, measurements obtained at ages eighteen and twenty-six, while first appearing to indicate adverse effects of marijuana smoking on lung function, ultimately revealed that this resulted from tobacco smoking and being overweight, confounding "third" variables. Of course, we would not have discovered this had it not been our practice to consider alternative explanatory factors. Second, and perhaps surprisingly, evidence obtained at age thirty-two actually indicated that those who smoked marijuana had *greater* lung capacity than nonusers! Why might that be the case? We suspect it could result from the practice of "holding in" marijuana smoke in order to secure more of its psychotropic properties.

Going forward, it will be interesting to determine whether the same proves true of vaping, which has been linked to serious lung problems, sometimes leading to death, and edibles, as the former means of using cannabis doesn't typically involve as much inhaling and the latter doesn't require any at all. If under these conditions future work fails to chronicle a link between cannabis use and greater lung capacity, that would provide support for our inference as to why such a relation emerged in the Dunedin Study.

With this background, let's turn to our health-related findings at age thirty-eight. Most notably and in contrast to the effects of tobacco, even persistent cannabis dependence proved to be all but unrelated to physical health. In fact, of our many health assessments, only periodontal health proved to be related to cannabis use in a negative manner. Specifically, repeated dental exams across the years revealed that marijuana smoking was associated with poorer periodontal health at age thirty-eight years and greater decline in periodontal health from age twenty-six to age thirty-eight. This was true even after controlling for the "pack years" of smoking tobacco—that is, dosage of tobacco use over the twelve-year period of study. We should note, however, that even though we did not detect evidence of damaging effects of cannabis use on lung function at midlife, many frequent cannabis users did acknowledge symptoms of bronchitis—symptoms that improved upon desisting from smoking marijuana.

Even though cannabis use proved generally unrelated to physical health, this was by no means the case with respect to tobacco use. It proved to be associated with poor lung function, increased systemic inflammation, and poor metabolic health at age thirty-eight, as well as greater decline in physical health from ages twenty-six to twenty-eight years. Even though tobacco and cannabis consumption both involve smoking, or at least did when the Dunedin Study members were growing up, it should be clear that the two types of smoking pose strikingly different risks for physical health. In drawing this conclusion, we do not mean to minimize the adverse effects of cannabis smoking on periodontal health or the apparent effects of quitting on symptoms of bronchitis, only to make clear that these two substances that are smoked should not be equated when thinking about their long-term effects on physical health. Indeed, once again we can wonder why smoking marijuana has been considered unacceptable—and illegal—for so long while smoking tobacco has been tolerated.

GENERAL CONCLUSION

Perhaps the first thing to be said regarding what we discovered during our developmental adventure studying cannabis as part of our effort to illuminate effects of peer-initiated marijuana use in the Dunedin Study is something we have not explicitly stipulated to this point: in all our research on this subject, we have never found evidence that occasional recreational cannabis use by adults is harmful. Having said that, whatever the pleasures of such use, our long-term investigation of its effects does indicate that its potentially problematic consequences should not be treated glibly in the case of users who are adolescents or who used it on a near-daily basis for many years. It is especially important to appreciate that whereas the first findings we shared indicated that it was individuals who initiated cannabis use in adolescence were the ones whose mental health and neuropsychological functioning were compromised, our subsequent research revealed far more general effects: adverse consequences of persistent cannabis use extended to real-world economic and social functioning of virtually all persistent users, irrespective of whether they started smoking cannabis in adolescence. At the same time, however, we could detect almost no adverse effects of even persistent cannabis use on diverse aspects of physical health—with the exception of periodontal health.

Now some might argue that the real-life, untoward effects we chronicled could just be an indirect consequence of those smoking marijuana getting caught up in the legal system, being arrested for using an illegal substance. In other words, it is not cannabis smoking, even persistent smoking, that matters but rather getting entangled with the courts for doing so. In line with this argument, one well-known and one-time cannabis user, President Barack Obama, once asserted that "cannabis doesn't cause harm; it's getting a criminal record for cannabis that causes all the harm." Well, we actually evaluated this claim, Mr. President, and found it wanting. When we eliminated from our analysis of the real-world consequences of persistent cannabis use all study members who had drug convictions, the results remained unchanged. Thus, even cannabis users who had avoided coming to the attention of the police showed downward social mobility and poor financial and family-life outcomes in middle age.

What perhaps makes these and other cannabis-related results particularly disconcerting is that the cannabis available today is much more potent in terms of THC content—the psychoactive component responsible for marijuana's "high"—than was the case when our thirty-eight-year-old study members were adolescents and even young adults. As we said earlier, you've come a long way, Mary Jane, and apparently not necessarily for the good. Although this new reality may have limited consequences for physical health, it seems likely that it would have implications for mental health, neuropsychological functioning, and work and family life.

In light of this observation, the question must be entertained as to whether those who turn fifteen or thirty-eight in the twenty-first century and have smoked much more potent marijuana early in life or persistently in adulthood will be affected in the same way as such individuals were a generation or more ago. Given what the Dunedin Study findings indicate—and as we have already implied—we suspect not. And, given what we now know that we did not in the 1970s and 1980s about how the brain, especially the prefrontal cortex, continues to develop into the third decade of life, there is reason to believe that our findings likely underestimate adverse effects of early and persistent cannabis use in the twenty-first century.

We should point out before closing this chapter that there remain strong forces pushing against the message that our results deliver—that notable psychological and social problems are associated with cannabis use, at least persistent use, whether just for those who start using cannabis in adolescence or for those who continue their heavy use into midlife. Indeed, we know firsthand about the proclivity of some to "shoot the messenger" who reports findings that others simply find hard to embrace. This is because we actually found it challenging to get the results of our third study on real-life outcomes published. Some reviewers of our work that we submitted to scholarly journals appeared to reject our scientific report not so much as a result of fundamental flaws in our methods and measures but because they were concerned about the message our science might be sending and even what our motives were.

Notably, the same thing occurred when we initially tried to get our data on physical health published. Now the issue was not that we were unfairly producing scientific evidence against cannabis use, perhaps exaggerating its negative effects for personal reasons, but doing just the opposite! "You can't say that marijuana is not bad for health, as this will lead more people to use it" was the sentiment we encountered. In the case of research on the effects of marijuana, it looks like scientists are doomed to be damned if they do and damned if they don't find negative effects. We certainly have been vilified (and celebrated) by both anti-cannabis and pro-cannabis advocacy groups.

We see serious problems with this approach to evaluating research, as we made clear in Chapter 8, which focused on our day-care adventure. As scientists, we do not regard it as our job to make people feel better or worse by what well-designed empirical inquiry and fairly derived results reveal. Rather, our job is to be open minded, prepared to let the scientific chips fall where they may. Just as importantly, we do not think those who re- port unpopular findings should be castigated for doing so, as is sometimes the case. Remember: if the weatherman says it is going to rain tomorrow, it is not because he is against sunshine! The same appreciation needs to be applied when it comes to any scientific finding that emerges from high- quality research. We need to distinguish between what many of us want or would like to believe—and even hope emerges from sound scientific inquiry—and what the dispassionately collected and evaluated data actu- ally reveal.

In conclusion, let us make one important policy-related point: Now that cannabis is legal or quasilegal in so many places, there is a special need to ensure that adolescents find it extremely difficult to obtain—and that everyone be alerted to its negative consequences for social and economic success when persistently used from adolescence through midlife. It seems possible that the legalization of marijuana might actually facilitate this goal. After all, two of the reasons for legalization are to undermine criminal en- terprises that sell marijuana to young people and to raise funds for treating those who seem to be unable to stop using cannabis on their own. Let's hope legalization proves successful in both regards.

PART V

GENETICS

12

Is Smoking in Our Genes?

Despite the fact that the smoking of cigarettes occurs much less frequently in the United States and in much of the Western world these days than it once did, it remains a problem in many places, and perhaps no place more so than in China. Cigarette smoking is a costly and prevalent public health problem. *The Economist* magazine reported in 2017 that the estimated worldwide annual cost of smoking as a result of ill health and lost productivity was $1.4 trillion, with almost 40 percent of this expense falling on developing countries, those least able to afford it. Indeed, the US Centers for Disease Control and Prevention attributed more than four hundred thousand American deaths and $95 billion in lost productivity to tobacco smoking at the turn of the twenty-first century.

So why do people in a highly educated, advanced, technological society such as the United States continue to smoke cigarettes, especially when in many places they now must stand outside in the freezing cold or in the brutal heat of summer to do so? For quite some time, the evidence has been incontrovertible that smoking is bad for your health, as already noted with respect to mortality risks, by increasing the likelihood of lung cancer and cardiovascular disease. Indeed, the evidence was sufficiently persuasive some forty years ago that it stimulated the father of one of the authors to give up his thirty-year, pack-a-day habit of smoking unfiltered Camel cigarettes. It's hard to imagine he would have lived ninety years—especially while overweight—had he not done so.

Health concerns also played a role in Terrie Moffitt's giving up her own pack-a-day habit at age twenty-six after starting to smoke at age seventeen—just like many other teens did in rural North Carolina, where tobacco was the cash crop and cigarettes were inexpensive. In fact, it was when Terrie's grandfather—who had smoked most of his life—died of lung cancer that she realized that whatever the short-term benefits of smoking, including seeming "cool," the long-term costs were just too great. Richie Poulton also spent (too) many years smoking what used to be called "death sticks," but he eventually smartened up, too—though only after his wife told him "no kids until you do." Of the four authors, only Avshalom Caspi continues to smoke cigarettes, though he is what is referred to as a "chipper," someone who seems not to be addicted, able to enjoy an occasional cigarette, including days without any cigarettes, while finding it easy to quit periodically.

These personal experiences led us on our developmental adventure seeking to better understand why we still find people smoking cigarettes. It would seem indisputable that developmental and environmental factors make a difference. Most people who end up addicted to nicotine start smoking in adolescence, often because of peer pressure. In too many cases, this is because they are seeking social acceptance, to enhance their reputation, to be "grown up," and/or, like the authors during their teenage years, to be "cool." Perhaps, though, the best evidence that environmental factors matter comes from research linking the increased price of cigarettes with decreased smoking, especially among the young. But genetics, as we will see in this first chapter addressing this topic, matters, too, at least in terms of who moves quickly from trying cigarettes to becoming hooked on them—becoming addicted to nicotine.

Hardly a day goes by without a report in the popular press or on social media announcing that some aspect of human functioning has been found to be influenced by a person's genes. The subject of a media story based on a scientific report may be a mental disturbance such as schizophrenia or autism, a psychological phenomenon such as loneliness, or a behavioral issue such as risk taking. In many respects, this should be expected, as it appears that no matter where genetically oriented investigators point their scientific telescope, they find evidence of the role of genes in contributing to almost any phenotype. Phenotype refers to any observable characteristic of an individual. Your height, sexual preference, and whether you smoke are all phenotypes. Given widespread evidence that genetic makeup contributes to almost every phenotypic characteristic, what should really be newsworthy is when a phenotype is identified that does not show evidence of genetic influence!

That a phenotype is at least partly genetic can be and often is misunderstood. One such misunderstanding is that DNA is destiny: if you have genes for X, then you will develop X; end of story. There are multiple reasons why that need not be the case, however. Most importantly, there is a long chain of biological (and sometimes psychological and behavioral) events linking genotype with phenotype. All that genes do (which is not intended to make light of their importance) is code for or create proteins, and this is only the beginning of the creation of curly hair, math talent, or sexual preference. Because so much transpires as genetic influence travels along this path, it is often the case that a genetic possibility does not get realized. Here we are dealing with probabilism again, rather than determinism. And even when there is statistical evidence of associations between genotype and phenotype, thereby implicating genetics, it is well appreciated by scientists that exactly how the former comes to be related to the latter still remains very much a mystery. This does not mean that it is unknowable or that no steps in the process have been illuminated, only that we do not yet have a complete map of the complex pathways by which a genotype develops into a phenotype, especially in an organism as complex as the human.

This is especially true with respect to the very complex phenotypes that are the subject of this book, including temperament, self-control, ADHD, pubertal timing, bullying, marijuana use, and tobacco smoking. This is not unusual in science. Long before it was understood exactly how smoking affected health—that is, the biological mechanism(s)—evidence existed that smoking was statistically related to a variety of diseases. One might even wonder why it would even make sense to delve deeply into the biological or psychological and behavioral processes linking any predictor, such as genes, with any supposed outcome, such as smoking, before it is established that the predictor actually is empirically related to the outcome. Note that throughout our work discussed in this book, we routinely first determined whether a predictor of interest actually succeeded in forecasting an outcome of interest before seeking to illuminate the development processes responsible for the predictor-outcome association under investigation. After all, why even consider evaluating whether, as hypothesized, variable B serves as the mechanism linking variable A with C if, on initial analysis, it turns out that variable A does not even predict variable C.

In referring to the complex chain of events linking genotype to pheno-type, we would err if we only conveyed a sense that the chain is comprised of biological processes going on inside the body or in the mind. This is because environmental exposures and experiences can also serve as critical links in the complex chain of influence that turns a genotype into a pheno-type. Recall in this regard two developmental processes we introduced early in this book when discussing the developmental legacy of early tempera-ment in Chapter 2, "niche picking" and "evocative effects." Central to the niche-picking idea is an appreciation that individuals are often producers of their own development—that is, organisms with agency. They are not just passive recipients of their developmental experiences or environmental exposures but are also their architects and engineers, even if unwittingly.

The genetics of intelligence and divorce represent examples of such pro-cesses. In the niche-picking case, genetics and intelligence may go together because those with certain genes find reading and learning more interesting, fun, and thus attractive than do others of a different genetic makeup. As a result, they end up more intelligent not simply because it is in their genes but rather because there is something about their genes that inclines them to do things—such as go to the library and be attentive in school—that foster intellectual development. In the case of divorce, it may be that the genes of some individuals contribute to their being poor at judging others and thus they select inappropriate and problematic partners, or their genes may influence their tendency to be argumentative, depressed, or a poor communicator, and it is through such social and emotional processes that the genotype and phenotype come to be linked. The central point here is that if mediational processes linking the genotype and phenotype don't occur for some reason(for example, schooling doesn't exist or divorce is outlawed), then the would-be genetic effects in question could not be fully realized. In such cases, genetics cannot be destiny. Therefore, once more we see how development, in this case dealing with genetic influence, is prob-abilistic, not deterministic.

The other indirect process worth considering again is the evocative one. Now it is less where a person goes—to the library to get more books or to the bar to find a problematic mate—than how others react to a person's behavior and how this feeds back to shape the person's development and functioning. Returning to the topic of intelligence, we can think about the child who, for genetic reasons, has a large appetite for learning. As a result, she is given more extracurricular, afterschool lessons in music, art, languages, or computer technology. Such experiences provide additional cognitive stimulation, which results, ultimately, in more knowledge.

It is also easy to imagine such an evocative process operating in the case of divorce. Consider individuals who, for genetic reasons, may be very sexually motivated, even inclined to seek sexual variety, and end up having multiple extramarital affairs, only to have their spouses initiate divorce proceedings. Again, it is not that divorce is directly a function of one's genetic makeup but rather that psychological and behavioral inclinations that are influenced by one's genotype result in responses from others that contribute to the individual's phenotype, in this case their becoming a divorcee.

Because this notion that genetics need not be destiny is such an important issue and reports of genetic effects are so often misunderstood, let's consider two individuals who are, for genetic reasons, inclined to be intellectually curious. One has parents who respond favorably to that disposition, whereas the other has parents—who may be poor, highly stressed, and/or uneducated—who find the child's behavior, such as asking many questions, irritating and respond harshly to it. In the case of divorce, consider the person who is just as motivated as another to pursue extramarital affairs but lives on a remote farm far away from others and so has no real opportunity to realize such ambitions.

If nothing else, what these examples illustrating how genotypes can require certain contextual conditions to develop into phenotypes make clear is that genes operate in an environmental context. Thus, even evidence that a phenotype is genetically linked (that is, heritable) does not mean that only genetic makeup matters. Just as there appears to be little in human development and behavior that seems to be free of genetic influence, there is little that is entirely immune to environmental influence. Nurture and nature play a role, though the exact degree will likely vary depending on the phenomenon—the phenotype—to be explained. Such nature-nurture interplay will be the primary focus of Chapters 14 and 15.

Before considering how genetic effects are studied by students of human development, as a prelude to discussing our research on the genetics of smoking, there is another important point to be made about the role of context when considering genetic effects: all evidence documenting genetic effects is specific to the population being studied unless proven otherwise. Thus, just because intelligence or divorce is found to be related to genetics in one place and time does not necessarily mean that it would be so at another place or at another time, at least not to the same degree. Even if someone claims, hyperbolically, that "divorce is in our genes"—as a result of evidence that divorce is heritable—that does not mean this is true in every population, everywhere in the world, at every point in human history. After all, how could divorce be genetically shaped in a society that does not allow it? Or how could alcoholism prove heritable in a country in which it is illegal to consume alcohol and alcohol cannot be obtained? There is even some suggestive, if not conclusive, evidence that while intelligence is highly heritable in affluent American communities, it is much less so in economically impoverished ones, perhaps because the conditions do not exist for intelligence to flourish in the latter contexts, thereby constraining the expression of genetic differences. Never forget that nature depends on nurture.

STUDYING GENETIC EFFECTS

When it comes to illuminating the role of genes in shaping human development and functioning, for good (for example, intelligence) or ill (for example, crime), scientists have relied on ever-developing tools for doing so. Indeed, one can distinguish at least two waves of inquiry when it comes to studying psychological and behavioral development, as well as physical health: "quantitative behavioral genetics" and "molecular genetics." The second—and later—"wave" involves the actual measurement of genes. This was one of our most interesting developmental adventures, and it will be the focus of this chapter and Chapters 13–15. Quantitative behavioral genetics, on the other hand, emerged before the technology to measure individual genes even existed. Because this prior method of inquiry provided the foundation on which the later method built, we consider it first.

Behavioral Genetics

Without measuring genes, how could one document genetic effects? There are actually several ways of accomplishing this. To appreciate them, we have to remember some basics of biology and inheritance, most notably that the closer a relative is to an individual biologically, the more genes they share in common. Here we are referring to those genes on which humans vary. Perhaps surprisingly, these make up only a small percentage—about 5 percent—of the entire human genome! Identical twins, such as Jay Belsky and his brother, share 100 percent of those genes on which humans vary, whereas first-degree relatives, such as parent and child and biological siblings (and fraternal twins), share 50 percent of such genes. Second-degree relatives, such as a grandchild and grandparent or a nephew and his uncle, share 25 percent of these genes. First cousins, who are third-degree relatives, share 12.5 percent of the genes on which humans vary. A parent and an adopted child share none of these genes, with the same being true of an adopted child and her sibling who is the biological child of the adoptive parent. Given such foundational understanding, behavior genetics is based on the notion that if a phenotype is heritable, persons who have more of their genes in common will be more similar to each other, and people who are less genetically related will be less similar to one another.

Thus, if a phenotype is heritable, we would expect that identical twins would be more similar on that phenotype than would fraternal twins; that the similarity between the biological parent and biological child would be greater than that of the adoptive parent and adoptive child; that a first-degree relative such as a sibling or parent would be more similar to each other than to a second-degree relative, such as an uncle or aunt; and that first-degree relatives would be more similar to each other than to a third-degree relative such as a first cousin. This basic approach to investigating genetic effects was invented by Sir Francis Galton, Charles Darwin's cousin, in the late 1800s.

As noted at the beginning of this chapter, patterns of similarity based on genetic relatedness have been documented repeatedly in research on almost every possible phenotype one can think of. In other words, genetic influence seems ubiquitous, which again is not to say that differences between people are entirely genetic—nurture matters, too—only that genetic influence is widespread. To be frank, that should be indisputable in the twenty-first century, but so should the claim that genes are not the only source of influence when it comes to most phenomena that are of interest to students of human development and concern health and well-being.

Molecular Genetics

One of the great frustrations of any kind of behavioral-genetic research involving the comparison of groups of people with different degrees of shared genes—identical versus fraternal twins, biological versus adoptive siblings, or first-degree versus second-degree relatives—is that it cannot tell us which particular genes are potentially influential even when evidence of heritability emerges, and there are millions of genetic variants to consider. One ends up with a kind of "black box" understanding: there is something about genetic makeup that matters and accounts for differences in their functioning across individuals, but that is about all we can say.

Toward the end of the twentieth century, a radical change took place in the kind of genetic insight that developmental scholars could achieve because of advances in technology for actually measuring genes. It is important to appreciate that this genotyping technology enabled, among other things, the linking of specific genes with specific psychological and behavioral phenomena in so-called genotype-phenotype research, such as that reported in this chapter and Chapter 13. It is also important to appreciate that molecular-genetic research has gone through a series of phases or waves because of the ever-decreasing cost of measuring genes. Thus, the first wave of genotype-phenotype inquiry focused on single "candidate" genes presumed to influence a particular phenotype based on some understanding of the underlying biology of the phenotype (that is, "biological plausibility").

But as the cost of sequencing, that is measuring, actual genes came down and more and more genes could be sequenced, efforts to link genes with phenotypes focused on multiple genetic variants and thereby the creation of "polygenic risk scores" based on many genes. Exactly which genes should be combined in the formation of such a polygenic score to predict a particular phenotype—smoking in this chapter and educational achievement (and life success) in Chapter 13—was determined by extremely large genome-wide association studies (GWAS). These genetic "discovery" investigations involved thousands or even tens or hundreds of thousands of individuals on whom there was genetic data and information pertaining to a particular phenotype. In a "theory-free" statistical manner not guided by any biological insight, it simply became a question of which of the thousands or even millions of genetic variants were statistically more frequent among cases with the phenotype under investigation (for example, ADHD) compared to controls who lacked the phenotype. What GWAS made clear was that genetic effects are complex; that almost all phenotypes of interest are influenced by very many genes; that each of these many genes has a very small effect; and that, as a result, it made little sense to focus on one gene at a time.

Given the organization of this book, especially in terms of this chapter and Chapters 13–15, focused on genetic effects, we need to make clear that even though in this chapter and Chapter 13 we will be focusing on GWAS-based research and in Chapters 14 and 15 on candidate-gene-based research, this order of presentation is actually the reverse of how genetic research advanced as well as of the sequence in which we conducted our own genetic research. We and others carried out candidate-gene work before GWAS-related work, so why not tell the story of our research using a "historical" frame of reference, discussing what came first before what came later? The answer to this question centers on the fact that the two sets of work considered different empirical questions, and we considered it more important to let conceptual considerations rather than historical ones guide us.

A core difference between our later genetic work, which we discuss first (here and in Chapter 13), and our earlier genetic work (on antisocial behavior and depression which we consider thereafter) concerns the focus of inquiry. Whereas GWAS work addresses *genotype-phenotype associations,* our (and others') candidate-gene work addresses *gene-environment interaction.* The latter differs from the former in that it does not ask simply whether variation in genes predicts variation in some phenotype but rather whether environmental effects (which have been so much a focus of this book to this point) actually vary depending on an individual's genetic makeup. We consider this a more complex issue, so we postpone covering it until somewhat later.

Let us make two more historical points before turning to our primary focus, the genetics of smoking. To date, it has proven extremely difficult to investigate gene-environment interaction using polygenic risk scores based on multiple genes, if only because such efforts demand even larger sample sizes than GWAS-related genotype-phenotype work does. Having said that, we need to acknowledge that the study of the genetics of human development and health has moved beyond a focus on candidate genes. This is because of the surprising discovery, already highlighted, of how small the effects of individual genes, all by themselves, turn out to be.

LINKING SMOKING GENOTYPE WITH PHENOTYPE

As the technology to measure multiple genes and create polygenic risk scores advanced, the Dunedin Study was positioned to ask questions based on the GWAS findings of extremely large investigations—ones with sample sizes that put ours to shame in some respects. Even with one thousand study members, the Dunedin Study was not in a position to carry out GWAS "discovery" research, which involves identifying which genetic variants—out of tens or hundreds of thousands—prove most and least related to a particular phenotype; it was simply far too small for that. Nevertheless, it was ideally positioned to create a polygenic risk score for each study member *based on findings that emerged in large GWAS research* conducted by others in order to examine relations between genetics and human-development phenotypes. That is how we went about investigating the genetics of smoking. With genetic information on study members available, we created a polygenic risk score for each study member based on GWAS "discovery" research that alerted us to the particular genes that could be used to predict the number of cigarettes smoked per day by adults.

But, in investigating the genetics of smoking, we must acknowledge that we were initially limited—mostly by money. Even though GWASs of smoking on which we based our own polygenic scores revealed very many genetic variants were associated with smoking, we had assayed early on in the Dunedin Study only a limited number of genes, only six of which had been linked to smoking in GWAS. This limitation existed because when we began genetic work the cost of assaying genes was so expensive. Thus, our polygenic risk score for smoking was based on only six genetic variants rather than all those that GWAS has since identified. As we will see in Chapter 13, once the price of assaying genes decreased substantially and we were able to assay many more genes of study members, we could create polygenic risk scores based on millions of genetic variants!

Even with a limited "polygenic risk score" pertaining to quantity of cigarettes smoked in a day by adults, we sought to extend discovery research on the genetics of smoking in a number of ways. First, being developmental scholars, we desired to cast the issue of genetics of smoking in developmental perspective. Thus, in our genetics-of-smoking adventure, we sought to determine whether six of the previously identified genetic markers of quantity of smoking *by adults* that comprised our polygenic score collectively predicted smoking *by adolescents.*

This issue is of critical importance for two reasons. First, most smokers develop the habit in adolescence, usually in the context of peer pressure. Second, from the standpoint of public health, intervention to disrupt effects of genetic risk is likely to be most effective early in the development of nicotine dependence rather than after years or even decades of addiction to nicotine. Just as important is that it is not a foregone conclusion that genes associated with a phenotype in adulthood are necessarily related to the same phenotype in adolescence. So genes related to smoking, or any other phenotype, in middle-aged adults are not necessarily (all) the same ones related to the phenotype in adolescence. That sounds hard to believe, but it is true. Thus, it was an open question whether smoking-related genes identified in GWAS of adults would also prove to be related to smoking in our New Zealand adolescents.

The second way in which we extended prior work while adventuring in the world of smoking genetics was to distinguish and investigate different smoking phenotypes, with special concern for the *development* of smoking. Thus, as we will delineate, we moved beyond simply asking whether our six-gene, polygenic smoking score predicted the average number of cigarettes smoked each day by study members in both adolescence and adulthood to consider other indices of smoking. One such phenotype we highlight now, *rapid progression to heavy smoking,* is particularly important, as it is a signal of heightened risk of nicotine dependence in adulthood. What needs to be appreciated at this juncture, perhaps extending the comment made in the previous paragraph about different periods of life, is that just because one set of genes may play a role in shaping one smoking phenotype (for example, started smoking) does not necessarily mean it plays a role in shaping any or all other smoking-related ones (for example, became addicted to nicotine). In the same way that it is an empirical question whether genes related to smoking in adulthood also predict smoking in adolescence, it could not be assumed that our polygenic risk score derived from GWASs of number of cigarettes smoked in a day by adults would predict different smoking phenotypes, even measured in adulthood, to say nothing of in adolescence.

The third way in which we sought to extend research on the genetics of smoking was to evaluate whether our phenotypic measures of smoking in adolescence accounted for already established genetic effects of smoking in adulthood. Consider the possibility, for example, that the genes that play a role in how much one smokes early in a smoker's career might be different from those that play a role in maintaining a one- versus two-pack-a-day habit decades later. Thus, it remained possible that the genes associated with smoking in adolescence and adulthood would not be entirely the same.

Exploring this fundamental development issue, then, was important not just from the perspective of basic science. The truth is that what we discovered during this adventure could be of importance to applied science because it could have ramifications for intervention to prevent or inhibit smoking. This would be the case if smoking phenotypes in adolescence were found to be related to our (adult-GWAS derived) polygenic risk score and accounted for effects of this same polygenic score on smoking in adulthood. This is because that would imply that those very genes already identified in GWAS of *adult* smokers could be used to identify individuals at heightened risk of becoming smokers before they do so—in adolescence or even earlier in life. Indeed, such a discovery might afford targeting teens most at risk for becoming smokers—because of their high polygenic smoking scores—for programs aimed at preventing smoking or reducing it. Of course, this would require that the relation between smoking genes and smoking be strong enough in adolescence to indicate that such targeting could prove efficient and effective.

DO GENES THAT PREDICT SMOKING IN ADULTHOOD PREDICT SMOKING IN ADOLESCENCE?

Because we had followed study members for so long and because we repeatedly asked them detailed questions about their cigarette-smoking (and other risk-taking) behavior over many years as part of the Dunedin Study, we were positioned to create many smoking-related "outcomes" to associate with our six-gene, polygenic risk score. Indeed, we created and distinguished two sets of smoking phenotypes so that we could evaluate how our polygenic score related to smoking in adolescence and again in adulthood when study members were thirty-two and thirty-eight years of age. The smoking-related "outcomes" we focused on in this first stage of our genetics-of-smoking adventure will become evident as we share our results.

The first thing we found was that our polygenic smoking score did *not* distinguish those study members who smoked from those who did not, or even the age when the smokers started smoking. In other words, the six genes we put together based on GWAS research showing that these genes (and others) predicted the number of cigarettes adults smoked per day could not be used to identify study members who did or did not start smoking or those who started at a young or older age, at least not in the Dunedin Study. These results underscore a point made earlier: different genes may influence different aspects of smoking (for example, smoking versus not smoking, speed of becoming addicted, amount of smoking).

These null findings led us to turn our attention exclusively to those individuals who initiated smoking at some point in the hope of illuminating the *development* of their smoking habit. When we did this, we discovered that study members at higher genetic risk of smoking—those with a higher polygenic risk score—were more likely to progress to smoking twenty or more cigarettes per day once they started and progressed to this high level of smoking more rapidly than peers who had also started smoking but had lower polygenic scores. Thus, even though our polygenic score could not predict who would and would not try smoking, it could predict the *development* of smoking addiction.

Among those who had smoked even a single cigarette, just under 20 percent "converted" to smoking every day—becoming "daily" smokers—by age fifteen, and these study members who experienced such "early conversion" had higher polygenic scores than those who took more time before smoking even one cigarette per day. Another 10 percent of smokers progressed to smoking twenty cigarettes per day by age eighteen, reflecting rapid progression to heavy smoking, and these individuals also scored higher on the polygenic index than those who took longer to reach this high level of cigarette smoking. In sum, *higher polygenic scores were related to developing the smoking habit earlier and faster following one's first cigarette rather than later and more slowly.*

What about smoking in adulthood? Would our GWAS-derived polygenic score based on one adult phenotype—number of cigarettes smoked per day—predict other adult smoking phenotypes in the Dunedin Study? It turned out that it did. Having a higher polygenic score predicted greater accumulation of "pack years" by age thirty-eight. (Pack years are defined as the number of cigarettes smoked per day divided by twenty—the number of cigarettes in a pack—and multiplied by the number of years smoked at that rate through thirty-eight years of age.) Study members at greater genetic risk also were more likely to become nicotine dependent—defined by the number of years between initiation and meeting standard criteria for "needing" to smoke, based on symptoms such as needing a cigarette upon waking up, smoking even when having a cold or flu, and smoking many cigarettes per day (see Figure 12.1). These same individuals with high polygenic scores also were more chronically nicotine dependent, meeting criteria for dependence for more years of their lives. Individuals with higher polygenic scores were also most likely to rely on smoking as a means of coping with stress, most likely to fail in their efforts to quit smoking between the ages of eighteen and thirty-two, and least likely to have quit smoking in their thirties (Figure 12.2).

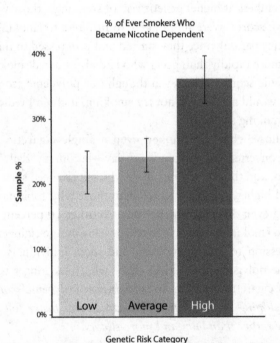

FIGURE 12.1. Percentage of study members who had ever smoked and became nicotine dependent as a function of being at low, average, or high genetic risk. Reformatted from Belsky, D.W., Moffitt, T.E., Baker, T.B., Biddle, A.K., Evans, J.P., Harrington, H., Houts, R., Meier, M., Sugden, K., Williams, B., Poulton, R., & Caspi, A. (2013). Polygenic risk and the developmental progression to heavy, persistent smoking and nicotine dependence. *JAMA Psychiatry, 70*, 534–542, figure 4B. Reproduced with permission. Copyright © 2013 American Medical Association. All rights reserved.

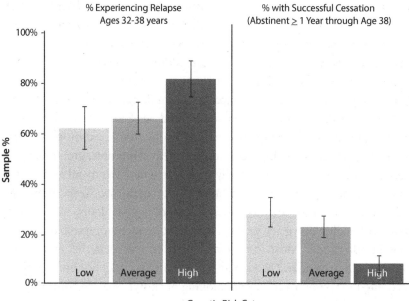

FIGURE 12.2. Percentage of study members who returned to smoking after quitting ("relapse") between ages thirty-two and thirty-eight (left panel) and who successfully quit smoking for at least a year ("cessation") by age thirty-eight (right panel) as a function of being at low, average, or high genetic risk. Reformatted from Belsky, D.W., Moffitt, T.E., Baker, T.B., Biddle, A.K., Evans, J.P., Harrington, H., Houts, R., Meier, M., Sugden, K., Williams, B., Poulton, R., & Caspi, A. (2013). Polygenic risk and the developmental progression to heavy, persistent smoking and nicotine dependence. *JAMA Psychiatry, 70*, 534–542, figure 4C. Reproduced with permission. Copyright © 2013 American Medical Association. All rights reserved.

Clearly, we had evidence that in both adolescence and adulthood some aspects of smoking—specifically the *development* of smoking once one started—was in the genes (in our Dunedin sample).

DOES ADOLESCENT SMOKING ACCOUNT FOR GENETIC RISK OF ADULT SMOKING?

Given these links between our polygenic smoking score and multiple smoking phenotypes in both adolescence and adulthood, in the next stage of our genetics-of-smoking adventure we turned to our core developmental question: does genetic risk associated with adult smoking in GWAS research account for adolescent smoking? Recall that this is an important question and not one that was addressed in GWAS of *adult* smoking on which we based our own work. Recall, too, that in addressing this issue we hoped to gain insight into whether it might make sense to target adolescents at high genetic risk of smoking for participation in smoking-prevention programs.

To address the developmental issue at hand, we first created a new adult smoking measure that reflected smoking problems, based on pack years smoked by age thirty-eight, nicotine-dependent symptoms, and number of ages at which we interviewed study members where the member reported that efforts to quit smoking had failed. Once again, we were "lumping" indicators of what we sought to measure: smoking problems. As expected, those with higher polygenic scores did experience more total smoking problems in adulthood. Most important, however, was that this association linking the polygenic risk score with adult smoking could be almost entirely accounted for by two adolescent-smoking phenotypes: early conversion to smoking at least one cigarette per day, thus becoming a "daily" smoker, and rapid progression to smoking twenty or more cigarettes per day, thus becoming an addicted smoker. These results therefore indicated that the *genetic foundations* of adult smoking identified in GWAS discovery research on adults are operative much earlier in life than GWAS research indicated. Even if the GWAS of smoking was focused on the genetics of adult smoking, such work we found was also informative about the development of adolescent smoking.

CONCLUSION

The fact that the polygenic risk-of-smoking score we created, based as it was on prior GWAS discovery research, did not distinguish between those who did and did not become smokers was more or less what we expected when we launched our developmental adventure studying the genetics of smoking. This is because the genes identified in the prior GWAS discovery research—on which we based our polygenic risk score—predicted quantity of cigarettes smoked in a day among adults, not initiation of smoking. In other words, the genetic risks captured in our polygenic risk score would seem to reflect the body's response to nicotine, not a young person's propensity to initiate smoking. What genes, if any, might be related to this latter phenotype remain to be determined. Perhaps they could be related to susceptibility to peer pressure, given that adolescents often try smoking in response to friends' encouragement of smoking.

Consistent with the view that our polygenic score was tapping *susceptibility to nicotine addiction* were the findings showing that the developmental progression of smoking behavior proved to be related to the score. Recall that among individuals who initiated smoking, those at higher genetic risk progressed more rapidly to heavy smoking and nicotine dependence; were more likely to become persistent heavy smokers and persistently nicotine dependent; and also had more difficulty quitting their smoking habit than did those smokers with lower polygenic scores. One finding we have not yet mentioned that surprised us was that "chippers" such as Avshalom Caspi, who seem to enjoy an occasional cigarette (that is, not necessarily every day) but are not physiologically addicted to nicotine scored lowest of all study members on our polygenic smoking score, even lower than those who never smoked. This finding once again underscores the fact that our polygenic score seemed to be tapping susceptibility to become nicotine dependent rather than, perhaps, susceptibility to social pressure to try smoking. So who is pressuring Avshalom Caspi to smoke these days?

While our genotype-phenotype findings involving smoking are in line with what some other investigatory teams have reported, our research was the first to track the relations of particular genetic risks to the *development* of smoking behavior—from initiation, through conversion to daily smoking, and progression to heavy smoking, nicotine dependence, and struggles with cessation through midlife. This, of course, was because the long-term nature of the Dunedin Study and its rich and repeated measurements of smoking behavior positioned us to do so, whereas prior work could not. This unique situation also enabled our discovery that genetic influences on adult smoking problems are mediated via—or derive from—an adolescent pathway involving progression from smoking initiation to heavy smoking. In other words, the genetics of adult smoking are, as noted earlier, already operative in the second decade of life. Thus, those who smoke a lot in midlife for reasons related to their genetic makeup do so as a result of the rapid development of the smoking habit two decades or more earlier in life.

Such empirical observations are consistent with the view of some pediatricians that some adolescents after only experimental use of tobacco quickly become regular smokers and nicotine dependent. Early identification of these individuals—before any such experimentation and subsequent dependence has occurred—would seem an appropriate and now potentially realizable public health goal. In fact, our work suggests that it might be worth trying two different things. First, teens could be genotyped and simply informed about their personal risk of becoming addicted to tobacco even before they begin to experiment, potentially preventing those most likely to find it difficult to stop smoking from starting in the first place (and saving an awful lot of money). This might be especially helpful if they received other messages indicating that smoking was no longer "cool" and what lifetime expenditures by addicted smokers amount to (that is, thousands of dollars). Second, the same information on adolescents' genetic makeup could be used, initially on a small-scale basis, to identify high-risk adolescents in order to target them for more intensive smoking-prevention treatments. If initial trials proved effective, there would be a basis for expanding such efforts.

Readers should appreciate, however, that such screening and targeting could prove ineffective, and one reason for this could be that the power of our polygenic score to predict smoking phenotypes, though noteworthy, was limited, with the same being true of polygenic scores based on many more GWAS-identified genes of quantity of smoking in adulthood. Ultimately, this is why we are only comfortable advancing the idea of small-scale trials rather than any broader effort. Having said that, one might also imagine using a polygenic risk score in combination with other known risks—such as having a parent, older sibling, or friend who smokes, aspiring to be like older kids who smoke, or experiencing lots of peer pressure to smoke. There is every reason to believe that such a polygenic-plus-environment risk score based on genetic *and* environmental factors would prove more powerful in identifying youths most at risk than one based solely on genetic information.

Experience teaches us that some people will object to using genetic information to screen individuals—even on an experimental-trial basis—and then differentially treat those scoring high on a polygenic index of smoking, including treating them preferentially with respect to participation in smoking-prevention programs. Many have understandable, but we think exaggerated, fears of the misuse of genetics, often based on the sordid history of the eugenics movement of many decades ago. The question one must ask in the face of such objections, however, is why it is okay to screen for breast-cancer genes but not genes related to behavior, such as smoking (which has a cancer risk not unlike carrying BRCA, the breast-cancer gene). If it is because the predictive power of genes for serious medical conditions is greater, then that is a most reasonable, even persuasive, argument; it suggests that if and when the power of genetic prediction of behavior increased, then it would be appropriate to target on the basis of better evidence.

But experience also teaches us that even such better—meaning stronger—evidence will not be sufficient for many. This is because too many people today still distinguish body, mind, and behavior, somehow thinking that while the body is genetically influenced, this is not so in the case of the mind and behavior. We strongly advocate moving beyond such false distinctions. After all, evidence now indicates that gut bacteria are related to psychological functioning, no doubt via the vagal nerve connecting gut and brain. So treating the body and mind and thus the body and behavior as somehow fundamentally different seems a seriously outdated way of thinking about humans, genetics, and human development. Simply put, it is long past time to abandon the mind-body duality; we are dealing with a systemically integrated organism, not an individual with separate parts that follow entirely different rules.

13

Genetics of Life Success?

In Chapter 12, we introduced GWAS—genome-wide association studies—which investigate whether and how thousands or even millions of genetic variants, measured using whole-genome scans obtained on thousands or even tens or hundreds of thousands of individuals, are related to a phenotype of interest. Recall in this regard that when studying smoking genetics in the Dunedin Study (Chapter 12), we relied on genes discovered in prior research that included tens of thousands of adults. Because it is often the case that no single investigation includes a sufficient number of participants to carry out a GWAS, most such "discovery" research involves the collaboration of many teams of investigators that have separately gathered data on the phenotype of interest, such as smoking, while also collecting DNA from their research participants. Thus, in conducting a GWAS, the data collected by many investigatory teams are routinely combined to create a sample large enough to allow whole-genome analysis to be carried out. This is one reason why published reports of such studies can have scores of authors.

Two important characteristics of GWAS need to be highlighted for the purposes of this chapter, because it is focused on our developmental adventure investigating the genetics of success in life. The first characteristic is that the many studies that are combined to create samples large enough to conduct whole-genome research in which thousands or millions of genetic variants are statistically evaluated for their association with a particular phenotype often differ from each other in character and complexity. Thus, although they can be combined based on their common measurement of DNA and a particular phenotype such as smoking, they vary greatly in terms of other phenotypes and environmental exposures that they have and have not measured. Thus, whereas one data set that is contributed to a GWAS might have lots of information on physical health, it may lack information on mental health, the reverse may be true in other data sets. Consequently, the same set of studies that is used to conduct a GWAS of a particular phenotype cannot necessarily be combined to carry out a GWAS on some other phenotype and thus determine whether genes associated with one outcome are also associated with another outcome. As we will see, the availability of many different phenotypes that could be linked to the same set of genes to address this issue was a major strength of the Dunedin Study when it came to investigating the genetics of success. But we are getting ahead of our story.

The second important point to make about GWAS, indeed about all research examining genotype-phenotype associations—that is, what genetic variants are associated with a particular phenotype—is that they are fundamentally correlational in character. And the mantra that every student of human development memorizes early on in his or her education is that "correlation is not causation." This, of course, is why we have repeatedly challenged the associations we discerned in addressing multiple topics throughout this book in an effort to discount alternative explanations of our findings. Whether genotype-phenotype research focuses on one or a few candidate genes or thousands or even millions of genetic variants as in GWAS, those that distinguish who rapidly becomes addicted to nicotine and who does not, for example, cannot be presumed to be identifying genes that actually exert a *causal* influence. This is because some of the genes identified may be correlated with the phenotype in question just because they themselves are closely related—statistically or physically (that is, in close proximity within the genome itself)—to other genes that actually exert causal influence.

Ultimately, understanding the workings of the genome and, specifically, whether and how particular genes come to causally influence particular phenotypes does not end with GWAS. In many respects, it is just the beginning, potentially affording scientists insight into what biological mechanisms might be involved in linking a genotype with a phenotype. For example, if it is known from other work that some of the genes that emerge from a whole-genome study play a role in inflammatory processes or are related to metabolism, then that provides investigators with insight as to where to look when it comes to "turning up the power of the microscope" to inquire in more detail into the biological processes by which genotypes develop into phenotypes if and when they do.

As it turns out, it may not only be the case that some GWAS-identified "nicotine-addiction genes" discussed in Chapter 12 do not actually play a causal role in determining who rapidly becomes an everyday smoker, a pack-a-day smoker, and/or a smoker who finds it difficult to give up the habit. It may also be that referring to such genes in such terms—even if they do play a causal role—on the basis of GWAS findings may be as misleading as it is illuminating. We say that because two things about genotype-phenotype associations are now well appreciated. First, because whole-genome research is identifying so many genes related to virtually all phenotypes investigated, there is ever more reason to believe that many genes exert only a very small effect on the phenotype in question, if it is actually causally influencing the phenotype (and not just correlated with it). Thus, it is exceedingly rare for a phenotype to be associated with only a single gene or even very few genes, especially the phenotypes—or developmental outcomes—that are the focus of this volume. Consequently, diseases that are a function of a single genetic mutation, as some very rare diseases are (for example, Huntington's disease), turn out not to be very good models of how genes influence the phenotypes that most interest students of human development.

The second critical point to be made about genotypes and their relation to phenotypes is that many, even most, genes are systematically related to many different phenotypes. *Pleiotropy* is the scientific term used to refer to this biological reality. What this means is that supposed "smoking genes" identified in GWAS of smoking may emerge in other whole-genome studies focused on entirely different phenotypes. It's not hard to imagine, for example, that genes related to addiction to nicotine could relate to readiness to become addicted to other substances. Please appreciate that even if this proved to be so, it would not preclude the possibility that such apparent "addiction genes" could even be related to phenotypes having nothing to do with addiction.

In fact, the phenomenon of pleiotropy may account for why the human genome proved to be so much smaller—in terms of total number of genes—than many thought would be the case when this was first determined. After all, if a particular gene influences many phenotypes, then one would not need as many genes to help assemble and develop *Homo sapiens* as would be needed if every gene influenced only a single phenotype. As an analogy, if a builder required one hammer to build a deck, another to put shingles on the roof of a home, and still another to install a kitchen counter, then his toolbox would need to include more tools than if a single hammer could serve these three functions—and even others, such as breaking a window to rescue a dog in a house fire.

Consideration of the small effects of individual genes and their likely effects on multiple phenotypes raises the issue central to the developmental adventure that is the focus of this chapter, the genetics of life success, which, admittedly, has taken awhile to get to: could it be that the genes associated with one phenotype and so labeled—as in "smoking genes"—are actually associated with many other phenotypes to such an extent that labeling them the way they have been labeled is as misleading as it is informative? For example, imagine we identify, via GWAS, 873 genetic variants related to divorce upon comparing the whole genomes of thousands of individuals who never divorced with those of thousands of others who did divorce. Now one may be inclined, perhaps understandably, to label these distinguishing genes as "divorce genes." But what if many of these 873 genetic variants also distinguished people who were and were not argumentative, did and did not lose their jobs, and/or perennially bet on the losing team rather than the winning one? Besides perhaps helping to account for why some individuals were more likely to get divorced than others—because they were argumentative, had difficulty holding onto a job, and picked problematic mates—wouldn't such a finding call into question the appropriateness of referring to the set of genes in question as "divorce genes"? In other words, given pleiotropy, even if specific genes are associated with a particular phenotype, it does not logically follow that all these genes are exclusively associated with that one phenotype.

EDUCATIONAL ATTAINMENT GENES?

This kind of thinking led us to wonder about genes that GWAS research on educational attainment identified—in more than one discovery study—as distinguishing more and less educated individuals. More specifically, we wondered whether research on "educational attainment" genes might not fully characterize what they were associated with, influenced, and thus reflected. Might they also be related to many other aspects of life success, not just how many years of education an individual achieved, especially in the years following the completion of formal schooling? If so, that would suggest that referring to them as "education genes" would be misleading, insufficiently reflecting the core principle of modern-day genetics—pleiotropy. That would be especially true if putative "educational-attainment" genes predicted other aspects of life success even after taking into account years of education. Unfortunately, GWAS studies of educational attainment have not been positioned to address this issue because not all studies that are combined to allow GWAS of educational attainment and involve thousands of individuals also measure the same noneducation phenotypes that might be regarded as indicators of life success. The question their participants had answered was simply, "What is your highest academic degree?" The GWAS to find genes linked to variation in educational attainment has now included more than a million participants, which was possible simply because "highest degree" is a check box filled in by participants in virtually every study ever done, including those that collected DNA.

This is where the Dunedin Study comes in, affording the opportunity to determine whether putative educational-attainment genes predict much more than years of schooling—even after controlling for years of schooling. Using much more genetic information available on study members than we had when we carried out our earlier genetics-of-smoking research discussed in Chapter 12, we could now create a putative "educational-attainment" polygenic score for every Dunedin Study member and determine whether this multigene index predicts not just educational achievement but many other aspects of life success as well. To this end, we created a polygenic score comprised of more than two million genetic variants, and each variant was specifically weighted to reflect the degree to which it predicted educational attainment in several large GWAS discovery studies.

In addition to determining whether genetic discoveries for educational attainment also predicted success-related outcomes beyond schooling, we asked two related follow-up questions addressing issues of development in our adventure focused on the genetics of success. First, are child, adolescent, and young-adult ways of functioning that precede final educational attainment or eventual life success also related to the polygenic "educational-attainment" score? In other words, does a polygenic score that predicts academic accomplishment by the end of the second decade of life and beyond also predict functioning much earlier in life? This, more or less, is the same developmental issue we addressed in Chapter 12 when we asked whether genes found to predict smoking in adulthood also did so in adolescence. Second, if genes that relate to success in adulthood also predict phenotypes much earlier in life, do such early-life characteristics help to account for the process by which a genotype develops into a phenotype? That is, are they part of the pathway to life success connecting genes to achievement and success in adulthood? We addressed this issue in Chapter 12 as well, when we found that our polygenic smoking score came to be related to adult smoking phenotypes via genetic effects on adolescent smoking.

The two questions just raised are important not just from the perspective of basic science, wanting to know about "how" development operates, but also from the perspective of applied science. If developmental-behavior paths could be identified by which genes seemed to exert their predictive magic, then those paths could become targets of intervention, especially for those children whose genetic makeup does not seem to advantage them in terms of succeeding in multiple aspects of life. Notably, this is exactly the logic behind much genetically oriented cancer research. First, find the genes associated with cancer, then illuminate the (biological) pathways linking genotype with cancer phenotype, and then target these pathways with drugs to prevent or treat those genetically disposed toward the cancer. In other words, a tried-and-true model of enhancing well-being in the case of those at genetic risk of cancer could be applied to development and behavior. The targets of intervention in this case might not be physiological or biochemical but instead psychological and behavioral. This analysis returns us, of course, to the idea that closed the previous chapter—the need to move beyond mind-body duality thinking, appreciating that mind, behavior, and biology do not follow entirely different rules.

BEYOND EDUCATIONAL SUCCESS

Once we developmental (and now genetic) adventurers had provisioned ourselves with a polygenic "educational-attainment" score for each Dunedin Study member, the next step in setting up research on the genetics of life success was to create measures of success in schooling and beyond. Schooling success was measured simply by determining the highest academic degree that the study member had earned by their thirty-eighth birthday. This was an important measure because if our polygenic score considered by GWAS investigators to reflect educational-attainment genes did not predict education in the Dunedin Study, then we would have had to terminate the research; there would be no grounds for going forward.

Fortunately, this did not prove to be a problem. Just as in the original GWAS discovery research, study members with higher polygenic scores achieved more years of formal schooling, whereas those with lower scores achieved less education by age thirty-eight (Figure 13.1). In fact, the association we detected between these two variables was modest—of virtually the same magnitude as in the original GWAS discovery research. Because the association was modest, it should by no means be inferred that the polygenic index was an overwhelming determinant—or at least predictor—of educational attainment. Clearly, factors other than genetic makeup matter; the relation between even millions of genes comprising

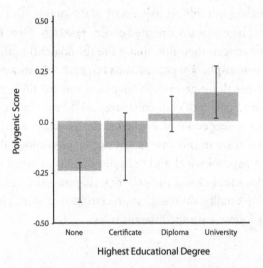

FIGURE 13.1. Association between polygenic score and educational attainment, showing that the greater the attainment, the higher the polygenic score. Reformatted from Belsky, D.W., Moffitt, T.E., Corcoran, D.L., Comingue, B., Harrington, H., Hogan, S., Williams, B.S., Poulton, R., & Caspi, A. (2016). The genetics of success: How single-nucleotide polymorphisms associated with educational attainment relate to life-course development. *Psychological Science*, *27*, 957–972, figure 1a. Copyright © 2016 The Authors. Reproduced with permission of SAGE Publications, Inc.

our polygenic score and educational attainment was probabilistic, not deterministic.

Having replicated the findings from discovery research, we were positioned to implement the next step of our investigatory plan, trying to predict success beyond school by using the "educational-attainment" polygenic score. To this end, we created two composite measures, each based on several other component measures. The first, labeled adult attainment, was based on diverse information collected at age thirty-eight, some using questionnaires completed by the study member, some from questionnaires completed by friends or relatives about the study member, some from interviews with the study member, and some from administrative records. Thus, the adult-attainment measure was based on the study member's occupational prestige (for example, being a doctor is more prestigious than being a nurse), annual income, total assets (for example, cash, stocks, home, and car), problems with credit, difficulty paying bills, days receiving social-welfare benefits, and formal credit score. These were combined in such a way that a higher score on this composite index reflected greater life success and a lower score less success.

Just as anticipated, we found that the polygenic "educational-attainment" index also predicted more general adult attainment. By age thirty-eight, study members with higher polygenic scores were more likely than those with lower scores to be employed in more prestigious occupations, to earn higher incomes, to have accumulated more assets, to report fewer difficulties paying their bills, to rely less on social-welfare benefits, and to have better credit scores.

Upon generating these results, we turned our attention to our second measure of postschooling success, social mobility. This phenotypic outcome was based on a comparison of the prestige of the occupation of the study member's parents with the education, occupation, and adult attainment of the study member. Whereas most study members (like others of their generation) were upwardly mobile, being at a higher social-class level than their parents, some were downwardly mobile, being at a lower social-class level than their parents. Consider in this regard two middle-aged male participants in the Dunedin Study (whose names have been changed to protect their identities, as has been our practice throughout this book). Peter, who had a college degree, was employed as an accountant. Because his father was only a high-school graduate and worked in a factory, Peter experienced upward mobility. In contrast, Charles, who was a clerk in a retail store, had a parent who was a teacher and thus experienced downward social mobility.

Given what we have already reported, it will not be surprising to learn that what we should now refer to as the polygenic education-*and*-adult-attainment index also predicted social mobility; the polygenic scores proved to be an index of educational attainment *and* adult attainment *and* social mobility (that is, not just educational attainment). In fact, even after taking into account the study member's social class as a child, those with higher polygenic scores earned higher education degrees and were employed in more prestigious occupations than their peers with lower polygenic scores.

Of special significance was the discovery that the power of the polygenic score to predict such success in life was virtually the same for children who grew up in families of low, middle, and high social class. No matter what the child's beginnings—in terms of the social status of the child's family while growing up—those with higher polygenic scores *within each social stratum* were more likely to experience upward mobility, whereas those with lower scores were more likely to be downwardly mobile. Consequently, study members from low-SES backgrounds who had high polygenic scores were more likely than their fellow low-SES study members to climb the socioeconomic ladder, whereas those from high-SES backgrounds with high polygenic scores were less likely to fall in class than their high-SES counterparts with low polygenic scores, thus remaining in the high social class they were born into.

To be honest, it would have been shocking had we not found that so-called education-attainment genes predicted postschooling life success. From a purely logical—and sociological—standpoint, if the polygenic index predicts educational success, as it does, and educational success predicts many features of life success, as it surely does, it would be highly likely that the polygenic index would also predict postschooling life success. Indeed, such an inferential analysis suggests that the reason why so-called educational-attainment genes predict life success is because of the role that educational success plays in promoting life success. One might even regard this as an almost algebraic law of human development, at least in the modern postindustrial Western world: when domino A, representing educational-attainment genes, falls down, it routinely knocks over domino B, representing actual educational attainment, which then knocks over domino C, representing life success.

But is this the entire story? Do educational-attainment genes predict life success only as a result of and via educational attainment? Metaphorically, what happens to domino C if one takes away domino B and knocks down domino A? We accomplished this by statistically controlling for—and thus discounting the effect of—educational attainment when predicting life success. Thus, our metaphorical question became, "Is domino A heavy enough to shake the table and thus knock over domino C or at least make it seriously wobble in the absence of domino B?" The answer is "yes." Even with educational attainment controlled, the polygenic score still predicted adult attainment. Of importance, though, was that under these predictive conditions the predictive power of the polygenic index was cut virtually in half. This means that even if education is clearly part of the explanation as to how so-called education genes come to predict adult attainment, it is not the entire story. Let's now extend our life-success adventure to look more closely at the role of genetics in the *development* of life success.

POLYGENIC CORRELATES EARLIER IN LIFE

However interesting the findings summarized to this point documenting pleitropy and thereby highlighting the problem of labeling the set of genes in question as genes for "educational attainment" may be, it was the issue of pathways from genotype to phenotype that proved most exciting to us as developmental scholars. Thus, the second stage of our adventure investigating the genetics of success was designed to answer the question, "How—at the psychological, behavioral and social level—does a genotype develop into a phenotype?" As the first step in addressing this issue, we determined whether accomplishments in childhood, adolescence, and even adulthood also proved to be associated with our polygenic score reflecting educational attainment and life success. If they did, they could serve as "B" candidates in our domino metaphor and we could then investigate whether these links between genes and early-life functioning could help account for the already documented links between genes and life success. We would be well positioned to investigate possible pathways accounting for how our genetic measurements came to be associated with adult development.

In seeking to better understand the developmental process, we cast our investigatory net rather widely, drawing on a large number of measurements obtained between the time children were three and eighteen years of age. We conceptualized these as possible mediators—that is, domino Bs—that might link genotype with adult phenotype. As a result, we discovered that children with higher polygenic scores and thus with a greater likelihood of life success differed from their agemates very early in life. Although the polygenic score proved unrelated to the age at which motor milestones such as crawling, walking, and jumping were achieved early in life, other developmental milestones pertaining to language did relate to study members' genetic makeup. Specifically, those study members with higher polygenic scores began talking earlier than those who had lower scores and were also somewhat quicker to begin communicating using sentences (that is, putting two or more words together). Those with higher polygenic scores also acquired reading skills at younger ages. In fact, test scores administered repeatedly between ages seven and eighteen revealed that children with higher polygenic scores were not only better readers but improved their reading performance at a faster rate over time and thus achieved their peak reading performance (on the tests) at a younger age.

Perhaps not surprisingly, then, when we asked study members to bring to the project office their official exam records, which included scores on standardized tests administered to all students by the New Zealand Ministry of Education, those with higher polygenic scores outperformed their peers with lower polygenic scores on tests administered when they were fifteen, sixteen, and seventeen years of age. In line with these findings was evidence from questionnaires and interviews indicating that study members with higher polygenic scores aspired, at age eighteen, to higher levels of education, desiring, in particular, to attend university. They also aspired to work in more prestigious, "professional" occupations, such as being a doctor or an engineer.

Perhaps more interesting or at least less obvious as a plausible pathway from genes to life success was what we learned about geographic mobility in adulthood. In considering the forthcoming results, it should be appreciated that overseas work experience is common for New Zealanders. By age thirty-eight, more than one-third of study members had worked in a foreign country for a period of at least twelve months, with Australia being the commonest destination. But it is work experience beyond Australia that is most prestigious to New Zealanders, referred to as "the Big OE" (for "overseas experience"). Notably, study members with higher polygenic scores were more likely to have an OE, and at age thirty-eight, these higher polygenic scorers were more likely to be working overseas, even beyond Australia, than those with lower polygenic scores.

A focus on "planfulness" revealed that such differences in overseas experiences between those with higher and lower polygenic scores were not an accident or a result of some random opportunity that befell them. From questionnaires mailed to friends and relatives who knew the study members well at ages thirty-two and thirty-eight, we learned that those with higher polygenic scores proved better at managing money. Indeed, interviews with study members themselves in the fourth decade of life about their financial circumstances revealed the same. Thus, it was not the case that genetic makeup forecast only language and academic-related skills and credentials.

Findings further indicated that the greater skills and success of study members with higher polygenic scores extended to their mating. Even though genetic makeup did not distinguish study members who were and were not in a serious relationship, those with a higher polygenic score and involved in such relationships were partnered with someone who was more likely to have a college degree and an income above that of the national median than those also in relationships but with lower polygenic scores. Apparently, then, the former individuals bolstered their own socioeconomic advantages that they accrued through their educational and occupational attainments by partnering with socially advantaged mates. It would seem, then, that those who were genetically, educationally, and occupationally rich got relationally richer, too!

FROM GENOTYPE TO PHENOTYPE

It is one thing to learn that a supposed polygenic score for "educational attainment" not only predicts multiple aspects of life success in adulthood and even that the same polygenic score is associated with many aspects of cognitive, motivational, social, and financial functioning earlier in life, but it is another to determine whether the latter is the means to the former. In other words, do child, adolescent, and even adult capabilities associated with the polygenic score prove to be pathways by which a genotype develops into a phenotype? That is the issue to which we next turned our attention as adventurers, whether, again metaphorically, domino B links domino A, representing genotype, with domino C, representing life success. Recall that we regarded this issue as critically important for identifying potential targets of intervention if we discovered that the personal characteristics under investigation functioned as the means by which genetic makeup came to be associated with multiple aspects of life success.

With this concern in mind, we focused on three sets of possible mediators linking genotype to phenotype: cognitive skills, as measured by standardized tests, given the obvious possibility that intelligence may ultimately be responsible for many of our findings; noncognitive abilities, most notably self-control; and interpersonal skills, given ever-growing evidence that these are as important if not more important than intellectual ability when it comes to life success (as discussed in detail in Chapter 3); and, finally, physical health, given the possibility that it may just be the case that good health is the means by which genetic makeup comes to influence life success.

With measurements of these domains of functioning in hand, we asked whether if we took these "intermediate phenotypes" into account (domino B), they would explain how our polygenic index (domino A) came to predict life success (domino C). As a first step in addressing this issue, we had to determine whether the polygenic index was reliably associated with the personal characteristics outlined in the preceding paragraph. Results indicated that the polygenic index predicted both cognitive and noncognitive skills, even if not physical health. Consistent with observations already made, study members with higher polygenic scores outperformed those with lower scores on IQ tests administered at ages five, seven, nine, and eleven. In fact, the former children evinced a faster rate of intellectual development through age thirteen. Study members scoring higher on the polygenic index also were observed and reported to have more self-control when it came to managing their impulses, emotions, and behavior across the first decade of life than those with lower polygenic scores. Finally, at ages three, five, seven, and nine, those with higher polygenic scores were rated as more friendly, confident, cooperative, and/or communicative, resulting in better overall interpersonal skills, than those with lower scores. This means that these indicators of cognitive and noncognitive skills are plausible "intermediate phenotypes" that could mediate or help to explain how a genotype becomes a phenotype, even if the same was not true of indices of physical health.

As it turned out, these cognitive and noncognitive "intermediate phenotypes" did statistically mediate and thus helped account for the effect of the polygenic index on life success (that is, genes→cognitive/noncognitive skills→life success). In so doing, they revealed possible developmental pathways by which a genotype developed into a phenotype. In fact, cognitive ability, self-control, and interpersonal skill accounted for about 60 percent of the association linking genetic makeup with educational attainment and almost 50 percent of that with adult attainment. Although such findings do not conclusively prove that modifying these intermediate phenotypes for the better would result in increased life success, the results of our observational study certainly point in that direction.

CONCLUSION

In case this is news to you, life, or at least the biology of life, is apparently unfair. We are led to offer this as a core conclusion of our developmental adventure investigating the genetics of life success simply because none of us gets to choose our parents, yet genes inherited from them give some of us more of a head start in life than others. As we have seen, this biological inheritance results in increased or decreased chances of developing verbal and reading skills earlier and faster in childhood; of having higher aspirations in adolescence regarding what will be achieved in life educationally and occupationally; of securing overseas schooling and/or work experience in young adulthood; and, by midlife, of being financially planful and in a relationship with an educationally and financially advantaged partner. These same inherited genes seem to affect one's chances of developing more or fewer cognitive and noncognitive skills in childhood. Perhaps most significantly, these personal attributes appear to be at least somewhat responsible for why those with a particular genetic makeup—a result of having particular parents whom they did not choose—proved more or less likely to become occupationally, financially, and socially successful, experiencing upward social mobility.

Though it is tempting to regard the multiple observations just made as implying that biology is destiny, there are at least two reasons why perhaps we should not. The first has to do with the predictive power of genetic makeup, the second with the implications of our work for intervention. Let's consider each in turn.

The Limits of Genetic Prediction

Whatever our success in predicting life success and in showing that a set of genes found to predict educational attainment in GWAS discovery research and in the Dunedin Study predicts much more than that—and not just because they are related to educational success—the fact is that the predictive power of our polygenic index was limited rather than overwhelming. In other words, there is a lot about educational, occupational, financial, and relationship success that could not be explained by the set of genes that comprised our polygenic index. Importantly, the same is true of our ability to predict, using the polygenic index, many of the "intermediate phenotypes" we focused on in attempting to illuminate developmental pathways pertaining to how a genotype becomes a phenotype.

There are at least two possible reasons why our prediction proved limited. One is that we based our polygenic index only on research linking genes with educational attainment. Thus, it is certainly possible, even likely, that had there existed GWAS discovery research linking genes with our adult-attainment and social-mobility outcomes, or the intermediate phenotypes we studied to illuminate how genotype comes to be related to phenotype, we could increase predictive power by including any additional identified genes in our polygenic index.

But no matter how many genes we might identify in discovery research, the second reason why our polygenic prediction proved limited is founded on the results of many GWAS studies of many different phenotypes. These indicate that the power of genes alone to predict virtually all phenotypes investigated to date leaves a lot of variation in how people function and develop unaccounted for. In fact, one of the great conundrums of genetic science is that while behavior genetics research, discussed in Chapter 12, that does not include measuring genes indicates that about 50 percent of many phenotypes are heritable, the percentage variation of the very same phenotype that even polygenic scores explain remains for the most part in the single digits! This contrast is referred to in the scholarly literature as the "missing heritability" problem. Why do polygenic scores based on even millions of genetic variants account for so little of the difference between individuals when twin, adoption, and other family studies suggest that genetics is responsible for so much more of the variation?

Ultimately, there is every reason to presume that if GWAS discovery studies were carried out on any or all of the life-success or intermediate phenotypes we focused on in our investigation and we were able to include their results in our polygenic score, there would no doubt still be much variation in how people develop and function that simply could not be explained by genes alone. In other words and importantly, the limits of our ability to predict almost any aspect of development, including life success, using just genetic information make it highly likely that there are many nongenetic factors not at all related to genetic makeup that contribute to virtually all aspects of human development. Genes, then, are probabilistically influential, at least for the phenotypes that we have focused on. Just knowing about genes provides only limited, though noteworthy, predictive power.

Intervention Implications

If the power of genetics to account for all the variation we can observe in human functioning and development is ultimately limited, representing our first reason for not concluding that biology is destiny, what is the second reason to which we alluded earlier? It is simply that, as noted in Chapter 12, all estimates of genetic influence are population specific, meaning specific to the time, place, and people studied. This might be read to suggest that our findings are restricted to New Zealanders born in a single twelve-month period in the early 1970s who grew to midlife at the end of the twentieth century and the very beginning of the twenty-first, but that is not what we mean; and this is because there are lots of reasons to expect that our findings generalize well beyond that narrow frame of reference. Most obviously, the genetic "discovery" research on which we based our polygenic score was conducted not in New Zealand but elsewhere in the Western world. This means that, at the very least, the ability to predict educational attainment—and we suspect much more—using the polygenic index that we used is not restricted only to where and when the original discovery research was carried out or where and when our life-success research was conducted.

If that is so, then why is it important to highlight the fact that estimates of genetic influence are population specific? The reason is that the world as we know it is not the only possible world that could be. That is why our findings pertaining to the mediation of genetic effects are so significant. As we have noted repeatedly, those findings have important implications, suggesting that if nongenetic means of promoting language and reading skills and self-control and interpersonal skills could be identified and implemented—perhaps even targeting those whose genetic makeup puts them at risk of limited life success—then the genetic effects detected in our work could be altered. In fact, in such a world, they could even be reduced substantially. Imagine, for example, a society in which multiple—and effective—efforts were made to foster the very "intermediate-phenotype" skills we identified as mediating the genetic effects on life success, especially in the case of those children whose genetic makeup puts them at risk of limited life success. This could well result in those whose genetic makeup now proves related to limited life success being far more likely to experience greater life success. Were that so, the power of genes to predict life success would be reduced, as those with more rather than fewer "life-success" genes would end up developing more rather than less like each other.

This analysis makes clear, yet again, that biology need not be destiny and that development is probabilistic, not deterministic. In the same way that it may be possible to counteract the effect of cancer genes, via pharmacology, once biological pathways to cancer are understood, there is reason to believe that it should be possible to counteract the effect of genes for limited life success with developmental interventions to promote cognitive and noncognitive skills and perhaps so much more.

14

Child Maltreatment, Genotype, and Violent Male Behavior

There is little in life that results from a single cause. Recall in that regard that we ended Chapter 5, which focused on why parents parent the way they do, by noting that even though we found that how girls were reared as children and adolescents provided predictive insight into their own parenting as adults, parenting was "multiply determined." In other words, even though mothering appeared to be intergenerationally transmitted—and our most recent work revealed that this wasn't just a case of genetic effects masquerading as environmental ones—how one is reared as a child is not the only force shaping future parenting. The temperament and behavior of the child, the quality of the parent's relationship with his or her partner, and the stresses and strains experienced at work are also likely to shape parenting, to name just a few sources of influence.

Relatedly, in Chapter 7 we learned that while the early sexual maturation of girls participating in the NICHD Study of Child Care and Youth Development was linked to their sexual behavior in adolescence, the presence of boys, especially older boys, also mattered. Thus, when these two factors co-occurred, Dunedin female study members who matured early and attended coed schools were especially likely to violate norms of good behavior at age thirteen and engage in delinquent behavior at age fifteen. Yet when girls who were just as physically mature attended an all-girls school, such adverse effects of early maturity did not emerge. In other words, the all-girls school functioned as a protective factor, promoting resilience, whereas attendance at a school with boys operated in reverse fashion, amplifying the effect of early maturity on girls' problem behavior. In this chapter and Chapter 15, we extend our work on the multiple determinants of development and resilience by focusing on both genetic and environmental influences and, most importantly, how they interact in shaping human development, specifically antisocial behavior in this chapter and depression in Chapter 15.

Particularly in this chapter, we further develop the theme of whether and how childhood experiences shape functioning later in life by adding information on genetics, specifically a singular candidate gene, to that on childhood. Recall that in Chapter 12 we distinguished the candidate-gene approach from the GWAS-derived, multigene—or polygenic—approach that informed our investigations of the genetics of smoking (Chapter 12) and life success (Chapter 13). Recall as well our discussion in Chapter 12 as to why after focusing on the polygenic genetic approach—which emerged after initial candidate-gene work in both our own research program and the broader field of human development—we reverse sequenced our presentation of these strategies for studying genetic influence. Whereas we used the later-emerging, polygenic approach to illuminate genotype-phenotype links in Chapters 12 and 13, here and in Chapter 15 we use the earlier-emerging, candidate-gene approach to illuminate gene-environment interaction (GXE), or how genetic variation proves influential in terms of whether developmental experiences and environmental exposures influence development.

DETERMINANTS OF ANTISOCIAL BEHAVIOR

Antisocial behavior, like so much else of development, is well studied and known to be influenced by a variety of factors. So when it came to selecting an environmental factor and a genetic factor to focus on in our adventure investigating the developmental origins of antisocial behavior in adulthood, we turned to prior research on this topic to guide us. Notably, because we were interested in investigating how genes and environment interact or work together in shaping development, we had to consult two separate bodies of scholarly literature. This was because those investigating each of these sources of influence tend not to consider (in any detail) the other source (that is, genetics, not environment, and environment, not genetics).

On the environmental side, child maltreatment turns out to be a well-established correlate and predictor of antisocial behavior. This should not be read to mean, however, that every maltreated child becomes an antisocial adult. Indeed, there is informative scholarly literature, referred to in Chapter 5, on "breaking the cycle" of the intergenerational transmission of child maltreatment. It helps to explain why some children do and others do not succumb to this anticipated effect of child abuse. In fact, even though maltreatment increases the risk—a statement of probability, not certainty—of later criminality by about 50 percent, it remains the case that most maltreated children do not become delinquents or criminal adults.

This reality that not all maltreated children develop in the same way—another case of probabilistic development—was brought home to us rather dramatically in the case of two boys enrolled in the Dunedin Study, James and Arthur (which again are not their real names). Both came from the kinds of homes where physical abuse is most likely to occur. In each household, there were problems with parents' alcohol consumption, and in each home there was little routine and much disorder and chaos. In each family, parents not only treated these boys harshly but also engaged in domestic violence. Yet, for some reason, only James developed the kind of behavior problems we were led to expect would emerge from a rearing environment like this.

How might we explain this "inconsistency" in the effect of maltreatment on male antisocial behavior, evident both in the case of the two boys just discussed and in the research literature itself on effects of child maltreatment? We wondered, in fact, whether genetics could help to explain why some children exposed to child abuse become antisocial whereas others do not. Indeed, it was this possibility that led us to undertake our first GXE research—using a single candidate gene. This was our first step into the scientific world of molecular genetics—the measurement of actual genes (rather than the behavioral-genetic focus on the relatedness of individuals, be they twins, parent and child, or parent and adopted child). We were off on another adventure in human development. Let us repeat here what we stipulated in Chapter 12 when discussing and distinguishing candidate-gene and polygenic research—that when this first work of ours investigating the influence of genes on development was undertaken, the cost of assaying genes was much higher than it was when the polygenic research discussed in Chapters 12 and 13 was undertaken. Thus, we were limited in the number of genes we could afford to assay and focus on.

When it came to selecting a gene to include in our GXE work, we chose a functional polymorphism in the promoter of the monoamine oxidase A gene, hereafter referred to as *MAOA*. The *MAOA* gene is located on the X chromosome; whereas males have only one X sex chromosome, the other being Y, females have two X chromosomes. This complicating factor, along with the greater propensity for males to engage in antisocial behavior, led us to focus exclusively on men in this genetically informed research. Functionally, the *MAOA* gene encodes the *MAOA* enzyme, which metabolizes—that is, breaks down—neurotransmitters (in the brain) such as norepinephrine (NE), serotonin (5-HT), and dopamine (DA), rendering them inactive; neurotransmitters are the molecules that carry signals between nerve cells. Critically for our purposes, genetic deficiencies in *MAOA* activity—that is, low levels of the enzyme resulting from a particular variant or version of this gene—had already been linked with aggression in mice and humans by other investigators. In fact, this is exactly why we selected this "candidate" gene for our very first GXE study. The existing evidence indicated, as pointed out in the next paragraph, that it was "biologically plausible" that this particular gene could play a role in accounting for who does and does not become an antisocial adult as a result of being maltreated as a child.

Before proceeding further to consider the evidence that made the case for focusing on the *MAOA* polymorphism, we should make clear again that our focus on a single candidate gene in the two GXE adventures discussed in this book—in this chapter and Chapter 15—was consistent with how such work was done in the 2000s. Whole-genome GWAS methods were ten years in the future. At the time the Dunedin team first began using measured genes, genotyping was still carried out by hand, one genetic marker at a time. About then, in the late 1990s, the field was beginning to notice that some of the findings of connections between candidate genetic markers and psychiatric conditions were not replicating: one team of investigators would report something to great fanfare, but the next team could not detect the same thing. Thus, even though one team of investigators might report in a publication that variation across individuals in a particular gene was systematically associated with a particular phenotype, some subsequent investigations failed to document the same relation.

We reasoned that this inconsistency across research studies might occur if the participants in these investigations differed in the social or environmental causes of their mental disorder. It had long been established that mental disorders had environmental causes (for example, child maltreatment, stressful life events, toxic exposures, and so forth), but in the initial headlong rush to test candidate genes in genotype-phenotype work, this established fact was being sidelined. We chose *MAOA* as a promising candidate gene that had been associated with antisocial behavior and then tested the hypothesis that only if study participants had suffered child maltreatment would their *MAOA* status, risk or nonrisk, predict whether they would become antisocial. Our goal was to see whether findings of candidate gene studies would prove more replicable if the environment was brought back into the picture. This thinking likewise drove our work the next year on the serotonin transporter gene, life stress, and depression (Chapter 15).

As already noted, the research discussed in these two chapters was carried out some ten years before GWAS-based genetic work became the strategy of choice for investigating genetic influence in humans—using polygenic scores, as discussed in Chapters 12 and 13. So even though the GXE adventures we share are perhaps a bit "dated," we have devoted chapters to them because they reveal, in concert with GWAS work, how research on the genetics of human development has changed and probably will continue to change. To summarize briefly what was made clear in Chapter 12, first there was behavior-genetic work using twin and adoption studies that did not measure genes but only how similar related individuals were to each other (for example, parent-child, sibling-sibling, adopted children) as a proxy for shared genes, then there was candidate-gene work, and then came GWAS-related work. What came next was epigenetics, the focus of Chapter 16. What comes after that remains to be seen.

Returning to the issue of evidence underscoring the "biological plausibility" of studying *MAOA* in the hope of illuminating the determinants of antisocial behavior, research on rodents—or "animal models"—proved informative. Increased aggression and increased levels of brain NE, 5-HT, and DA characterize the biology of mice that have had the gene encoding *MAOA* "knocked out," meaning eliminated from their genome by microbiologists. Just as important, when the process is reversed, aggression is reduced. Even more notable, perhaps, is that human studies also point to the role of *MAOA* in aggressive behavior. Especially informative was the discovery of a rare genetic condition in a single family lineage in the Netherlands in which no *MAOA* enzyme could be produced; this is the equivalent of a "knockout" in the case of humans. And Dutch males in these families have proven to be notoriously violent individuals across multiple generations. These observations suggested to us that low levels of the enzyme, caused by a low-activity rather than high-activity variant of the *MAOA* gene, could play a role in violent behavior. Having said that, it remained the case when we launched our GXE work focused on maltreatment and *MAOA* that the association between *MAOA* and aggressive behavior was, despite the evidence from the rather unique Dutch family, inconclusive in research on humans.

Nevertheless, when we developmental detectives put together the two observations that child maltreatment and *MAOA* were each inconsistently related to antisocial behavior, it suggested to us the following GXE hypothesis: *men were most likely to become violent if they had been maltreated as children and carry certain variants of the MAOA gene.* In other words, when two risk conditions co-occurred, one involving exposure to maltreatment and the other to a particular genotype, adult violence was most likely to develop. This was, by the way, a form of what is known as the "diathesis-stress hypothesis" in research on psychopathology. Diathesis refers to an underlying or latent "vulnerability" that puts one at risk of developing a problem, but according to this hypothesis, the problem only arises when a particular stress is experienced or encountered. This is why the diathesis-stress hypothesis is sometimes labeled—in a more user-friendly way, as we did in Chapter 8 when discussing effects of day care—the "dual-risk hypothesis."

The diathesis of interest in our work was genetic makeup, specifically the low-activity rather than high-activity variant of the *MAOA* gene, and the stress was exposure to child maltreatment while growing up. In other words, unless both conditions obtained, we did not expect adult violence to emerge—because the underlying vulnerability or diathesis would not be provoked or realized. This is kind of like "it takes two to tango." Having only one condition, the stress or the diathesis, is insufficient to get the (violence) job done. You need both.

GENETIC VARIATION

As we made clear in Chapter 12, most of the genes we *Homo sapiens* carry are the same in every one of us—no matter where we live or what race or ethnicity we are. That is why we all have two eyes, two arms, two legs, two lungs, a heart, and so on. But a small percentage of genes, around 5 percent, vary across individuals, and these are referred to as polymorphisms, a term we introduced earlier in this chapter. In the case of *MAOA*, these variants are labeled as low and high activity, reflecting the extent to which the *MAOA* enzyme is expressed due to the gene, resulting in the breakdown, respectively, of a little or a lot of the previously mentioned neurotransmitters. Individuals carrying the low form, which results in limited *MAOA* enzyme activity, are hyperresponsive to threats, making them likely to react to perceived danger in an hostile manner. The opposite is presumed in the case of high *MAOA* activity. Thus, we predicted that male study members would be most likely to become antisocial adults if they were exposed to child maltreatment while growing up *and* carried the low-activity variant of *MAOA*.

MEASURING CHILD MALTREATMENT

Fortunately, most of the children participating in the Dunedin Study did not experience child maltreatment, but some did. Evidence of childhood maltreatment during the first decade of life (ages three to eleven years) was ascertained using behavioral observations and parental reports during study members' childhoods, and retrospective reports by study members themselves about their rearing in childhood once they reached adulthood. We drew on multiple sources of information collected over many years to make an informed judgement as to which study members experienced maltreatment while growing up. Let's begin by considering the earliest relevant measurements that informed our ultimate determination of maltreatment status.

As reported in Chapters 2, 3, and 5, mother-child interactions were observed during the child's age-three assessment. This included rating the extent to which mothers engaged in specific problematic parenting behavior, such as being consistently negative in their affect, being otherwise harsh in dealing with the child, being rough in handling the child, and making no effort to help the child. In all, there were eight such ratings, and if mothers engaged in two or more such behaviors, they were classified as rejecting; 16 percent met this criterion.

When children were seven and nine years of age, mothers indicated on a checklist whether they engaged in any of ten harsh disciplinary practices, such as smacking or hitting the child with something. Remember, back in the 1970s, physical punishment was rather widely practiced, more so than today, at least in the English-speaking world, so parents were typically quite willing to report engaging in such child-rearing practices. Nevertheless, harsh parenting as we operationalized it reflected parenting that was unusually harsh for the era and the culture. In Chapter 5, we commented on how often abusive parents justify such behavior by saying things like, "What's wrong with smacking? That's how my parents raised me and I turned out okay." Parents who scored in the top 10 percent of the measure of harsh discipline were classified as unusually harsh.

Because the experience of family disruption has also been linked to antisocial behavior, the 6 percent of the sample that experienced two or more changes in their primary caregiver during the first decade of life were classified as having suffered disruptive caregiver changes. We also interviewed study members about victimization at age twenty-six, and 3 percent reported multiple episodes of severe physical punishment (for example, strapping leaving welts or whipping with electric cords) resulting in lasting bruising or injury before age eleven; we classified them as physically abused. Unwanted sexual contact was also assessed retrospectively in another part of the age-twenty-six interview, dealing with reproductive health. Five percent of study members were classified as sexually abused because they reported having their genitals touched, being forced to touch another's genitals, or attempted and/or completed sexual intercourse before age eleven (5 percent of sample).

With all this abuse-relevant information in hand, we derived a cumulative exposure index for each child by counting the number of maltreatment experiences during the first decade of life. Thus, the more a child was judged to be rejected, was considered to have experienced unusually harsh punishment, was discovered to have experienced two or more changes in primary caregiver, and was believed to have experienced physical or sexual abuse, the more likely we judged them to be victims of child maltreatment. As it turned out, approximately two-thirds of the study members experienced no maltreatment, a little more than one-quarter had a single indication of maltreatment, and just under 10 percent had two or more maltreatment-related experiences. We categorized and labeled the first group as "not maltreated," the second as "probably maltreated," and the third group as having experienced "severe maltreatment."

TESTING A GXE INTERACTION

When it came to testing our diathesis-stress or dual-risk hypothesis about how a history of child maltreatment and the *MAOA* polymorphism interact to predict antisocial behavior, our investigation had three important advantages relative to much prior work. First, in contrast to genetic studies that begin with a clinical or special sample—say of criminals convicted of violent offenses—we were studying a representative general population. This enabled us to avoid potential distortions in associations between predictor and outcome variables that can emerge when "special" samples are the focus of inquiry, as discussed in Chapter 1 when considering the utility of prospective—rather than retrospective—studies. Second, as already noted, our sample has well-characterized environmental-adversity histories, given the detailed information we had on study members' childhoods between ages three and eleven, most of it prospectively collected. Let us note as an important aside that the three maltreatment groups did not differ in their genetic makeup. If they had, this would have posed an interpretive problem— because then we could have been dealing with a situation in which a child's genetic makeup influenced the likelihood of being maltreated. In such a situation, there is a risk that gene-environment correlation could be mistakenly interpreted as a GXE interaction.

The third major strength of the study pertained to the outcome we were seeking to predict. Antisocial behavior was rigorously measured across different developmental periods. The fact is that antisocial behavior is a complicated phenotype, and the different approaches we used to measure it have different strengths and weaknesses. Thus, we relied on four different sets of measurements when it came to evaluating the extent to which each study member engaged in antisocial behavior. In adolescence, we relied on a formal psychiatric diagnosis of conduct disorder based on a standardized clinical interview carried out by a trained evaluator when study members were eleven, thirteen, fifteen, and eighteen years of age. Study members were considered conduct disordered if they received a formal psychiatric diagnosis at any of these ages. When it came to assessing criminal convictions—for violent crimes—we relied on court records obtained with the cooperation of the Australian and New Zealand police. Among male study members, 11 percent had been convicted by age twenty-six for violent crimes such as common assault, aggravated assault with intent to injure with a weapon, domestic violence, manslaughter, and rape, for a total of 174 convictions. At age twenty-six, we used a standard personality assessment completed by study members that included items related to violence to create an index of disposition toward violence; illustrative items were "when I get angry I am ready to hit someone" and "I admit that I sometimes enjoy hurting someone physically." Finally, we relied on information provided by friends or relatives at age twenty-six pertaining to study members' violent behavior. These informants who knew the study member well were asked about seven cardinal symptoms, including "has problems controlling anger," "blames others for own problems," "does not show guilt after doing something bad," and "(not a) good citizen."

The fact that all four sets of information pertaining to study members' propensities toward violence proved to be substantially related to each other statistically made clear that they were tapping the same underlying disposition. Being the "lumpers" (rather than "splitters") that we are, this led us to create a composite index of antisocial behavior. This summary index reflects whether the study member met diagnostic criteria for adolescent conduct disorder, was convicted of a violent crime, scored in the top quartile of the sample on self-reported disposition toward violence, and fell in the top quartile of the sample on informant-reported symptoms of antisocial personality disorder.

Results of our statistical analyses provided strong support for our GXE hypothesis. Indeed, irrespective of whether we focused on the composite index of antisocial behavior or separately on each of its four components that we initially lumped together, the same picture emerged. Figures 14.1

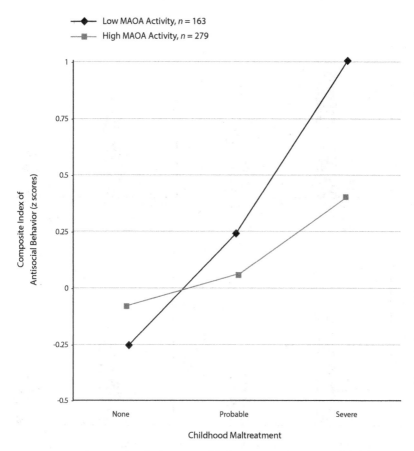

FIGURE 14.1. Average level of antisocial behavior as a function of child maltreatment and *MAOA* genotype. Reformatted from Caspi, A., McClay, J., Moffitt, T.E., Mill, J., Martin, J., Craig, I.W., Taylor, A., & Poulton, R. (2002). Role of genotype in the cycle of violence in maltreated children. *Science, 297*, 851–854, Figure 1. Reproduced with permission from AAAS.

and 14.2 reveal that while antisocial behavior is greater the more certain it is that the study member was subject to maltreatment as a child (that is, severe>probable>none), this dose-response relation proved especially pronounced in the case of individuals carrying the low-activity rather than high-activity *MAOA* gene variant, just as predicted by the diathesis-stress/dual-risk thinking that informed our work. In fact, no matter how we measured antisocial behavior, it was the *combination* of the low-activity *MAOA* genetic variant *and* exposure to probable—but especially

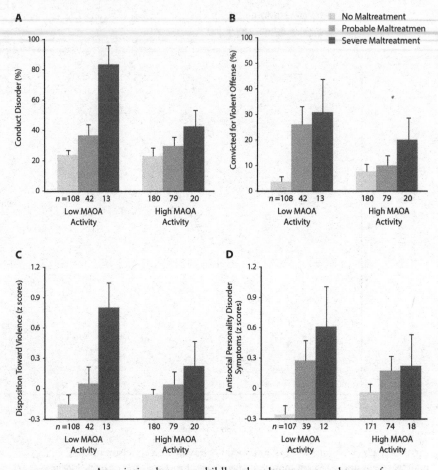

FIGURE 14.2. Association between childhood maltreatment and types of antisocial behavior as a function of *MAOA* genotype. Caspi, A., McClay, J., Moffitt, T.E., Mill, J., Martin, J., Craig, I.W., Taylor, A., & Poulton, R. (2002). Role of genotype in the cycle of violence in maltreated children. *Science, 297*, 851–854, figure 2A and B. Reproduced with permission from AAAS.

severe—maltreatment that generated the greatest amount of problematic functioning.

· CONCLUSION

In addition to documenting the GXE interaction just highlighted, and thus once more the probabilistic nature of development—because not every maltreated boy grew up to become an antisocial man—we should make clear two additional findings stemming from our developmental adventure studying genetics and environment simultaneously. First, even if child maltreatment proved especially problematic for males carrying the low-activity variant of *MAOA*, it was also, even if less so, the case that childhood exposure to maltreatment, all on its own, predicted higher levels of antisocial behavior—that is, irrespective of genetic makeup. To repeat, though, not every maltreated child developed into an antisocial young adult. Notably, however—and this is the second additional finding to consider—this general effect of maltreatment was not true of genetic makeup. So just knowing whether a study member carried the low-activity or high-activity variant of *MAOA* failed to distinguish males in terms of their violent behavior. Thus, it was principally the *co-occurrence* of a particular rearing history and a particular genotype that made our male study members especially prone to behave in antisocial ways.

Having the low-activity *MAOA* variant would therefore seem to *amplify* the risk of antisocial and violent behavior among those exposed to both probable and, especially, severe maltreatment. In fact, even though individuals having the combination of the low-activity *MAOA* genotype and maltreatment comprised only 12 percent of the male birth cohort, they accounted for almost half—44 percent—of the cohort's violent convictions. In other words, the males experiencing the "dual risk" in question were doing four times their share of rape, robbery, and assault relative to all other study members. Moreover, 85 percent of cohort males having a low-activity *MAOA* genotype who were severely maltreated developed some form of antisocial behavior (as reflected in our four individual outcomes graphed in Figure 14.2).

Numerous biological and psychological processes have been proposed in an effort to explain why and how experiences of maltreatment develop into antisocial behavior. These emphasize, among other things, hormones, brain structures and processes, sensitivity to threats, and proclivity to spend time with others who are aggressive, delinquent, or violence prone. But there is no conclusive evidence that any of these processes can account for the progression from child maltreatment to later criminal behavior. As should be well appreciated by now, some youngsters make the progression but others do not. Our work indicates that genetic differences among maltreated children may make a difference; they certainly did in the Dunedin Study.

To bring home the point that biology, including genetics, is not destiny, it must be emphasized that if study members carried the "risk" gene—the low-activity *MAOA* variant—but were not subject to child maltreatment, they were no more likely than those carrying the low-risk genetic variant to engage in violent or otherwise antisocial behavior. In fact, careful inspection of far left side of Figures 14.1 and 14.2 actually indicates that those with the high-risk, low-activity genetic variant actually scored lower on our antisocial outcomes if not maltreated than those who carried the low-risk, high-activity genetic variant who also were not maltreated. It would be a mistake to breathe too much meaning into this observation, given the small difference we are highlighting. Nevertheless, it stimulates us to think in terms of an alternative to the prevailing diathesis-stress or dual-risk model that has productively informed so much work on GXE interaction.

To sense where we are going, reexamine Figures 14.1 and 14.2, asking yourself how the data might have looked had we not simply focused on problematic parenting in the form of child maltreatment and its absence but also considered especially supportive parenting. In fact, imagine that the horizontal axis in each figure is extended leftward of the vertical axis and that the farther to the left one moved on this horizontal axis, the more positive and supportive parenting became. Thus, the extreme left side of the horizontal axis would denote especially sensitive, supportive, and nurturing parenting and the right side severe maltreatment. Now, with this rejiggering of the figures in mind, continue to plot—or extend—the graphed lines in the figures of the low- and high-*MAOA* activity groups downward and to the left. What happens? It is something that a focus exclusively on environmental adversity could never reveal—that those individuals most susceptible, for genetic reasons (that is, the low-activity subgroup), to the adverse effects of maltreatment could also be individuals who benefit the most from positive parenting, as they would manifest the least antisocial behavior. Were that the case, as we are proposing it might be given this thought experiment, it would imply that diathesis-stress and dual-risk thinking represent only half the story of GXE interaction and could even prove misleading.

It would not be just that some individuals are more vulnerable to adversity but also that some individuals are more susceptible to parenting and perhaps other environmental influences "for better and for worse." In other words, they are more susceptible to both negative and positive environmental effects. After all, in our thought experiment, the low-activity *MAOA* carriers would not only evince the most antisocial behavior if severely maltreated but also the least if cared for especially well. As it turns out, there is an emerging school of thought influencing how we think about GXE and person-X-environment interaction more generally that emphasizes this possibility. It is referred to as the "differential susceptibility" perspective because it stipulates that some children are more susceptible than others to environmental influences expected to undermine well-being *and* to those presumed to foster it.

Jay Belsky proposed the notion that children have differential susceptibility to environmental influences, an idea that pediatrician and public health researcher W. Thomas Boyce explores in detail in his 2019 book *The Orchid and the Dandelion*. The title refers to two types of children. Orchid children are considered highly sensitive and therefore very much affected by their developmental experiences (for example, supportive and unsupportive parenting) and environmental exposures (for example, poverty and affluence). Just like orchids, they thrive when cared for well but die when this is not the case. Dandelion children are just the opposite, as they seem more or less impervious to their developmental and rearing experiences, even to the point of being entirely unaffected by them. We are not fans of this typological approach because it risks classifying all children as one of these two kinds. Figures 14.1 and 14.2 alert us to a more nuanced view that recognizes a gradient or continuum of susceptibility to environmental influences or developmental plasticity. Simply put, whereas some children are extremely susceptible, others are less so, still others not at all.

While we cannot know whether the gradient approach to the differential-susceptibility framework applies to our study members given how we designed our investigation, focusing only on problematic, not supportive parenting, we highlight it to encourage readers to think about development differently than many do—and indeed how we did when we launched our adventure investigating GXE interaction. To be specific, entertain the possibility that those children who in studies like our own turn out to function most poorly in the face of adversity because of their genetic makeup (or even some other factor, such as temperament) could very well develop best if exposed to a supportive or enriched rearing environment.

In concluding this chapter, let us make one more observation about the possible limits of our GXE research. Unlike the prior work on genetics—of smoking and life success—presented in Chapters 12 and 13, our GXE research examining the differential effects of child maltreatment, like that on depression in Chapter 15, focused on a single "candidate" gene. As we indicated, we selected the *MAOA* polymorphism because of animal and human evidence that indicated it was biologically plausible that it could interact with an environmental exposure, in our case maltreatment, to predict adult antisocial behavior. But this choice of ours should not be read to suggest that it is the only polymorphism that might interact with maltreatment to undermine well-being. Given that, as we noted in Chapter 12, most phenotypes are influenced by a myriad of genes, each with a small effect, nothing could be further from the truth, in all likelihood. The challenge going forward, then, will be to include multiple genes linked to antisocial behavior, perhaps based on GWAS research, and determine whether a derived polygenic score would also interact with maltreatment to predict antisocial behavior in the way that we found *MAOA* did.

15

Life Stress, Genotype, and Depression in Young Adulthood

Depression is a common and serious malady that adversely affects how you feel, the way you think, and how you act. Fortunately, it is also treatable. Depression causes feelings of sadness and/or an inability to experience pleasure. It can result in a variety of problems, both emotional and physical, while reducing a person's capacity to function at work and at home. Symptoms of depression can vary from mild to severe. They can include one or more of the following: feeling sad or having a depressed mood; losing interest or pleasure in activities once enjoyed; changes in appetite; weight loss or gain that does not involve dieting; difficulty falling or staying asleep or sleeping too much; loss of energy or increased fatigue; increase in purposeless, dysfunctional physical activity, such as hand-wringing or pacing, or slowed movements and speech; feeling worthless or guilty; difficulty thinking, concentrating, or making decisions; and thoughts of death or suicide.

Sadly, depression is pervasive. In 2015, about 16 million American adults—almost 7 percent of the adult population in the United States—had a major depressive episode in the past year. The American Psychiatric Association defines a major depressive episode as "a period of two weeks or longer during which there is either depressed mood or loss of interest or pleasure and at least four other symptoms that reflect a change in functioning, such as problems with sleep, eating, energy, concentration, and self-image." Additionally, the episode must be accompanied by clinically significant distress or impairment in social, occupational, or other important areas of daily life. Major depression takes the most years off American lives and accounts for the most years lived with disability of any mental or behavioral disorder. It is also expensive: from 1999 to 2012, the percentage of Americans on antidepressants rose from an estimated 6.8 percent to 12 percent. The global depression drug market is slated to be worth over $16 billion by 2020—and this does not include self-medication via cannabis, alcohol, and other nonprescription substances.

Given depression's prevalence and discomfort, it is not surprising that great efforts have been made not only to treat it but also to identify its causes, and the latter is the focus of the scientific adventure we discuss in this chapter, again from the perspective of a gene-by-environment (GXE) interaction, as described in Chapter 14. In a notable modification of our concern with the influence of childhood and adolescent experiences on later development, in this chapter we focus on adult experiences, particularly on negative or stressful life events. It is well established that such experiences can play a role in precipitating depression. These events can take a variety of forms, involving employment, as when one loses a job either because the business fails or one is fired; financial, as when an investment goes bad or one has insufficient funds to pay bills and becomes indebted; and social, as when one experiences the breakup of an intimate relationship or the death of a loved one. Housing events can also precipitate depression, as when one's house burns down or one becomes homeless for other reasons. Then, of course, there are negative health-related events, such as being diagnosed with cancer or another terminal or seriously debilitating condition.

But the power of negative life events to predict depression turns out to be similar to what we learned in Chapter 14 about the effects of child maltreatment on violent behavior in men. Not only are findings concerning the effect of serious life events on depression inconsistent, but it is well appreciated that not everyone reacts the same way to the same adversity. Once more, we are dealing with a probabilistic rather than deterministic effect. This observation calls to mind Dunedin Study interviews at age twenty-six with two young women, whom we will refer to as Charlotte and Olivia, about their social relationships. Both had recently experienced a breakup with a boyfriend, and in each case these women had been dumped rather than being the one doing the dumping. In both cases, the relationships had lasted several years, leading these young women to believe there was the possibility of a long-term future, perhaps even marriage. But while Charlotte was emotionally devastated by the experience, meeting criteria for major depression when we administered the standard psychiatric interview we gave every twenty-six-year-old participating in the Dunedin Study, Olivia proved resilient to this stressor. Even though she was clearly disappointed that the relationship did not work out, she was not despondent; she did not believe, as Charlotte did, that she would probably never find another man to love her and would probably have to spend the rest of her life on her own. In fact, Olivia was rather optimistic, commenting that "there's lots of fish in the sea."

Such observations make it clear that serious negative life events are a "risk factor" for depression. The very terminology of "risk factor" conveys an important but too often misunderstood point when thinking in cause-and-effect terms. So let's review what was highlighted way back in Chapter 8, as well as in Chapter 14, that while something like the dissolution of a close relationship increases the probability that a person will become depressed, it by no means guarantees it. Indeed, it is well appreciated that such risks are typically realized when other risk conditions co-occur. For example, the probability of the undesired end of a relationship leading to depression is greater if it coincides with another serious life event, say the loss of a job or the death of a loved one.

But in our work, informed as it was by the diathesis-stress (or dual-risk) model of psychopathology, also introduced in Chapter 14, we investigated not only the accumulation of serious life events but rather, once again, the possibility that because of differences in their genetic makeup some people succumb to adversity whereas others do not. In other words, genotype is once again the diathesis, this time making one vulnerable to becoming depressed in the face of many negative life events; but in the absence of such adversity, the vulnerability would not, or at least be less likely to, be realized. Once more, we theorized that it would take "two to tango"—adversity in the form of negative life events *and* a certain genetic makeup—to precipitate depression. Put another way, each of these inconsistently detected correlates of depression functioned as clues to us developmental detectives when undertaking our adventure studying GXE interaction once again.

WHAT GENE?

In Chapter 14, we reviewed our earliest work on GXE interaction focused on the *MAOA* polymorphism because of theory and evidence linking it to violent behavior. When we did our candidate-gene work investigating such interaction, also in the 2000s—before GWAS-based polygenic scores became the "go to" strategy (as discussed in detail in Chapter 12)—*MAOA* was not the appropriate candidate when it came to studying the etiology of depression in young adulthood. Instead, we focused on another polymorphism, the serotonin transporter, otherwise referred to as *5-HTTLPR*. The serotonin transporter comes in two versions, which are referred to as short (s) and long (l). Each of us inherits one such allelic variant from each of our parents. As a result, *HTTLPR* can take the form of ss, ll, or sl. When the same allelic variant is inherited from both parents, in this case l or s, the person is said to be "homozygous" for that variant, whereas when an individual carries one of each variant, sl, that person is said to be "heterozygous."

We selected *5-HTTLPR* as the genetic focus in our research on the etiology of depression for two reasons—because of evidence of its functionality and because of research indicating that it moderates (that is, modifies) response to stress. Functionally—at the cellular level—short alleles are associated with reduced "uptake" of serotonin, a neurotransmitter, from the synapse connecting two neurons in the brain, whereas long alleles are associated with greater uptake of serotonin. In other words, the two variants differentially affect how long this neurotransmitter remains in brain synapses. The longer it remains, it is thought, the greater the calming effect of serotonin. This would seem to suggest that individuals who carry short alleles, perhaps especially two, would be at higher risk of depression, because they would benefit less from the calming effect of serotonin.

Beyond this speculation, there are empirical reasons to believe that variation in the serotonin transporter polymorphism is related to depression. Indeed, complementing the previously cited inconsistent evidence linking the short allele directly with depression are repeated indications that variation in the serotonin transporter interacts with stress to produce depression-like behavior and/or a physiological response related to depression. In this regard, first consider animal research. Mice with one or two short alleles exhibit more fearful behavior when stressed, as well as greater increases in a stress hormone, than do those with two long alleles, but these differences in emotional and physiological functioning as a result of genotype fail to materialize in the absence of stress. Next, consider research on a highly social species of monkey, the rhesus macaque, indicating that individual animals carrying the short allele display decreased serotonergic activity compared to those with long-allele homozygotes when reared in a stressful, socially isolating condition, yet no such neurotransmitter difference is observed between such genetically different monkeys when they are housed with other monkeys while growing up. Finally, in humans, neuroimaging studies show that people carrying one or two s alleles exhibit greater neuronal activity in one part of the brain that responds to stress, the amygdala, than individuals homozygous for the long allele. In all cases, differences in behavioral and physiological functioning emerge as a result of genetic variation, *but only under stressful conditions*. This, by definition, is evidence of a GXE interaction.

Based on this evidence available at the time we began this adventure investigating the causes of depression, we suspected that variation in *5-HTTLPR* moderates psychopathological reactions to stressful experiences. Thus, we specifically hypothesized that *study members carrying two short alleles would be most likely to become depressed or exhibit symptoms of depression when they experienced multiple stressful life events* and that this would also be the case among those with a single s allele relative to those with no s alleles: the ll carriers. Consistent with the already cited work, we further expected that there would be no differences between s and l carriers in terms of depression when study members did not experience a negative life event. In other words, as the extent of exposure to negative life events increased—say, from no such events to one, two, three, and four or more—the differences in depression between ss, sl, and ll carriers would become increasingly evident, with s carriers showing greater psychopathology than ll carriers, especially under ever more stressful circumstances in their lives.

TESTING THE GXE INTERACTION

To test our predictions, once we had genotyped study members, we turned to our data pantry and accessed information on negative life events and depression that we had collected. To assess exposure to and experience of negative life events, we relied on a method we developed called the life-history calendar. This involves walking study members through a timeline of their life, year by year and month by month, since we last saw them, to review things that happened to them. This has proven to be a much more accurate way of gathering information about life experiences than simply asking questions about whether this or that happened to a person or even just asking whether anything problematic had occurred over some period of time. So when we saw study members at age twenty-six, we administered the life-history calendar covering the previous five years, from their twenty-first to twenty-sixth birthdays.

From the events that were reported and recorded, we identified negative or stressful ones involving employment problems (long-term unemployment, being made redundant, losing a job because the company moved, or being fired); financial problems (problems with debt, such as having items repossessed, not having enough money to pay for food or household expenses, lacking money for medical expenses, or difficulty paying bills); housing problems (homelessness or multiple residence changes); health problems (a disabling physical illness lasting a month or more or a disabling injury); and relationship problems (being involved in a physically violent relationship or the breakup of a cohabiting, intimate relationship). Overall, 30 percent of the study members experienced no stressful life events over the five years under consideration, 25 percent experienced one event, 20 percent had two events, 11 percent had three events, and 15 percent reported four or more events.

When it came to assessing depression, we relied on a standard psychiatric interview, also administered at age twenty-six, but by a person who was not involved in collecting the life-event information (so their judgements could not be biased by such knowledge). The interview focused on feelings of depression experienced over the preceding twelve months. It yielded a continuous measure of the number of depressive symptoms (for example, can't sleep, worry all the time), as well as a formal psychiatric diagnosis of a major depressive episode, as previously defined. Overall, 17 percent of study members (58 percent female, 42 percent male) met criteria for a major depressive episode in the previous calendar year. This rate is comparable to that documented in the United States for individuals of the same age and sex.

In addition to testing our GXE hypothesis on the diagnostic outcome of major depressive disorder and, separately, on the number of depressive symptoms, we also examined suicidal inclinations; 3 percent of the study members reported suicide attempts or recurrent thoughts about suicide in the context of a depressive episode. Finally, at age twenty-six, we secured information about study members from people who knew them well, via a mailed questionnaire that asked them, among other things, to rate the study member on four different symptoms: "feels depressed, miserable, sad, or unhappy," "feels that no one loves them," "seems lonely," and "talks about suicide." Thus, we ended up with four indicators of depression—number of depressive symptoms, diagnosis of major depression, suicide ideation and/or attempt, and evaluation of depression by a friend or family member.

We these data in hand, we were almost ready to test our GXE hypothesis, but before we could do so, we needed to determine whether study members with many or few negative life events differed from each other genetically. If that was the case—for example, those homozygous for the short allele experienced more negative life events than others did—it would raise the possibility of gene-environment correlation, referred to in Chapter 14, and thus selection effects. In fact, if study members with and without short alleles also differed in terms of their experience of negative life events, we could not go forward with our GXE inquiry. Fortunately, this was not the case. Knowing a person's 5-HTTLPR genotype provided no insight into his or her negative life experiences, because genotype was independent from environment.

Our first step in directly testing our hypothesis provided support for it. Exposure to many negative life events more strongly predicted experiencing more depressive symptoms for study members carrying an s allele (ss or sl) than it did for those carrying two l alleles. This remained the case even when we took into account—that is, statistically discounted—the effects of depressive symptoms we had measured at age twenty-one. This latter result meant that the GXE prediction of depressive symptoms at age twenty-six could not be attributed to earlier depression leading to later depression. In fact, it meant that more stressful life events predicted an *increase* in depressive symptomology from age twenty-one to age twenty-six for those carrying short alleles. As Figure 15.1A indicates, the experience of lots of negative life events was associated most strongly with more depressive symptoms in the case of ss homozygotes, making them the most vulnerable to adversity, and least strongly for ll homozygotes, making them resilient

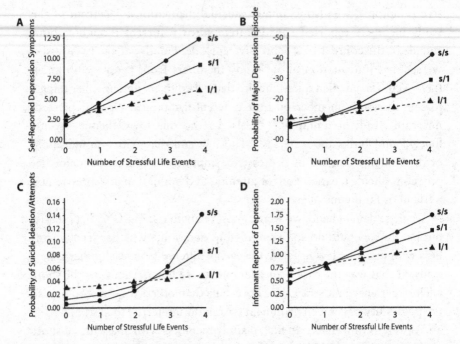

FIGURE 15.1. Association between number of stressful life events (between ages twenty-one and twenty-six years) and depression-related outcomes at age sixteen as a function of 5-HTT genotype (s = short allele; l = long allele). Caspi, A., Sugden, K., Moffitt, T.E., Taylor, A., Craig, I.W., Harrington, H., McClay, J., Mill, J., Martin, J., Braithwaite, A., & Poulton, R. (2003). Influence of life stress on depression: Moderation by a polymorphism in the 5-HTT gene. *Science, 301*, 386–389 figure 1. Reproduced with permission from AAAS.

in the face of adversity, with sl heterozygotes falling between these two groups. Clearly, the more s alleles a study member carried, the more adverse the effect of lots of negative life events.

Also noteworthy is that the same pattern of results emerged when we considered different ways of measuring depression—risk of a major depressive episode (Figure 15.1B), likelihood of thinking about or attempting suicide (Figure 15.1C), and even reports of depressive symptoms by informants who knew the study members well (Figure 15.1D). In all cases, s carriers, and especially ss homozygotes, proved to be more adversely affected than ll homozygotes by negative life events, with no genotypic differences in depression emerging when study members reported no or even very few stressful life events. Thus, no matter how we measured depression, a classic, diathesis-stress-related GXE interaction emerged.

A POSSIBLE ALTERNATIVE EXPLANATION

However convincing our GXE findings first appeared, we appreciated that they could reflect something else going on other than s-allele carriers being more susceptible to the adverse effects of negative life events on depression. This was because the results we have shared also would have emerged if study members who experienced more rather than fewer negative life events differed from each other genetically in a way that affected their exposure to stressful life events. Were this the case, it could indicate that our would-be measure of environmental stress was actually a measure of genetic makeup more or less "masquerading" as a measure of the environment. Consider this thought experiment: imagine we found that people who eat a lot end up heavier than those who eat less, but it turned out that eating a lot resulted from genetic makeup. Were that so, it would be a mistake to conceptualize a measure of eating as solely an index of experience rather than of genetic makeup.

So even though we had already ruled out this kind of misspecification of *5-HTTLPR* when we found that this *particular* genetic factor was not related to stressful life events, it remained possible that *other* genes that we had not measured still could be. If that were so, our findings would actually be the result of a gene-X-gene (GXG) interaction rather than a GXE interaction—since our supposed environmental index ("E") actually was a measure of G, genetics. Because we did not have measures of all other possible genes when we carried out our depression work early in our program of genetics research, we could not directly address the concern under consideration.

It occurred to us, however, that we could evaluate the alternative GXG possibility indirectly. If the alternative GXG explanation was responsible for our apparent GXE results, then it should be the case that life events would interact with *5-HTTLPR* in predicting depression even when those life events occurred *after* an episode of major depression. This would be a case of *post*diction, which is not logically possible because it would reflect an environmental experience in the future (negative life events) forecasting something in the past (depression), rather than *pre*diction (that is, something earlier predicting something later). But if our measure of life events truly reflected environmental stress and was not a camouflaged index of genetic makeup, then the timing of life events relative to depression would matter. Indeed, predictor and outcomes would be "temporally ordered" in a manner consistent with causation, such that the would-be cause, life events, *precedes* the would-be consequence, depression. In other words, support for our interpretation of the GXE evidence would emerge if, as we had already found, *earlier* life events interacted with genetic makeup to predict *later* depression and, as we still needed to determine, *later* life events did not interact with genetic makeup in postdicting *earlier* depression.

To address this latter issue empirically, we reran our original statistical analysis, but in place of depression measured at age twenty-six, we used as the outcome to be explained depression measured at ages eighteen and twenty-one. In these two additional analyses, we were looking to see whether *later* life events, perhaps reflecting G, interacted with *5-HTTLPR* to postdict *earlier* depression. The results proved consistent with our original GXE interpretation in that later life events did not interact with genetic makeup to postdict earlier depression. When considered alongside our original GXE findings, these null results gave us confidence that we were not dealing with a GXG interaction masquerading as a GXE one.

CONCLUSION

In our second adventure investigating GXE interaction, we found further evidence that perhaps one reason prior research on environmental and genetic influences, investigated separately, proved inconsistent in predicting mental health was because some individuals, because of their genetic makeup, are more susceptible to the effects of adversity than others are. This observation is important because it raises the prospect that greater scientific progress might be made if instead of thinking about genes for this or that illness or psychopathology, we thought about genes for susceptibility to potential environmental influences. This, of course, would be consistent with the differential-susceptibility perspective introduced at the end of Chapter 14. Recall that this perspective raised the possibility that some individuals are more susceptible than others to both positive and negative environmental exposures and developmental experiences. Thus, imagine a science that sought to identify not just genes that supposedly "code" for some illness or malady but also genes that shape the way we respond to environmental insults—such as toxins or life stressors—and/or supports, such as high-quality schooling or positive life events. Should these prove identifiable, it could raise the possibility of targeting those individuals, for preventative purposes, who are most likely to succumb to some adversity and, for enhancement purposes, those individuals most likely to benefit from some forms of contextual enrichment.

However exciting the GXE results linking exposure to multiple life events and being a *5-HTTLPR* short-allele carrier seemed to be to us and many others, and however consistent our results were with the long-standing diathesis-stress model of psychopathology, our GXE work did not go uncontested. Even though we made clear that others needed to replicate our findings before any implications for service and practice should be drawn, we encountered a virtual tidal wave of criticism—or so it seemed. Although some of it was not unreasonable—rare is the perfect piece of scientific research—much of it seemed motivated by nonscientific factors. Many of our colleagues who defended us against criticism believed that we were attacked because as non-card carrying geneticists whose work emphasized the importance of the environment, we had succeeded where a lot of genetics-only research (that is, genotype-phenotype work) had failed. Moreover, in showing that it was a GXE interaction rather than genetics alone that was influencing depression, our results indicated, once again, that genetics is not destiny, an observation that upset the intellectual apple cart of some people.

In the years that followed the publication of our paper, much additional research has been done. One thing that has become clear to many is that problems with research on GXE interaction involving life events, *5-HTTLPR,* and depression may have as much to do with the now well-recognized limits of candidate-gene research (see the discussion in Chapter 12) as with poorly measuring stressful life events, relying on checklists rather than careful and probing interviews such as those we implemented in using our life-history calendar data-collection method.

As we reflected on our own findings, it occurred to us that there were at least two additional issues worth pursuing, one having to do with environmental exposures and the other with genotype. With regard to the former, we wondered, given our evidence that carrying short alleles increased the probability of becoming depressed in the face of multiple stressful life events, whether adversity experienced not just in adulthood but also in childhood would operate in a similar way. This led us to draw on our measure of child maltreatment described in Chapter 14 to determine if it, too, interacted with *5-HTTLPR* in predicting risk of a major depressive episode. As Figure 15.2 makes clear, it did, basically mirroring earlier findings involving stressful life events (see Figure 15.1B). What this means, of course, is that certain individuals (that is, *5-HTTLPR* short-allele carriers) are more susceptible to at least two different adversities experienced in two different life phases—maltreatment in childhood and stressful life events in young adulthood—when it comes to the risk of being depressed in young adulthood.

The second thing we wondered about was whether the risk of becoming depressed in the face of adversity was specific to *5-HTTLPR* and not another candidate gene we had already found (see Chapter 14) to be associated with males becoming more violent because of the experience of being maltreated in childhood. That is, did the *MAOA* polymorphism interact with stressful life events in predicting depression in the same dual-risk manner that *5-HTTLPR* did when interacting with negative life events? Results revealed that this was not the case. There was thus some genetic specificity to who succumbed to depression when exposed to multiple stressful life events.

Although much of this chapter has highlighted the disproportionate vulnerability of *5-HTTLPR* short-allele carriers to adversity when it comes to experiencing depression in young adulthood, we should not lose sight of

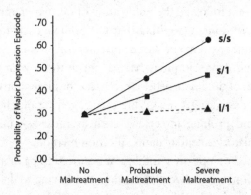

FIGURE 15.2. Association between childhood maltreatment (between the ages of three and eleven years) and adult depression (ages eighteen to twenty-six) as a function of 5-HTT genotype (s = short allele; l = long allele). Caspi, A., Sugden, K., Moffitt, T.E., Taylor, A., Craig, I.W., Harrington, H., McClay, J., Mill, J., Martin, J., Braithwaite, A., & Poulton, R. (2003). Influence of life stress on depression: Moderation by a polymorphism in the 5-HTT gene. *Science, 301*, 386–389, figure 2. Reproduced with permission from AAAS.

what the findings have to say about resilience. As we noted in Chapter 14, when it comes to the issue of factors and forces that seem to protect individuals from succumbing to the negative effects of adversity, attention is often—and not unreasonably—paid to environmental factors, such as having a good friend, or personal characteristics, such as having a high IQ or a good sense of humor. What both GXE studies covered in this chapter and Chapter 14 make clear is that genetic makeup also needs to be considered. Having one or especially two long *5-HTTLPR* alleles appears to make individuals relatively immune to the "depressionogenic" effects of negative life events in young adulthood and of maltreatment in childhood in the case of participants in the Dunedin Study. Given this result, it would seem once again too bad that you can't choose your parents!

16

Epigenetics, or Genes as Dependent Variables

Throughout the first fifteen chapters of this book, we have sought as much as possible to avoid reliance on scientific jargon while sharing the work we have done following thousands of children as they grow and develop. There is a need to diverge from that practice at least a little bit, however, as should be evident from the title of this chapter. In the parlance of science, when we investigate whether and how some factor, such as temperament in early childhood, or some experience, such as being bullied in middle childhood, predicts and perhaps influences some aspect of development (for example, antisocial behavior or depression), the predictor is referred to as the *independent* variable and the outcome being predicted is called the *dependent* variable. This is based on the presumption that the phenomenon being predicted (for example, amount of aggression) *depends* on the independent variable (for example, being bullied or not).

In all the genetic work we have discussed in Chapters 12–15, genes have been regarded, as is typical when thinking about human development, as an independent construct, a predictor of some phenotype. As we have seen, genes can serve as a predictor either on their own, as in Chapters 12 (smoking) and 13 (life success), or in interaction with some environmental condition, as in Chapters 14 (child maltreatment) and 15 (stressful life events). In fact, genes are typically regarded as "first causes," as they exist

from the moment of conception, thus preceding all phenotypic development. They are thereby thought to influence most, if not all, of how the
individual develops, even if they are not the sole source of influence. In this
chapter, however, we entertain the possibility that developmental experiences and environmental exposures can actually influence the functioning
of genes, thereby seeming to magically turn the first-cause independent variables into dependent variables! For most students of human development,
this is a rather radical view of how genes might influence psychological and
behavioral phenomena. Indeed, it serves to define an entirely new field of
genetics, referred to as *epigenetics,* for those studying environmental effects.

Although epigenetics is relatively new to students of human development, it is a field of inquiry with a substantial history. Indeed, it proved
central to understanding what once was one of the great mysteries of life:
How do cells in the eye, ear, leg bone, or heart "know" to become those
kinds of cells rather than some other kinds? Why don't heart cells turn up
in the eye, or eye cells in the heart? It turns out that embryologists have
long known that the answers to these questions involve the differential *expression* of genes. Thus, when a cell develops into heart muscle rather
than, say, your bicep or femur, it is because certain genes have been turned
on and become expressed, thereby stimulating the generation of proteins,
which launches the process of genetic influence, whereas other genes have
been turned off to ensure that they do not influence the protein-making process of genetic influence. It's almost like having the same alphabet of genes
in every cell in the body but with only certain "letters" used to "spell" certain "words"—or body parts. Metaphorically, then, only certain letters
are typed out to create the word *heart,* others to write *bicep,* and still others
to write *femur.* All this occurs during the embryological period of prenatal
development, that short period of gestation when all parts of the body get
defined and that occurs soon after the fertilized egg, the ovum, attaches itself to the intrauterine wall.

From the perspective of embryological epigenetics, once cells are defined
as heart, bicep, or femur cells, nothing changes (unless cancer strikes). Consequently, every "daughter" cell inherits the same alphabetical instructions as the "parent" cell when the older cell divides (before dying) to make
the new (replacement) cell. Thus, the genes in each subsequent generation
of heart, bicep, or femur cells get expressed in exactly the same way as in
the first generation. Until rather recently, our understanding of epigenetics

was that particular cells, carrying the full complement of the individual's genes, become distinctive parts of the body during the embryological period when specific genes are turned on and expressed and other genes are turned off—forever.

But something truly groundbreaking was reported early in the twenty-first century that radically challenged this established view of epigenetics. A team of Canadian researchers led by Michael Meany of McGill University discovered that how a mother rat, called a "dam," treated her newborn "pup" affected gene expression in the pup and thereby whether that baby rat grew up to be less rather than more anxious. When dams licked and groomed their newborns a lot rather than a little, the expression of a particular gene known to play a role in the rat's physiological response to stress was turned off, thereby making the rat less anxious as it developed. More specifically, the stress-related gene was chemically "turned off" when it had a methyl group attached to the gene when the dam engaged in a lot of licking and grooming, thereby resulting in a more stress-resistant pup. While there are other ways of affecting gene expression, this process of DNA *methylation*—which turns genes off—is the one that has been studied the most in humans and thus the one that we focus on in this chapter. To be clear, then, methylation is not a synonym for epigenetics or gene expression. Rather, it is one of several epigenetic mechanisms that regulate gene expression and thus perhaps can be influenced by developmental experiences and environmental exposures, thereby affecting phenotypic development.

The excitement that Meaney's research generated among students of human development is hard to convey. In one case, it led a distinguished scholar to write in the magazine of the Association for Psychological Science, which goes out to thousands of psychological and behavioral scientists each month, about how parenting affects gene expression and thereby psychological and behavioral development. What the scholar in question failed to acknowledge, however, so excited was he about the potential implications of the research for humans, was that the research in question was carried out on rats! This almost glib generalization of a finding about rats to people—without necessary cautions—was not uncommon. It also seems noteworthy that the same rodent research and what it might mean for the process of human development led to a cover story in the June 26, 2009, issue of *Newsweek*. It is easy to see why. Not only was it the case, as has long been appreciated, that genes affect development—as independent variables (that is, first causes)—but also developmental experiences, such as parenting, now seemed to be able to influence DNA methylation and thereby gene expression and consequently human development. Genes had become dependent variables! While they remained sources of influence on development, they now could be affected by other sources of influence—developmental experiences and environmental exposures. So, in addressing this topic in this chapter, we are returning to our theme of childhood influences on human development but extending it to consider the role of epigenetics in linking developmental experiences earlier in life, in this case in adolescence, and psychopathology later in life.

As increasing evidence seeming to document environmental effects on DNA methylation in humans appeared in the scientific literature, stimulated as it was by the original rodent research, we began to wonder about the confidence that could be placed in the findings being published and, especially, the conclusions being drawn based on the emerging evidence. Like so many others, we were greatly excited by the potential for epigenetics to dramatically alter how we think about nature and nurture, with the possibility of nurture shaping (the expression of) nature. At the same time, however, we wondered about how reliable—or replicable—the epigenetic findings being reported and involving DNA methylation would prove to be. While there was a burgeoning body of literature on the apparent environmental regulation of gene expression, as revealed in measurements of methylation, there was a lot of methodological variation across the published studies. They focused not only on many different environmental exposures (for example, early parental loss, child abuse, and parental mental illness) but also, when it came to the methylation of genes, on many different genes.

It also was rarely clear how many different environmental exposures and/or different genes many of these studies had examined. It is one thing to find that exposure X is linked to the expression of gene Y because of DNA methylation, but what if this same finding emerges when investigating how four different exposures (for example, poverty, sexual abuse, harsh punishment, and bullying) affect the methylation and thus expression of forty-five different genes? In such a case, we could have one result being heralded after a search of 180 possibilities! Were that so, there would be good reason to question whether the exciting result was real—to be believed—or just a function of chance.

In making these observations, we do not mean to demean those who were among the first to publish studies of environmental effects on the epigenome—that is, the methylation of genes—in humans. It is often the case that in the early phases of scientific inquiry consideration and empirical exploration of many possibilities makes sense. But the time eventually comes to move beyond the initial phase of excitement and get more focused—and rigorous—in evaluating an idea. So that is what we set out to do, relying as we did on the Environmental-Risk Study, in the epigenetic adventure that is the focus of this chapter. Just to be clear, our aim was not to disconfirm the results of others. We were open minded and hopeful, endeavoring to extend work in this area. Perhaps the best evidence of this is the amount of time, money, and effort we put into our epigenetic investigation, which should become evident.

We appreciated from the outset of our epigenetic adventure that if we wanted to investigate effects of developmental experiences and environmental exposures on DNA methylation, and thereby psychological and behavioral development, then the first thing we needed to do was provision our journey by identifying an independent environmental factor that we had reason to believe could influence and thus predict a particular dependent, developmental one. This was necessary because the presumption guiding epigenetic inquiry into human development was that (A) developmental experiences and environmental exposures affect (B) DNA methylation and thereby (C) psychological and behavioral development.

In view of our desire to test the hypothesis, as emerging theory stipulated (and limited evidence suggested), that the effect of A on C resulted from the effect of A on B followed by an effect of B on C, we planned five stages of inquiry. After identifying the environmental feature reflecting children's experience and the developmental phenotype we would seek to have it explain in stage 1 of our epigenetic adventure, stage 2 would be devoted to determining whether, as anticipated, the environmental exposure we selected did predict the developmental phenotype we selected. If it did not, there would be no reason to proceed with our journey, but if it did, stage 3 would commence, determining whether our environmental predictor, A, also predicted our would-be methylation mediator, B. Stage 4 would subsequently evaluate whether this mediator B itself predicted our developmental outcome, C. Finally, if stages 3 and 4 yielded promising results, in stage 5 we would determine whether the previously detected effect of A on C resulted from the mediational effect of B (that is, A→B→C).

STAGE 1: IDENTIFYING AND MEASURING PRE-DICTOR AND OUTCOME

After careful consideration, we decided that when it came to A, we would focus on the experience of victimization in adolescence, and when it came to C, we would focus on psychopathology in young adulthood. We chose victimization as our environmental exposure because, like limited licking and grooming by a mother rat and some of the conditions that human investigators of DNA methylation had focused on already (for example, child abuse), it is considered very stressful. We focused on psychopathology as our outcome phenotype to be explained because of extensive evidence that different types of victimization promote psychopathology. Also influencing this latter decision was the original rodent research showing that parental behavior affected the anxiety manifested by rats because of the methylation—or lack thereof—of a particular gene known to be associated with the physiological stress-response system.

When it came to investigating victimization, we decided to focus not on one particular form of victimization experienced by E-Risk Study members, such as child abuse, but instead many different ways in which an adolescent could be victimized. This decision was based on prior research indicating that multiple or "poly" victimization is considerably more powerful than the presence or absence of any particular experience of victimization as a predictor of psychiatric symptoms. In fact, existing evidence indicated that polyvictimized children tended to experience more symptoms than even children who were repeatedly exposed to one kind of victimization, be it child abuse or bullying by peers.

To assess victimization, we interviewed E-Risk Study members at age eighteen about their victimization experiences since leaving primary school at age twelve and entering secondary school. More specifically, we asked them questions about their experience of maltreatment, neglect, sexual victimization, family violence, peer or sibling victimization, internet or mobile phone victimization, and crime victimization. Just under two-thirds of adolescents reported experiencing no severe victimization, but almost

20 percent reported one such experience, just under 10 percent two experiences, and almost 7 percent three or more severe forms of victimization.

When it came to measurement of our dependent variable in the first step of the first stage of our multistage adventure, we relied on confidential interviews with study members at age eighteen about symptoms of mental disorders. More specifically, we assessed symptoms of five *externalizing* spectrum disorders (alcohol dependence, cannabis dependence, conduct disorder, tobacco dependence, and ADHD) and four *internalizing* spectrum disorders (depression, anxiety, post-traumatic stress, and eating disorder) that members experienced during the past year. We also assessed *thought-disorder* symptoms by gathering information about delusions and hallucinations, as well as experiences of unusual thoughts and feelings (for example, "my thinking is unusual and frightening" and "people or places I know seem different"). In addition to creating three distinct measures of externalizing, internalizing, and thought-disorder symptoms for analysis, we also created an index related to diverse symptoms based on evidence from our study and others that individuals often manifest a diversity of symptoms—referred to as "comorbidity"—that reflects psychopathology more generally; this index is referred to as *p* (representing "psychopathology"). The higher *p,* the more cross-disorder symptoms an individual manifests.

STAGE 2: VICTIMIZATION PREDICTING PSYCHOPATHOLOGY

Now that we had our independent and dependent variables in order, the next stage, still really a preliminary stage, of our epigenetic adventure involved determining whether, as hypothesized, adolescent victimization predicted early-adult psychopathology. Our initial effort addressing this issue revealed a dose-response relation between adolescent polyvictimization and each of the four indices of psychopathological symptoms outlined in the preceding paragraph. Thus, the more kinds of victimization a teenager experienced, the more externalizing, internalizing, and thought-disorder symptoms manifested (Figure 16.1) and, consequently, the higher the score on the index of *p* (Figure 16.2). Just as notable was that each separate type of adolescent victimization we assessed showed a similar dose-response relation to each of these four dependent variables. It is important to point

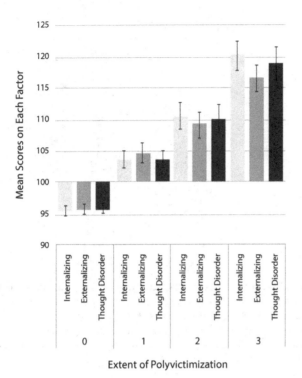

FIGURE 16.1. Mean levels of different psychopathological problems in early adulthood as a function of extent of polyvictimization. Reformatted from Schaefer, J.D., Moffitt, T.E., Arseneault, L., Danese, A., Fisher, H.L., Houts, R., Sheridan, M.A., Wertz, J., & Caspi, A. (2018), Adolescent victimization and early-adult psychopathology: Approaching causal inference using a longitudinal twin study to rule out alternative non-causal explanations. *Clinical Psychological Science*, Vol. 6(3) 352–371, figure 1. CC-BY.

out, however, that the deleterious effects of adolescent victimization on *p* were greatest in the case of maltreatment, neglect, and sexual victimization. Nevertheless, when all forms of victimization were considered simultaneously, each made an independent contribution to the prediction of *p*. In other words, every form of victimization exerted a unique—and additive—effect on *p*. This, of course, is why greater exposure to more types of victimization proved to be associated with a higher *p*.

Anyone who has read through even several of the preceding chapters in this book will be familiar with what comes next—because we most certainly did not stop here. As is our routine, we needed to challenge these initial findings in order to determine whether any or all four very plausible

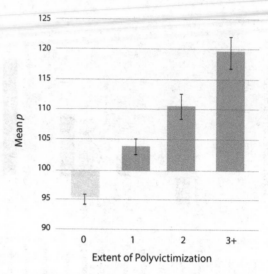

FIGURE 16.2. Average general-psychopathology score (p) in early adulthood as a function of extent of polyvictimization. Schaefer, J.D., Moffitt, T.E., Arseneault, L., Danese, A., Fisher, H.L., Houts, R., Sheridan, M.A., Wertz, J., & Caspi, A. (2018). Adolescent victimization and early-adult psychopathology: Approaching causal inference using a longitudinal twin study to rule out alternative non-causal explanations. *Clinical Psychological Science* Vol. 6(3) 352–371, figure 2a. CC-BY.

but noncausal explanations could account for our results. First, could the findings reported to this point—and that serve as the foundation for all that is to come—be an artifact of respondent bias? After all, the same person—the adolescent—provided information on both victimization experience and psychopathological symptoms? Isn't it possible, then, that an eighteen-year-old suffering from psychological problems could easily mischaracterize—and exaggerate—her victimization experience? If so, this would increase the likelihood that we would detect the victimization-psychopathology association that we did. Recall that this issue of biased memory was one that we discussed at length in Chapter 5 when considering the limits of retrospective studies and the strengths of prospective ones when investigating the intergenerational transmission of parenting. Recall as well that the general advantages of prospective over retrospective research on human development was also discussed in Chapter 1.

Fortunately, we had asked each twin in the E-Risk Study to report on their co-twin's victimization experience, and we did the same with parents, having them report separately on each twin's victimization experience. Thus, we could check whether findings linking greater polyvictimization with greater psychopathology would be similar if we relied on a child's victimization experiences *reported by others* who knew the child well. When we reran our analyses using these informant reports to predict each twin's p score, results revealed once more that greater polyvictimization, this time reported by a co-twin or parent, predicted more psychological symptoms, reported by the twin of interest. Apparently, response bias was not the cause of our findings. Thus, we could rule out the first noncausal and alternative explanation of the adverse effects of polyvictimization that we documented.

The second of four plausible noncausal explanations of our findings that we had to consider was that victimization was the consequence of earlier-in-life and thus preexisting psychiatric problems rather than adolescent polyvictimization. Thus, we posed the following question: could a process of "reverse causation" be at work, with earlier-in-life psychological difficulties leading to the victimization of teenagers rather than the other way around? To address this issue, we drew from our data pantry existing measures of mental health problems at age twelve, parent- and teacher-reported emotional and behavioral problems at age five, and family history of psychopathology. The fact that each of these measurements predicted psychiatric symptoms (that is, p score) at age eighteen meant that there was a very real possibility of reverse causation.

Yet, when we separately discounted the effects of each of these markers of prior psychological vulnerability—as well as all of them at the same time—greater polyvictimization in adolescence still predicted a higher p score. In other words, it was not the case that reverse causation was masquerading as victimization effects in our initial results, even if it was the case that there was a relation between early problems and victimization later in adolescence. In fact, our work revealed a cyclical relationship involving the factors and processes we were investigating: Early problems or the risk of them (that is, family history of psychopathology) predicted greater polyvictimization in adolescence, which itself predicted more psychiatric symptoms in early adulthood—in fact, more *types* of psychiatric symptoms.

When it came to our third plausible noncausal explanation, the issue to be addressed was strikingly developmental in character: Was victimization in childhood the reason why adolescent victimization predicted psychological problems in young adulthood? Might there in fact be a "sensitive" period such that victimization in childhood sets the stage for both future victimization in adolescence and psychopathological symptomology in young adulthood? To address this issue, we returned to the E-Risk data pantry to obtain information we had collected when children were five, seven, ten, and twelve years of age pertaining to whether they experienced severe exposure to domestic violence between the mother and her partner, frequent bullying by peers, physical maltreatment by an adult, sexual abuse, emotional abuse and neglect, and/or physical neglect. Fortunately, almost three-quarters of the E-Risk children had no severe victimization experiences, but 20 percent had one, almost 4 percent had two, and just under another 4 percent had three or more such experiences.

With the childhood-victimization data in hand, we re-evaluated the effect of victimization in adolescence on psychiatric symptoms at age eighteen after discounting childhood-victimization effects. Results revealed that even with the experience of being a victim in childhood taken into account, greater adolescent polyvictimization still predicted more psychiatric symptoms. But the evidence also indicated that victimization in childhood and in adolescence each independently and uniquely predicted our measure p, reflecting diverse psychiatric symptoms. In fact, our third challenge ultimately revealed that the best predictor of psychopathology at age eighteen was a study member's *cumulative* exposure to adversity across childhood and adolescence; it was not exclusively because of victimization in childhood or adolescence.

In some respects, addressing and overcoming the fourth and final plausible noncausal explanation of our core finding was the most demanding, but it was also the one that the E-Risk Study was specifically designed to address. This was because of the inclusion of identical twins, who share 100 percent of their genes, and fraternal twins, who share only 50 percent. As we have made clear repeatedly in this volume, genes can influence both environmental exposures—think niche picking and evocative effects, discussed in Chapter 2, on temperament—and developmental phenotypes that we treat as outcomes in most chapters (for example, antisocial behavior and gambling). If this is the case, then any association linking an environmental exposure, such as polyvictimization, with a developmental outcome, such as young-adult psychiatric symptoms, may not reflect a true environmental effect. It could emerge because of a common-gene effect. That would involve the same genes influencing both the probability of being victimized and of developing psychiatric symptoms. Were that the actual situation, it could mean that a genetic effect is masquerading as an environmental effect when it comes to our core finding of victimization predicting psychopathology.

Some of our evidence actually made this possibility a serious consideration that we had to entertain. The p scores and the victimization scores were more similar across identical twins than across fraternal twins. Findings such as these make it clear that both our victimization and psychiatric-symptom measures were at least partly a function of children's genetic makeup, even if such behavior-genetic evidence (see Chapter 12) cannot illuminate which genes are responsible for the differential similarity across identical and fraternal twins. But the critical issue was whether any such genetic influence was responsible for our initial evidence linking greater polyvictimization with more psychiatric symptoms, and it turned out that it did not.

The easiest way to share the evidence that this was the case is by sharing the the fact that when we considered all twins, irrespective of their identical or fraternal status and thus genetic similarity, the twin with greater exposure to victimization proved to have more psychiatric symptoms than his or her co-twin who experienced less victimization. This was true even when we restricted the focus to just identical twins. This latter result means that differences in psychopathology between identical twins that proved to be associated with differences between them in victimization could not result from genetic effects—because there are no genetic differences between identical twins. Ultimately, the evidence related to our fourth challenge revealed that the association between victimization and psychopathology symptoms could not be fully explained either by family-wide environmental factors that are shared by twins, whether fraternal or identical—such as living in a single- or two-parent household or in one in which there is a lot or a little chaos—or by genetic factors. In sum, victimization that was unique to a twin—not shared by a co-twin—was one reason why victimization proved to be associated with psychiatric symptoms.

Strikingly, we had evidence from the second stage of our epigenetic adventure that was as close as one could get in the course of an observational study of a truly causal effect of polyvictimization on psychopathology. So now that we discovered that the link between polyvictimization and psychopathological symptoms was real and not an artifact of a variety of alternative possibilities, we could move on to the next stage of our epigenetic adventure. Specifically, now that we knew that polyvictimization predicted—and clearly seemed to influence—psychopathology in young adulthood (A→C), the issue became whether this effect of victimization was caused by the epigenetic process of methylation, which turns off the expression of genes. Recall that to answer this complex question, what we had to do next, in stage 3 of our epigenetic adventure, was determine whether our polyvictimization index was related to the methylation of genes (A→B). If so, then we could proceed to see, in stage 4, whether epigenetic methylation related to psychopathological symptomology (B→C) and, if so, whether, in stage 5, epigenetics mediated the effect of polyvictimization on psychological problems (A→B→C).

STAGE 3: VICTIMIZATION AND EPIGENETICS

Before we could proceed to assay DNA to measure methylation, we had a big decision to make. In the original rodent work, investigators had "sacrificed"—meaning killed—rats in order to "harvest" their brain tissue so that the methylation of DNA in brain cells could be measured. Obviously, proceeding in a similar way with our E-Risk Study members was out of the question. In the one investigation that we are aware of that used human brain tissue to study epigenetic processes, the research was carried out after the study "participants" had died. So if we could not secure DNA from cells in the brain, where should it come from?

Ultimately, we decided on blood, so when E-Risk Study members were eighteen years of age, we arranged to draw blood from all who agreed to such a procedure—and almost all did. The reason that we chose to measure DNA methylation in blood cells was because the hypothesis underlying our inquiry, just like that of other epigenetic investigators, was that psychosocial stress experiences are converted to methylation via the sympathetic nervous system and, in particular, the hypothalmic-pituitary axis (HPA), effects that occur in peripheral circulating blood. In the conclusion of this chapter, we will return to this issue of the place in the body where one collects cells to assay DNA in order to measure methylation and thereby evaluate effects of developmental experiences and environmental exposures.

When it came to evaluating effects of victimization on the methylation of genes obtained in blood cells, we proceeded in two general ways. The two ways paralleled what we have seen already in molecular genetic work involving the whole genome and candidate genes. That is, we not only conducted an epigenome-wide association study (EWAS) that focused on methylation across the entire epigenome but also zeroed in on the methylation of several individual candidate genes that had been highlighted in other epigenetic work focused on the effects of adversity, including the original rodent research. In so doing, we cast our measurement net both very widely (EWAS) and very narrowly (candidate-gene focus). By proceeding in this way, we more or less insured ourselves against pursuing too narrow or too broad a focus. After all, if we focused only at the epigenome-wide level, we could end up missing methylation-related effects involving only specific candidate genes, as such gene-specific effects could be lost in a sea of genes. But if we focused only on those candidate genes that other adversity-related methylation studies had focused on, we could end up missing methylation-related effects occurring in places in the epigenome that had not been investigated before. (For a detailed discussion of the difference between genome-wide and candidate-gene work, see Chapter 12.)

An Epigenome-wide Approach

When it came to examining relations between polyvictimization and methylation of the entire epigenome, including candidate genes, our investigatory strategy was like the one already outlined in overcoming the fourth challenge we faced upon investigating the effects of polyvictimization on psychiatric symptoms. Thus, we evaluated whether differences in victimization experience between twins growing up in the same family were systematically associated with differences in the methylation of their genes. Thus, evidence of victimization effects on methylation would emerge if, in general, the one twin of a pair who experienced greater victimization systematically differed from their co-twin in terms of methylation. The empirical question thus became, "Do within-twin differences in victimization predict within-twin differences in methylation?" It is important to appreciate that when it came to the EWAS, our work involved making more than four hundred thousand comparisons of within-twin pairs! This was because of the numerous methylation sites on genes that are included in an EWAS. To ensure that any victimization effects we detected would likely reflect true effects on epigenetic methylation rather than a chance result, complex statistical adjustments, which we need not detail here, enabled us to reduce the risk that this would occur. Simply put, these adjustments took into account—and discounted—the possibility of chance results emerging simply because so many tests of so many methylation sites in the epigenome were evaluated.

Results of our analyses proved both interesting and surprising. To begin with, we discovered three distinctive effects of polyvictimization in adolescence on epigenetic methylation that survived our statistical adjustments to reduce the risk of chance results. Thus, we had reason to believe these three effects were not simply a function of the large number of methylation sites considered. But before we felt comfortable "breathing meaning" into these findings, we once again recognized the need to challenge them. Because we knew that victimization and cigarette smoking went together and that smoking exerted its own previously demonstrated effect on epigenome-wide methylation, we needed to ensure that a methylation-related effect of smoking was not masquerading as an effect of victimization in our E-Risk data. This became especially important to consider once our own data also revealed what prior studies had found and we just acknowledged—that smoking affected DNA methylation.

Notably, even after implementing the same statistical adjustment we had already used, eighty-three effects of smoking on epigenome-wide methylation emerged in the E-Risk data. Once we discounted these effects of smoking, the three effects on methylation that we originally discerned involving victimization in adolescence disappeared. In some respects, this was not really surprising—because the three original effects of victimization on methylation we detected were among the eighty-three detected not just in our work on smoking but in other EWASs on smoking as well. It would therefore seem that those three (of over four hundred thousand) original effects discerned were spurious—that is, artifacts of correlated smoking effects. In other words, these were three "findings" that we should not breathe meaning into.

Because we appreciated that "the absence of evidence is not evidence of absence," we did not throw in the towel and terminate our adventure in epigenetics at this point, even though we regarded the results just shared as disappointing. Instead, we chose to double-check what turned out to be our null epigenome-wide findings by repeating the work of our initial analysis, but this time focusing, separately, on potential effects of each of the seven distinct victimization experiences we originally measured in adolescence. This involved running the more than four hundred thousand comparisons seven times, once for each type of victimization! However huge the effort, it seemed worth undertaking because it remained possible that the decision to "lump" together different types of victimization to create our polyvictimization predictor variable obscured things more than it illuminated them. Perhaps specific forms of victimization uniquely affected the methylation of genes. As it turned out, adopting this "splitting" approach did not provide convincing evidence that particular victimization experiences influenced the methylation of the epigenome to any meaningful extent. In fact, although we detected eight associations—out of almost two million tested—that met statistical criteria after adjusting for multiple testing, none of them was repeated across victimization types. In other words, there was no consistent—or even semi-consistent—empirical "signal" that victimization affects methylation of particular sites on the epigenome.

Despite these further disappointing results, we were still not ready to throw in the towel and abandon our investigatory adventure. When climbing a mountain, just because one path uphill may be blocked by a rockslide is no reason to quit, at least not if you want to get to the summit, which we did. If, as many developmental theorists have argued, earlier-life experiences are more influential than later-life ones, perhaps it would be victimization in childhood rather than in adolescence that would reveal effects on the epigenome. Thus, our next effort mimicked what we had done previously, but now looking at whether victimization in childhood rather than during adolescence might be the source of influence on DNA methylation. But when we investigated effects of childhood polyvictimization, not even one effect met statistical criteria as being anything other than a product of chance—more disappointment.

Notably, however, when we proceeded to evaluate separately the effects of each of the six types of childhood victimization we had gleaned from E-Risk records, the results became more interesting—and promising. Not only were forty-eight effects linking victimization in childhood with the methylation of genes detected, all of which met statistical criteria for multiple testing, but thirty-nine of these involved sexual victimization. These findings would seem to indicate, consistent with some epigenetic theorizing, that childhood sexual victimization is associated with stable DNA methylation differences in whole blood in young adulthood. We needed to be cautious when it came to breathing meaning into these findings, however, because only twenty-nine of more than sixteen hundred twins studied had been sexually victimized according to our records. There was also the fact that the same sexual abuse/methylation associations were not observed when the focus of inquiry was on sexual victimization in adolescence. And just as important was that when we relied on retrospective reports of childhood adversity—discussed in great detail in Chapter 17—we discovered that adult recall of sexual abuse was related to methylation in a number of places in the epigenome, but none of these twenty-two detected effects overlapped with the thirty-nine methylation-related effects discerned when using sexual abuse based on records recorded in childhood as the predictor. In other words, while both prospective and retrospective measurements of sexual abuse in childhood predicted methylation, none of the methylated genes proved the same across the two analyses. Needless to say, it was hard to feel confident about even the sexual abuse findings that were emerging, given these differences in findings when using retrospective and prospective measurements of sexual victimization.

We still needed to ask about cumulative stress, just as we did when studying victimization effects on psychopathological symptoms, by considering effects of victimization experience chronically or recurrently. It is important to appreciate here that E-Risk Study members who experienced more forms of victimization in childhood also did so in adolescence. While we detected some limited and preliminary evidence that being subject to multiple types of victimization across both childhood and adolescence was related to DNA methylation, the few effects discerned disappeared once we again took tobacco smoking into account. For a second time, then, the initial finding, this time involving cumulative stress in the form of polyvictimization across childhood and adolescence, appeared to be spurious, an artifact of the (correlated) effect of smoking on epigenome-wide methylation. Needless to say, it was a good thing we opted for a conservative approach, challenging our initial findings—and thereby avoiding the mistake of prematurely embracing our initial findings and moving on as if we had truly discovered something.

A Candidate-Gene Approach

However disappointing our findings had proven to be to this point, we were still not ready to conclude that little was going on vis-à-vis the effects of victimization on the epigenetic mechanism of methylation, even though that was the emerging picture. There was still the possibility, as we indicated earlier could be the case, that our limited success was the result of casting our net too widely by adopting an epigenome-wide focus (that is, EWAS). Perhaps we needed to narrow the scope of our inquiry, zeroing in on the methylation of particular candidate genes, specifically those known to be related to the physiological stress response system and found in prior work by others to be related to indices of adversity. This led us to focus on six candidate genes. We will not specify or go into gory detail about them, given that we repeated all the analyses we described earlier when implementing the epigenome-wide approach for each of the six candidate genes and because this second major effort to detect victimization effects on epigenetic methylation proved just as limited as the previous phase of inquiry, if not more so. In other words, our strategy of "leaving no stone unturned" did not pay off in terms of detecting environmental effects on the epigenome.

What these disappointing results meant, given our planned five-stage epigenetic adventure, was that there was no basis for proceeding to the last two stages of our anticipated journey, testing whether epigenetic methylation predicted our psychopathology outcomes (stage 4: B→C) and whether it mediated the effect of victimization on psychopathology (stage 5: A→B→C). Because our environmental exposure, victimization stress (in its many varieties), did not consistently predict methylation of genetic markers at either the whole-epigenome or candidate-gene level—and therefore could not mediate the effect of victimization on psychopathology—our epigenetic inquiry came to an end. It should come as no surprise that after so much hunting and pecking, we were hugely disappointed.

CONCLUSION

At the time we undertook the work presented in this chapter, it was the most comprehensive investigation ever conducted of epigenetic alterations in humans' response to victimization stress in the first two decades of life.

Before carrying out the work, we identified environmental and developmental constructs we would focus on as the predictor and outcome of our epigenetic adventure (stage 1); hypothesized that not only would polyvictimization predict both psychiatric symptoms (stage 2), which it did, and DNA methylation (stage 3), which it barely did, but that methylation would predict psychiatric symptoms (stage 4) and even mediate the effect of polyvictimization on psychiatric symptoms (stage 5). Because of how limited the results proved to be in stage 3, there were insufficient empirical grounds for proceeding further with our original plan. It was time to terminate our investigation of the new genetics, epigenetics. But what should we make of what we found—or didn't find? Here we were of two minds.

Part of us felt like there was so little going on empirically linking our measures of victimization with methylation that there was very good reason to be skeptical about the early findings that had been reported by other investigators regarding the effects of developmental adversity on DNA methylation in humans. Not only did we have an excellent environmental predictor that was clearly and seemingly causally related to our ultimate outcome, psychiatric symptomology in young adulthood, but also this same predictor proved to be more or less unrelated to, barely related to, or at best inconsistently related to our methylation measurements. This was more or less true irrespective of whether we focused on the effects of childhood victimization, adolescent victimization, or cumulative victimization across both periods of development or whether we considered polyvictimization or specific forms of victimization. This disappointing state of affairs also characterized our efforts focused on methylation at the genome-wide level or more narrowly on specific candidate genes. Perhaps developmental scholars had gotten ahead of themselves, proving too willing to embrace evidence in prior work on the effects of adversity on DNA methylation in humans, work that was not as convincing as so much writing—in the scientific literature and in the popular press—presumed it to be. In other words, we were questioning not the original rodent research that got human developmentalists like ourselves so excited about genes as dependent variables but rather the diversity of findings emerging in the human literature on this subject.

We also appreciated the need to take seriously the adage we cited earlier in this chapter that "the absence of evidence is not evidence of absence." That was because however broad and deep our investigation—and it was very broad and very deep—it could not be regarded as the final say on the matter. To begin with, we focused only on one particular epigenetic process, methylation, although there are others that might be affected by victimization. Perhaps if we had been positioned to measure these other gene-expression mechanisms, more compelling evidence of effects of adversity on the epigenome would have materialized. Then there was the fact that we evaluated effects of victimization in childhood and adolescence. But what if adversity effects on methylation are most likely to prove evident even earlier in life, say in infancy or the preschool years? In the original rodent research, mothers' licking and grooming behavior, which proved so epigenetically influential, occurred in the opening days of life, the newborn period. Maybe the NICHD Study of Early Child Care and Youth Development, the focus of Chapters 7 and 8, would have been better positioned to reveal effects on methylation, since it began measuring children and their adversity-related experiences at six months of age. Unfortunately, that investigation never had the resources to address this issue, nor was the study of methylation even familiar to most developmentalists when that study was being conducted.

Another factor to consider when drawing conclusions about our mostly null findings concerns where we looked for adversity-related effects on methylation—in blood cells. Even though there is abundant reason to believe that effects of stress and adversity on methylation should prove evident in DNA found in blood cells, it remains possible that a better place to look for the effects we searched for was in the brain itself. Recall that this is where the original Canadian researchers looked when investigating genes as dependent variables in rodents or where other investigators looked when studying victims of suicide. But, of course, we had no access to brain cells, so we could not confirm or disconfirm this possibility that victimization effects could be specific to certain tissues of the body and not others, at least with respect to adversity effects on methylation.

Not to be missed, too, is the fact that however broad our genome-wide methylation assays were—leading us to undertake more than four hundred thousand comparisons in some analyses and more than two million overall—there were places in the epigenome that current technology did not enable us to investigate. The same point applies to our selection of candidate genes. Even though these were thoughtfully selected based on prior evidence linking adversity with methylation, our six candidate genes did not exhaust the list of possible candidate-gene suspects. Might a focus on others have yielded more convincing evidence of environmental effects on the epigenetic process of methylation—and thus genes as dependent variables?

Collectively, these considerations tempered our first set of thoughts. While it is true that there was nothing much going on in the E-Risk Study with regard to victimization effects on the methylation of genes—with the same proving true when we turned to the Dunedin Study to double-check some findings—that does not necessarily mean that had we looked, or been able to look, elsewhere that the findings would have been similarly disappointing. Only time will tell. Indeed, this last observation leaves us thinking about our epigenetic work and that of others in the following way. Going forward, the ball is now in the court of those who contend that adversity—or even positive and supportive experiences and exposures—affects gene expression via the epigenetic process of methylation in humans. But, to address this issue and provide convincing evidence, inquiries need to be more hypothesis driven rather than exploratory. Investigators need to be more specific about what they expect to find, meaning exactly where in the epigenome and in response to exactly what exposures and experiences they expect effects to prove detectable.

To repeat what we said earlier, in making these comments we do not mean to cast aspersions on those who have come before us, indeed whose shoulders we have stood on in order to carry out the work detailed in this chapter. Once again, we have come to neither praise nor bury Caesar—meaning the notion that stress and adversity affects gene expression via the epigenetic process of methylation and, thereby, psychological and behavioral functioning. We expected a greater harvest from our epigenetic work given all the effort we put into planting and nurturing the scientific trees we have focused on. While the behavioral fruit proved abundant in that victimization was clearly and apparently causally related to psychiatric symptoms in young adulthood, the same could not be said of the fruit of the methylation tree.

PART VI

AGING IN MIDLIFE

17

Childhood Adversity and Physical Health in Midlife

I t probably should have been pointed out many chapters ago, but it is not too late to make an important distinction when it comes to studying human development, especially with respect to the childhood and adolescent years. That distinction has to do with the fact that there are at least two types of developmental scholars. One kind is fascinated with the process of normative development—how the typical infant, child, or adolescent changes as he or she grows up. Such scholars investigate topics such as the emergence of language: how a typically developing baby who cannot speak words first starts to show evidence of understanding them, then deploys his or her first word, then puts two words together to make a first sentence, then even more words, and before too long is mastering the basics of grammar. Other scholars, interested in physical and physiological development, investigate the process of sexual maturation: how hormonal processes change and, with them, the body of the typically developing child as it becomes that of an adult during the pubertal transition. Likewise, students of social development similarly investigate how, on average, prosocial and antisocial behavior develop over time, from the infant, toddler, and preschool years well into adolescence.

Anyone who has progressed this far in this book—especially if reading the chapters sequentially—will appreciate that the kind of developmental inquiry just highlighted does not reflect our own intellectual inclinations and thus the kind of developmental adventures we pursue. We are members of a different developmental tribe, so to speak. Instead of being intrigued with normative patterns of typical development, it is *individual differences* that fascinate us. One truth about human development and thus virtually all aspects of body, mind, and behavior is that variation is the norm, not the exception—beyond the basics, of course, such as everyone having two arms, two legs, a gastrointestinal system, and, as a final example, the capacity to master language, barring any serious neurological problems or absence of exposure to language in everyday life. Many scholars work to describe the representative person, the average person, the person in the middle of this range of variation, but our interest has often been in the people out at the ends of the distribution, those whose characteristics and behavior are markedly different from the average guy or gal. Individual-difference scholars like us therefore want to understand why some people are seriously antisocial, depressed, or creative, to cite just three examples.

As should be apparent by now, we are led to ask, "Why do people of the same age, whether as infants, toddlers, children, adolescents, or adults, function so differently from one another?" Why do some begin routinely breaking rules early in life (Chapter 6) or, as we saw in Chapter 7, mature sexually earlier than others do? Is it their genes, their families, their peers, and/or their neighborhoods that shape these differences between people? And what are the consequences of early differences for the later developmental differences that are also so evident—in adolescence, in young adulthood, and, as this chapter and Chapter 18 will be concerned with, in middle age. This is the field of individual-differences research.

And, of course, it is what our book's second theme, addressing the child and adolescent origins of later-life functioning, has been all about. Here we extend that focus to address our third theme, which is really just an extension of the second, as it focuses on variation in physical health in midlife. So the question becomes, "Is such health in midlife related to experiences growing up and functioning earlier in life?" In other places in this book, we have touched on this issue; for example, when considering the physical health consequences of persistent marijuana smoking from adolescence onward (Chapter 11). But in this chapter and the next, it will be the primary concern.

It is interesting to observe that thinking about how psychological and behavioral development is shaped by earlier experiences in life has—from an individual-difference perspective—a remarkably long history, conceivably dating back to before the invention of writing. Certainly, Plato and Socrates were interested in this issue, and anyone who has studied even a little bit of philosophy has encountered the romantic idealism of Jean-Jacques Rousseau, the eighteenth-century French philosopher who argued that children were essentially born good and if left to their own devices would grow up to be sensitive, caring, cooperative individuals, so it was their families and society that more or less ruined some—if not most—of them. Perhaps this is why Rousseau himself seemed to have no qualms about abandoning his own numerous offspring. (Or maybe we are dealing with a case of "reverse causation": perhaps Rousseau abandoned his children first and subsequently developed his theory to justify the misdeed!)

The scientific study of the effect of childhood experiences on human development dates back to around the middle of the last century. Notably, most of this work, just like the preceding centuries of speculative thought, focused on how the nature and quality of rearing, typically in the family, shaped later psychological and behavioral development. This is what makes something that happened only about two decades ago—and is the focus of this chapter—so interesting. Although research on the effects of developmental experiences and environmental exposures in childhood *on psychological and behavioral development* later in life has continued unabated, what is perhaps more newsworthy is the relatively recent emergence of developmental theory and research focused on *physical health, or really ill health,* in midlife. Interest in this subject has given birth to an entirely new field of inquiry, that of the developmental origins of health and disease. It was launched not by psychologists, psychiatrists, or developmental scholars (that is, scientists like us), but instead by physicians who came to realize that poor health in middle age might have its roots in childhood and even before that, in utero—or even earlier, before conception! Today, this may seem rather obvious, but what seems rather surprising is how long it took developmental scholars to "get there."

Why was that? We suspect one reason is that for too long Western culture has distinguished mind and body—and in many respects still does—an idea we touched on at the end of Chapter 12 and also considered in Chapter 13.

Thus, the nature and character of the mind—and thus psychology and behavior—are regarded as fundamentally distinct from, even unrelated to, the body. By tradition, the mind and behavior have been the subjects of psychology and psychiatry, whereas the body has been the subject of biology and medicine. We can even see evidence of this dualist perspective in operation in some quarters today. Many don't bat an eyelash at the idea that genetic differences might lead doctors to treat each patient differently, because medical treatments that might benefit some do not seem to benefit others who are genetically different. Oncology—the study, diagnosis, and treatment of cancer—embodies this reality perhaps more than any other medical specialty. After all, the very notion of "personalized medicine" emerged in the treatment of cancer, as oncologists came to appreciate that cancers are very different from each other genetically. Thus, what works in destroying some cancers has no effect on others. This is great news for those with the "right" kind of cancer, but, sadly, is often life ending for those with other cancers.

Yet the idea that behavioral development might be thought of in similar terms is hard for many to swallow. As we have made clear, especially in chapters in Part V of the book, dealing with genetics, individuals who carry certain genes are more likely to develop, for example, antisocial behavior (Chapter 13) or to become depressed (Chapter 14) if maltreated in childhood than others who carry different genes. Yet, when the idea is even broached that one day, when more evidence is in hand, this could lead to treating individuals differently, all of a sudden some people are aghast, saying, "You can't treat people differently, perhaps targeting some for prevention or intervention programs before others; that is not fair." But why is it not fair if—and only if—the evidence becomes persuasive, as it is in the case of personalized cancer treatment? Why do so many seem to resist even entertaining the possibility of personalized treatment to prevent or remediate psychological and behavioral maladies? We are referring here to treatment that may benefit some but not others, as some emerging intervention work designed to prevent or remediate the development of problems in children already indicates is the case.

Our purpose in this chapter is not to resolve this issue of mind-body duality or really say anything more about it. We have raised it just to highlight why it may have taken so long for most developmental scholars to go on the adventure that is the focus of this chapter, investigating the developmental origins of health and disease (DOHD).

DEVELOPMENTAL ORIGINS OF
ILL HEALTH IN MIDLIFE

Most of the work on DOHD has relied on an approach to research that, as we have made clear repeatedly, beginning in Chapter 1, is inherently limited. This is because physicians, in much of their groundbreaking work seeking to illuminate whether and how adverse experiences in childhood and adolescence undermine adult health, have "looked back" on the lives of adult patients to see whether those who are healthier than others had different developmental experiences and environmental exposures while growing up. In other words, they have queried their adult patients about their childhoods.

Those of us who study psychological and behavioral development have long appreciated the serious limitations of this approach. Indeed, as pointed out in Chapter 1, they are the very reasons that longitudinal research like that central to this book is carried out. In order to illuminate how life experiences, whether in the family or beyond, affect development, they are best studied *as they occur.* Never forget that people can fail to remember even important aspects of their lives, and this may be especially true when what is not recalled was traumatic or otherwise painful. It is almost as though the mind buries the experience to protect the person from remembering it, even reliving it, a type of psychological defense. But this does not mean that such early-life adversities that are no longer remembered don't still play out and affect how people develop.

It is not only a failure to recollect what happened in childhood in one's family that can undermine our ability to understand how early family experiences affect later health and development. People can also distort what occurred during childhood. To repeat what we said when considering the intergenerational transmission of parenting in Chapter 5, such distortion can take at least two forms. The first to be considered is idealization, which involves casting one's childhood in a much more positive light than it actually merits. In such cases, details of supposedly supportive care are often lacking when it comes to descriptions of childhood, as idealizing individuals cannot get beyond broad generalizations, such as "I had great parents" or "My childhood was wonderful."

The second way that memory can be distorted is as a result of a negative mood or depressed state. In such cases, it is almost as though the person is seeing the world, including the past, through gray-tinted glasses. What too easily comes to mind when one is depressed, anxious, or hostile are the slights, offenses, and poor treatment received while growing up, even if these were not especially characteristic of their childhood. It is almost as though positive and supportive experiences in the family have become inaccessible.

As we watched more and more research get published and heralded in the popular press and on social media by physicians and now scholars from other fields about how "adverse childhood experiences"(ACEs) undermine physical health in middle age, we could not help but wonder about the validity of conclusions being drawn from such work. What was not clear was whether the medical researchers conducting this research on the developmental roots of ill health were oblivious to the risks associated with reliance on retrospective reports of childhood experiences or whether they were simply choosing to disregard concerns like those we have raised—and which have been discussed for decades in the psychological literature.

What we appreciated, however, was that we were once again in an ideal position to evaluate potential strengths and limitations of recollected assessments of ACEs while illuminating the developmental origins of health and disease. This was because we could examine the degree to which prospective and retrospective ACE measurements proved similar to one another and compare the power of ACE measurements based on each to predict health in midlife. This was because we measured retrospective ACEs for these specific purposes as part of the Dunedin Study when study members were thirty-eight years of age. Before reporting in some detail what we found in this phase of our ACE adventure, we summarize results of our prior ACE-related work investigating links between childhood adversity and future health.

CHILDHOOD ORIGINS OF HEALTH IN ADULTHOOD

In our first two investigations evaluating effects of childhood adversity on physical health in adulthood, we focused on what some have referred to as a family's "social address," in our case its socioeconomic status (that is, the study members' social-class origins). The term *social address*, coined by our previously mentioned professor at Cornell, Urie Bronfenbrenner, is meant to highlight that while social class identifies the social and economic position of a family in society, it cannot tell us for certain whether particular adverse experiences—such as child maltreatment or maternal depression—that we know occur more often in economically disadvantaged families are actually experienced by a particular child in a particular family and thus whether they prove to be developmentally influential. The same goes for other social-address characterizations of the family, whether concerned with its structure (for example, one or two parents) or its neighborhood location (for example, safe or dangerous), to cite just two ways of thinking about the family context. In other words, knowing that a child grows up in a lower-class family does not reliably tell us about her actual "lived experiences"—that is, for example, whether she was actually abused or had a depressed mother.

What made the introduction of ACE measurements by physicians so important was that it sought to move health-related developmental inquiry beyond the social-address approach to thinking about particular family influences. Thus, ACE measurements were designed to capture specific developmental experiences and environmental exposures thought to influence physical health and well-being. But before sharing our own health-related work that took us beyond the social-address approach, let's see what we learned using this less-than-ideal way of characterizing study members' families during their childhoods.

In our first investigation of the health legacy of childhood adversity, we evaluated whether a child's social-class origin and thus socioeconomic disadvantage while growing up predicted physical and dental health at age twenty-six. This work relied on repeated measurements of the occupational status of parents, averaged across the time when children were three, five, seven, nine, eleven, thirteen, and fifteen years of age. We proceeded this way not just for methodological reasons, being "lumpers" more than "splitters," but because socioeconomic status at a single point early in the life course does not necessarily capture cumulative exposure to disadvantaged—or advantaged—economic conditions while growing up. Our inquiry discounted any possible effects of pregnancy complications (for example, maternal diabetes, hypertension, and eclampsia) before the study members were even born, as well as their own health status at birth (for example, prematurity and birth weight), drawing on hospital records. We statistically controlled for the effects of these factors because we had already discovered that study members who grew up in families of low socioeconomic status experienced poorer health at birth, on average, so we didn't want any potential effects of childhood socioeconomic status on future health to be an artifact of this documented developmental reality.

Results revealed that three of four measurements of physical health—body-mass index, waist-hip ratio, and cardiorespiratory fitness, but not systolic blood pressure—showed a graded, dose-response relation with a child's social-class origin. As childhood economic disadvantage increased, so did indications of poor health in young adulthood. The same proved true of dental health, indexed by amount of plaque on teeth, bleeding of gums, periodontal disease, and decayed tooth surfaces. These phenotypes were all measured during dental exams administered to all study members at age twenty-six. The fact that all these detected effects of childhood economic disadvantage on physical and dental health remained even when study members' own occupational status at age twenty-six was controlled meant that the findings could not be the result of their social-class "destination"—that is, their socioeconomic status in adulthood.

When we saw study members again six years later, at age thirty-two, we focused specifically on cardiovascular disease risk. To this end, we relied on six biomarkers that we combined—being the "lumpers" that we are—to reflect elevated cardiovascular risk at age thirty-two: having high resting systolic blood pressure, elevated nonfasting total cholesterol, low nonfasting high-density lipoprotein cholesterol, high glycated hemoglobin concentration, low cardiorespiratory fitness, and being overweight. In line with the findings at age twenty-six, study members' social-class origin mattered. Those from chronically low-SES families were more than twice as likely as others to be at high risk for cardiovascular disease. Notably, these results remained, even if somewhat attenuated, when we took into account familial liability to poor health, indexed by whether either parent was a smoker, had a problem with alcohol, and/or had heart disease. The same was true when before evaluating childhood SES effects we took into account whether the study member showed evidence of poor health behaviors during adolescence, as indexed by smoking cigarettes, using alcohol or other illegal substances, and/or having a high body-mass index.

Given both sets of young-adult findings tied to the demographic characterization of the study member's family of origin—its socioeconomic status—we were especially interested in delving more deeply into the health-related legacy of childhood. Indeed, by investigating particular adverse childhood experiences, we could move beyond the family's social address to better understand whether and how actual "lived experiences", particularly adverse ones, which we know are more common in economically disadvantaged families, affected health in midlife. The first stage of the remainder of our ACE adventure, then, was designed to determine whether retrospective and prospective measurement of ACEs provided similar pictures of study members' developmental histories. In other words, how well did what study members recollected about their childhoods match up with what actually occurred, according to the information we had collected on them while growing up? The second stage involved comparing the power of these two developmental-history measurements to predict health at midlife. Here we sought to determine whether there were limitations of—or perhaps even advantages of—retrospective ACE measurements when it came to understanding the childhood roots of ill health in midlife. Given our preexisting views, we expected retrospective assessment of adverse childhood experiences to prove less powerful and informative when it came to predicting midlife health than prospective measurements obtained during childhood.

DO PROSPECTIVE AND RETROSPECTIVE ACES PAINT THE SAME PICTURE OF CHILDHOOD?

Because we wanted to be able to make comparisons between ACEs measured retrospectively and prospectively, we focused on experiences that were assessed both prospectively in childhood and retrospectively in adulthood. Indeed, we followed the approach articulated by the US Centers for Disease Control and Prevention when it came to conceptualizing ACEs. This meant measuring five types of child harm and five types of household dysfunction. When it came to harm, the focus was on physical abuse, emotional abuse, physical neglect, emotional neglect, and sexual abuse. Household dysfunction was defined in terms of incarceration of a family member, substance abuse by a household member, household mental illness, loss of a parent, and partner violence.

When it came to prospective measurement of these constructs, we returned to our data pantry and gathered records made during research assessments when children were three, five, seven, nine, eleven, thirteen, and fifteen years of age. These records were based on diverse sources. They included family contacts with social services and pediatricians, notes made by assessment staff who interviewed children and their parents, information obtained from researchers who observed mother-child interaction at the project office, records kept by public-health nurses who recorded conditions witnessed during home visits, and reports from teachers we surveyed about the child's behavior and performance. Information about parent criminality was obtained by means of questionnaires completed by parents.

To assess ACE-related experience in the family retrospectively, study members completed the same questionnaire at age thirty-eight that medical researchers had used in their work, the Childhood Trauma Questionnaire. To supplement the information secured using this measurement instrument, we also interviewed study members about their memories of exposure to family substance use, mental illness, incarceration, partner violence, and loss of a parent resulting from separation, divorce, death, or removal from home, as these topics were not covered in the questionnaire.

Once both sets of information were assembled, that on ACEs measured prospectively and retrospectively, coders were trained on definitions of ACEs provided by the Centers for Disease Control and Prevention. Then, each of the ten ACEs—five forms of physical abuse and five forms of household dysfunction—was scored as present or absent using this information from our data pantry. Thus, every study member received a prospective ACE score that ranged from one to ten, mirroring the way retrospective ACEs were quantified by medical researchers. It is important to note that those reviewing and coding our ACE-related prospective data had no knowledge of what study members had retrospectively reported at age thirty-eight.

Now we were positioned to evaluate the degree to which prospective and retrospective assessments of ACEs tell a similar story about childhood adversity. Did study members who scored high, medium, or low on the retrospective assessment of ACEs tend to score similarly on the prospective one? The answer was "yes," up to a point, but by no means to any great extent. While the two measures were not tapping entirely different things, neither were they tapping the same thing. In fact, when we closely examined the sixty study members who actually had four or more adverse family experiences according to (prospective) childhood records, more than half failed to (retrospectively) report this many all those years later. Just as noteworthy was that ten study members who experienced four or more adverse family experiences while growing up recalled experiencing none or just one!

But investigation of the mismatch between prospective evidence and recollection did not only reveal such "selective exclusion"—in midlife—of adversity experienced in childhood. Please appreciate that by using the term *exclusion* we do not mean to imply that this was done purposefully or consciously; until proven otherwise, we suspect childhood adverse experiences were simply not accessible to those study members who did not recollect them. Ten percent of study members who experienced none of the ten adverse experiences according to our prospective records recalled experiencing three or more! In other words, recollection led to both under- and overreporting of adverse family experiences in childhood. Despite our data making this rather clear, we would be remiss if we did not acknowledge that our prospective measure of ACEs was by no means foolproof. It certainly remains possible that the Dunedin Study data pantry lacked information on some study members' seemingly hidden adversities. Consider, for instance, that some study members recalled being a victim of sexual abuse as a child, whereas the (prospective) data pantry understandably had no record of this. It is also important to appreciate that an adverse childhood experience doesn't have to be real to have health consequences, if the patient believes in it fervently enough.

Recognizing the potential limits of even our prospective measurements, we decided to "turn up the power of the microscope" and examine the agreement between the two ACE measurements more closely, at the level of individual adverse family experiences rather than in terms of summary scores based on "lumping" diverse adversities together. Perhaps agreement and disagreement resulted from some types of adversity being easier and others more difficult to recollect accurately. That is just what we discovered. Indeed, agreement for each distinctive adversity ranged from excellent, in the case of loss of a parent, to extremely poor, in the case of emotional abuse. This suggested that the overall—and modest—level of agreement we initially detected between the two ACE scores was driven, even inflated, by the extremely high agreement on parental loss. In fact, when we eliminated this one item from the calculation of the ACE scores, the level of agreement between retrospective and prospective measurements dropped by 40 percent! And remember, it was not high to begin with. In other words, when we looked more closely at the ACE information, it became apparent that the concordance across prospective and retrospective measurements was even more limited than originally documented. Here, then, is concrete evidence suggesting that the ACE measurements based on the recall of adult patients should not be taken at face value in medical research on the developmental origins of health and disease—or in the treatment of patients by physicians.

PREDICTIVE POWER OF RETROSPECTIVE AND PROSPECTIVE ACES

Although it is certainly important to document and thus appreciate the fallibility of recollections of adverse childhood experiences, the question of greater importance to both science and health practice is how well ACEs recollected in adulthood relate to other aspects of functioning, especially relative to ACEs based on detailed records created during childhood and adolescence. If both retrospective and prospective ACE measurements similarly predict adult well-being, then the "slippage" or mismatch between prospective and retrospective measurements already documented becomes less problematic than it might appear at first.

Given our interest in comparing the power of retrospective and prospective ACE measurements to predict well-being in midlife, at age thirty-eight, we created four *subjective* measures of health, based on what study members told us, and two *objective* outcome measures, based on tests we administered and biological samples we collected. The first subjective outcome measure addressed physical health, reflecting how study members rated their overall health, ranging from poor to excellent. The second subjective measure addressed cognitive health and was based on study members' responses to nineteen questions about having difficulty with everyday tasks such as keeping track of appointments, remembering why they went to a store, and repeating the same story to someone. To measure the subjective outcome of mental health, we used an interview that assessed diverse symptoms of multiple mental health problems, including depression, anxiety, antisocial personality, and psychosis. Finally, the subjective measure of social health was based on a twenty-eight-item inventory pertaining to partner relationship quality, tapping open communication, shared activities and interests, balance of power, respect and fairness, emotional intimacy, and trust.

Turning to our two objective health outcomes, the first was based on multiple biomarkers obtained at age thirty-eight, including those reflecting cardiorespiratory fitness, pulmonary function, periodontal disease, systemic inflammation, and metabolic abnormalities (that is, waist circumference, high-density lipoprotein level, triglyceride level, blood pressure, and glycated hemoglobin). The second objective measure was of cognitive health and was based on an assessment of working memory that was part of a standardized intelligence test we administered at age thirty-eight.

With the measurements just described in hand, we proceeded to conduct our comparative analysis of how well retrospective and prospective ACE measurements predicted health in midlife. Several interesting findings emerged. In general, both prospective and retrospective ACE measurements modestly predicted self-reported and objectively measured health outcomes at age thirty-eight. Thus, no matter how we measured ACEs, prospectively or retrospectively, the evidence indicated, consistent with prior medical research, that greater childhood adversity was associated with (somewhat) poorer health in midlife. This was true whether the outcome to be explained was a subjective or an objective index of physical or cognitive health. Once again, we see evidence of probabilistic rather than deterministic development. Even among those scoring very high on ACEs, some were in good health, and even among those scoring very low, some were in poor health.

Further scrutiny of the data revealed that the retrospective ACE measurement generated the weakest and strongest associations with the health outcomes, and this was where things got especially interesting. When it came to predicting each of the four *subjective* self-reported measures of health, the retrospective ACE assessment proved to be a better predictor than the prospective ACE measure. Yet just the opposite proved true when the outcomes to be explained were the two *objectively* measured health outcomes. Now it was the prospective ACE assessment that proved to be a better predictor than the retrospective ACE measurement of our biomarker index of health and the cognitive assessment of working memory. It would therefore seem that if you want to know how ACEs might affect actual physical health in midlife, retrospective ACE reports are (somewhat) limited, but if you want to know about an individual's beliefs or feelings about his or her own health, then retrospective reports prove (somewhat) more informative.

CONCLUSION

Once more, we came to our research on the developmental origins of ill health neither to bury Caesar nor to praise him, metaphorically speaking. It was not the goal of our ACE adventure to prove that the retrospective approach to measuring adverse childhood experiences was without value or to demonstrate its utility. Rather, our goal was to understand, most notably, whether adversity actually and demonstrably experienced in childhood might actually predict and perhaps undermine physical health in adulthood. In other words, we wanted to know whether conclusions drawn on the basis of retrospective medical research held up when evaluated more rigorously.

Having said that, we must acknowledge that there were real limits to the rigor we could bring to this adventure. Perhaps most significantly, in the work reported, we were not positioned to discount some alternative explanations. Most notably, even though adversity in childhood predicted poorer objective health in midlife, the possibility remains that other factors—third variables—might have influenced both the predictor and outcomes that were the focus of this work. Most notably, certain unmeasured child characteristics—including genetic makeup—may have played a role in both the experience of adversity in childhood and poor health later in life. It is not hard to imagine, for example, that children who are less rather than more healthy or children of a certain genetic makeup could, under some circumstances, provoke adverse childhood experiences, just as discussed in Chapter 2, which focused on early temperament. We know, for example, that children with developmental disabilities are more likely than healthier children to be mistreated. So it remains possible that less healthy children or children of a certain genetic makeup—or those with both characteristics—might have ended up with poor health in midlife even in the absence of early-life adversity. We make this point just to alert the reader to the need to always entertain such possibilities when efforts have not or could not be undertaken to discount them.

In any event, the results of the Dunedin Study confirmed the general take-home message coming out of medical science. Adverse childhood experience not only compromises psychological and behavioral well-being, as we have seen throughout this book, but also appears to undermine physical health. This observation underscores the point made in Chapter16 that drawing strong lines between the mind and body is no longer a tenable way to think about human development, if it ever was.

It must also be appreciated that reliance on retrospective reports of childhood adversity is not without limits, both in terms of its accuracy and its power to predict physical health, especially when measured objectively using biomarkers. It is thus important for physicians who are incorporating ACE assessment into their medical practices to understand this and thus the limits of the information they are gathering. Just because a patient reports something about their childhood does not mean it necessarily occurred, and, just as importantly, just because someone does not report something does not mean it did not occur. This latter point recalls a point made about science in prior chapters, now extended to clinical practice, that absence of evidence is not evidence of absence. Whereas in the case of scientific research this aphorism pertains to breathing meaning into null findings (that is, what has not been detected), here it pertains to accepting at face value a claim that one or more particular adverse experiences that a patient contends did not happen actually did not occur.

Results of the Dunedin Study underscore two additional points that merit serious consideration by physicians. First, for different reasons, patients may underreport childhood adversities as well as overreport them. Second, indisputably objective *events,* such as the death of a parent, are more accurately recalled than more qualitative experiences, such as being emotionally abused. Notably, both these insights have been documented by others before us, as well as by ourselves in other work—decades ago. So, if physicians are going to ask adult patients to report on the adverse childhood experiences checklist in the hope of gaining insight into their health in midlife, both these points need to be understood. In the same way that developmental, psychological, and behavioral science need to be informed by medical science, the reverse is true as well.

18

Biological Embedding
of Childhood Adversity

More than any two chapters in this book, this one and Chapter 17 are tightly linked, which is not to say that Chapter 17 must be read before this one. We should point out, nevertheless, that Chapter 17's findings chronicling links between adversity in childhood and objectively measured physical health raise a fundamental scientific question that always arises in the scientifically minded when an association emerges connecting a would-be cause with a would-be consequence: how does the putative effect in question come to be realized?

In the current case, this question takes the form, "Through what mechanism or mechanisms might early-life adversity come to shape physical health in midlife?" While we will focus in this chapter on three distinct biological mechanisms, we should make clear that when it comes to illuminating how early-life adversity comes to be related to poor health in midlife, mediating processes need not be exclusively biological in character. Indeed, they could involve behavior, cognition, and emotion. Perhaps most important to consider in the current context are health behaviors involving inactivity, poor diet, and substance use (for example, smoking, excessive alcohol, and illicit drugs). Even though these are not a central focus of the adventure with which we are concerned in this chapter—biological mechanisms accounting for childhood roots of midlife health—that should not be read to imply that they do not play a role in explaining how childhood adversity comes to be linked to adult health.

Mechanism-oriented inquiry is of interest not only to the ivory tower, to researchers seeking to understand how development operates. This is because basic science insight into mechanisms can provide guidance when it comes to intervention and treatment—that is, applied science. This is an issue that we commented on earlier, perhaps most notably in Chapter 13, when we considered the genetics of success. Imagine that we cannot change an economically disadvantaged or adverse childhood environment, now found to forecast poor health in our study members' lives (Chapter 17), or biomarkers indexing poor health at ages twenty-six, thirty-two, and thirty-eight. This could be because we do not have the will, the knowledge, or the resources to do so effectively, or it could be because an adult's exposure to early-life adversity is the preexisting reality of his or her developmental history, which we cannot go back in time to reverse. Does this mean we are helpless to improve the individual's health?

The answer to this question need not be "yes." We are not, at least in principle, helpless to affect developmental trajectories established by earlier life forces that we cannot change. This is because if, in the current case, we understand the paths or mediating mechanisms that link exposure to adversity in childhood with later ill health, then those become potential targets of intervention. If we can effectively alter mediating mechanisms through some behavioral or pharmacological means, then what might have been a likely if not inevitable outcome, given the probabilistic nature of development, no longer needs to occur. This kind of thinking led us to examine in the biological-embedding adventure we discuss in this chapter three distinct biological processes that might mediate the established connection linking childhood adversity with age-related diseases: inflammation, stress physiology, and telomere erosion. The data on inflammation came from the Dunedin Study and the E-Risk Study, whereas that on stress physiology and telomere erosion came exclusively from the E-Risk Study.

Once more, we are obliged to alert the reader to the need to consider alternative explanations even when, as in the current inquiry, we are investigating potential biological mediators of early-life adversity effects on health in midlife. Thus, if and when we focus on associations linking adversities of different kinds (for example, maltreatment and bullying) with inflammation, stress physiology, and/or telomere erosion, we will, as is our practice, challenge our initial findings. For example, in this adventure seeking to understand the biological embedding of early-life adversity, we endeavor to discount potential confounding effects of characteristics of children (for example, birth weight, BMI, and intelligence), parents (for example, depression, parenting, and maltreatment), and the family (for example, SES). In so doing, we move beyond what we were able to do in Chapter 17 when examining links between adverse childhood experiences and health in adulthood.

INFLAMMATION

We chose to focus on inflammation—in three separate studies—because of preexisting evidence indicating that it is related to age-related disease. Inflammation is part of the complex biological response of body tissues to harmful stimuli, such as pathogens, damaged cells, or irritants, and is a protective response involving immune cells, blood vessels, and molecular mediators. The function of inflammation is to eliminate the initial cause of cell injury, clear out necrotic (dead) cells and tissues damaged from the original injury and the inflammatory process, and to initiate tissue repair.

Whatever the real and well-established benefits of inflammation, chronically high levels of it reflect abnormal functioning of the immune system. Consequently, such high levels of inflammation, as indexed by biomarkers such as C-reactive protein (CRP) in the blood, predict and can contribute to atherosclerosis, insulin resistance/diabetes, heart disease, and neurodegeneration/dementia in later life. Clearly, it is reasonable to hypothesize that inflammation may be part of the process by which childhood adversity becomes "biologically embedded," thereby undermining health. We focused specifically on levels of C-reactive protein in our inflammation-related research because it is considered one of the most reliable indicators of inflammation. In fact, it has recently been endorsed as an adjunct to traditional risk-factor screening for cardiovascular disease by the US Centers for Disease Control and Prevention and by the American Heart Association.

In our first two investigations of "biological embedding" of childhood adversity via increased inflammation, we examined links between a variety of adversity factors measured in childhood and inflammation assessed when study members were thirty-two years of age. Adversity was indexed in three different ways, having to do with social class, maltreatment, and social iso-lation. As in Chapter 17, social-class assessment was based on the status of parents' occupations as repeatedly measured from the time of the study member's birth to age fifteen. Child maltreatment over the first decade of life was operationalized in the same way as delineated in Chapter 14, with children being classified as not maltreated, probably maltreated, and se-verely or definitely maltreated based on their rearing experiences, which we measured as they were growing up. We relied on two questions admin-istered repeatedly to parents and teachers when children were five, seven, nine, and eleven years of age to assess social isolation. They addressed whether the child "tends to do things on his/her own; is rather solitary" and whether the child is "not much liked by other children." Blood drawn from study members at age thirty-two was used to measure C-reactive protein.

In the first of our two inflammation-related studies, both a history of childhood maltreatment and the experience of social isolation, although not social class, predicted increased inflammation, as reflected in elevated levels of C-reactive protein in the blood at age thirty-two. In fact, the evidence chronicled a dose-response relation between predictor and outcome. As the probability and severity of maltreatment increased—from none, to prob-able, to definite—so did the degree of inflammation. Because we knew—based on additional analyses of our data—that being born at low birth weight also predicted increased inflammation in adulthood, the findings linking childhood adversity with CRP levels discounted the effect of this condition. In other words, maltreatment and social isolation in childhood each forecast increased inflammation early in the fourth decade of life be-yond any effects of low birth weight.

At this juncture, it might be useful to return to and further develop an idea introduced in Chapter 17 dealing with adverse childhood experiences. Recall our distinction between measures of developmental experience based on a child's "social address"—such as social class—and those reflecting actual lived experiences, such as being maltreated. Recall that while such characterizations of childhood tend to be related to each other, one does not necessarily imply the other. Thus, even if child maltreatment is more likely among the economically disadvantaged than among the affluent, it occurs in both ecological niches. But only a direct measurement of something like maltreatment—or maternal depression, domestic violence, or insensitive parenting—can tell us with any real confidence whether such adverse experiences actually occurred in a child's life. At best, a social-address indicator such as social class is only a proxy for or probability statement about the likelihood that was the case, and a potentially inaccurate one at that. We suspect that this was why only maltreatment and social isolation, but not social class, predicted inflammation in our first study of inflammation.

Alternative Explanations

In our second study of inflammation, at age thirty-two, we evaluated whether the effect of maltreatment just reported proved independent of other risk factors. We explored maltreatment's effect after taking into account, in turn, three separate sets of additional risks. We pursued this follow-up work in response to three hypotheses that could challenge the claim that childhood adversity undermines adult health via increased inflammation. First, and in line with the "co-occurring risk hypothesis," we evaluated whether maltreatment predicted inflammation early in the fourth decade of life even when we controlled not just for birth weight but also for childhood SES and IQ (averaged across measurements at ages seven, nine, and eleven) as well. This approach was necessary to determine whether apparent effects of child maltreatment on inflammation might actually be caused by other co-occurring risk factors rather than maltreatment per se. Results failed to support the co-occurring risk-factor hypothesis. Even though maltreated children were more likely to experience the co-occurring early-life risks, these other risk factors did not fully explain or account for the inflammatory effects of maltreatment that we chronicled in our first study. Thus, maltreatment remained predictive of elevated CRP levels after taking other early-life risks into account.

The second alternative hypothesis that we evaluated was the "adult-stress hypothesis." It stipulates that childhood maltreatment may come to be related to inflammation in adulthood as a result of maltreated children achieving low occupational status, being depressed, and/or experiencing high levels of stress in adulthood. Again, these possibilities were evaluated to determine whether maltreatment's effect on inflammation was misspecified as resulting primarily from later-life experiences rather than childhood ones. Once more, we had to reject the hypothesis that only later-life conditions mattered. In fact, the results paralleled those presented in the preceding paragraph. Even though maltreated children were more likely to experience adult stress, these adult experiences did not fully account for its inflammatory effect. Thus, maltreatment remained predictive of elevated CRP levels after taking these other adult conditions into account.

Finally, we evaluated the "health-behavior hypothesis," which raised the possibility that the effect of maltreatment on adult inflammation at age thirty-two could be because adults maltreated in childhood showed evidence of metabolic syndrome (for example, being overweight, having high blood pressure, or having high cholesterol), being a smoker, being physically inactive, or having a poor diet. Once more, these possibilities were evaluated to determine whether maltreatment's effect on inflammation was misspecified, resulting from health-related conditions later in life rather than maltreatment in childhood. The health-behavior hypothesis also failed to fully account for our data. As before, even though maltreated children were more likely to be in poor health and to engage in health-damaging behavior in adulthood, these other outcomes of maltreatment did not fully explain the effects of maltreatment on inflammation. Once again, maltreatment remained predictive of elevated CRP levels after taking these other factors into account.

In fact, when we proceeded to take all three sets of alternative explanatory factors into account simultaneously rather than focusing on each set one at a time, the association between maltreatment and inflammation remained. Maltreated children suffered from elevated levels of inflammation, and this could not be entirely accounted for by a myriad of other factors, conditions, and behaviors known to be related to child maltreatment and/or inflammation.

Inflammation Earlier in Life

Having addressed several challenges to—or alternative explanations of—the effect of maltreatment on inflammation at age thirty-two, as developmental scholars we wondered whether the documented adverse effect of maltreatment on inflammation might actually have been evident decades earlier. In other words, could we have detected the longer-term effect of adversity on inflammation that was actually evident much earlier in life? Or might we have detected a delayed inflammatory response to maltreatment? Unfortunately, the Dunedin Study was not positioned to address this issue because we had not measured inflammation when study members were children (in the 1970s and 1980s). In fact, the New Zealand project was launched long before students of human development became fascinated with the developmental origins of health and disease. Recall our repeated observation that scientists often find themselves in situations after data collection has been completed where they wished they had measured something they had not.

Fortunately, we had our later-launched Environmental-Risk Study to turn to in order to address the issue at hand. Recall from Chapters 1, 9, and 10 that the E-Risk Study followed some one thousand pairs of British twins from ages five to eighteen. Included in its battery of measurements was that of C-reactive protein at age twelve. These were derived from small quantities of blood—blood spots—obtained by means of pinpricks to a child's finger. In this project, too, child maltreatment was measured across the first decade of life. In our E-Risk work, however, we extended our focus to consider effects of depression, which was also assessed at age twelve, via a standardized questionnaire completed by the child concerning his or her feelings.

The availability of information on both child maltreatment and childhood depression enabled us to compare four groups of children in order to evaluate the effects of childhood adversity on inflammation early in the second decade of life. One group was comprised of children who had been neither maltreated nor depressed, another comprised children maltreated but not depressed, the third group of children were depressed but not maltreated, and the fourth group of children were both maltreated and depressed. Results revealed that the children who were both maltreated and depressed had the highest C-reactive protein levels and differed most from the comparison group comprised of children with neither condition. Notably, the children who only experienced maltreatment or were only depressed did not differ from this comparison group in their C-reactive protein levels at age twelve. Importantly, the elevated inflammation evident in the "dual-risk" group—those experiencing both maltreatment and depression—could not be explained by a variety of other factors known to be related to inflammation, including childhood SES, sex, zygosity (that is, fraternal versus identical twins), body temperature, or waist-hip ratio.

When considered in their entirety, the results of our three investigations of inflammation, two based on the Dunedin Study and one on the E-Risk

Study, proved consistent with the hypothesis that inflammation may be one pathway by which childhood adversity comes to be related to age-related diseases—one that may actually endure from childhood to adulthood. For the next stage of our biological-embedding adventure, we turned our attention to stress physiology.

STRESS PHYSIOLOGY

The second piece of biological-embedding research we present builds on the work reported in Chapter 9 on the effects of bullying. Recall that we found in that E-Risk research that at age twelve bullying during childhood predicted emotional and behavioral problems and self-harming behavior and, at age eighteen, overweight status. These findings led us to focus on a particular aspect of stress physiology—blunted cortisol reactivity. We investigated this potential biological-embedding mechanism because extensive theory and research suggested that early-life stress might alter mental and physical health by affecting hypothalamic-pituitary-adrenocortical (HPA) axis activity. This is an integrated neurobiological pathway linking the nervous and endocrine systems.

The HPA axis underlies both adaptive and maladaptive responses to stress. Adaptive responses are characterized by a relatively rapid increase in cortisol, the hormonal end product of the HPA axis, when faced with a stressor, followed by its progressive decline. This is what happens when we are, say, frightened by a loud noise or forced to swerve our car quickly to avoid an accident. It is a process that protects us by quickly mobilizing our capabilities to cope with a surprising or threatening situation that catches us off guard. As we recover from our fright, elevated cortisol levels decline, rather quickly assuming their baseline level.

But when individuals are repeatedly exposed to unanticipated and uncontrollable sources of stress, this functional response can weaken, such that there is no or only a little spike in cortisol level when confronting a stressor. Essentially, the system seems overworked, exhausted, and no longer functioning properly. Think about it as Megan Gunnar, a developmental psychologist at the University of Minnesota, taught us to. Imagine a new rubber band or one that is rarely used. When you stretch it out, it springs right back to its original size. But what happens if you keep repeatedly stretching it, almost but not quite beyond its breaking point? Eventually it loses its elasticity. This more or less describes the conditions that give rise to a *blunted* cortisol response. Whereas a person who has not been repeatedly stressed can mount a spike in cortisol release, one that mobilizes coping but quickly declines after the stress passes, there is no such spike or only an attenuated one when stress is more or less chronic. At least that is what theory and some evidence indicated when we undertook our second study of the effects of bullying.

Given how stressful being bullied can be, we wanted to know whether those E-Risk children who were bullied displayed a blunted cortisol response when we experimentally subjected them to stress. To this end, we drew on two widely utilized and effective stress-evoking procedures, known as the Children's Paced Auditory Serial Addition Task (PST) and the Triers Social Stress Test (TSST), both of which were videotaped while the children completed them. The PST, which we administered first, is based on the claim that solving math problems in your head, without paper to write on, is stressful, especially when others are watching, so this is exactly what is involved in this investigatory procedure. The TSST is based on the notion that speaking in public is stressful. It thus involves having the twelve-year-old speak in front of an unknown and inexpressive judge and an interviewer about their most unpleasant experience at school. In both situations, the children are aware they are being videotaped, which is intended to add to the stress.

In order to assess blunted cortisol response, we collected five samples of saliva, which we sent to a laboratory to assay cortisol. Saliva was collected by having children use a straw to pass the saliva into a small container. The first samples were collected twenty and two minutes before the mental-math test, the third immediately after it, and the final two samples at twenty-five and thirty-five minutes after the start of the tasks. This allowed us to plot children's cortisol response before, during, and after the stressors and thereby characterize the trajectory of cortisol levels over time. Based on the ideas already outlined, we hypothesized that children who were subject to bullying would show evidence of blunted cortisol: a smaller spike or increase in cortisol in their saliva across the five saliva-measurement occasions than other children.

To increase the confidence we could place in results if they proved consistent with our hypothesis, we restricted this second study to identical twins (who share 100 percent of their genes) who were discordant for bullying according to maternal reports when the twins were seven, ten, and twelve years of age. By discordant we mean that one twin was bullied and the other twin was not—like Joshua and Jack, whom we introduced in Chapter 9. By proceeding in this way, we essentially had a genetic control for each bullied twin. This meant that any cortisol differences that might emerge between bullied and nonbullied twin pairs could not be attributed to genetic factors—since each pair of identical twins had identical genotypes—and would have to be the consequence of an environmental exposure.

When it came to evaluating our hypothesis, it was important that bullied and nonbullied identical twins have similar levels of cortisol in their saliva before starting the mental-math test. Fortunately, this was the case. As a result, we would be comparing like with like, so any differences that might emerge—consistent or inconsistent with our hypothesis—could not be attributed to the two groups being different in their salivary cortisol levels before being subject to our experimental procedures designed to promote stress. Comparisons of the two groups of twins revealed that while nonbullied twins showed the expected increase in cortisol by thirty-five minutes following the PST, their bullied twins did not exhibit this increase (see Figure 18.1). That is, the cortisol response of twins who had been bullied was blunted. In fact, the results of our experimental manipulation of stress revealed an inverse dose-response relation between degree of bullying experienced and cortisol reactivity. The more frequently, chronically, and severely children were victimized by bullying, the smaller their physiological response to stress. As Megan Gunnar might say, their "rubber bands" had been stretched so often that they had lost their "elasticity."

Even though our investigatory strategy—comparing identical twins discordant for bullying—discounted the possibility that our findings were a result of genetic effects masquerading as environmental ones, there remained some alternative explanations of our findings that we needed to check out in the course of our second biological-embedding adventure. One was that individual factors preceded bullying victimization and accounted for our findings. This could have been the case had the bullied and nonbullied twins differed in birth weight, IQ, and/or emotional problems and behavioral problems, but this was not the case when we checked. It also turned out that bullied twins and their nonbullied siblings did not differ in terms of the warmth that mothers expressed toward each twin at age five, before

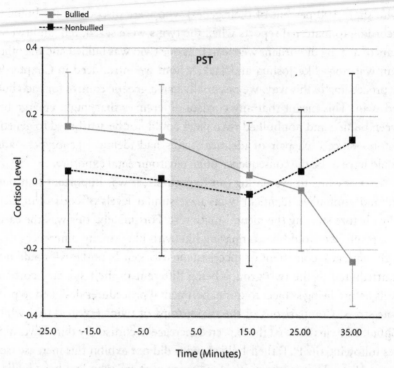

FIGURE 18.1. Average level of cortisol from twenty-five minutes before to thirty-five minutes after psychosocial stress test (PST) for bullied and nonbullied monozygotic twins. Reformatted from Ouellet-Morin, I, Danese, A., Bowes, L., Shakoor, S., Ambler, A., Pariante, C.M., Papadopoulos, A.S., Caspi, A., Moffitt, T.E., & Arseneault, L. (2011). A discordant monozygotic twin design shows blunted cortisol reactivity among bullied children. *Journal of the American Academy of Child & Adolescent Psychiatry, 50*, 574–582, figure 1. Reproduced with permission from Elsevier.

bullying victimization occurred, and whether they experienced maltreatment if residing in a home where such treatment had occurred. In other words, these dynamic family processes could not be responsible for the cortisol differences detected between twins discordant for bullying. The children's body-mass index (BMI), pubertal maturity, and own perpetration of bullying, or the stress and negative affect they experienced during the mental-math test also did not distinguish the two groups of twins. These latter results meant that neither individual factors concomitant with bullying victimization nor differences in emotional experience during the mental-math stressor could account for our results showing that bullied twins had a more blunted cortisol response than their genetically identical nonbullied twin. A second way, then, that childhood adversity—in this case bullying—becomes biologically embedded is via stress physiology.

There has been some discussion in the scientific literature suggesting that this "downregulation" of the HPA axis that we found to be associated with bullying may be adaptive. It is thought that it may serve to protect the still-developing brain from the harmful effects of prolonged exposure to elevated levels of cortisol resulting from chronic stress. Even if this is so, it does not mean that this protective adaptation is cost-free. Alterations in primary stress mediators—such as cortisol and catecholamines—promote adaptation to the changing environment. Persistently low cortisol secretion, however, may increase the future risk of poor physical and psychological health. This is because low cortisol levels have been associated with reduced attention, impaired working memory, and reduced responsiveness to reinforcement and punishment. Moreover, because cortisol affects the amplitude and length of proinflammatory response, persistently low cortisol levels may result in sustained overactivity of the immune system and thus increased risk of autoimmune disorders. In sum, even if there is some biological "wisdom" in the downregulation of cortisol in the face of chronic stress, this process still carries health-related costs.

TELOMERE EROSION

Development is, to say the least, a dynamic and complex process, and this is true whether we are considering social, emotional, cognitive, behavioral, or biological functioning. In the case of the biological embedding of childhood adversity, this means that there are other places to look besides inflammation and stress physiology when it comes to illuminating how adversity goes from outside to inside the body to eventually undermine physical health. This led to our work on telomeres and, specifically, telomere erosion—the shortening of telomeres over time.

What are telomeres? To answer this question, it helps to remember that our bodies are dynamic—meaning changing—entities. Thus, the cells of your eyes that help you read these words are not the same ones that were there a while ago, and they won't be the ones helping you read in the future. This is because cells "turn over," with existing ones eventually dying and being replaced by new ones through a process of cell division and thereby replication. Every time this occurs, that cap on the end of the chromosome—the telomere—shortens. You can think of telomeres like the ends of a shoestring, which keep the string from unraveling. Imagine that every time you tied a shoe the tapelike substance wrapped around the end of the string shortened; in time, it would cease to exist and the string would unravel. That is what happens with chromosomes. A cell line exists for only so long, and after enough cell divisions have occurred, the telomere no longer caps the end of the chromosome and cell death occurs.

As a result of this process, some have come to think of the telomere as a "biological clock" that reflects the age of the cell: the shorter the telomere, the older the cell and thus the older the individual, biologically speaking. Evidence that telomeres shorten with age is certainly consistent with this view. It also turns out that they are shorter in adults suffering from age-related diseases than in their healthy counterparts of the same chronological age. Most important for purposes of this stage of our biological-embedding adventure, however, is evidence that children whose childhoods are characterized by adversity have shorter telomeres than those of other children of the same chronological age. Strikingly, research even documents an association between adversity and telomere length on the first day of postnatal life. Newborns whose mothers have experienced more stress during pregnancy have shorter telomeres than other newborns! Apparently, adversity accelerates biological aging of cells even before postnatal life begins.

It is one thing to discover that adversity is related to shorter telomeres measured at a single point in time, whether in childhood or adulthood, but another to link adversity to the actual erosion process or shortening of telomeres over time. Such evidence would imply that adversity accelerates aging and, if linked to future poor health, that this is another biological-embedding mechanism by which childhood adversity goes "underground" and "gets under the skin," influencing physical health. We therefore sought to extend work on adversity and telomere length by investigating whether exposure to violence in childhood predicted actual *change* in telomeres from ages five to ten years in the E-Risk Study, not just in the length of telomeres at one point in time. We predicted that children exposed to more violence than others would show greater erosion of telomeres over this five-year time span.

To get a good estimate of children's exposure to violence, we drew on interviews conducted with E-Risk mothers when their twins were five, seven, and ten years of age. As part of these extensive interviews, mothers were queried about three different types of violence to which each of their children might have been exposed. In the case of *domestic violence,* the mother reported whether either she or her partner had ever engaged in any of twelve specific behaviors, such as kicking the partner or threatening him or her with a knife. A child was considered subject to *bullying victimization* based on mothers' open-ended responses to questions, as described in Chapter 9. Recall that a child was considered bullied when another child said mean and hurtful things; made fun of the twin or called the twin mean and hurtful names; completely ignored or excluded the twin from their group of friends or left the twin out of activities on purpose; hit, kicked, or shoved the twin or locked him or her in a room; told lies or spread rumors about the twin; or engaged in similarly hurtful acts.

Physical maltreatment, the third type of violence exposure we focused on, was determined based on extensive records kept by researchers who conducted home visits to E-Risk families and on information provided by mothers during detailed questioning about child-rearing practices. Behavior qualifying as maltreatment included documented actions such as the mother smacking the child weekly and leaving marks or bruises; the child being repeatedly beaten by a young-adult stepsibling or being routinely smacked by the father when he was drunk, "just to humiliate" the child; and the child being fondled sexually and often slapped by the mother's boyfriend.

As was the case in the Dunedin Study, research workers made clear to the E-Risk mothers that they were obliged to seek help for families if a child was judged to be in ongoing danger. Indeed, they conveyed this information twice during the home visit. Therefore, any mother whose narrative included information indicating that the child was still in danger knew that they were in essence asking the research team to intervene. Such intervention involved going with the mother to the family doctor (all children are registered with a doctor in the United Kingdom) and reporting the situation together. In this way, we ensured that a medical professional known to the family and responsible for the child's well-being took over the case. This enabled us to meet legal requirements for reporting dangerous conditions for a child in a manner that was acceptable to the families, as well as our own ethical responsibilities. It may seem that mothers would conceal abuse out of fear of reprisal, but because mothers were repeatedly interviewed about harm to their children over the course of home visits at five, seven, ten, and twelve years of age, sooner or later they felt comfortable revealing their child's mistreatment. We intervened with several families over the years, but no family dropped out of the study as a result.

With the diverse data we had in hand pertaining to children's exposure to domestic violence, bullying, and physical maltreatment, we data "lumpers" created a composite measure of *cumulative violence exposure*. About half the children were judged not to have been exposed to violence, about one-third were exposed to one type of violence, and just over 15 percent were exposed to two or more types of violence.

To measure telomere length at ages five and ten years, cheek cells were obtained by rubbing the inside of the child's mouth with a Q-tip-like object. These were brought to our London lab for DNA extraction and ultimately telomere-length measurement.

When it came to determining whether greater exposure to violence predicted greater telomere erosion (that is, faster shortening) over the five-year period of study, we discovered that it did. Children who experienced two or more types of violence exposure showed accelerated telomere erosion from age five to age ten compared to children who had one type of violence exposure or who were not exposed to violence at all (Figure 18.2). This was so even when we took into account a host of alternative explanatory factors, those "third variables" we have referred to throughout the book, including children's sex, body-mass index, and physical health, and family socioeconomic deprivation. In other words, violence exposure predicted accelerated shortening of telomeres beyond any effects of these other factors.

Despite investigations earlier than our own documenting links between adversity in childhood and shorter telomeres—measured at a single point in time—our study was the first to shed light on how adversity affects the *development* of telomeres. Thus, consistent with our hypothesis, it was the first to show that exposure to adversity in the form of psychological and physical violence predicts the actual shortening or erosion of telomeres over time. It thus seems reasonable to infer that in children exposed to two or more types of violence, cells were aging, biologically speaking, faster than their agemates' cells. The more general issue of pace or rate of aging is the focus of the next chapter.

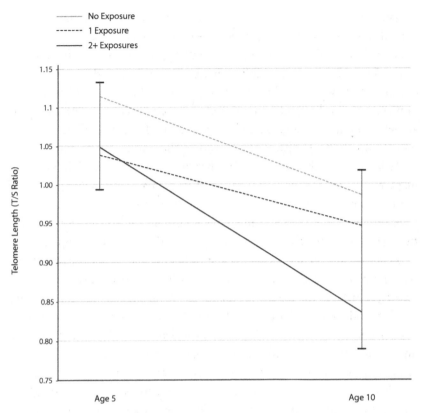

FIGURE 18.2. Association between cumulative violence exposure and telomere length at five and ten years of age. Reformatted from Shalev, I., Moffitt, T.E., Sugden, K., Williams, B., Houts, R.M., Danese, A., Mill, J., Arseneault, L., & Caspi, A. (2013). Exposure to violence during childhood is associated with telomere erosion from 5 to 10 years of age: a longitudinal study. *Molecular Psychiatry, 18*, 576–581, figure 2.

CONCLUSION

When considered in their entirety, the results of our adventure in biological embedding provided support for the hypotheses we set out to test, thereby extending the research reported in Chapter 17 linking such adversity with poor physical health in midlife. We first saw evidence of this when we endeavored to predict levels of C-reactive protein in the blood when members of the Dunedin Study were thirty-two years of age. It was very important that the associations detected linking greater childhood adversity and increased inflammation could not be fully accounted for by other factors known to be related to inflammation. In our first inflammation-related study, this proved true as well—when both child maltreatment and social isolation remained predictive of inflammation beyond effects of low birth weight. In our second inflammation-related study, this was also the case, this time when child maltreatment remained predictive of inflammation even after taking into account other indicators of early-life adversity, as well as adult stress and health behavior. In our final inflammation-related inquiry involving E-Risk children rather than adult participants in the Dunedin Study, it should be recalled that the combination of child maltreatment and depression was related to increased inflammation that also could not be accounted for by a variety of potentially confounding factors. This third inflammation-related study was very important because it made clear that even by age twelve, adversity effects on inflammation are operative.

Since we published those studies of inflammation, as measured with C-reactive protein, a new test for inflammation has been designed, called suPAR, shorthand for soluble urokinase plasminogen activator receptor. We are now finding, in both the Dunedin and E-Risk studies, that children who had adverse childhood experiences show elevated suPAR as adults; in fact, adding suPAR and C-reactive protein together triples the size of the adversity effect, making it much stronger. This illustrates that part of our adventure is keeping up with the latest measurement tools—and "lumping" related measurements together to get a stronger "signal" of their power to predict developmental outcomes of interest.

Just as importantly, our other E-Risk work focused on stress physiology and telomere length revealed that exposure to bullying and violence was associated with, respectively, blunted cortisol reactivity and accelerated telomere erosion, once again with confounding factors controlled. What makes these findings, like the age-twelve inflammation results, particularly significant is that they indicate that the effect of adversity on processes of biological embedding involves not only some kind of delayed response, which could have been the case. Instead, our work investigating inflammation and stress physiology in twelve-year-olds and telomere shortening across the second half of the first decade of life makes clear that these biological-embedding processes found to be associated with adversity are actually occurring during the period of stress exposure. Prior work, including our own on inflammation at age thirty-two, left this issue unclear.

Four additional points need to be highlighted. The first is that even though we found repeatedly, that childhood adversity affected biological processes in ways known to undermine health—even after discounting the effects of numerous alternative explanatory factors—the effects in question were probabilistic, not deterministic. Thus, some children exposed to the very adversities we studied did not evince elevated levels of inflammation or accelerating telomere erosion, and some not exposed to the same adversities did. Exactly why this was the case was not something we focused on but clearly merits additional work in the future. For now, we can just repeat the mantra that runs throughout this volume, that development is probabilistic, not deterministic.

The second point is that even if our findings are consistent with the claims that heightened inflammation, indexed by elevated C-reactive protein levels; maladaptive stress physiology, indexed by blunted cortisol reactivity; and accelerated biological aging, indexed by greater telomere erosion, may mediate and thus be responsible for the effects of childhood adversity on health later in life, our research has not yet provided evidence of this. Before we can complete the necessary research to test whether inflammation, blunted cortisol reactivity, and/or telomere erosion links childhood adversity with actual age-related diseases such as diabetes, we have to wait for our E-Risk twins and Dunedin Study participants to get older. Once again, we are back to being fruit growers; we have planted trees but need to wait for them to mature before we can harvest the fruit.

Our third point is that the findings emanating from our biological-embedding research raise new questions about biological processes implicated in the association between childhood adversity and poor adult health. One is whether the biological-embedding processes we have studied are related to each other. Certainly one possibility is that stress physiology affects inflammation and thereby accelerates telomere erosion. However plausible this sounds, subsequent work in the Dunedin Study indicated that diverse putative indicators of biological aging, at least at age thirty-eight, were not related to each other. Whether the same would be true in childhood remains to be determined.

Whatever the case, it seems almost certain that other biological-embedding processes are at work in the process of health and human development beyond the ones we have considered in the current developmental adventure. The point is that there is probably a complex chain of influence by which adversity moves from outside the body to inside it to affect inflammation, stress physiology, telomere length, and, eventually, physical health. It should be clear by now that human development is complicated. This is why in Chapter 1 we likened it to meteorology. In so many respects, we and others studying the biological embedding of childhood adversity are only at the beginning when it comes to illuminating this process.

Our fourth and final—and perhaps most important—point actually reiterates one made at the very beginning of this chapter, so here we remind the reader of the potential intervention implications of the results of our work illuminating biological-embedding processes in childhood. To the extent that future inquiry reveals that the processes under consideration here—inflammation, blunted cortisol reactivity, and telomere erosion— actually function as part of a causal pathway linking childhood adversity to age-related diseases, it would highlight potential biological targets of intervention, thus moving us from basic to applied science. One might imagine a time when children, adolescents, or even adults exposed to adversity in childhood could be treated pharmacologically—or even behaviorally—in ways that downregulate inflammation, recover the "elasticity" of the cortisol response, and/or slow or perhaps even reverse telomere erosion that has resulted from maltreatment, social isolation, bullying, depression, and many more conditions of childhood adversity. Beyond being fascinating in its own right, this is one reason why mechanistic-oriented developmental inquiry of the kind presented in this chapter is so important. It holds the promise of revealing potentially influential targets of intervention. In other words, the work we presented here might have been conducted in the ivory tower, but we hope it will not stay there.

19

Aging Fast, Aging Slow

L ife is funny, and so is (the perception of) time. Remember in childhood how you couldn't wait to grow up—to be able to go to school, to be able to stay up later, to be able to drive, and to go away to college? It couldn't happen fast enough. It always seemed to take forever for these milestones—and associated opportunities—to arrive.

Now fast-forward to the second half of the life course—if you haven't already gotten there. We are talking about the late thirties or early forties, given that the average American life span is currently seventy-eight years. Who is in a rush to get older? Yet, at the same time, the older we get, the faster time seems to be moving, so the faster we seem to be aging. "How did I reach forty, fifty, or even sixty years of age so quickly?," many of us wonder, "Wasn't I just starting a career, switching jobs for the first time, having children? So how has my career already peaked or how did my children become parents themselves so quickly? Wasn't I attending their childhood sports events and recitals just a short time ago?"

Then there is the fact that some of us feel old before our time whereas others feel just the opposite. "Boy, I can't wait to retire," some fifty-year-olds think, "I'm so tired all the time; I wish I didn't need the money." Yet others, even some who are much older, can't even imagine retiring and seem to have more energy than teenagers, going skiing, hiking, and/or biking every chance they get.

Then, of course, there is the fact that some of us—who are the same thirty, forty, or fifty years of age—look so different from others our (chronological) age or even older and carry ourselves differently. Why are one woman's eyes shiny, her skin smooth, and her hair lustrous, whereas another woman the same age looks years older? Is it just the makeup and the hairdresser? As we watched the Dunedin Study members return to the research unit every five years or so in adulthood, we could not help but reflect on observations like those just made and questions like those just raised.

All this was brought home to us in a rather dramatic way one day at the research unit when phase 38 was under way. Two study members, Oliver and Michael, arrived at about the same time for their all-day visit to be interviewed, to take tests of physical fitness and cognitive functions, to provide blood samples, to have their teeth examined, and to have a variety of other procedures performed that we used to gather information on the individuals we had now been following for almost four decades. It was simply hard to believe that both men were thirty-eight years old. Oliver had a twinkle in his eyes, a mouthful of shiny white teeth, a thick head of hair that was graying only around the temples, and walked briskly, with shoulders straight and head held high. Michael, in contrast, was pale by comparison, had teeth that were discolored or missing, walked slowly, with slumped shoulders, and had hair that had gone quite gray. Had someone not known that these middle-aged men were born just a few weeks apart, it would have been a no-brainer to claim that Michael was substantially older than Oliver.

Observations such as these, along with research being carried out by other investigatory teams around the world, made us curious about the process of accelerated aging, leading some to age more rapidly, both biologically and physically, than others. Indeed, these observations stimulated the final developmental adventure we take you on in this book, related as it is to the childhood roots of health in midlife. It's probably not surprising that we middle-aged authors are very intrigued by this topic of the process and pace of aging. Jay Belsky has been swimming a mile four to six times each week for some forty years in an effort to age well (and eat whatever he wants). Avshalom Caspi takes a draconian approach to diet, eating only roots, stems, leaves, and seed pods most of the time. Terrie Moffitt eats cake, dyes her hair red, and reads literary novels with elderly characters who serve as role models of a good old age. And Richie Poulton gets his heart rate up by grappling with the intricacies of New Zealand politics and the excitement of watching the All Blacks, the famous New Zealand rugby team!

Just as we had before, we again realized that the Dunedin Study was well positioned to address the pace of aging. Our great advantage relative to other investigations of the aging process was that we did not have to rely on a retrospective approach that involved interviewing aging individuals about their pasts—because we already had collected a wealth of data on study members long before they reached midlife. Once more, we were not at risk of falling into the measurement trap of thinking that information collected on a retrospective basis is accurate, especially as we had repeatedly found this was not the case. Recall from Chapter 17 that when we compared what adult study members told us after they had grown up about childhood and adolescence with information we had gathered when they were children and teenagers, it did not match up as well as many might suppose it would have. Some individuals remembered their earlier life as though looking through rose-colored glasses, seeming to have forgotten the stressors and strains they lived through, whereas others wore gray-colored ones, which cast too much of their past in too dark a light.

Discovering whether some individuals seem to age quickly whereas others age more slowly by midlife, while illuminating the potential causes and consequences of such variation, is more than just a theoretical or academic exercise. Indeed, what makes the adventure we share in this chapter so noteworthy is that by 2050 the world population age eighty and older will more than triple, approaching four hundred million individuals! And, as populations age, the global burden of disease and disability is rising. From the fifth decade of life, advancing age is associated with an exponential increase in the burden of many chronic illnesses, including diabetes, heart disease, dementia, and obesity. The most effective means of reducing the disease burden and controlling health-care costs is to delay this progression by extending not the life span but the *health* span, defined as years of life lived free of disease and disability.

Some might think it was too early to investigate the issue of aging fast versus aging slow when study members were thirty-eight years of age, but a key to extending the health span is addressing the problem of aging itself, including intervening to reverse or delay the march toward age-related disease when people are still relatively young. Waiting until individuals are much older than thirty-eight to inquire into the nature and determinants

of variation in the rate of aging, as is rather routine in so much aging research, results in addressing the issue at a point when many individuals have
already developed age-related diseases. As we will see, age-related changes
in physiology accumulate before age forty, often affecting organ systems
years before diseases are diagnosed. Waiting to study aging until people are
in their sixties, seventies, or eighties risks missing the boat.

To gain insight into variation in aging, our pace-of-aging adventure proceeded in four stages. In the first, we used diverse physiological measurements obtained at age thirty-eight to distinguish study members who were
biologically older and younger—even though they were the same chronological age. In the second stage, we drew on data gathered over the preceding
twelve years to assess the pace of aging between ages twenty-six and thirty-
eight. This would enable us to determine whether those study members who
proved to be biologically older than agemates in midlife had in fact aged
faster, biologically speaking, beginning in their twenties, if not before. We
predicted that this would be the case. Stage 3 was designed to move us beyond biomarkers reflecting physiological condition to assess what might be
considered more everyday indicators of aging—such as cognitive ability and
motor skills—in order to determine whether these varied as a function of the
biological age of our thirty-eight-year-olds. In other words, were biomarkers
and psychological and behavioral phenotypes systematically related? Again,
we suspected that this would be the case. Finally, we sought to illuminate the
childhood antecedents of variation in the pace of aging, returning we developmental scholars once again to the childhood roots of health. This led us to
consider the social-class origins of study members, their exposure to adversity
in childhood, their health, their intelligence, and their self-control, as well as
how long their own grandparents lived. Anyone who has read this volume
this far will anticipate that we predicted that poor functioning in childhood
and greater exposure to adversity would forecast a faster pace of aging.

CHARACTERIZING ACCELERATED
AGING IN MIDLIFE

Our first task was to create a composite measure of biological aging in
midlife, so we decided to exclude from our work eleven study members who
by this young age already showed evidence of age-related diseases, including

type-2 diabetes, myocardial infarction, and stroke. We reasoned that including these strikingly unhealthy few could distort results that would otherwise emerge. With this modest modification of our sample, we proceeded to combine ten biomarkers assessed at age thirty-eight to create an index of biological aging of each study member, specifically measures of sugar in the blood (glycated hemoglobin), lung capacity (forced expiratory volume in one second, FEV1), kidney function (creatinine), liver function (urea nitrogen, albumin, and alkaline phosphatase), immunocompetence (cytomegalovirus IgG), inflammation (C-reactive protein), blood pressure (systolic), and total cholesterol. We chose each of these biomarkers because previous research by another investigatory team studying accelerated aging had found that every single one predicted, by itself, higher mortality than predicted by chronological age.

Once again, and like most scientists, we were standing on the shoulders of those who preceded us, having their prior work inform our own—just as we did when relying, as outlined in Chapters 12 and 13, on the GWAS findings of large "discovery" studies to guide our own genetic research. Given its appropriateness, let us again quote English poet John Donne's 1624 poem "Devotions Upon Emergent Occasions" that "no man is an island entire to itself; every man is a piece of the continent, a part of the main."

When we plotted our composite biomarker score for each of our study members, the distribution took the form of a lovely bell curve, clearly documenting substantial variation in their biological ages. Those aging especially fast or slow were few in number, whereas many more were aging at the expected pace. We figured this out by comparing the data on our thirty-eight-year-olds with data collected in the other study already alluded to that originally developed the biological-age index we used. Because that other study included many people of many ages, we could use data from that study to determine the biological age of each of our thirty-eight-year-olds by comparing the score each study member had on the biological-aging index with how old the people in the other study were when they scored similarly on the same composite index of biological age. Thus, whereas Oliver was judged to be thirty-four years old "inside" (that is, biologically speaking), Michael's biomarker composite score indicated he was as old inside as a typical forty-seven-year old. While a few of our thirty-eight-year-olds were under thirty years of age biologically speaking and somewhat more were, like Michael, over forty-five years of age biologically, most had a biological age between thirty-five and forty years.

THE PACE OF AGING

Recall that the second stage of our pace-of-aging adventure, after documenting variation in biological age in midlife, was to determine whether those study members who were biologically older at midlife got there because they had been aging more rapidly earlier in life. We predicted, not surprisingly, that this would be the case. To address this pace-of-aging hypothesis, we created a different composite index of biological aging, based on eighteen biomarkers. Each was measured during earlier phases of the Dunedin Study, when study members were twenty-six and thirty-two, as well as at age thirty-eight. Thus, we relied on all the biomarkers in the Dunedin data pantry that were repeated at those three ages. Seven of the eighteen component measures were the same as those included in the already-described index of biological age at age thirty-eight (that is, glycated hemoglobin, FEV, creatinine, urea nitrogen, mean arterial blood pressure, and total cholesterol). To these we added ten biomarkers reflecting cardiorespiratory fitness (VO2Max), waist-hip ratio, forced vital capacity ratio (FEV1 / FVC), body-mass index, lipoprotein (a), triglycerides, periodontal disease, white blood cell count, high-density lipoprotein (that is, "good" cholesterol), and apolipoprotein B100 / A1 ratio. The final biomarker making up the pace-of-aging index was leukocyte telomere length, discussed in Chapter 18, which is a measure of DNA that reflects the lengths of the caps at the ends of each chromosome. Recall that these shorten every time a cell replicates itself and, as a result, become shorter with age.

With our new composite biomarker measurement in hand—at three different points in time—we could evaluate whether, as anticipated, the degree of change over time in our now eighteen-item biomarker index would distinguish those study members who appeared to be aging faster and more slowly as determined by the thirty-eight-year, ten-biomarker index of biological age. The results were consistent with our prediction: the faster the pace of aging—as indexed by greater deterioration from age twenty-six, to age thirty-two, to age thirty-eight across multiple biological systems—the older the study member's biological age when thirty-eight years old. Needless to say, Oliver's pace of aging proved to be substantially slower than Michael's over the dozen years that preceded our biological age measurement at age thirty-eight.

Our results therefore indicated that a substantial component of individual differences in biological age at midlife emerges between young adulthood and midlife, if not before. This observation underscores the point made earlier that aging appears to be not just a phenomenon of the aged. Looking forward, we are now forced to wonder whether those who were biologically older at age thirty-eight (such as Michael) than their chronological agemates (such as Oliver)—and who we now know aged more rapidly from twenty-six to thirty-eight—will age even faster biologically as they get chronologically older. And if so, will they experience shorter health spans and life spans as a result? To gain some insight into this issue, we proceeded to stage 3 of our adventure studying the pace of aging.

BEYOND BIOMARKERS

Recall that the third issue we addressed in our research on midlife aging concerned whether those study members found to be biologically older at age thirty-eight, apparently because their biological systems had deteriorated more rapidly over the preceding twelve years, would also manifest evidence of accelerated aging in their brains and the rest of their bodies. To test the prediction that they would, we examined physical capabilities, such as climbing stairs and participating in strenuous sports, as well as cognitive decline across more than two decades of life. The latter focus was addressed by drawing on repeated measurements of IQ obtained when study members were seven, nine, eleven, thirteen, and thirty-eight years of age. We also took advantage of photos taken of study members' faces at age thirty-eight to see whether these also showed evidence of more rapid aging in the case of individuals who were biologically older. Additionally, we asked study members about their own health and used sophisticated optometric instruments to examine blood vessels in the eyes of study members.

Given the results already considered, it was not surprising to learn that the brains and other body parts of biologically older and younger thirty-eight-year-olds—who remember were the very same chronological age—proved to be different. The first evidence consistent with this claim is that study members who were biologically older at age thirty-eight performed less well on objective tests of physical functioning at that age (Figure 19.1). They had more difficulty with balance, more limited fine-motor capabilities (tested using a pegboard), and weaker grip strength. These observations were consistent with study members' own reports of their physical limitations. Those who were biologically older at age thirty-eight claimed to have more difficulty climbing stairs, walking more than two-thirds of a mile, and participating in strenuous sports than did fellow study members of the same age who were biologically younger. Notably, these results based

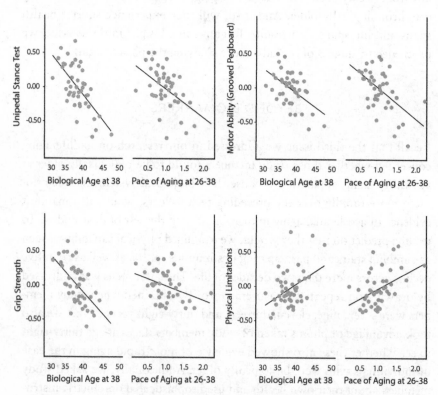

FIGURE 19.1. Associations between biological age and pace of aging and diverse aspects of physical health in middle age. Reformatted from Belsky, D.W., Caspi, A., Houts, R., Cohen, H.J., Corcoran, D.L., Danese, A., Harrington, H., Israel, S., Levine, M.E., Schaefer, J.D., Sugden, K., Williams, B., Yashin, A.I., Poutlton, R., & Moffitt, T.E. (2015). Quantification of biological aging in young adults. *PNAS*, E4104-E4110, figure 5.

on reports of physical limitations were consistent with study members' own evaluations of their physical health: those who were biologically older at age thirty-eight characterized themselves as in poorer health than did age-mates who were biologically younger.

It was not just the body that was functioning more poorly among the biologically older thirty-eight-year-olds. They also scored lower than other study members on the IQ test administered at age thirty-eight. This was because, these biologically older thirty-eight-year-olds experienced greater decline than biologically younger study members in cognitive functioning from age seven to age thirty-eight (Figure 19.2). Of course, study members still retained mental abilities and knowledge from their younger years, but

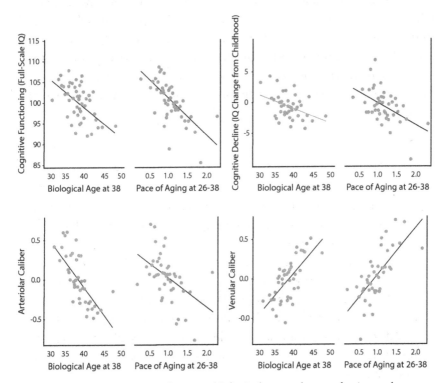

FIGURE 19.2. Associations between biological age and pace of aging and cognitive competence and risk of stroke in middle age. Reformatted from Belsky, D.W., Caspi, A., Houts, R., Cohen, H.J., Corcoran, D.L., Danese, A., Harrington, H., Israel, S., Levine, M.E., Schaefer, J.D., Sugden, K., Williams, B., Yashin, A.I., Poutlton, R., & Moffitt, T.E. (2015). Quantification of biological aging in young adults. *PNAS*, E4104-E4110, figure 6.

for those aging fast, the speed with which they could process information had slowed considerably.

The two-dimensional photographs of blood vessels in the retinas, taken with special optometric equipment, told a similar story, as is evident in the bottom two graphs in Figure 19.2. To understand the findings, however, one needs to appreciate that narrower arterioles (which take oxygen-enriched blood *to* the eye from the lungs) are associated with increased risk of stroke, and wider venules (which take oxygen-depleted blood *from* the eye to the lungs) are associated with increased risk of dementia. Biologically older thirty-eight-year-olds had both narrower arterioles and wider venules, so they appeared at greater risk of both stroke and dementia!

Finally, faces told a similar story. Evaluators given the task of judging a study member's chronological age after viewing a (nonsmiling) photograph taken at age thirty-eight rated those who scored biologically older at age thirty-eight as looking older. For this finding to be fully appreciated, it should be made clear that these trained raters, working only from the photographs, were undergraduates at Duke University in the United States who knew absolutely nothing about the study members, including their real chronological age.

CHILDHOOD ORIGINS OF THE PACE OF AGING

We next turned our attention to what must be regarded as a fundamental question about life span: are development and experience in childhood related to the pace of aging? To address this issue, we drew on measurements we introduced in earlier chapters of this book, with one exception. Thus, when it came to predicting variation in the pace of aging, we focused on childhood social class, adverse childhood experiences, childhood health, childhood IQ, and childhood self-control, but to this set of previously described developmental constructs we added "grandparental longevity," operationalized as the oldest age to which any of a study member's four grandparents lived.

Our findings were in line with expectations. Study members with shorter-lived grandparents, who grew up in households of lower social class, who experienced more frequent adverse childhood experiences, who scored lower on IQ tests, and who had more limited self-control all showed evidence of accelerated biological aging during their twenties and thirties (see Figure 19.3). In fact, not only did each of these factors by themselves predict the pace of aging, but also their power to predict how quickly study members were aging increased when we lumped them all together to create a composite index of the cumulative risk of fast aging.

As a second way of looking at the relation between childhood antecedents of the pace of aging, we divided the study members into three groups: those 15 percent or so who were aging most slowly according to our biological index, those 15 percent or so who were aging most rapidly, and the remaining 70 percent or so, who were aging at a more or less average pace. Notably, most of those in the slowly aging group had none of the family and childhood risk factors for accelerated aging, such as low family SES,

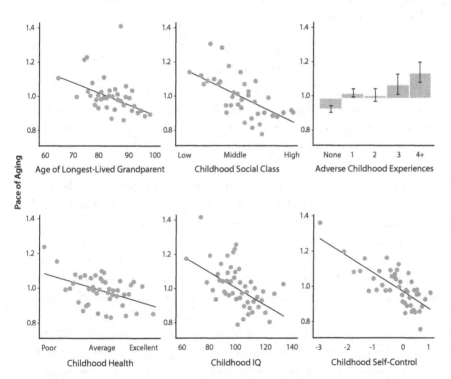

FIGURE 19.3. Associations between aspects of children's families, experiences, and well-being and pace of aging in middle age. Reformatted from Belsky, D.W., Caspi, A., Cohen, H.J., Kraus, W.E., Ramrakha, S., Poulton, R., & Moffitt, T.E. (2017). Impact of early personal-history characteristic on the Pace of Aging, *Aging Cell*, 16 644–651, figure 2. CC-BY.

low IQ, and poor childhood health. In contrast, more than 40 percent of the rapidly aging study members were classified as high risk on multiple family and childhood characteristics. It would therefore seem that indicators of childhood adversity and early child development probabilistically forecast a faster pace of aging. We say probabilistic because, once more, prediction here was by no means perfect. So, obviously, there are some individuals who by one means or another avoid the accelerated aging that might otherwise be expected of them on the basis of their childhoods. At the same time, there are also some who age more rapidly than one might expect based on their early-life experiences and condition. It will take future work to identify what resilience and vulnerability factors might help explain these exceptions to our findings and expectations. As we have noted previously, insight here could, in principle, be used to develop interventions to slow or perhaps even reverse the kind of accelerated biological aging we have detected.

CONCLUSION

The evidence we have shared indicates that aging is not a phenomenon restricted to the old. Even by age thirty-eight, just about halfway through the average American's life span, some of us are biologically older than others. This is because even by midlife there is evidence of individual differences in the pace of aging, with this difference beginning in the mid-twenties, if not earlier. That being biologically older is associated with a host of real-world limitations and characteristics is just as notable. Those who are biologically older are less physically capable, experience more rapid intellectual decline, and simply look older. More troubling than the latter is that blood vessels in the eye suggest that those who are biologically older are at greater risk of developing dementia and having a stroke than those aging more slowly.

The health conditions just described are especially expensive to deal with—whether speaking in terms of time, energy, and money or of individuals, families, and society more generally. This is why accelerated aging is—or at least should be—a major public-health concern. That our findings suggest that it could be possible to identify those who are experiencing accelerated biological aging well before it becomes obvious opens up the prospect of doing so to decelerate the pace of aging. What remains to be determined, of course, is whether identifying and targeting those who are aging rapidly could lead to interventions that could decelerate the aging process—or even possibly reverse it. That achieving such goals would yield benefits—to individuals, to their loved ones, and to society—clearly seems evident based on our results.

In addition to distinguishing those study members aging fast and slow at age thirty-eight and linking such variation to the pace of aging based on repeated biological measurements obtained in their twenties and thirties, our developmental adventure also revealed childhood antecedents of the pace of aging. Given what we learned in Chapter 17 regarding the developmental origins of health and disease, we must acknowledge that our results were not surprising. Nevertheless, it remains noteworthy that we could predict the pace of aging across a twelve-year period (from ages twenty-six to thirty-eight) by considering factors other than adverse childhood experiences, including poorer childhood health and low child IQ. Recall that we observed that the relationship between personal-history risk factors and biological aging was cumulative: more risks predicted a faster pace of aging.

Once again, we feel justified in heralding the fact that the discoveries we have shared could not have emerged without the great investment made—by ourselves, our collaborators, our funders, and, of course, study members—in carrying out a multidisciplinary, prospective study of an entire birth cohort, starting very early in life and continuing to midlife (and we hope beyond). For example, retrospective investigation of accelerated aging simply could not have revealed the cognitive decline we found associated with it. Had we only measured traditional psychological constructs, such as intelligence or perceived health, and not invested in biological assessments well before they bore empirical fruit, we could not have discovered that accelerated biological aging began in the third decade of life—and probably earlier (see Chapter 15). And had we not studied an entire birth cohort but rather a sample of highly motivated volunteers or a select sample of only those aging very well and very poorly, we would be on much weaker ground when generalizing our results to a larger population.

We should again underscore the fact that those who launched the Dunedin Study so many years ago could not have imagined the work we have just reported—and so much more covered in other chapters of this book—if only because accelerated aging was so much less of an issue back in the early 1970s, when the demographics of Western industrial societies were so different from what they are today. Also, so many of the biological measurements we drew on simply did not exist back then. It is only because those Dunedin Study investigators who preceded us cut down the trees, turned over the soil, and planted the seeds that they did that we have been able to harvest the fruit of this inquiry, having toiled ourselves in continually fertilizing those trees and using as ingredients the fruits they yielded to cook up the many meals we have delivered throughout this book.

PART VII

CONCLUSION

20

Miles to Go Before We Sleep

Readers familiar with twentieth-century American poet Robert Frost will appreciate that the title of the final chapter of this book is taken, with slight revision, from one of the lines of one of his most well-known poems, "Stopping by Woods on a Snowy Evening." The poem's narrator describes pausing on a long journey to admire the beauty of a winter landscape before continuing onward. To our way of thinking, this perfectly captures what we have tried to do in this volume. We have paused midway in our decades-long adventure studying human development, we hope from the womb to the tomb, to take stock of and share with readers what we regard as some of our most interesting findings while illuminating how we go about our work.

We selected the word *adventure* as a description throughout this book because that is what our programs of research have been and continue to be for us, a sensibility that we hope we have conveyed and that the reader has shared. Indeed, as mentioned in the preface, we originally thought we would use *Adventures in Human Development* as the title of the book. Even though we often know where we are going and what we are likely to find—recall our reliance on the metaphors of treasure hunter, chef, and fruit grower—there have been other times when we have been uncertain, posing developmental questions rather than testing particular hypotheses, leading us to use the metaphor of explorer. Irrespective of whether we were testing a formal prediction, we have repeatedly been surprised in our research endeavors—both by what we ended up studying and by what we did and did not discover. With regard to the former, none of us would have predicted so long ago when we started our journey that we would investigate family influences on female pubertal development (Chapter 7), cardiovascular disease in midlife (Chapter17), or the genetics of success (Chapter 13), to cite but a few examples. With regard to the latter, we never would have predicted that smoking cannabis would be related to increased lung function (Chapter 11) or that the stress of polyvictimization would not prove to alter epigenetic methylation (Chapter 16).

Given the wide array of topics we have investigated and shared in this book, it seems noteworthy that we never started out as the multidisciplinary scientists we have become. What we discovered in the course of our own professional development was simply that to understand the development of mind and behavior, we had to spread our net widely and learn from what was being discovered outside our original disciplines of developmental and clinical psychology. One consequence of our own intellectual journey is that we no longer find it easy to say exactly who we are or what we do when we are asked—whether by the person seated next to us on a plane, the friend of a friend we encounter at a party, or a relative at a family gathering. Neither "psychologist," "health researcher," nor even "developmental scientist" seem to do the trick, and too often when we say we study "human development," people ask, "What's that?" This too often requires a long-winded explanation. Now we are often inclined to stipulate simply that we study "how we become who we are."

A guiding philosophy of science that embraces both theory-guided inquiry and theory-free empiricism has been central to our scientific adventures. This means that in some cases hypotheses that we tested derived directly from theoretical claims. Recall in this regard our attempts to test Moffitt's theory of antisocial behavior, which highlighted the distinction between life-course-persistent and adolescent-limited delinquency (Chapter 5), or Belsky's recasting of development in an evolutionary perspective, leading to our work investigating the effects of childhood adversity on pubertal timing (Chapter 6). But we also shared investigatory adventures that were not guided by theory but instead sought to answer a developmental question we found interesting. Consider in this regard the work shared about how temperament in early childhood is related to development much later in life (Chapter 2) and how day care affects child development (Chapter 8). While we might have had some general conceptual ideas in addressing these issues—for example, whether development is continuous or discontinuous in the case of early temperament and later development—the research undertaken was not based on any particular developmental or psychological theory. To repeat what we said earlier, when we had a clear road map enabling us to advance testable hypotheses, we functioned as treasure hunters knowing what we were looking for or as chefs knowing what we would prepare, but when this was not the case, our adventure was more like that of an explorer, prepared for whatever turned up but having little idea what that might be.

In drawing a distinction between theory-based and theory-free inquiry, we cannot help but recall how the former used to be heralded and the latter treated as a poorer relative. One of the fascinating things that has transpired over the course of our careers is how theory-free work has been "rebranded" from what used to be disparagingly referred to as "dust bowl empiricism" (a reference to the Midwestern United States, where this kind of inquiry was supposedly highly regarded). But with the arrival of big-data science—such as seeing which of millions of genetic polymorphisms are related to some phenotype (for example, smoking addiction)—it became widely appreciated that in many cases theory could not handle all the information that has become available. Therefore, the strategy became "let the computer figure it out" rather than "here is how things likely work so let's find out if they do." We actually practiced this former approach ourselves when investigating the developmental legacy of early-childhood temperament (Chapter 2). Recall that we simply asked the computer to process, using sophisticated multivariate analysis, our multiple measurements of child behavior in order to identify types of children. We did not start with a theory of the types of children that would be revealed, even if we were aware that some other investigators had ideas about this.

A commitment to dispassionate inquiry has also been central to our philosophy of science. By this we mean that we didn't set out to "find" something, such as negative or positive effects of cannabis on psychological and behavioral development and physical health (Chapter 11), even when we had strong bases for particular predictions. Instead, we committed ourselves to illuminating how development operates. So even when we hypothesized—or just hoped—that results would turn out one way rather than another, we disciplined ourselves so as not to let those preferences bias our investigation. While we probably cannot be 100 percent certain that we succeeded in realizing this ambition, we did bend over backward to avoid such intellectual "contamination." Perhaps the best evidence of this was our repeated efforts to challenge our initial findings even when they were consistent with what we expected. In the final analysis, we have been—and remain—dyed-in-the-wool empiricists. Wherever the chips fall is where we also land.

Like Frost's traveler, we still have miles to go before we sleep. Although the NICHD Study of Child Care and Youth Development was terminated when the children were fifteen years of age, having answered the core questions that it was funded by the government to address, the Dunedin Study and the Environmental-Risk Study are ongoing. Indeed, to repeat what was said in Chapter 1, participants in the Dunedin Study were most recently reassessed in 2018–2019 at age forty-five—including in an MRI brain scanner—and as we write these words, we are gearing up to see the E-Risk Study participants again in their mid-twenties. We do not envision these data collections to be the end of the research road by any means. We hope to continue to follow both samples as long as funding and our own abilities permit. And if and when our abilities do not permit, we hope that others will pick up where we left off, just as we once picked up from the founders of the Dunedin Study so many years ago.

As we trust this book has demonstrated, longitudinal studies like those that are its focus are treasures that just keep giving. We have noted repeatedly that such long-term investigations, which are so challenging to maintain once launched, continue to prove their scientific value long after the original data were collected. What continues to surprise and fascinate us, even though perhaps it should not, is how the emergence of new scholarly questions and new measurement technologies—such as the methylation assays reported in Chapter 16 to investigate epigenetic mechanisms and the just-concluded brain imaging of forty-five-year-old members of the Dunedin Study—enable us to investigate issues that were never even imagined when some of the childhood data to be used in addressing the new questions were gathered.

It is not just new measurements that make these studies so valuable. Being able to repeat measurements over time is essential if we want to learn about how humans develop and change. As one example, just consider how in Chapter 18 we used repeated measurements of biomarkers obtained at ages twenty-six, thirty-two, and thirty-eight to investigate the pace of aging, thereby enabling us to discover that those aging faster and more slowly were already on their developmental paths by the middle of their third decade of life, if not earlier. Recall, too, how in Chapter 11 we relied on repeated measurements of intelligence to illuminate the long-term effects of persistent cannabis use, enabling us to distinguish between those whose cognitive capabilities were and were not declining, even if only by a modest amount.

As we go forward, we expect to repeat many measurements while also implementing new assessments resulting from technological advances and/or the aging of our study members, which we hope will enable us to make new discoveries. In fact, these might result from addressing questions that we cannot even imagine at present. But instead of going there right now, let us take stock of how far we have come by returning to the themes that we stipulated in Chapter 1 would emerge in this book.

The Child as the Father of the Man

The first theme to consider is the long-standing notion that how children think, feel, and behave early in their lives foreshadows how they will develop in the future, which we addressed in Part II. Perhaps the best way to summarize what we learned is that while it is certainly—and repeatedly—the case that individual differences in children within the first decade of life can forecast how they will function decades later, the power to predict later development from childhood measurements is often, though not always, limited. This is because development is not over even by the end of the first decade of life. At least some people continue to grow and change.

Having qualified any claims of inevitable strong continuity between early and later development, we nevertheless should not lose sight of our discovery that temperament at age three predicted how some children functioned much later in life. Recall that we found that many of those young children who were especially undercontrolled or overcontrolled continued to manifest these early temperamental styles as they aged (see Chapter 2). This led us to characterize the former as "moving against the world" and the latter as "moving away from the world." Related to these findings was evidence that children who manifested low or high levels of self-control in many aspects of their functioning across the first decade of life still behaved similarly decades later (see Chapter 3) across many domains of life (for example, work, family, and health). We also discovered that even if a formal psychiatric diagnosis of ADHD in childhood did not predict clinical levels of this disorder decades later (see Chapter 4), it remained the case that those children and adolescents so diagnosed continued to behave in ways consistent with their childhood condition.

Influence of Childhood Experiences within and beyond the Family

In Parts III and IV, we discuss our discovery that developmental experiences and environmental exposures within and beyond the family certainly appeared to influence how children develop. For example, in Chapter 5, we considered the evidence pertaining to the intergenerational transmission of parenting, which indicated that how girls, but not boys, were reared predicted how they related to their own three-year-olds. In Chapter 8, we noted that whereas good-quality day care seemed to enhance, somewhat, cognitive-linguistic development, lots of time spent in day care over months and years appeared to foster, at least to some degree in the American context, aggression and disobedience in childhood and risk taking and impulsivity in adolescence. Chapters 6 and 7 pointed out that adverse family environments (for example, conflicted relationships, inconsistent parenting) promoted early and enduring antisocial behavior, especially when children began life with neuropsychological deficits and behavioral limitations (Chapter 6), and even accelerated the sexual maturation of girls (Chapter 7). Chapter 11 made clear that even if persistent cannabis use, typically initiated in the presence of peers, had few negative effects on physical health, the same was decidedly not the case when it came to mental health. Chapter 9 discussed how being bullied by peers and/or growing up in a disadvantaged neighborhood undermined well-being, with the latter adverse effect actually amplified when more affluent families lived nearby.

Some of these and other observations are consistent with what are frequently regarded as commonsense claims (for example, day care carries developmental risks), whereas others may not be (for example, adolescent misbehavior is just a passing phase). Besides pointing out that one person's common sense is not always another's (for example, day care is good for children, day care is bad for children; adolescent delinquency is or is not a passing phase), our research made clear that common sense can be wrong: misbehavior in adolescence is not always just a passing phase (Chapter 6), and high-quality care does not attenuate, much less ameliorate, the negative effects of lots of time spent in day care initiated in infancy and continuing until the start of formal schooling (Chapter 8). We have often found when we share our findings that some will assert that they are just common sense, sometimes implying that the research that yielded a particular result was a waste of time, money, and effort. We encourage such critics to appreciate that sometimes common sense is not as common—that is, widely shared—as often presumed, to say nothing of it not accurately reflecting the nature of development. For both these reasons, we regard longitudinal research as very important, especially when it comes to understanding topics like those addressed in this book, most of which are difficult if not impossible to study experimentally and deal with real-world issues and problems that children, families, and society more broadly face.

Now that we have commented on the putative wisdom of common sense, we need to make two more points about the influence of experiences and exposure within and beyond the family. The first is that whatever the power to predict later development documented herein, the results we shared were never so strong as to imply that our foci of inquiry (child-rearing, day care, bullying, and neighborhood deprivation) were so great as to powerfully determine how children would grow and develop. This is our way of again underscoring the critical point that development is an ongoing process that is determined by many, often interacting, factors and forces, just like the weather. That is why it is probabilistic and not deterministic, another theme repeatedly highlighted in this book. In the same way that knowing only the humidity or barometric pressure cannot tell you everything you need to know to make an accurate precipitation forecast, knowing just one thing about development—be it how a child was reared or what a child's neighborhood was like—is likely to be equally limiting. This is not to say that it is unimportant, only that many other forces and factors need to be considered because the predictive power of any one force or factor will be limited most of the time.

Genetics

The second additional point we want to make about familial and extrafamilial influences on development that we studied leads us directly into another theme of this book: the influence of genetics. With rare exceptions, our observational work could not fully discount the possibility that genetics was influencing our results. This is why we qualified our claims in the preceding paragraphs and throughout the book when discussing putative effects of the developmental experiences and environmental exposures we studied. We should point out here that some scholars might reasonably object to the very notion of studying development, including environmental effects, by ruling out genetic effects. Separating nature and nurture is impossible, even silly, some thoughtful critics would claim. After all, were one a chemist, would one ever investigate the properties of water (H_2O) by controlling the effects of H to illuminate the effects of O? Even if there is some merit to this point of view, the fact remains that behavioral and development scientists do see value in efforts to separate effects of nature and nurture while also examining their interplay, just as we have in Chapters 14 and 15, focused on gene-X-environment interaction.

For this reason, we stipulated in a number of chapters the possibility that the environmental forces we investigated (for example, parenting, day care, and neighborhood) could have predicted the aspects of development they did because of genetic influence on both the environmental exposure and the developmental outcome. Consider in this regard the possibility that some boys destined, for genetic reasons, to become antisocial adults actually provoke the harsh discipline they receive, which itself is a function of the genes that their harsh parents shared with their offspring. By repeatedly challenging our findings and thus discounting many alternative—and commonsense—explanations of why we discerned what we did, we nevertheless reduced the likelihood that the environmental effects we chronicled were simply a function of genetics. Having said that, let's be clear that only rarely could we eliminate genetic influence virtually in its entirety, most notably when we compared the development of identical twins in the same family who were and were not bullied (Chapter 10) and who did and did not experience polyvictimization (Chapter 16). That is why our research chronicled in Part V focused on genetics.

What did we learn? First, the power of either a few or even many GWAS-derived genetic variants to predict the developmental phenomena we targeted—smoking, life success, antisocial behavior, and depression—again proved to be real but limited, which once more should not be read to mean unimportant. To repeat, development is multiply determined and probabilistic. As Chapter 14, focused on genetics and antisocial behavior, and Chapter 15, focused on genetics and depression, made abundantly clear, when it comes to understanding development, it is useful to think in terms of both nature and nurture. Recall in this regard that findings pertaining to effects of nurture—as reflected in child maltreatment vis-à-vis antisocial behavior and stressful life events vis-à-vis depression—were "conditioned" by nature. Study members who were genetically different were consequently differentially affected by the developmental experiences and environmental exposures we investigated. Therefore, the too general belief that child abuse leads to aggression is another commonsense claim that needs qualification. The same, of course, proved true when it came to the adverse effect of stressful life events on depression. Recall, however, that when, consistent with prevailing epigenetic thinking, we sought to determine whether exposure to diverse forms of victimization turned off gene expression—by measuring methylation of DNA at the epigenome and candidate-gene levels— we found little evidence to support this view.

Aging in Midlife

Part VI sought to highlight the theme that it is not only mental health but also physical health that is rooted in childhood, clearly implying that a developmental perspective is essential when seeking to understand why people in midlife differ in their physical well-being. Recall in this regard that, perhaps most notably, we discovered that the more adverse experiences (for example, maltreatment) and exposures (for example, family members with mental health problems) children had growing up, the poorer their physical health was by age thirty-eight (Chapter 17). Recall as well that we could detect in three of four cases that problematic childhoods affected would-be biological embedding processes, thereby "getting under the skin" (Chapter 18). Then there was the fact that by midlife—and even earlier—it was clear, based on multiple biomarkers and even pictures of faces, that not only did some individuals age faster than others but also once again adversity in childhood and adolescence contributed to these differences.

Developmental Mechanisms

In so much of the work we shared, we sought to move beyond chronicling links between childhood experiences and exposures and psychological, behavioral, and physical development later in life, including physical health. Central to our developmental adventures were efforts to explore, where possible, the developmental mechanisms by which such effects might be realized. Indeed, this was exactly why we sought to investigate potential biological-embedding processes in Chapter 18.

As we have noted repeatedly, it is one thing to know that a particular way of functioning early in life (for example, childhood ADHD; see Chapter 4) or a specific experience (for example, maltreatment; see Chapter 14) affects a specific aspect of development but another to understand *how* such effects come to be. Thus, sometimes we focused on the social and behavioral experiences that mediated the effects being investigated and at other times we explored plausible biological mediators, even if we did not formally test their mediational effect. With regard to the former, consider our findings highlighting how the "snares" of adolescence—such as school failure, drugs, and teenage pregnancy—helped to explain how early-onset antisocial behavior came to be related to problematic functioning, including criminal behavior, in adulthood (Chapter 6). With regard to biological processes, we discovered that early-life adversity proved related to telomere erosion, inflammation, and stress physiology (Chapter 18). However, we could only advance an inferential argument that these processes contribute to poor health in adulthood—by mediating the effect of early-life adversity—because the youth of our study members does not yet position us to test whether these mechanisms of biological embedding undermine health later in life. Recall, though, that when we addressed what could be regarded as another process of biological embedding, epigenetic methylation, in Chapter 16, we detected little evidence that genes function as dependent variables, being regulated by victimization experiences.

Resilience

We saw repeatedly in this book that factors and forces that undermine human development can be prevented from working their black magic. Here we are referring to the recurring theme of resilience that kept emerging from our developmental adventures. Even if family conflict accelerated the sexual maturation of girls, we discovered that attachment security in infancy could buffer and prevent this development outcome from being realized (Chapter 7). Although we found that girls who are more physically mature engaged in more risk taking, we also learned in Chapter 7 that this did not happen when they attended all-girl schools. Recall also how supportive families protected bullied children from succumbing to the otherwise untoward consequences of bullying (Chapter10). We also discovered that not just social experience could play a role in resilience but genetic factors mattered, too. Dunedin Study males who had been maltreated as children but carried high-activity alleles of the *MAOA* gene were far less likely than carriers of the low-activity genetic variant to become antisocial adults (Chapter 14).

Implications for Intervention

A point we made repeatedly across a number of chapters was that appreciating resilience, especially factors promoting it, and understanding developmental mechanisms instantiating effects of childhood on later development were particularly important because of their potential to illuminate targets of intervention. This is true whether the goal is to prevent a problem from developing in the first place, remediate one already established, or simply promote well-being even among those not manifesting any dysfunction. Consider those circumstances where we cannot change a child's or adolescent's early-life functioning or lived experiences. Insight into mechanisms affected by these circumstances that influence later development raises the prospect of modifying social, behavioral, and biological mediators in the hope of redirecting previously established developmental trajectories. That is one reason why development remains open ended, at least in principle, rather than being fully determined by how a child functions early in life or by what happens to him or her while growing up. Just as we know we can increase water pressure in a home by replacing or patching a leaking section of rusted pipe that connects the line from the water company into a home with the home's bathtub tap, understanding the pipeline(s) of development should enable us to enhance human functioning.

But, having said that, we also feel a need to make clear that, with few exceptions, there is typically no direct line from evidence to practice and policy, even though so much rhetoric coming from scientists would seem to indicate otherwise (that is, because the evidence indicates X, we should or must do Y). Just because something is found to promote a favored outcome (for example, academic achievement) or a disfavored one (for example, cognitive decline) does not automatically lead to a particular action that should be taken, even if it does point to one or more that could be taken. Perhaps the best evidence of this is to be found in the laws regulating the sale and smoking of tobacco. Given the overwhelming evidence that such behavior is unhealthy, even costing societies millions of dollars in health-related costs, one reason that we allow it—but certainly not the only one—is that we value freedom and individual choice. In other words, beliefs and values will almost always play a role in determining a response to scientific evidence. While there may be some scientific findings that carry a moral imperative, this is by no means routinely the case.

All this is not to say that scientists should not engage in policy advocacy based on their scientific understanding of a particular phenomenon, but it does imply that when they put on their advocacy hats, they cannot claim to be operating purely as scientists. Their attitudes and values, as well as their scientific understanding, come into play, and, sadly, this too often seems insufficiently recognized or appreciated. The reality often is that open-minded people, including scientists, can come to opposite or at least alternative views as to what should—or should not—be done even when considering the same evidence. This is typically because they weigh and value the evidence differently.

To bring this point home, just consider the following question. Given the evidence reported in Chapter 8 that early, extensive, and continuous child care (of the kind routinely available in the United States) appears to promote somewhat increased levels of aggression and disobedience in childhood and promote risk taking and impulsivity in adolescence, what should the policy response be, if any? Whereas some might conclude that families should use less day care and that family-leave policies should be expanded, others will see things differently. The latter might say that these seemingly negative effects are too modest, and the benefits of the mother's employment—in terms of income, career development, and psychological well-being—too great, so every effort should be made to expand the availability and affordability of high-quality day care, including for very young infants. The difference of opinion indicates that even open-minded people, to say nothing of closed-minded ones, can value different things and hold different beliefs about what is best for children, for parents, for families, and even for societies.

Even if we favor some service and policy responses to particular findings—and we authors don't necessarily agree among ourselves on this all the time—that does not mean our expertise grants us superior status when it comes to deciding what should be done. While we may have special expertise when it comes to human development, that is not going to be the case for so much more that determines—or should or could determine—what is decided. After all, we are not economists, philosophers, or historians, to cite but three potentially informative perspectives. There is also the fact that our scientific expertise does not mean that our beliefs and values should trump those of others.

Future Directions

Having reviewed the core themes and related ideas to emerge from our book, let us take a moment in closing to share some of our ambitions for the future—what we are already planning to investigate as well as hoping to be able to address sometime in the future. The eleven hundred British E-Risk Study twin pairs will soon enter "emerging adulthood" in their mid-twenties. We have eagerly awaited this for over two decades because adult twins offer the opportunity for a strong test of the effects of social experience on physical and mental health development. When they were toddlers, twins of a pair went everywhere in one double stroller, seeing the world from a united point of view. In childhood, most of their experiences were the same as well. For example, pairs generally attended the same school and were often in the same classroom, exposed to the same teacher and instructional style. But, as adults, they will venture into separate lives, have different experiences with partners, have different experiences with work, and no doubt become parents at different times in their lives. Some twins will go to jail, while their co-twins will not; some twins will smoke, while their co-twins will not; some twins will build large friendship networks, while their co-twins will become socially isolated; and, as a final example, some twins will become vegetarians, while their co-twins will eat meat. We look forward to this opportunity to hold family and genetic background constant while seeking to illuminate the effects of such divergent life experiences. In keeping with the themes in this book, we expect some, but by no means perfect, continuity from early life. We also expect that some study members who were otherwise at risk for problematic development will prove resilient. It will be our job to understand the process by which such developmental outcomes were avoided, but it will also likely be the case that some E-Risk children who seem to be developing well will end up not fulfilling their earlier developmental promise, so it will also be our goal to understand why.

There are also exciting new questions on the horizon for the one thousand Dunedin Study members who have entered midlife—and thus exciting new adventures on the horizon for us developmental explorers. Our plan is to continue to track each study member's personal pace of aging when they are in their fifties and sixties, again using the many biological markers we measured repeatedly at ages twenty-six, thirty-two, thirty-eight, and forty-five. Repeated measures of telomere length and epigenetic methylation will enable us to test whether changes in the pace of aging also track changing genomic systems. We will investigate what factors from study members' childhoods speed up or slow down the pace of their aging, and whether a lifelong accumulated history of psychiatric illness is linked to faster aging. We will also be able to evaluate whether and how an individual's pace of aging relates to changes in adaptive functions, including physical fitness, cognitive functions, and MRI-assessed brain structure and function, as well as sensory functions of hearing, taste, and vision. In keeping with the themes in this book, we expect continuities from early life, but we will also look for experiences and characteristics that single out the study members who show the most resilience, remaining conspicuously young in body and young at heart compared to their Dunedin agemates. As we have said already, miles to go before we sleep.

BIBLIOGRAPHY

INDEX

BIBLIOGRAPHY

CHAPTER 1

NICHD Early Child Care Research Network (Ed.). (2005). *Child care and child development: Results of the NICHD Study of Early Child Care and Youth Development*. New York: Guilford Press.

Poulton, R., Moffitt, T. E., & Silva, P. A. (2015). The Dunedin Multidisciplinary Health and Development Study: Overview of the first 40 years, with an eye to the future. *Social Psychiatry and Psychiatric Epidemiology, 50,* 679–693.

CHAPTER 2

Caspi, A. (2000). The child is father of the man: Personality continuities from childhood to adulthood. *Journal of Personality and Social Psychology, 78,* 158–172.

Caspi, A., & Silva, P. A. (1995). Temperamental qualities at age three predict personality traits in young adulthood: Longitudinal evidence from a birth cohort. *Child Development, 66,* 486–498.

Newman, D. L., Caspi, A., Silva, P. A., & Moffitt, T. E. (1997). Antecedents of adult interpersonal functioning: Effects of individual differences in age 3 temperament. *Developmental Psychology, 33,* 206–217.

Robins, R. W., John, O. P., Caspi, A., Moffitt, T. E., & Stouthamer-Loeber, M. (1996). Resilient, overcontrolled, and undercontrolled boys: Three replicable personality types. *Journal of Personality and Social Psychology, 70,* 157–171.

Slutske, W. S., Moffitt, T. E., Poulton, R., & Caspi, A. (2012). Undercontrolled temperament at age 3 predicts disordered gambling at age 32. *Psychological Science, 23,* 510–516.

CHAPTER 3

Moffitt, T. E., Arseneault, L., Belsky, D., Dickson, N., Hancox, R. J., Harrington, H., Houts, R., Poulton, R., Roberts, B. W., Ross, S., Sears, M. R., Thomson, W. M., & Caspi, A. (2011). A gradient of childhood self-control predicts health, wealth, and public safety. *Proceedings of the National Academy of Sciences, 108*, 2693–2698.

Moffitt, T. E., Poulton, R., & Caspi, A. (2013). Lifelong impact of early self-control: Childhood self-discipline predicts adult quality of life. *American Scientist, 101*, 352–359.

CHAPTER 4

Agnew-Blais, J. C., Polanczyk, G. V., Danese, A., Wertz, J., Moffitt, T. E., & Arseneault, L. (2016). Evaluation of the persistence, remission, and emergence of attention-deficit/hyperactivity disorder in young adulthood. *JAMA Psychiatry, 73*, 713–720.

Arseneault, L., Agnew-Blais, J., & Moffitt, T. E. (2017). Child vs adult onset attention-deficit/hyperactivity disorder-reply. *JAMA Psychiatry, 74*, 422–423.

Moffitt, T. E., Houts, R., Asherson, P., Belsky, D. W., Corcoran, D. L., Hammerle, M., Harrington, H., Hogan, S., Meier, M. H., Polanczyk, G. V., Poulton, R., Ramrakha, S., Sudgen, K., Williams, B., Rohde, L., & Caspi, A. (2015). Is adult ADHD a childhood-onset neurodevelopmental disorder? Evidence from a four-decade longitudinal cohort study. *American Journal of Psychiatry, 172*, 967–977.

CHAPTER 5

Belsky, J., Hancox, R. J., Sligo, J., & Poulton, R. (2012). Does being an older parent attenuate the intergenerational transmission of parenting? *Developmental Psychology, 48*, 1570–1574.

Belsky, J., Jaffee, S., Sligo, J., Woodward, L., & Silva, P. (2005). Intergenerational transmission of warm-sensitive-stimulating parenting: A prospective study of mothers and fathers of 3-year olds. *Child Development, 76*, 384–396.

Wertz, J., Moffitt, T. E., Agnew-Blais, J., Arseneault, L., Belsky, D. W., Corcoran, D. L., Houts, R., Matthews, T., Prinz, J. A., Richmond-Rakerd, L. S., Sugden, K., Williams, B., & Caspi, A. (in press). Using DNA from mothers and children to study parental investment in children's educational attainment. *Child Development*.

CHAPTER 6

Moffitt, T. E. (2018). Male antisocial behavior in adolescence and beyond. *Nature Human Behaviour, 2,* 177–186.

Moffitt, T. E., & Caspi, A. (2001). Childhood predictors differentiate life-course persistent and adolescence-limited antisocial pathways in males and females. *Development and Psychopathology, 13,* 355–375.

Moffitt, T. E., Caspi, A., Dickson, N., Silva, P., & Stanton, W. (1996). Childhood-onset versus adolescent-onset antisocial conduct problems in males: Natural history from ages 3–18. *Development and Psychopathology, 8,* 399–424.

Moffitt, T. E., Caspi, A., Harrington, H., & Milne, B. J. (2002). Males on the life-course persistent and adolescence-limited antisocial pathways: Follow-up at age 26 years. *Development and Psychopathology, 14,* 179–207.

Odgers, C., Caspi, A., Broadbent, J. M., Dickson, N., Hancox, B., Harrington, H. L., Poulton, R., Sears, M. R., Thomson, M., & Moffitt, T. E. (2007). Conduct problem subtypes in males predict differential adult health burden. *Archives of General Psychiatry, 64,* 476–484.

Odgers, C. L., Moffitt, T. E., Broadbent, J. M., Dickson, N., Hancox, R. J., Harrington, H., Poulton, R., Sears, M. R., Thomson, W. M., & Caspi, A. (2008). Female and male antisocial trajectories: From childhood origins to adult outcomes. *Development and Psychopathology, 20,* 673–716.

CHAPTER 7

Belsky, J., Steinberg, L., Houts, R., Friedman, S. L., DeHart, G., Cauffman, E., Roisman, G. I., Halpern-Felsher, B., Susman, E., & The NICHD Early Child Care Research Network. (2007). Family rearing antecedents of pubertal timing. *Child Development, 78,* 1302–1321.

Belsky, J., Steinberg, L., Houts, R. M., Halpern-Felsher, B. L., & The NICHD Early Child Care Research Network. (2010). The development of reproductive strategy in females: Early maternal harshness→earlier menarche→increased sexual risk taking. *Developmental Psychology, 46,* 120–128.

Caspi, A., Lynam, D., Moffitt, T. E., & Silva, P. (1993). Unraveling girls' delinquency: Biological, dispositional, and contextual contributions to adolescent misbehavior. *Developmental Psychology, 29,* 19–30.

Caspi, A., & Moffitt, T. E. (1991). Individual differences are accentuated during periods of social change: The sample case of girls at puberty. *Journal of Personality and Social Psychology, 61,* 157–168.

Moffitt, T., Caspi, A., Belsky, J., & Silva, P. (1992). Childhood experience and the onset of menarche: A test of a sociobiological model. *Child Development, 63,* 47–58.

Ramrakha, S., Paul, C., Bell, M. L., Dickson, N., Moffitt, T. E., & Caspi, A. (2013). The relationship between multiple sex partners and anxiety, depression, and substance dependence disorders: A cohort study. *Archives of Sexual Behavior, 42,* 863–872.

Sung, S., Simpson, J. A., Griskevicius, V., Kuo, S. I., Schlomer, G. L., & Belsky, J. (2016). Secure infant-mother attachment buffers the effect of early-life stress on age of menarche. *Psychological Science, 27,* 667–674.

CHAPTER 8

Belsky, J., Vandell, D., Burchinal, M., Clarke-Stewart, K. A., McCartney, K., Owen, M., & The NICHD Early Child Care Research Network. (2007). Are there long-term effects of early child care? *Child Development, 78,* 681–701.

McCartney, K., Burchinal, M., Clarke-Stewart, A., Bub, K. L., Owen, M. T., Belsky, J., and the NICHD Early Child Care Research Network. (2010). Testing a series of causal propositions relating time in child care to children's externalizing behavior. *Developmental Psychology, 46,* 1–17.

NICHD Early Child Care Research Network. (1997). The effects of infant child care on infant-mother attachment security: Results of the NICHD Study of Early Child Care. *Child Development, 68,* 860–879.

NICHD Early Child Care Research Network. (1998). Early child care and self-control, compliance and problem behavior at 24 and 36 months. *Child Development, 69,* 1145–1170.

NICHD Early Child Care Research Network. (1999). Child care and mother-child interaction in the first three years of life. *Developmental Psychology, 35,* 1399–1413.

NICHD Early Child Care Research Network. (2000). The relation of child care to cognitive and language development. *Child Development, 71,* 958–978.

NICHD Early Child Care Research Network. (2001). Child care and family predictors of preschool attachment and stability from infancy. *Developmental Psychology, 37,* 847–862.

NICHD Early Child Care Research Network. (2002). Child care and children's development prior to school entry. *American Education Research Journal, 39,* 133–164.

NICHD Early Child Care Research Network. (2003). Families matter—even for kids in child care. *Journal of Developmental and Behavioral Pediatrics, 24,* 58–62.

NICHD Early Child Care Research Network. (2003). Does amount of time spent in child care predict socioemotional adjustment during the transition to kindergarten? *Child Development, 74,* 976–1005.

NICHD Early Child Care Research Network. (2003). Early child care and mother-child interaction from 36 months through first grade. *Infant Behavior and Development, 26,* 345–370.

NICHD Early Child Care Research Network (Ed.). (2005). *Child care and child development: Results of the NICHD Study of Early Child Care and Youth Development*. New York: Guilford Press.

NICHD Early Child Care Research Network. (2005). Early child care and children's development in the primary grades: Follow-up results from the NICHD Study of Early Child Care. *American Educational Research Journal, 43,* 537–570.

Vandell, D. L., Belsky, J., Burchinal, M., Steinberg, L., Vandergrift, N., & the NICHD Early Child Care Research Network. (2010). Do effects of early child care extend to age 15 years? *Child Development, 81,* 737–756.

CHAPTER 9

Jaffee, S. R., Caspi, A., Moffitt, T. E., Polo-Tomos, M., & Taylor, A. (2007). Individual, family, and neighborhood factors distinguish resilient from non-resilient maltreated children: A cumulative stressors model. *Child Abuse and Neglect, 31,* 231–253.

Odgers, C. L., Caspi, A., Russell, M. A., Sampson, R. J., Arseneault, L., & Moffitt, T. (2012). Supportive parenting mediates neighborhood socioeconomic disparities in children's antisocial behavior from ages 5 to 12. *Development and Psychopathology, 24,* 705–721.

Odgers, C. L., Donley, S., Caspi, A., Bates, C. J., & Moffitt, T. E. (2015). Living alongside more affluent neighbors predicts greater involvement in antisocial behavior among low income boys. *Journal of Child Psychology and Psychiatry, 56,* 1055–1064.

Odgers, C. L., Moffitt, T. E., Tach, L. M., Sampson, R. J., Taylor, A., Matthews, C. L., & Caspi, A. (2009). The protective effects of neighborhood collective efficacy on British children growing up in deprivation: A developmental analysis. *Developmental Psychology, 45,* 942–957.

CHAPTER 10

Baldwin, J. R., Arseneault, L., Odgers, C., Belsky, D. W., Matthews, T., Ambler, A., Caspi, A., Moffitt, T. E., & Danese, A. (2016). Childhood bullying victimization and overweight in young adulthood: A cohort study. *Psychosomatic Medicine, 78,* 1094–1103.

Bowes, L, Maughan, B., Caspi, A., Moffitt, T. E., & Arseneault, L. (2010). Families promote emotional and behavioural resilience to bullying: Evidence of an environmental effect. *Journal of Child Psychology and Psychiatry, 51,* 809–817.

Fisher, H. L., Moffitt, T. E., Houts, R. M., Belsky, D. W., Arseneault, L., & Caspi, A. (2012). Bullying victimization and risk of self harm in early adolescence. *BMJ, 344,* e2683.

CHAPTER 11

Arseneault, L., Cannon, M., Poulton, R., Murray, R., Caspi, A., & Moffitt, T. E. (2002). Cannabis use in adolescence and risk for adult psychosis: Longitudinal prospective study. *BMJ, 23*, 1212–1213.

Caspi, A., Moffitt, T. E., Cannon, M., McClay, J., Murray, R., Harrington, H., Taylor, A., Arseneault, L., Williams, B., Braithwaite, A., Poulton, R., & Craig, I. W. (2005). Moderation of the effect of adolescent-onset cannabis use on adult psychosis by a functional polymorphism in the catechol-O-methyltranserase gene: Longitudinal evidence of a gene X environment interaction. *Biological Psychiatry, 57*, 1117–1127.

Cerda, M., Moffitt, T. E., Meier, M. H., Harrington, H., Houts, R., Ramrakha, S., Hogan, S., Poulton, R., & Caspi, A. (2016). Persistent cannabis dependence and alcohol dependence represent risks for midlife economic and social problems: A longitudinal cohort study. *Clinical Psychological Science, 4*, 1028–1046.

Hancox, R. J., Poulton, R., Ely, M., Welch, D., Taylor, D. R., McLachlan, C. R., Greene, J. M., Moffitt, T. E., Caspi, A., & Sears, M. R. (2010). Effects of cannabis on lung function: A population-based cohort study. *European Respiratory Journal, 35*, 42–47.

Hancox, R. J., Shin, H. H., Gray, A. R., Poulton, R., & Sears, M. R. (2015). Effects of quitting cannabis on respiratory symptoms. *European Respiratory Journal, 46*, 80–87.

Meier, M., Moffitt, T. E., Cerda, M., Hancox, R., Harrington, H. L., Houts, R., Poulton, R., Ramrakha, S., Thomson, M., & Caspi, A. (2016). Physical health problems associated with persistent cannabis versus tobacco use at midlife: A population-representative longitudinal study. *JAMA Psychiatry, 3*, 731–740.

Meier, M. H., Caspi, A., Ambler, A., Harrington, H., Houts, R., Keefe, R. S. E., McDonald, D., Ward, A., Poulton, R., & Moffitt, T. E. (2012). Persistent cannabis users show neurospsychological decline from childhood to midlife. *Proceedings of the National Academy of Sciences, 109*, E2657–E2664.

Meier, M. H., Caspi, A., Cerda, M., Hancox, R. J., Harrington, H., Houts, R., Poulton, R., Ramrakha, S., Thomson, W. M., & Moffitt, T. E. (2016). Associations between cannabis use and physical health problems in early midlife: A longitudinal comparison of persistent cannabis vs tobacco users. *JAMA Psychiatry, 73*, 731–740.

Taylor, D. R., Fergusson, D. M., Milne, B. J., Horwood, L. J., Moffitt, T. E., Sears, M. R., & Poulton, R. (2002). A longitudinal study of the effects of tobacco and cannabis exposure on lung function in young adults. *Addiction, 97*, 1055–1061.

CHAPTER 12

Belsky, D. W., Moffitt, T. E., Baker, T. B., Biddle, A. K., Evans, J. P., Harrington, H., Houts, R., Meier, M., Sugden, K., Williams, B., Poulton, R., & Caspi, A. (2013). Polygenic risk and the developmental progression to heavy, persistent smoking and nicotine dependence. *JAMA Psychiatry, 70,* 534–542.

CHAPTER 13

Belsky, D. W., Moffitt, T. E., Corcoran, D. L., Comingue, B., Harrington, H., Hogan, S., Williams, B. S., Poulton, R., & Caspi, A. (2016). The genetics of success: How single-nucleotide polymorphisms associated with educational attainment relate to life-course development. *Psychological Science, 27,* 957–972.

CHAPTER 14

Caspi, A., McClay, J., Moffitt, T. E., Mill, J., Martin, J., Craig, I. W., Taylor, A., & Poulton, R. (2002). Role of genotype in the cycle of violence in maltreated children. *Science, 297,* 851–854.

CHAPTER 15

Caspi, A., Holmes, A., Uher, R., Hariri, A., and Moffitt, T. E. (2010). Genetic sensitivity to the environment: The case of the serotonin transporter gene (*5-HTT*), and its implications for studying complex diseases and traits. *American Journal of Psychiatry, 167,* 509–527.

Caspi, A., Sugden, K., Moffitt, T. E., Taylor, A., Craig, I. W., Harrington, H., McClay, J., Mill, J., Martin, J., Braithwaite, A., & Poulton, R. (2003). Influence of life stress on depression: Moderation by a polymorphism in the 5-HTT gene. *Science, 301,* 386–389.

CHAPTER 16

Marzi, S. J., Sugden, K., Arseneault, L., Belsky, D. W., Burrage, J., Corcoran, D., Danese, A., Fisher, H. L., Hannon, E., Moffitt, T. E., Odgers, C. L., Pariante, C., Poulton, R., Williams, B. S., Wong, C. C. Y., Mill, J., & Caspi, A. (2018). Analysis of DNA methylation in young people reveals limited evidence for an association between victimization stress and epigenetic variation in blood. *American Journal of Psychiatry, 175,* 517–529.

Schaefer, J. D., Moffitt, T. E., Arseneault, L., Danese, A., Fisher, H. L., Houts, R., Sheridan, M. A., Wertz, J., & Caspi, A. (2018). Adolescent victimization and early-adult psychopathology: Approaching causal inference using a longitudinal twin study to rule out alternative non-causal explanations. *Clinical Psychological Science, 6,* 352–371.

CHAPTER 17

Danese, A., Moffitt, T. E., Harrington, H., Milne, B. J., Polanczyk, G., Pariante, C. M., Poulton, R., & Caspi, A. (2009). Adverse childhood experiences and adult risk of factors for age-related disease. *Archives of Pediatric and Adolescent Medicine, 163,* 1135–1143.

Melchior, M., Moffitt, T. E., Milne, B. J., Poulton, R., & Caspi, A. (2007). Why do children from socioeconomically disadvantaged families suffer from poor health when they reach adulthood? A life-course study. *American Journal of Epidemiology, 166,* 966–974.

Ouellet-Morin, I., Danese, A., Bowes, L., Shakoor, S., Ambler, A., Pariante, C. M., Papadopoulos, A. S., Caspi, A., Moffitt, T. E., & Arseneault, L. (2011). A discordant monozygotic twin design shows blunted cortisol reactivity among bullied children. *Journal of the American Academy of Child & Adolescent Psychiatry, 50,* 574–582.

Poulton, R., Caspi, A., Milne, B. J., Thomson, W. M., Taylor, A., Sears, M. R., & Moffitt, T. E. (2002). Association between children's experience of socioeconomic disadvantage and adult health: A life-course study. *The Lancet, 360,* 1640–1645.

Reuben, A., Moffitt, T. E., Caspi, A., Belsky, D. W., Harrington, H., Schroeder, F., Hogan, S., Ramrakha, S., Poulton, R., & Danese, A. (2016). Lest we forget: Comparing retrospective and prospective assessments of adverse childhood experiences in the prediction of adult health. *Journal of Child Psychology and Psychiatry, 57,* 1103–1112.

Shalev, I., Moffitt, T. E., Sugden, K., Williams, B., Houts, R. M., Danese, A., Mill, J., Arseneault, L., & Caspi, A. (2013). Exposure to violence during childhood is associated with telomere erosion from 5 to 10 years of age: A longitudinal study. *Molecular Psychiatry, 18,* 576–581.

CHAPTER 18

Belsky, D. W., Caspi, A., Houts, R., Cohen, H. J., Corcoran, D. L., Danese, A., Harrington, H., Israel, S., Levine, M. E., Schaefer, J. D., Sugden, K., Williams, B., Yashin, A. I., Poulton, R., & Moffitt, T. E. (2015). Quantification of biological aging in young adults. *Proceedings of the National Academy of Sciences,112,* E4104–E4110.

Caspi, A., Harrington, H. L., Moffitt, T. E., Milne, B., & Poulton, R. (2006). Socially isolated children 20 years later: Risk for cardiovascular disease. *Archives of Pediatric and Adolescent Medicine, 160,* 805–811.

Danese, A., Caspi, A., Williams, B., Ambler, A., Sugden, K., Mika, J., Werts, H., Freeman, J., Pariante, C. M., Moffitt, T. E., & Arseneault, L. (2011). Biological embedding of stress through inflammation processes in childhood. *Molecular Psychiatry, 16,* 244–246.

Danese, A., Moffitt, T. E., Harrington, H., Milne, B. J., Polanczyk, G., Pariante, C. M., Poulton, R., & Caspi, A. (2009). Adverse childhood experiences and adult risk of factors for age-related disease. *Archives of Pediatric and Adolescent Medicine, 163,* 1135–1143.

Danese, A., Pariante, C. M., Caspi, A., Taylor, A., & Poulton, R. (2007). Childhood maltreatment predicts adult inflammation in a life-course study. *Proceedings of the National Academy of Sciences, 104,* 1319–1324.

Ouellet-Morin, I., Danese, A., Bowes, L., Shakoor, S., Ambler, A., Pariante, C. M., Papadopoulos, A. S., Caspi, A., Moffitt, T. E., & Arseneault, L. (2011). A discordant monozygotic twin design shows blunted cortisol reactivity among bullied children. *Journal of the American Academy of Child & Adolescent Psychiatry, 50,* 574–582.

Rasmussen, L. J. H., Moffitt, T. E., Arseneault, L., Danese, A., Eugen-Olsen, J., Fisher, H., Harrington, H., Houts, R., Matthews, T., Sugden, K., Williams, B., & Caspi, A. (in press). Improving the measurement of stress-related inflammatory burden in young people: A longitudinal cohort study. *JAMA Pediatrics.*

Rasmussen, L. J. H., Moffitt, T. E., Eugen-Olsen, J., Belsky, D. W., Danese, A., Harrington, H., Houts, R. M., Poulton, R., Sugden, K., Williams, B., & Caspi, A. (2018). Cumulative childhood risk is associated with a new measure of chronic inflammation in adulthood. *Journal of Child Psychology and Psychiatry, 60,* 199–208.

Shalev, I., Moffitt, T. E., Sugden, K., Williams, B., Houts, R. M., Danese, A., Mill, J., Arseneault, L., & Caspi, A. (2019). Exposure to violence during childhood is associated with telomere erosion from 5 to 10 years of age: A longitudinal study. *Molecular Psychiatry, 18,* 576–581.

CHAPTER 19

Belsky, D. W., Caspi, A., Cohen, H. J., Kraus, W. E., Ramrakha, S., Poulton, R., & Moffitt, T. E. (2017). Impact of early personal-history characteristics on the pace of aging: Implications for clinical trials of therapies to slow aging and extend healthspan. *Aging Cell, 16,* 644–651.

Belsky, D. W., Caspi, A., Houts, R., Cohen, H. J., Corcoran, D. L., Danese, A., Harrington, H., Israel, S., Levine, M. E., Schaefer, J. D., Sugden, K., Williams, B., Yashin, A. I., Poulton, R., & Moffitt, T. E. (2015). Quantification of biological aging in young adults. *Proceedings of the National Academy of Sciences,112,* E4104–E4110.

Belsky, D. W., Moffitt, T. E., Cohen, A. A., Corcoran, D. L., Levine, M. E., Prinz, J. A., Schaefer, J., Sudgen, K., Williams, B., Poulton, R., & Caspi, A. (2018). Eleven telomere, epigenetic clock, and biomarker-composite quantifications of biological aging: Do they measure the same thing? *American Journal of Epidemiology, 187,* 1220–1230.

INDEX

Page numbers in *italics* refer to figures.